Potential Designs for Clarion's Knives

I didn't make the initial knife sketches for *Ghost Urn*. The editor put in a new order with me, saying "Rikudo-shi shouldn't do all the work. Let's give Shirow Masamune something to do too." In response, I made these for *Pandora in the Crimson Shell* on March 30, 2014.

Potential Designs for Clarion's Knives

Since it'd be a hassle to draw them like this over and over, just work with your impression from these sketches and make them more suitable for drawing in the manga. Also, they have a sort of bloodthirsty vibe that doesn't really match the feel of the manga, so maybe make them a bit cuter somehow.

Anyway, I'm imagining a reverse hold with the tip of the blade pointing toward the elbow. I'm picturing the shorter types as one in each hand. The blade thickness is less like a knife and more like brass knuckles with spikes.

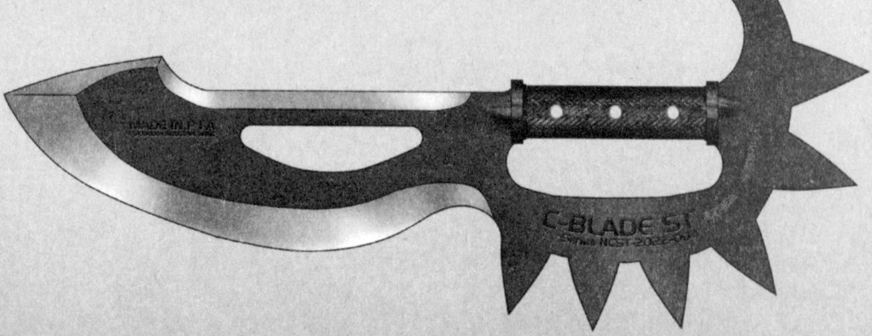
C-BLADE ST

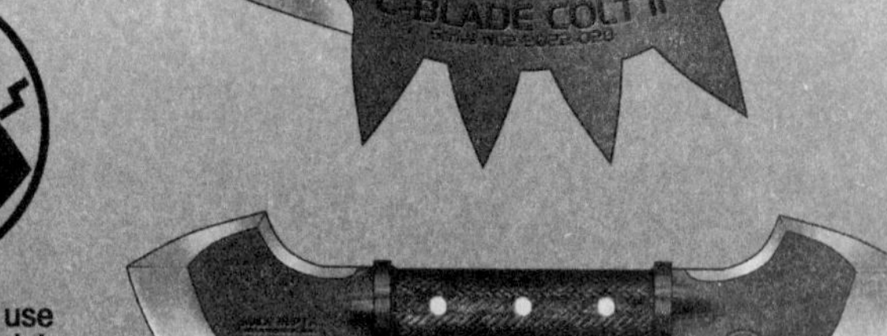
C-BLADE COLT II

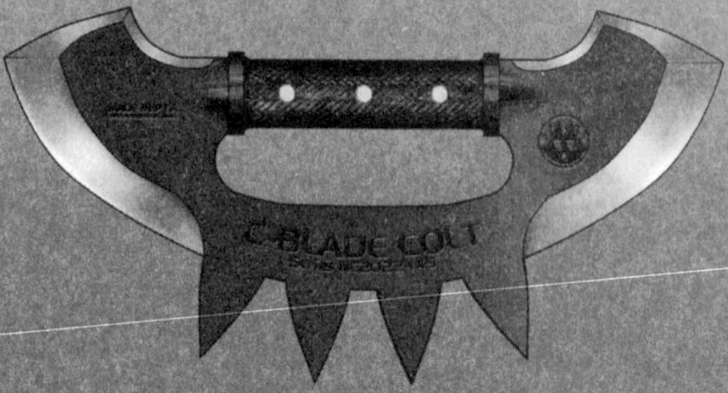
C-BLADE COLT

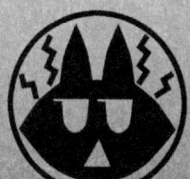

If you can make use of these, please do! But if using them would be difficult, there's no need to bend over backward to make them work.

Greetings! (For the sixth time!)

So! Everything you've seen up until this point--the two protagonists, the five evil women (and the side characters), the overview of the island, Buer--has been based on designs I created for the initial concept. (Not including the text.) (That early on, very little text was involved.)

Apparently, there's been an announcement that *Pandora in the Crimson Shell* will be in color when it's released digitally, but what that means is that it'll be colored as was always intended, not just that we added color to it after the fact. Bearing in mind that this was originally proposed as an anime project, it was originally conceived to include color. When it was compiled into manga volumes, it was black and white, and the version with corrections and adjustments for the print version did come out first, but the black-and-white version was actually the second one made.

Also, because we were originally planning this for anime, other anime people did character designs in the initial stages too, not just me and Rikudou-shi. There were different looks for Nene, Clarion, and the others for use in the anime. But once the anime *Ghost Um* project was set aside, those designs were pragmatically repurposed for a completely different TV anime (which was also different from 2014's *Ghost in the Shell: ARISE*). That makes it tricky for us to show you those designs here, but it's possible that you've seen a character elsewhere whose look and movements could have belonged to Nene. (LOL)

Now, as I said before, it didn't seem right to make Rikudou-shi do all the work, so I was told to create new designs (for characters and equipment) in addition to the initial project designs. I think you'll get to see more of the images I was commissioned to do in the future--watch this space! It's more on the level of putting out more simplified ideas than the chapter subplots you've seen related to the first *Ghost in the Shell S.A.C* or *ARISE*, but...well, I'm sure those will be story ideas, too.

June 18, 2014
Shirow Masamune

row Masamune Shirow Masamune Shirow Masamune Shirow Mas

GHOST URN-EPISODE.log —— The story so far!

Deep beneath Cenancle, the massive boring machine Buer's rest is frequently disturbed by the American Empire's attempts to unearth it--attempts that make Buer run amok and throw the island into chaos!

Clarion has infiltrated the empire's secret base in hopes of keeping Nene safe, but Colonel Kurtz sends a combat android after Clarion to keep her from disrupting his plan to acquire Buer. As for Nene, her worry for Clarion sends her after her friend--accompanied by Buer's perverted central control unit...

udou Koushi Rikudou Koushi Rikudou Koushi Rikudou Koushi Riku

GHOST URN-CHARACTERS — Main Characters

Nanakorobi Nene
A girl whose brain was implanted into an entirely artificial body after an accident when she was young. Nene has one of the few full-body prosthetics in the world!

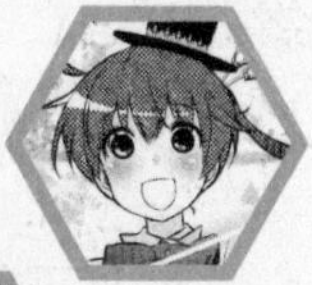

Clarion
A combat android owned by Uzal. Clarion has many top-secret, illegal programs tucked away inside her.

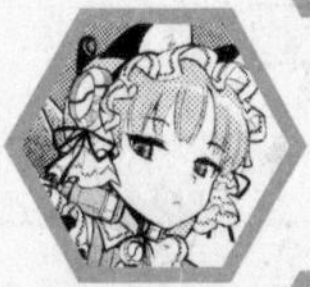

Uzal Delilah
The mysterious Uzal (real name: Sahar Schehera) is a well-known international businesswoman, but she has plenty of secrets. She vanished during the chaos when Buer ran wild.

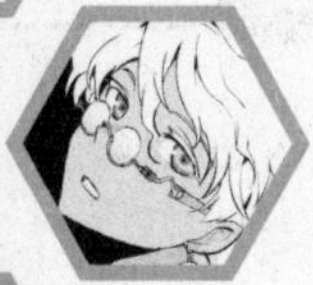

Korobase Takumi
Age unknown. She heads up the Korobase Foundation, which controls cybrain marketing, but has a pathological fear of people.

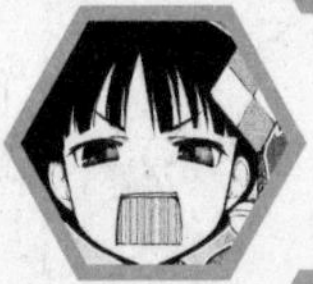

Massive boring machine Buer: Central Nervous Unit
The central control unit for the large multi-legged boring machine Buer. As Buer's actual body is currently dormant underground, the central nervous unit is accompanying Nene. This pompous-sounding entity provides a constant stream of perverted, leering commentary.

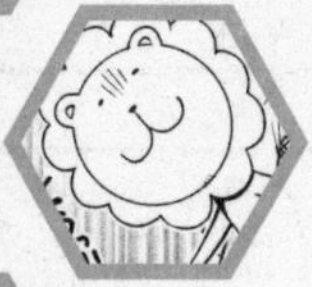

Vlind
A perky, enthusiastic freelance reporter who dreams of taking her place among the top idols *and* the top reporters in the world! Dragging her two staffers in her wake, she's working hard to conquer mass media.

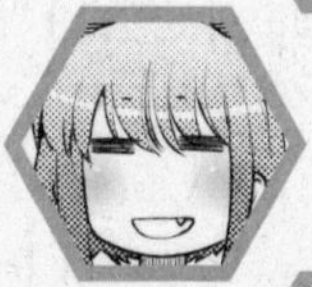

Colonel Kurtz
A member of the American Imperial army. He's aiming to seize control of Buer, the machine Uzal left behind.

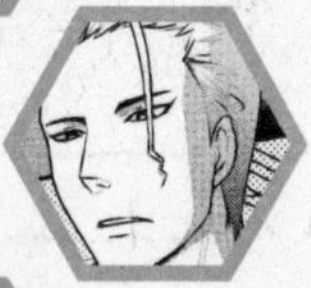

Robert Altman
A captain with the Cenancle Defense Forces, currently under the command of Special Military Advisor Kurtz. A passionate tough guy who loves justice and peace.

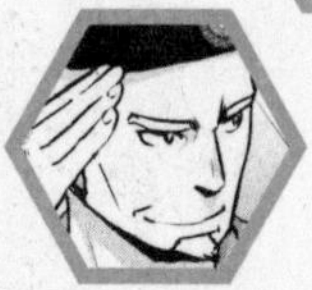

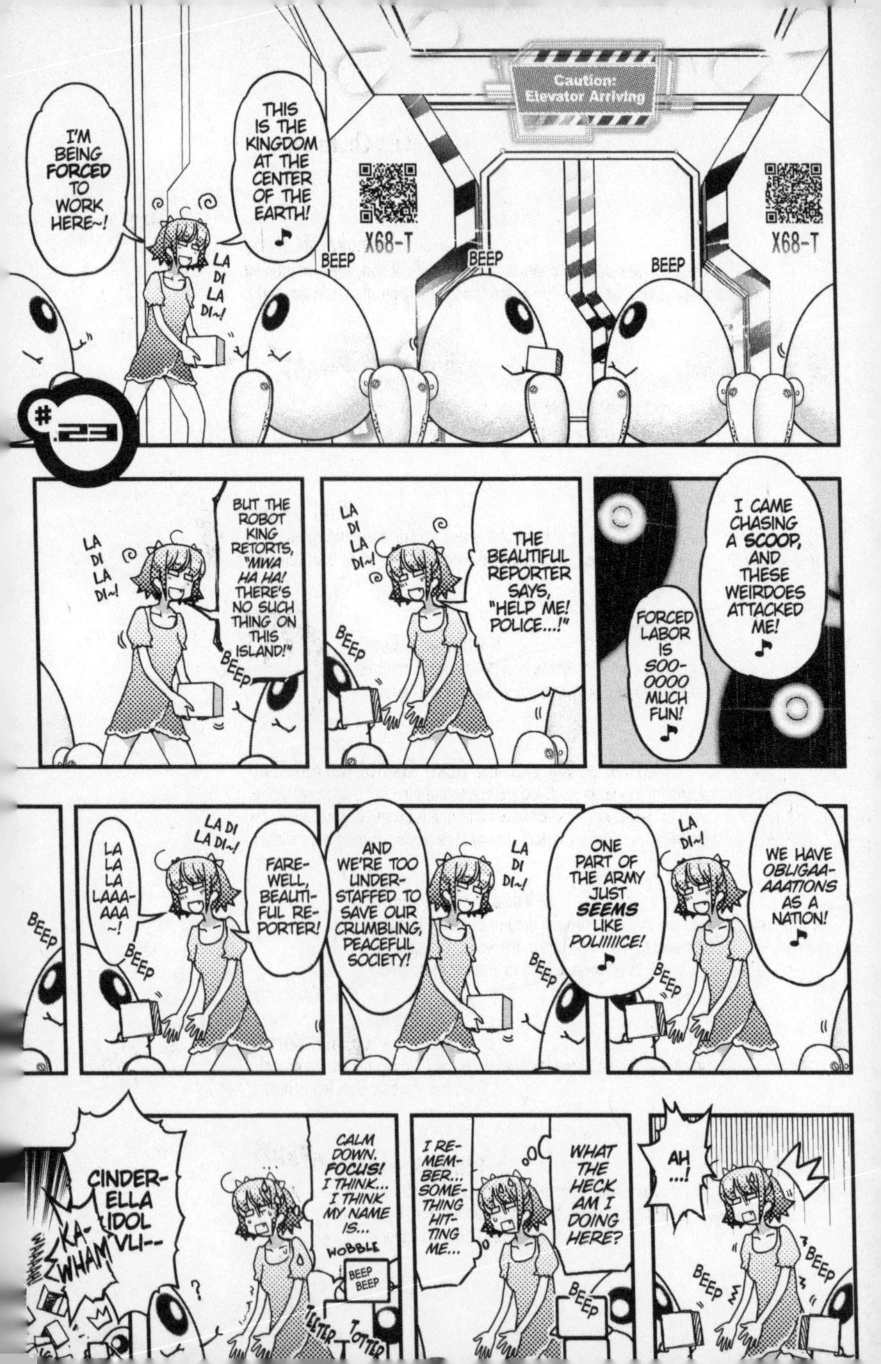
Caution: Elevator Arriving
X68-T
X68-T
BEEP
BEEP
BEEP
THIS IS THE KINGDOM AT THE CENTER OF THE EARTH! ♪
I'M BEING FORCED TO WORK HERE~!
LA DI LA DI~!
#.23
I CAME CHASING A SCOOP, AND THESE WEIRDOES ATTACKED ME! ♪
FORCED LABOR IS SOO-OOOO MUCH FUN! ♪
LA DI LA DI~!
THE BEAUTIFUL REPORTER SAYS, "HELP ME! POLICE...!"
BEEP
BUT THE ROBOT KING RETORTS, "MWA HA HA! THERE'S NO SUCH THING ON THIS ISLAND!"
LA DI LA DI~!
BEEP
LA DI~!
WE HAVE OBLIGAA-AATIONS AS A NATION! ♪
ONE PART OF THE ARMY JUST SEEMS LIKE POLIIIIIICE! ♪
BEEP
LA DI DI~!
AND WE'RE TOO UNDER-STAFFED TO SAVE OUR CRUMBLING, PEACEFUL SOCIETY!
BEEP
LA DI LA DI~!
FARE-WELL, BEAUTI-FUL RE-PORTER!
LA LA LA LAAAA-AAA~!
BEEP
BEEP
AH ...!
BEEP
BEEP
WHAT THE HECK AM I DOING HERE?
I RE-MEMBER... SOME-THING HIT-TING ME...
BEEP
CALM DOWN. FOCUS! I THINK... I THINK MY NAME IS...
WOBBLE
BEEP BEEP
TEETER TOTTER
CINDER-ELLA IDOL VLI--
KA-WHAM

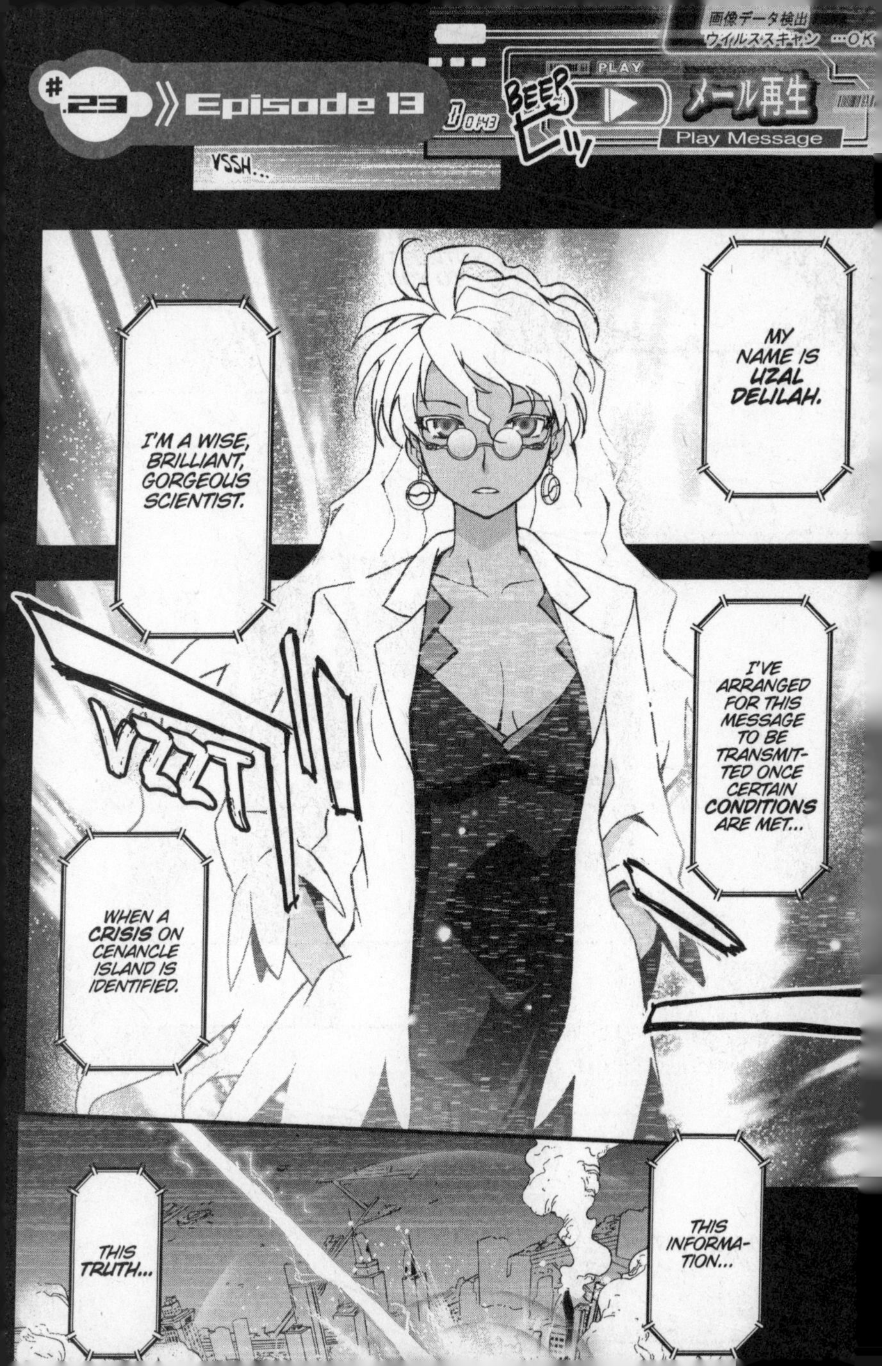
#.23 Episode 13
画像データ検出
ウイルススキャン …OK
PLAY
メール再生
Play Message
BEEP
ピッ
VSSH...
MY NAME IS UZAL DELILAH.
I'M A WISE, BRILLIANT, GORGEOUS SCIENTIST.
I'VE ARRANGED FOR THIS MESSAGE TO BE TRANSMIT-TED ONCE CERTAIN CONDITIONS ARE MET...
VZZT
WHEN A CRISIS ON CENANCLE ISLAND IS IDENTIFIED.
THIS INFORMA-TION...
THIS TRUTH...

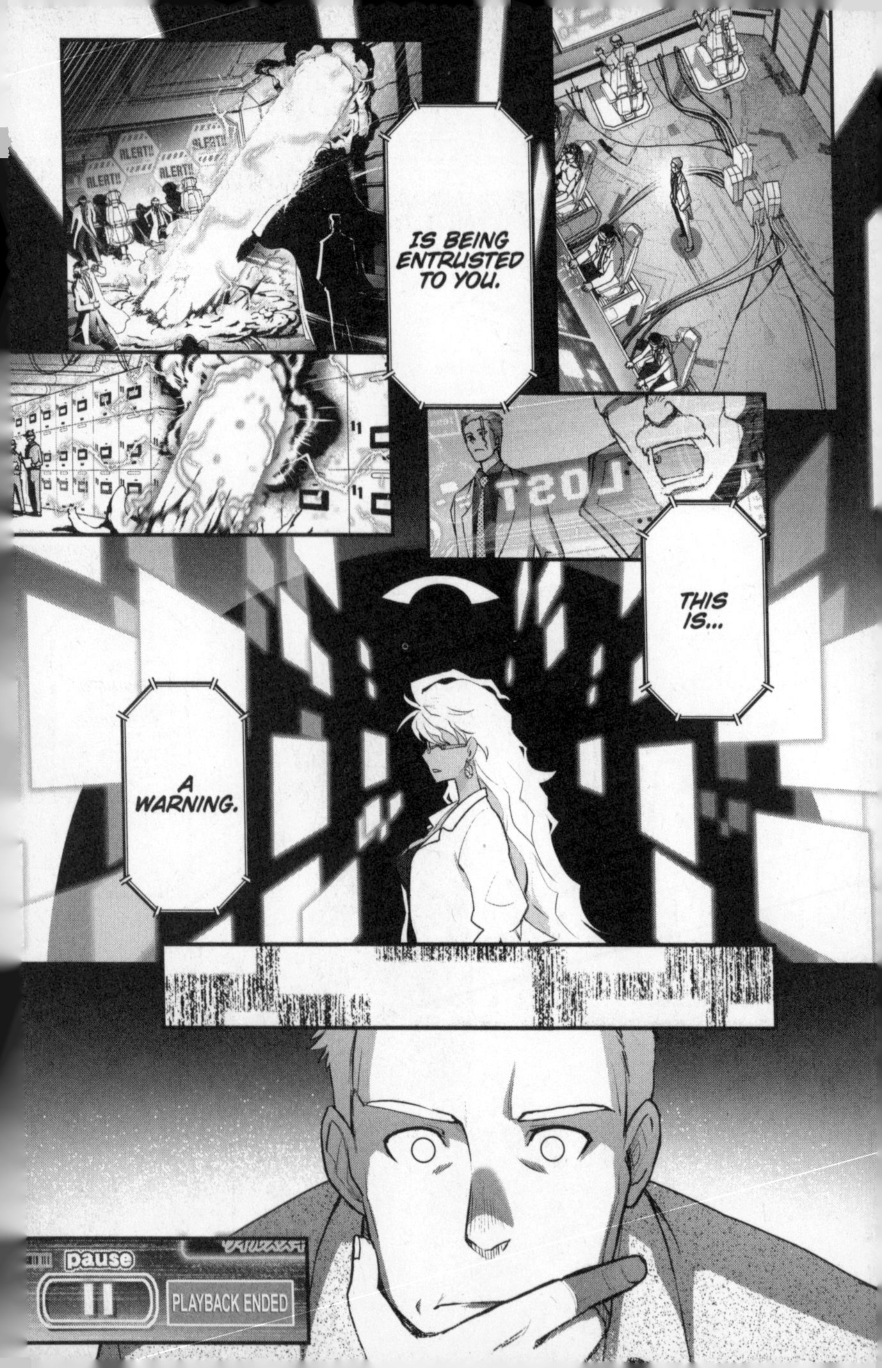
IS BEING ENTRUSTED TO YOU.
ALERT!!
ALERT!!
ALERT!!
ALERT!!
ALERT!!
LOST
THIS IS...
A WARNING.
pause
PLAYBACK ENDED

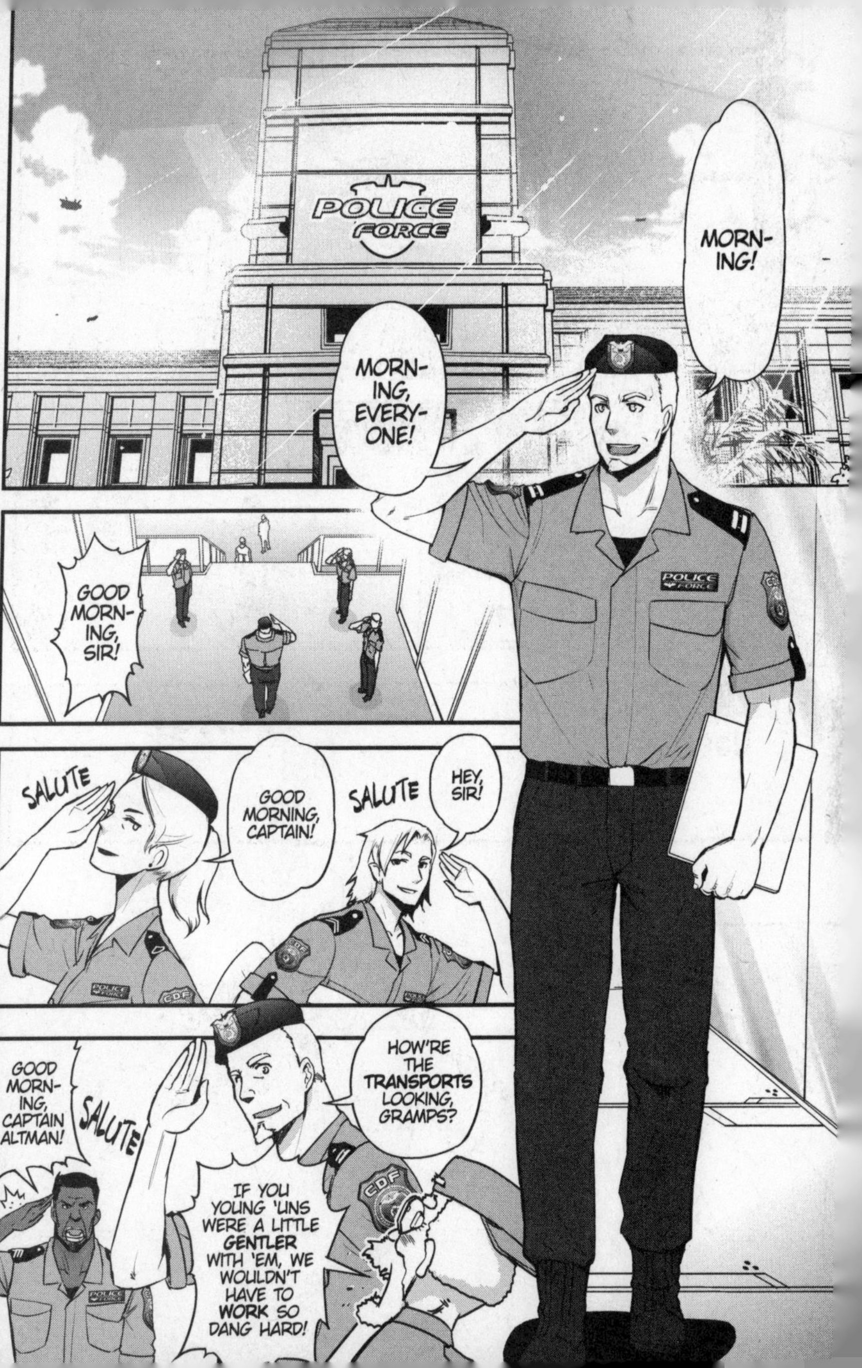
POLICE FORCE
MORN-ING!
MORN-ING, EVERY-ONE!
GOOD MORN-ING, SIR!
HEY, SIR!
SALUTE
GOOD MORNING, CAPTAIN!
SALUTE
HOW'RE THE **TRANSPORTS** LOOKING, GRAMPS?
SALUTE
GOOD MORN-ING, CAPTAIN ALTMAN!
IF YOU YOUNG 'UNS WERE A LITTLE **GENTLER** WITH 'EM, WE WOULDN'T HAVE TO **WORK** SO DANG HARD!

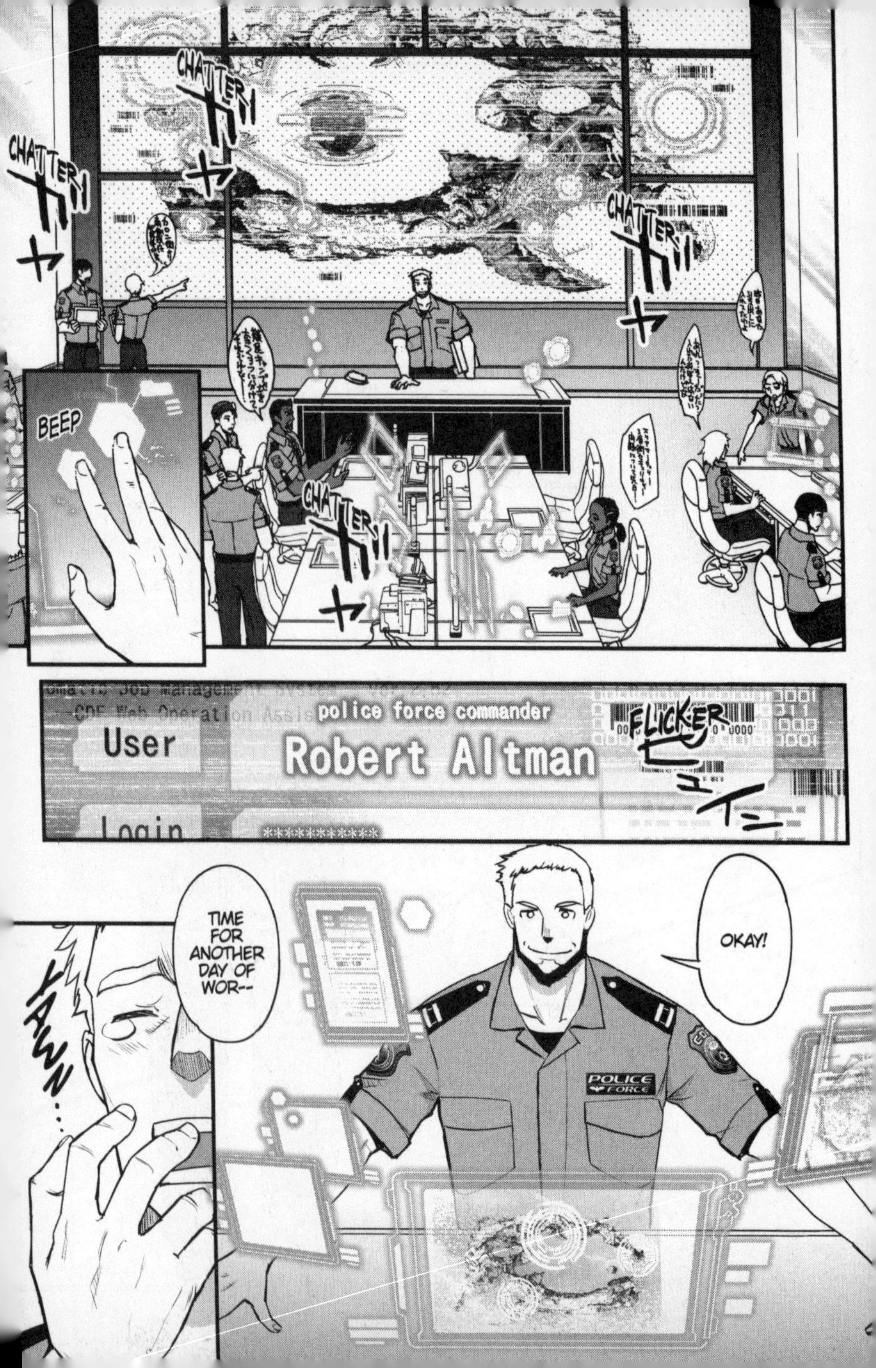
CHATTER
CHATTER
CHATTER
CHATTER
BEEP
police force commander
User
Robert Altman
FLICKER
Login
****
OKAY!
TIME FOR ANOTHER DAY OF WOR--
YAWN...

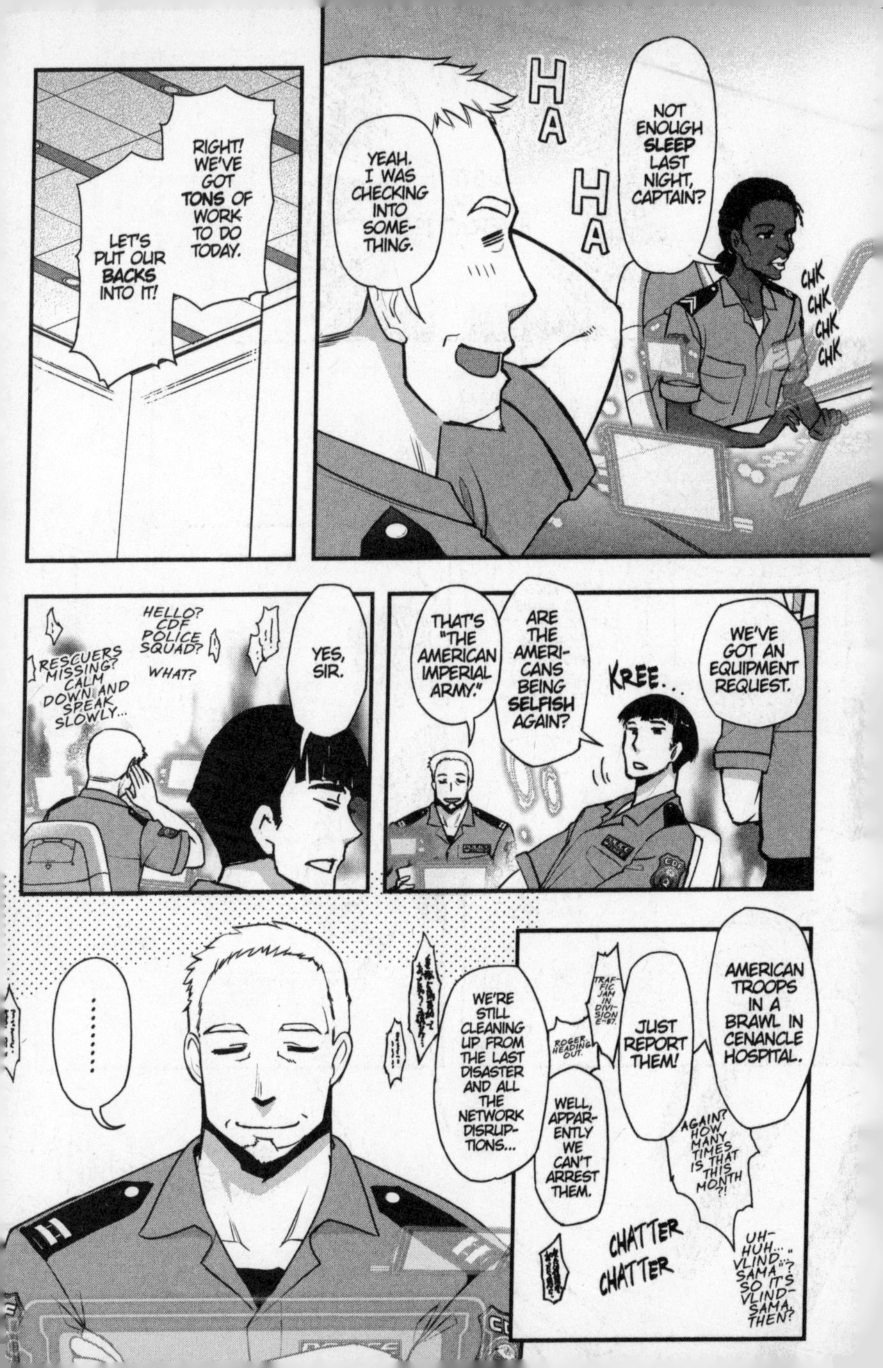
HA HA HA HA
NOT ENOUGH SLEEP LAST NIGHT, CAPTAIN?
CHK CHK CHK CHK
YEAH. I WAS CHECKING INTO SOME-THING.
RIGHT! WE'VE GOT TONS OF WORK TO DO TODAY.
LET'S PUT OUR BACKS INTO IT!
WE'VE GOT AN EQUIPMENT REQUEST.
KREE...
ARE THE AMERI-CANS BEING SELFISH AGAIN?
THAT'S "THE AMERICAN IMPERIAL ARMY."
YES, SIR.
HELLO? CDF POLICE SQUAD?
WHAT?
RESCUERS MISSING? CALM DOWN AND SPEAK SLOWLY...
AMERICAN TROOPS IN A BRAWL IN CENANCLE HOSPITAL.
JUST REPORT THEM!
AGAIN? HOW MANY TIMES IS THIS MONTH?!
TRAF-FIC JAM IN DIVI-SION E-87.
ROGER, HEADING OUT.
WE'RE STILL CLEANING UP FROM THE LAST DISASTER AND ALL THE NETWORK DISRUP-TIONS...
WELL, APPAR-ENTLY WE CAN'T ARREST THEM.
CHATTER CHATTER
UH-HUH... "VLIND-SAMA"? SO IT'S VLIND-SAMA, THEN?
......

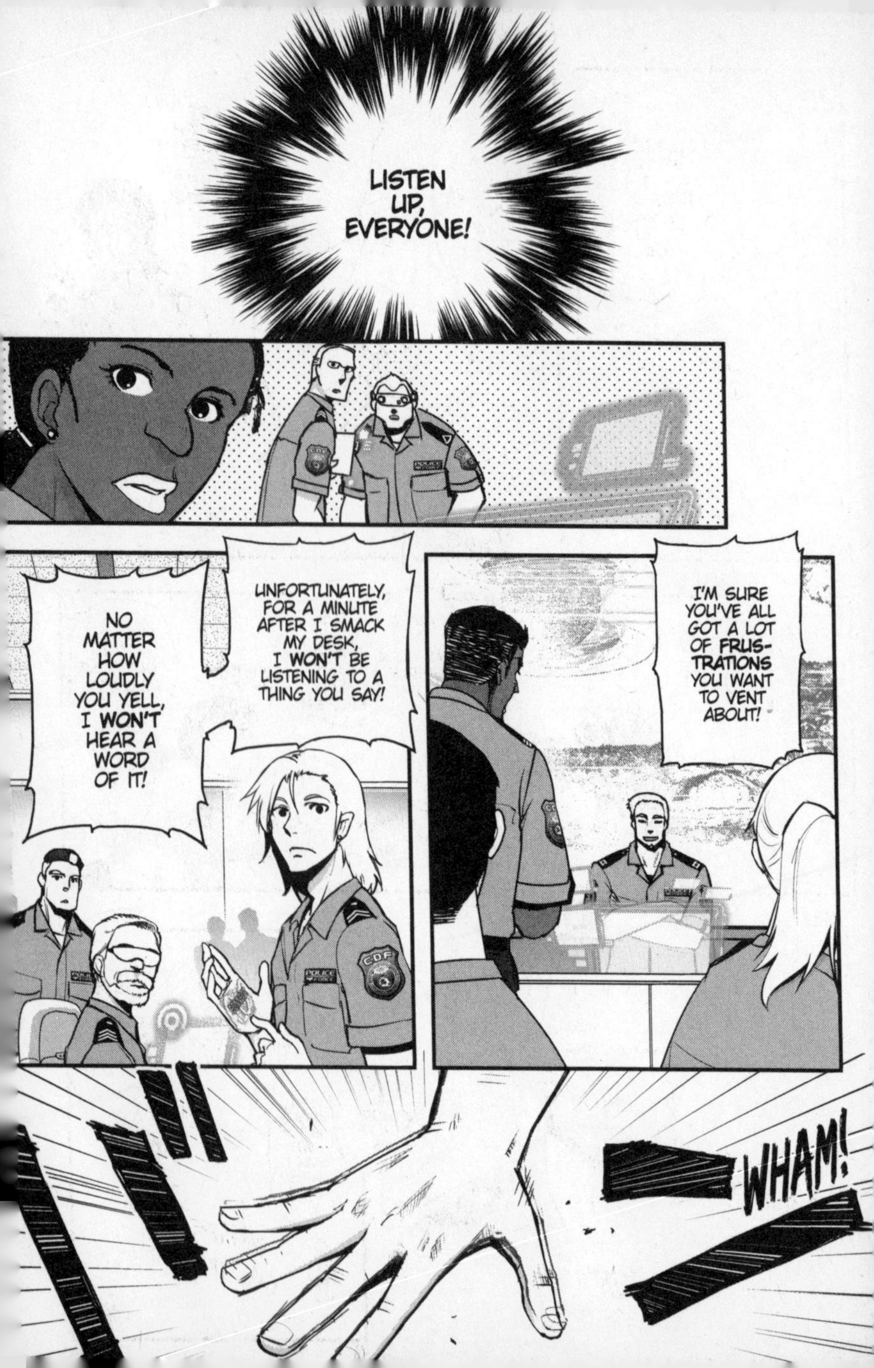
LISTEN UP, EVERYONE!
I'M SURE YOU'VE ALL GOT A LOT OF FRUS-TRATIONS YOU WANT TO VENT ABOUT!
UNFORTUNATELY, FOR A MINUTE AFTER I SMACK MY DESK, I WON'T BE LISTENING TO A THING YOU SAY!
NO MATTER HOW LOUDLY YOU YELL, I WON'T HEAR A WORD OF IT!
WHAM!

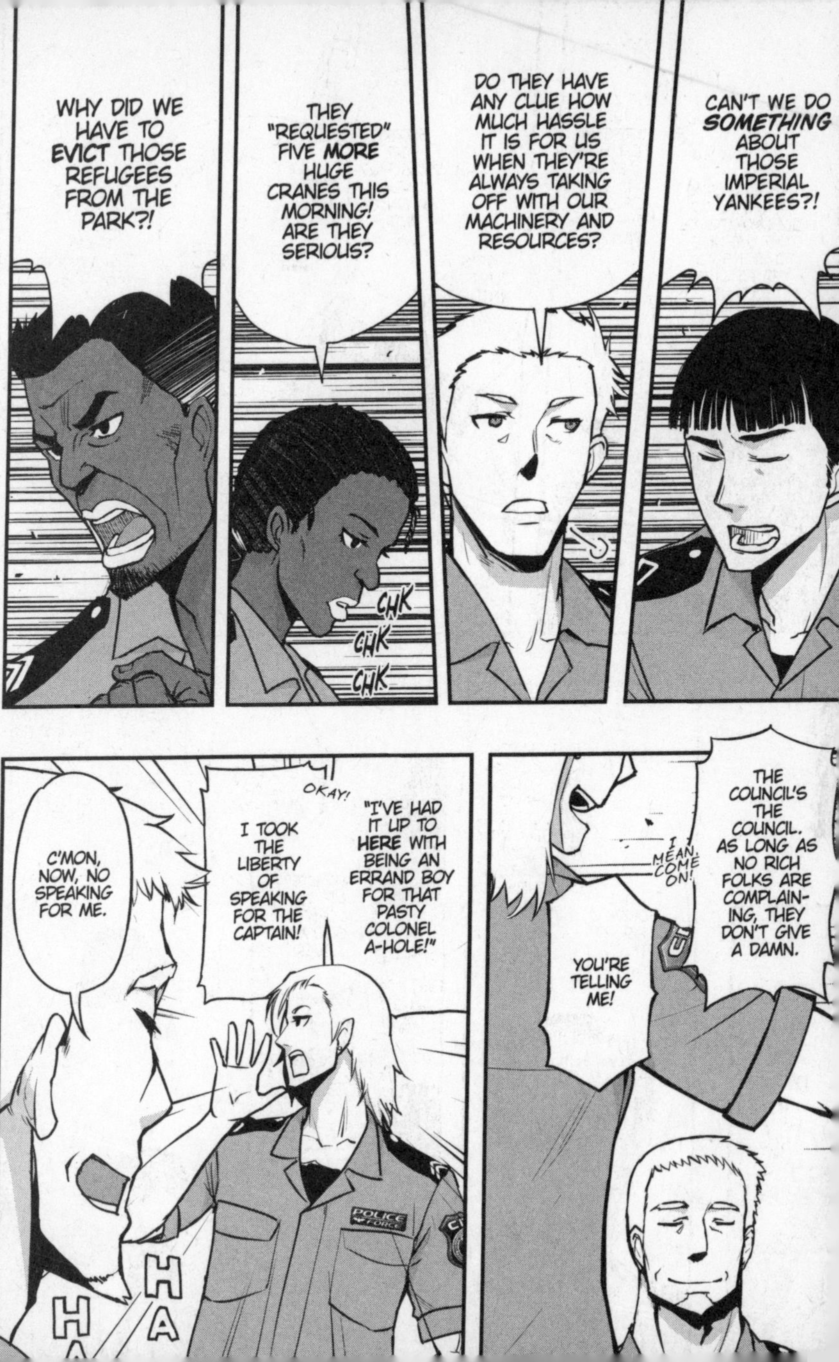

CAN'T WE DO SOMETHING ABOUT THOSE IMPERIAL YANKEES?!
DO THEY HAVE ANY CLUE HOW MUCH HASSLE IT IS FOR US WHEN THEY'RE ALWAYS TAKING OFF WITH OUR MACHINERY AND RESOURCES?
THEY "REQUESTED" FIVE MORE HUGE CRANES THIS MORNING! ARE THEY SERIOUS?
CHK
CHK
CHK
WHY DID WE HAVE TO EVICT THOSE REFUGEES FROM THE PARK?!
THE COUNCIL'S THE COUNCIL. AS LONG AS NO RICH FOLKS ARE COMPLAIN-ING, THEY DON'T GIVE A DAMN.
I MEAN, COME ON!
YOU'RE TELLING ME!
OKAY!
"I'VE HAD IT UP TO HERE WITH BEING AN ERRAND BOY FOR THAT PASTY COLONEL A-HOLE!"
I TOOK THE LIBERTY OF SPEAKING FOR THE CAPTAIN!
C'MON, NOW, NO SPEAKING FOR ME.
HA
HA

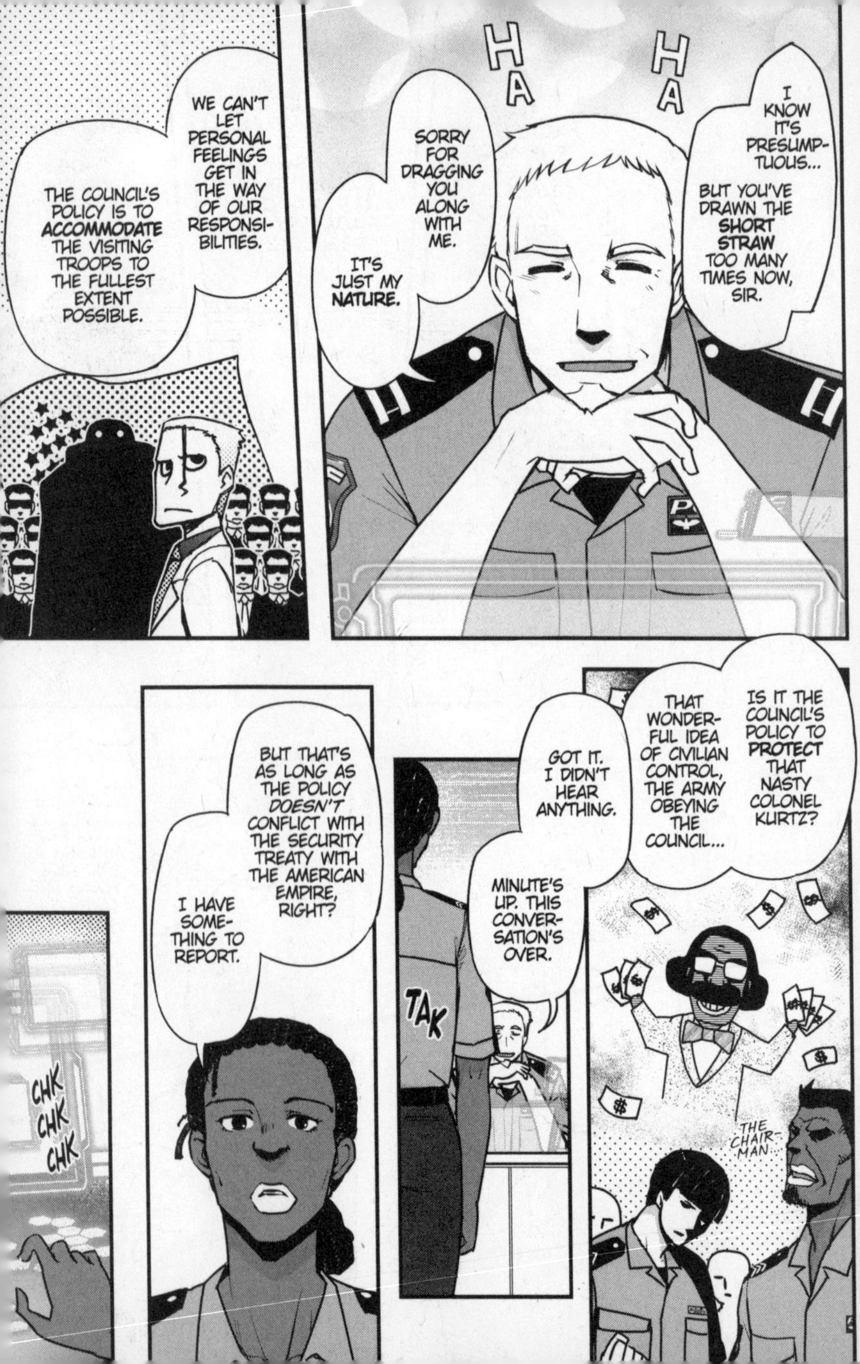
HA HA
I KNOW IT'S PRESUMPTUOUS...
BUT YOU'VE DRAWN THE **SHORT STRAW** TOO MANY TIMES NOW, SIR.
SORRY FOR DRAGGING YOU ALONG WITH ME.
IT'S JUST MY **NATURE.**
WE CAN'T LET PERSONAL FEELINGS GET IN THE WAY OF OUR RESPONSIBILITIES.
THE COUNCIL'S POLICY IS TO **ACCOMMODATE** THE VISITING TROOPS TO THE FULLEST EXTENT POSSIBLE.
IS IT THE COUNCIL'S POLICY TO **PROTECT** THAT NASTY COLONEL KURTZ?
THAT WONDERFUL IDEA OF CIVILIAN CONTROL, THE ARMY OBEYING THE COUNCIL...
THE CHAIRMAN...
GOT IT. I DIDN'T HEAR ANYTHING.
MINUTE'S UP. THIS CONVERSATION'S OVER.
TAK
BUT THAT'S AS LONG AS THE POLICY *DOESN'T* CONFLICT WITH THE SECURITY TREATY WITH THE AMERICAN EMPIRE, RIGHT?
I HAVE SOMETHING TO REPORT.
CHK CHK CHK

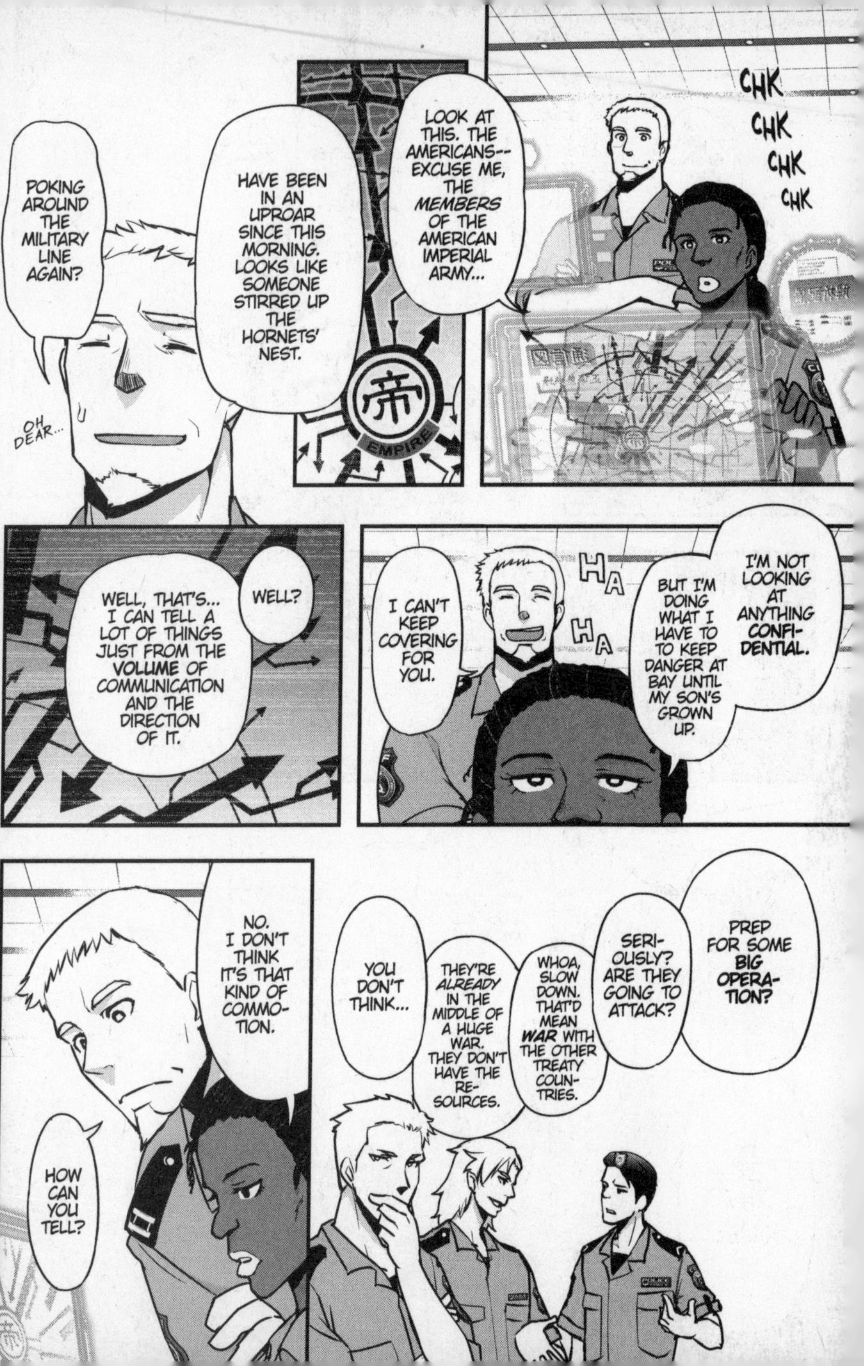
CHK CHK CHK CHK
LOOK AT THIS. THE AMERICANS-- EXCUSE ME, THE MEMBERS OF THE AMERICAN IMPERIAL ARMY...
EMPIRE
HAVE BEEN IN AN UPROAR SINCE THIS MORNING. LOOKS LIKE SOMEONE STIRRED UP THE HORNETS' NEST.
POKING AROUND THE MILITARY LINE AGAIN?
OH DEAR...
I'M NOT LOOKING AT ANYTHING CONFIDENTIAL.
BUT I'M DOING WHAT I HAVE TO TO KEEP DANGER AT BAY UNTIL MY SON'S GROWN UP.
HA HA
I CAN'T KEEP COVERING FOR YOU.
WELL?
WELL, THAT'S... I CAN TELL A LOT OF THINGS JUST FROM THE VOLUME OF COMMUNICATION AND THE DIRECTION OF IT.
PREP FOR SOME BIG OPERATION?
SERIOUSLY? ARE THEY GOING TO ATTACK?
WHOA, SLOW DOWN. THAT'D MEAN WAR WITH THE OTHER TREATY COUNTRIES.
THEY'RE ALREADY IN THE MIDDLE OF A HUGE WAR. THEY DON'T HAVE THE RESOURCES.
YOU DON'T THINK...
NO. I DON'T THINK IT'S THAT KIND OF COMMOTION.
HOW CAN YOU TELL?

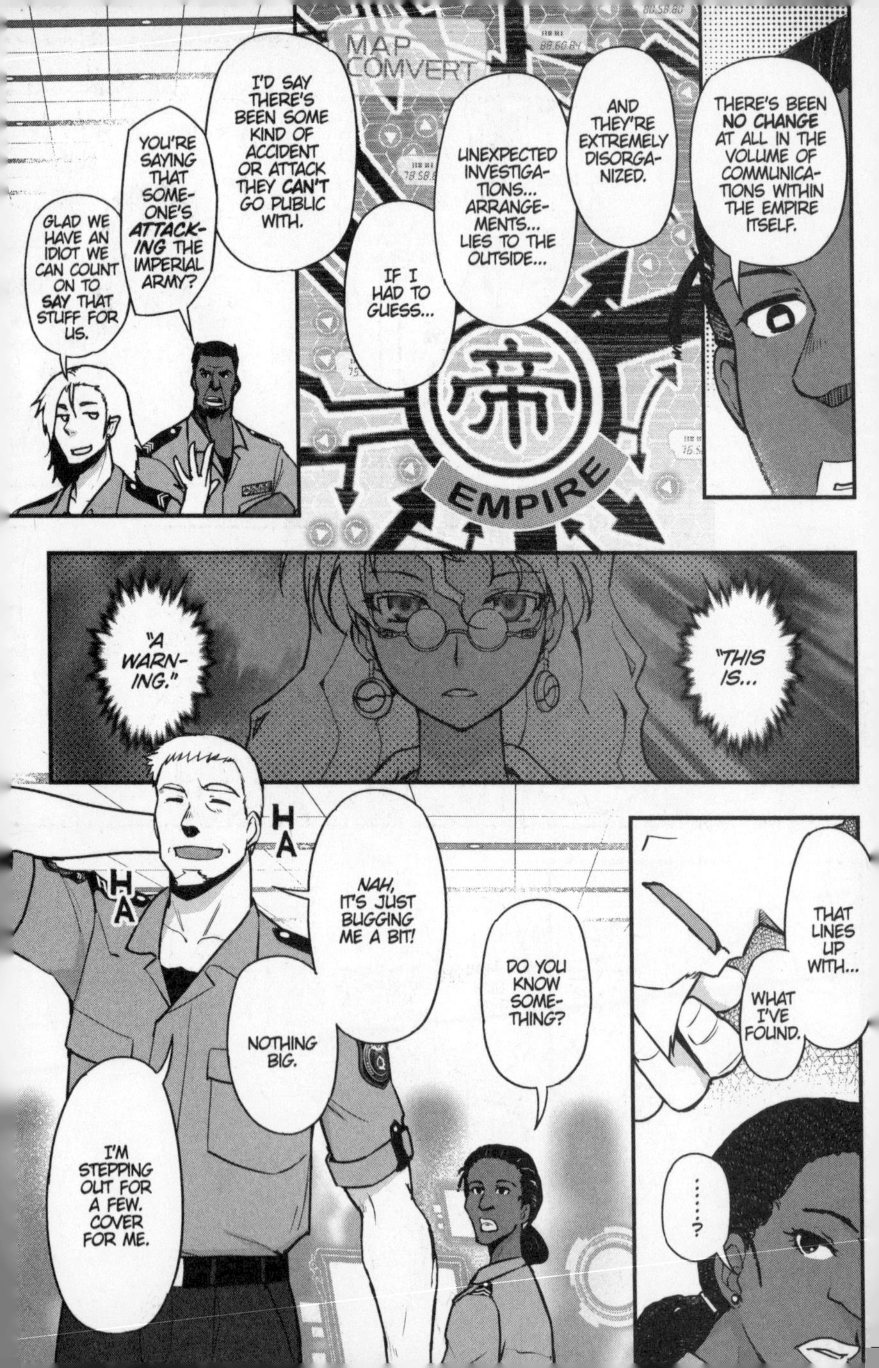

THERE'S BEEN NO CHANGE AT ALL IN THE VOLUME OF COMMUNICATIONS WITHIN THE EMPIRE ITSELF.
MAP COMVERT
AND THEY'RE EXTREMELY DISORGANIZED.
UNEXPECTED INVESTIGATIONS... ARRANGEMENTS... LIES TO THE OUTSIDE...
IF I HAD TO GUESS...
I'D SAY THERE'S BEEN SOME KIND OF ACCIDENT OR ATTACK THEY CAN'T GO PUBLIC WITH.
帝
EMPIRE
YOU'RE SAYING THAT SOMEONE'S ATTACKING THE IMPERIAL ARMY?
GLAD WE HAVE AN IDIOT WE CAN COUNT ON TO SAY THAT STUFF FOR US.
"THIS IS...
"A WARNING."
THAT LINES UP WITH...
WHAT I'VE FOUND.
......?
DO YOU KNOW SOMETHING?
NAH, IT'S JUST BUGGING ME A BIT!
HA
HA
NOTHING BIG.
I'M STEPPING OUT FOR A FEW. COVER FOR ME.

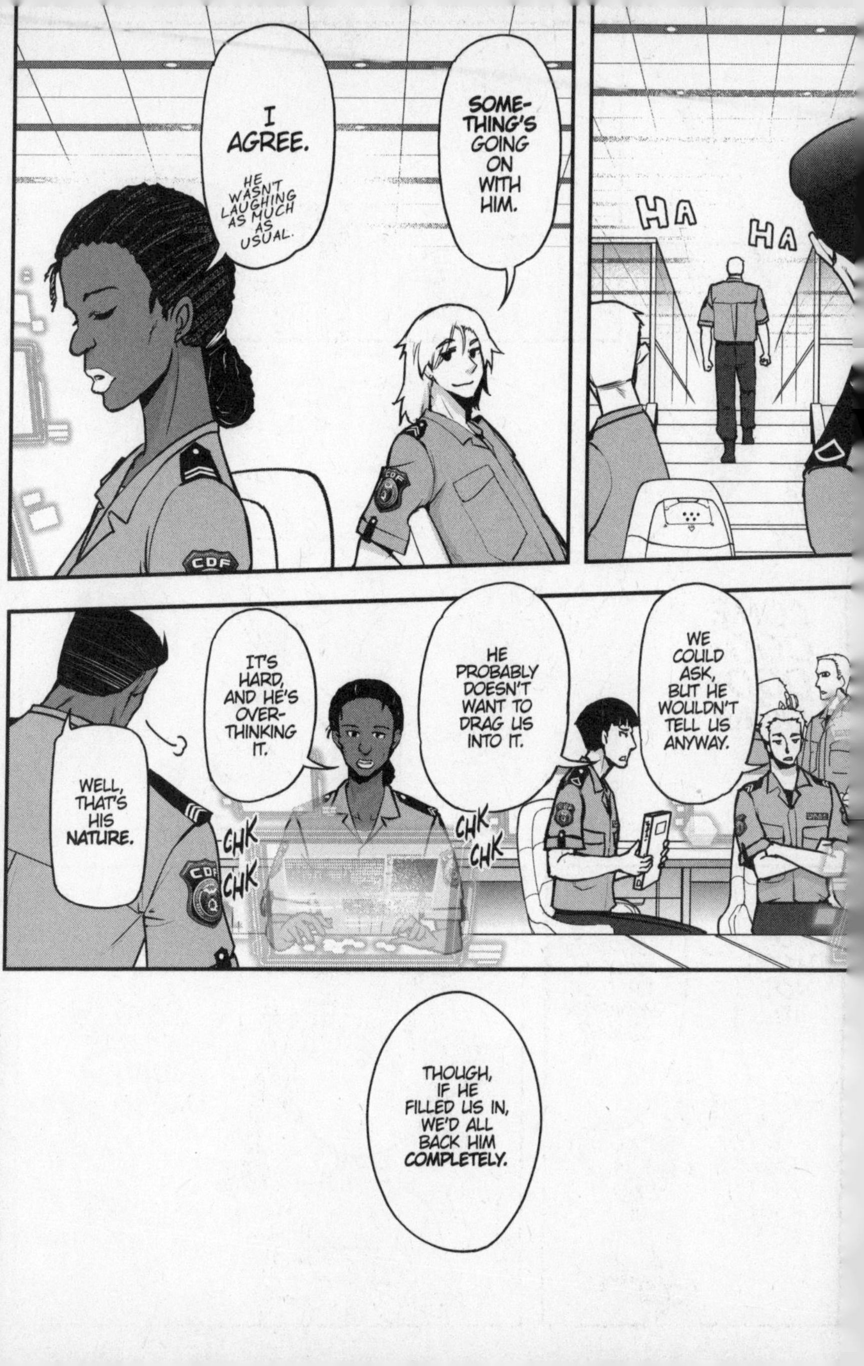
HA HA
SOME-THING'S GOING ON WITH HIM.
I AGREE.
HE WASN'T LAUGHING AS MUCH AS USUAL.
WE COULD ASK, BUT HE WOULDN'T TELL US ANYWAY.
HE PROBABLY DOESN'T WANT TO DRAG US INTO IT.
CHK CHK
IT'S HARD, AND HE'S OVER-THINKING IT.
CHK CHK
WELL, THAT'S HIS NATURE.
THOUGH, IF HE FILLED US IN, WE'D ALL BACK HIM COMPLETELY.

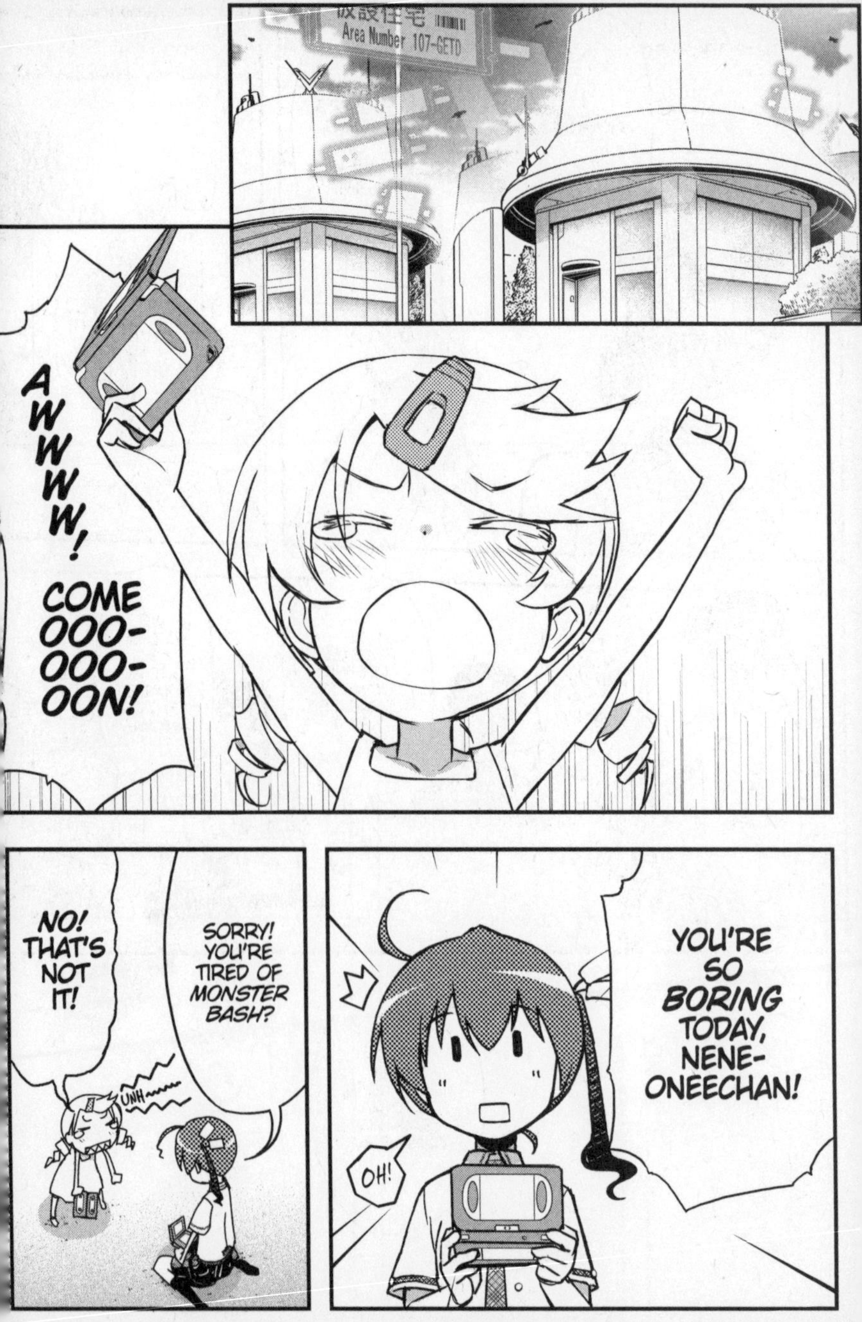
Area Number 107-GETD
AWWWWW! COME OOO-OOO-OON!
YOU'RE SO *BORING* TODAY, NENE-ONEECHAN!
OH!
SORRY! YOU'RE TIRED OF MONSTER BASH?
NO! THAT'S NOT IT!
UNH~~~

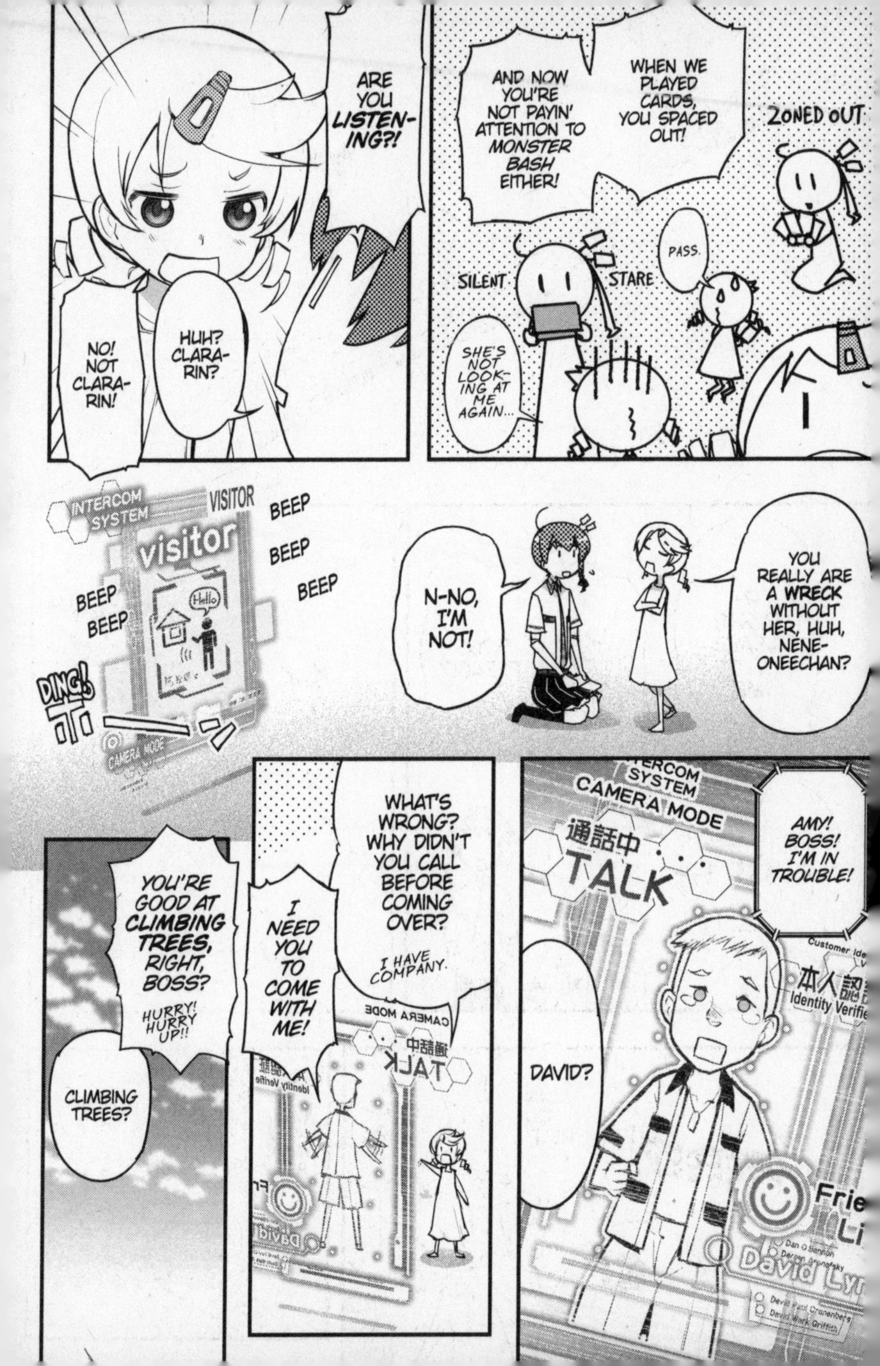
ZONED OUT
WHEN WE PLAYED CARDS, YOU SPACED OUT!
AND NOW YOU'RE NOT PAYIN' ATTENTION TO MONSTER BASH EITHER!
PASS.
SILENT STARE
SHE'S NOT LOOKING AT ME AGAIN...
ARE YOU LISTENING?!
HUH? CLARA-RIN?
NO! NOT CLARA-RIN!
YOU REALLY ARE A WRECK WITHOUT HER, HUH, NENE-ONEECHAN?
N-NO, I'M NOT!
BEEP BEEP BEEP
VISITOR
INTERCOM SYSTEM
visitor
Hello
BEEP BEEP
DING!
CAMERA MODE
INTERCOM SYSTEM CAMERA MODE
通話中 TALK
AMY! BOSS! I'M IN TROUBLE!
DAVID?
WHAT'S WRONG? WHY DIDN'T YOU CALL BEFORE COMING OVER?
I HAVE COMPANY.
I NEED YOU TO COME WITH ME!
YOU'RE GOOD AT CLIMBING TREES, RIGHT, BOSS?
HURRY! HURRY UP!!
CLIMBING TREES?

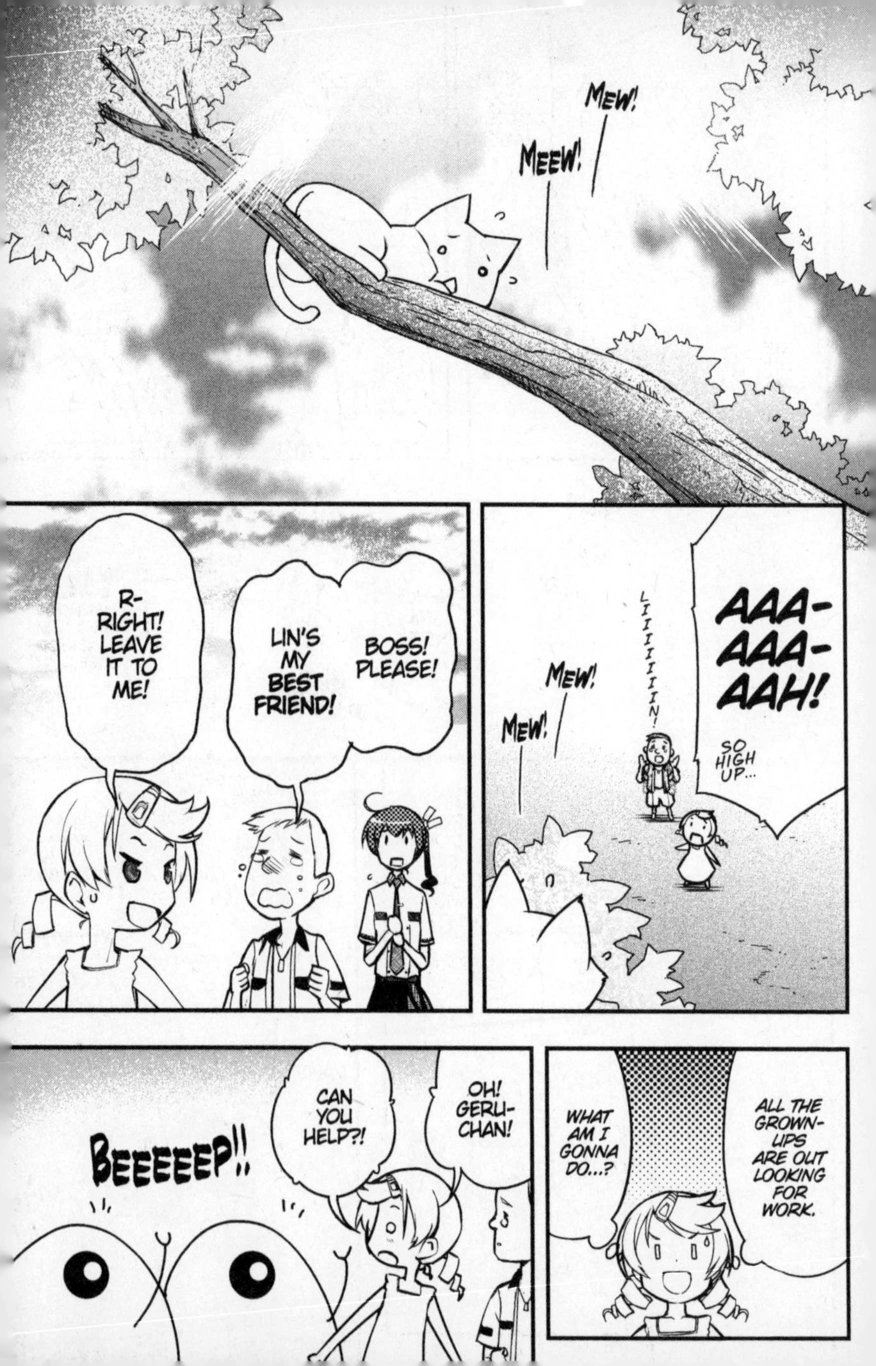
MEW!
MEEW!
AAA-AAA-AAH!
SO HIGH UP...
LIIIIIIIIN!
MEW!
MEW!
BOSS! PLEASE!
LIN'S MY BEST FRIEND!
R-RIGHT! LEAVE IT TO ME!
ALL THE GROWN-UPS ARE OUT LOOKING FOR WORK.
WHAT AM I GONNA DO...?
OH! GERU-CHAN!
CAN YOU HELP?!
BEEEEEEP!!

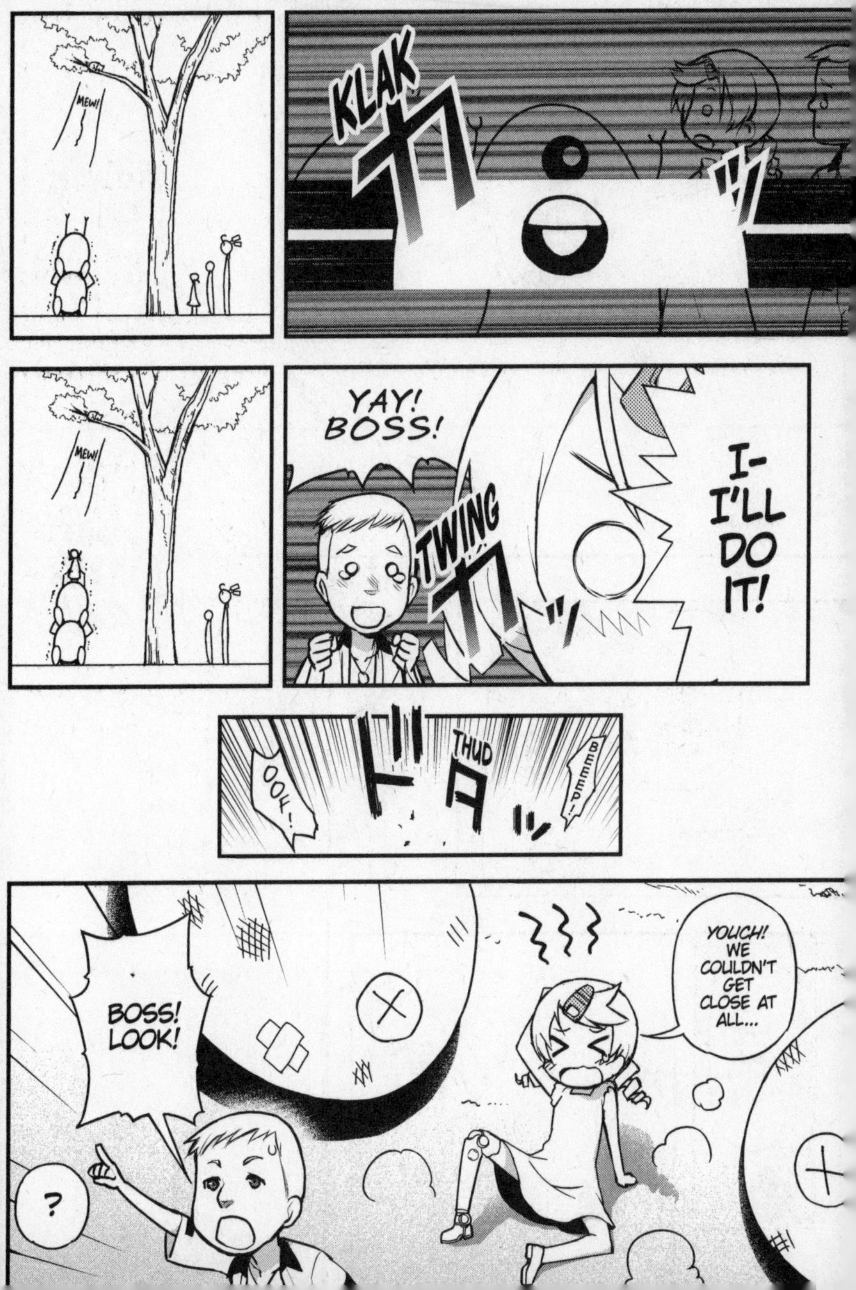
KLAK
MEW!
I- I'LL DO IT!
YAY! BOSS!
TWING
MEW!
BEEEP!
THUD
OOF!
YOUCH! WE COULDN'T GET CLOSE AT ALL...
BOSS! LOOK!
?

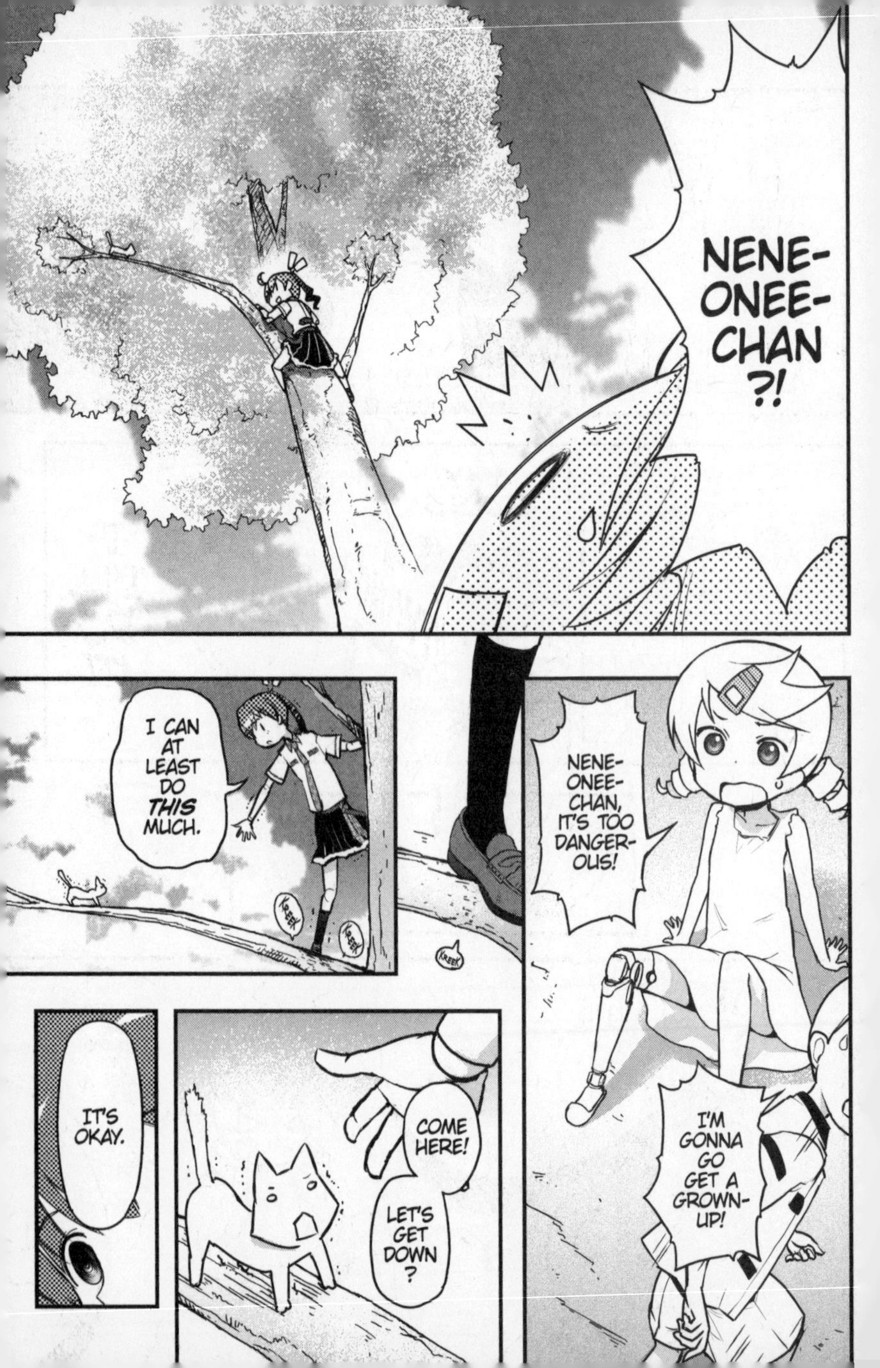
NENE-ONEE-CHAN?!
NENE-ONEE-CHAN, IT'S TOO DANGER-OUS!
I'M GONNA GO GET A GROWN-UP!
I CAN AT LEAST DO THIS MUCH.
KREEK
KREEK
KREEK
COME HERE!
LET'S GET DOWN?
IT'S OKAY.

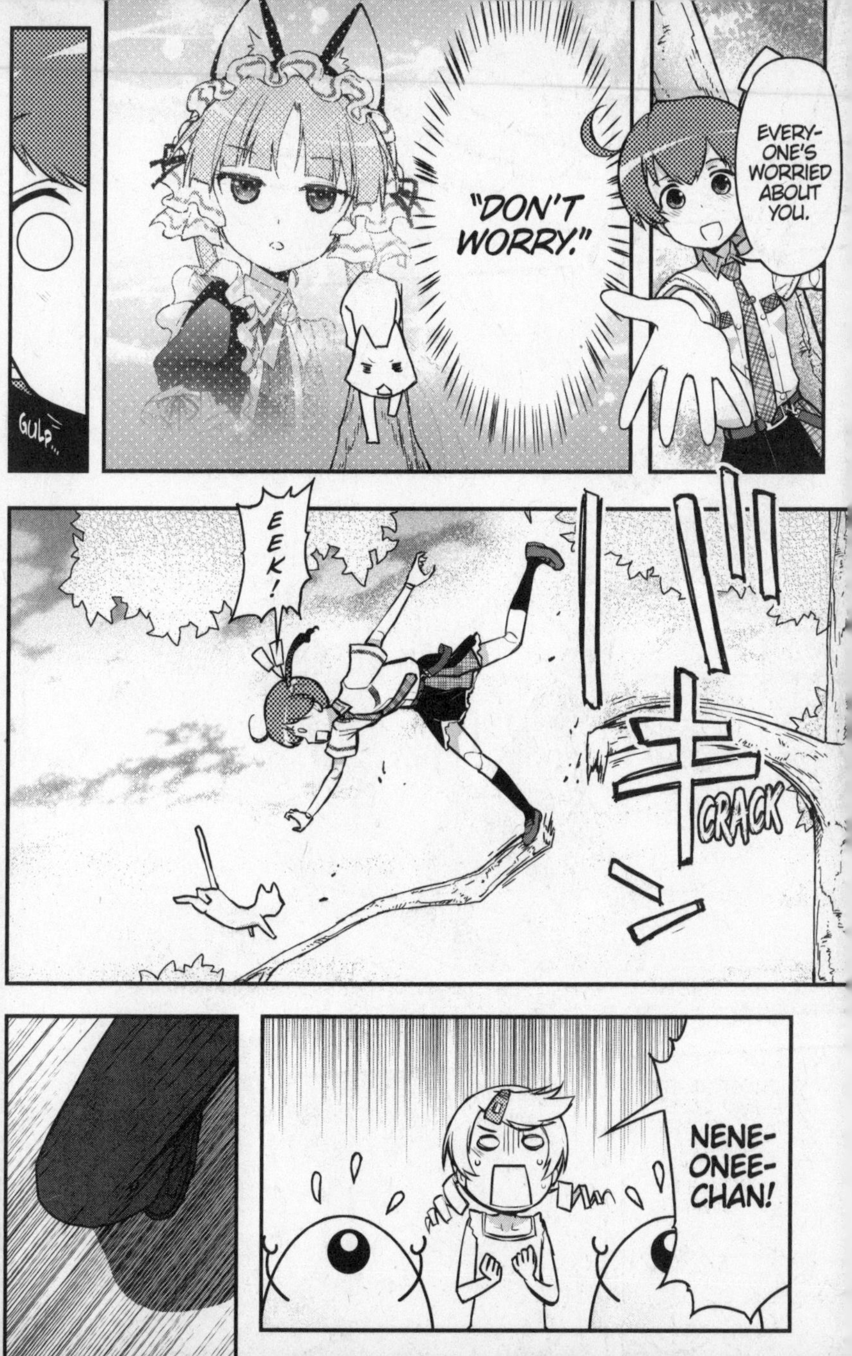
EVERY-ONE'S WORRIED ABOUT YOU.
"DON'T WORRY."
GULP...
EEK!
CRACK
NENE-ONEE-CHAN!

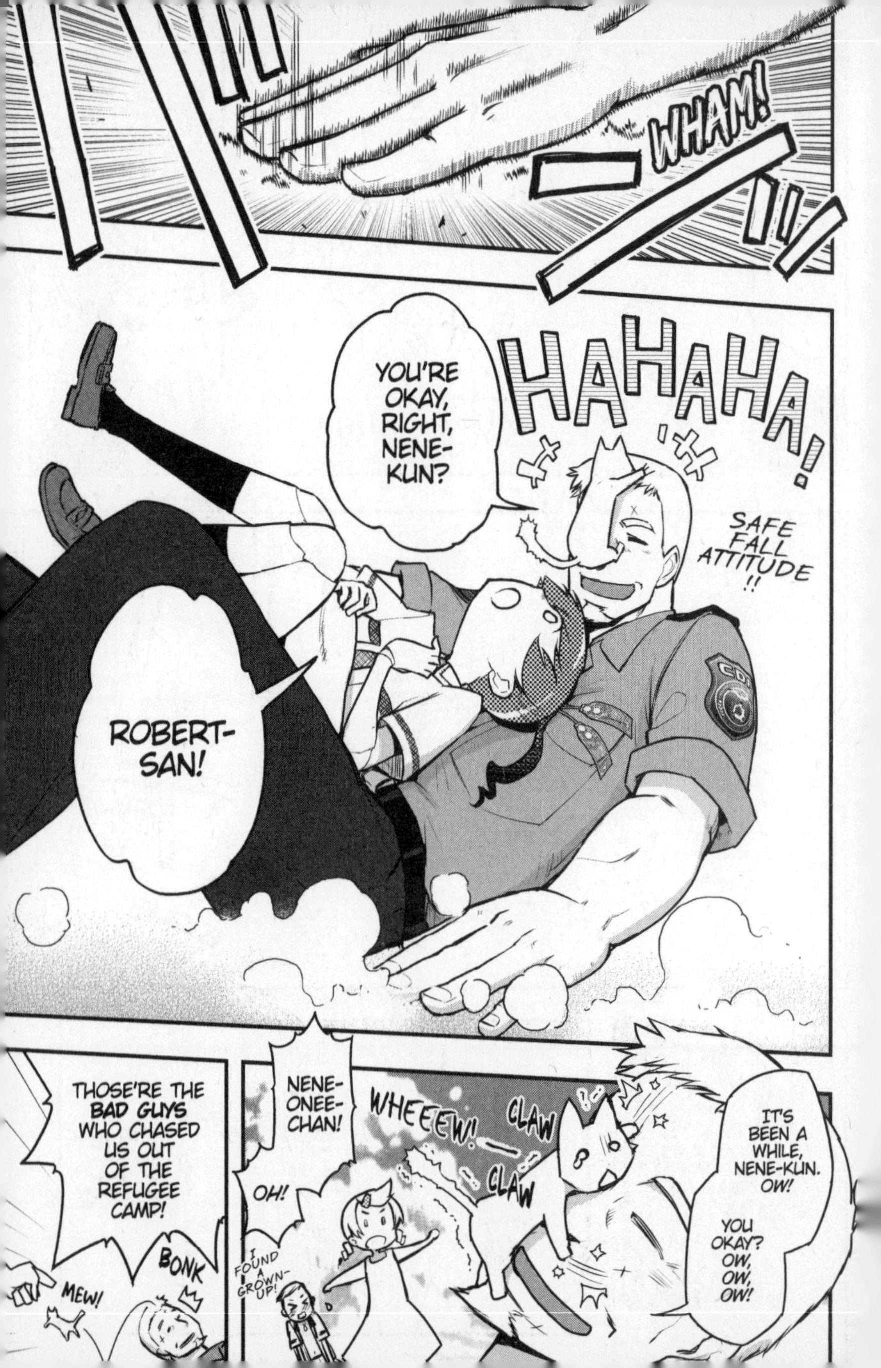
WHAM!
HAHAHA!
YOU'RE OKAY, RIGHT, NENE-KUN?
SAFE FALL ATTITUDE!!
ROBERT-SAN!
IT'S BEEN A WHILE, NENE-KUN. OW!
YOU OKAY? OW, OW, OW!
CLAW
CLAW
WHEEEW!
NENE-ONEE-CHAN!
OH!
I FOUND A GROWN-UP!
THOSE'RE THE BAD GUYS WHO CHASED US OUT OF THE REFUGEE CAMP!
BONK
MEW!

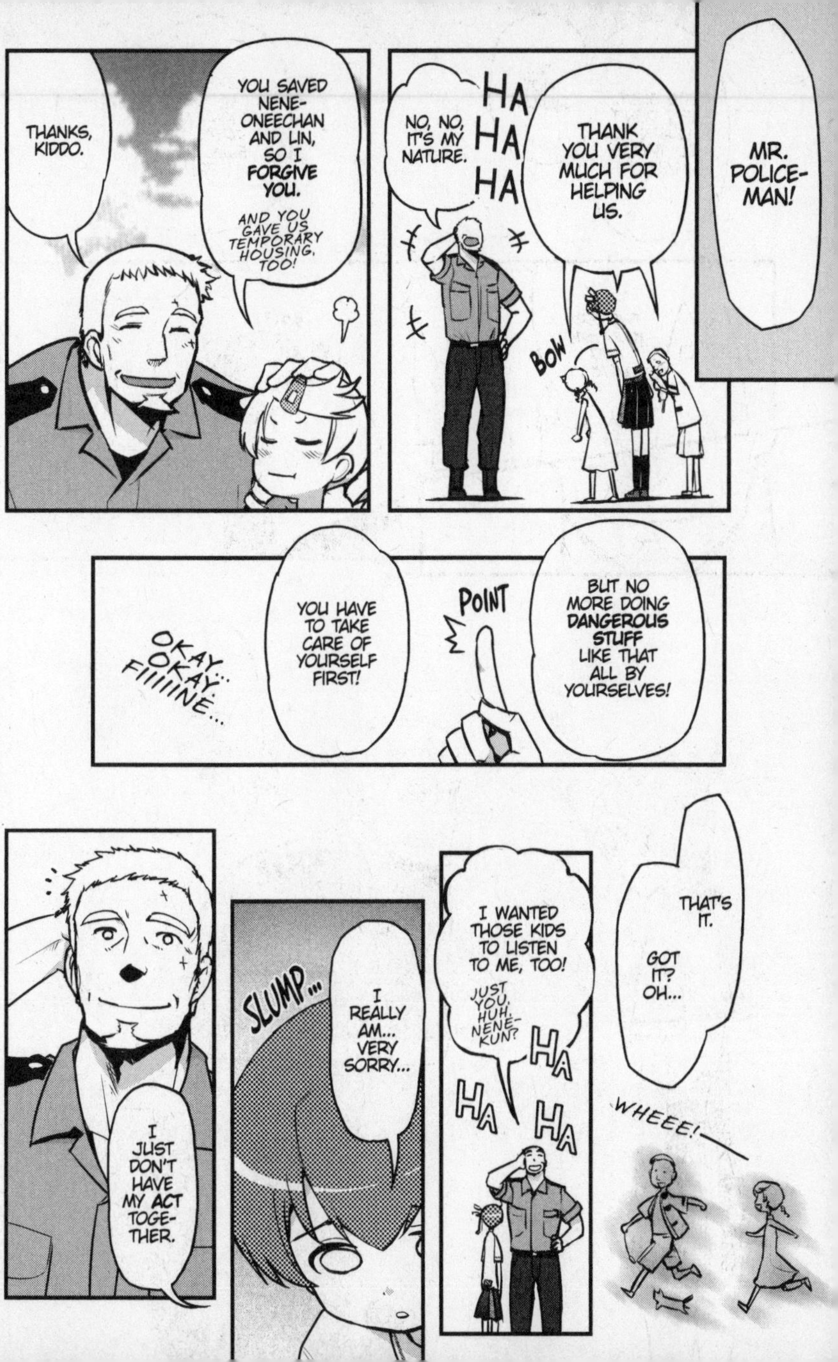
MR. POLICE-MAN!
THANK YOU VERY MUCH FOR HELPING US.
HA HA HA
NO, NO, IT'S MY NATURE.
BOW
YOU SAVED NENE-ONEECHAN AND LIN, SO I FORGIVE YOU.
AND YOU GAVE US TEMPORARY HOUSING, TOO!
THANKS, KIDDO.
BUT NO MORE DOING DANGEROUS STUFF LIKE THAT ALL BY YOURSELVES!
POINT
YOU HAVE TO TAKE CARE OF YOURSELF FIRST!
OKAY... OKAY. FIIIIINE...
THAT'S IT.
GOT IT? OH...
WHEEEE!
I WANTED THOSE KIDS TO LISTEN TO ME, TOO!
JUST YOU, HUH, NENE-KUN?
HA HA HA
SLUMP...
I REALLY AM... VERY SORRY...
I JUST DON'T HAVE MY ACT TOGE-THER.

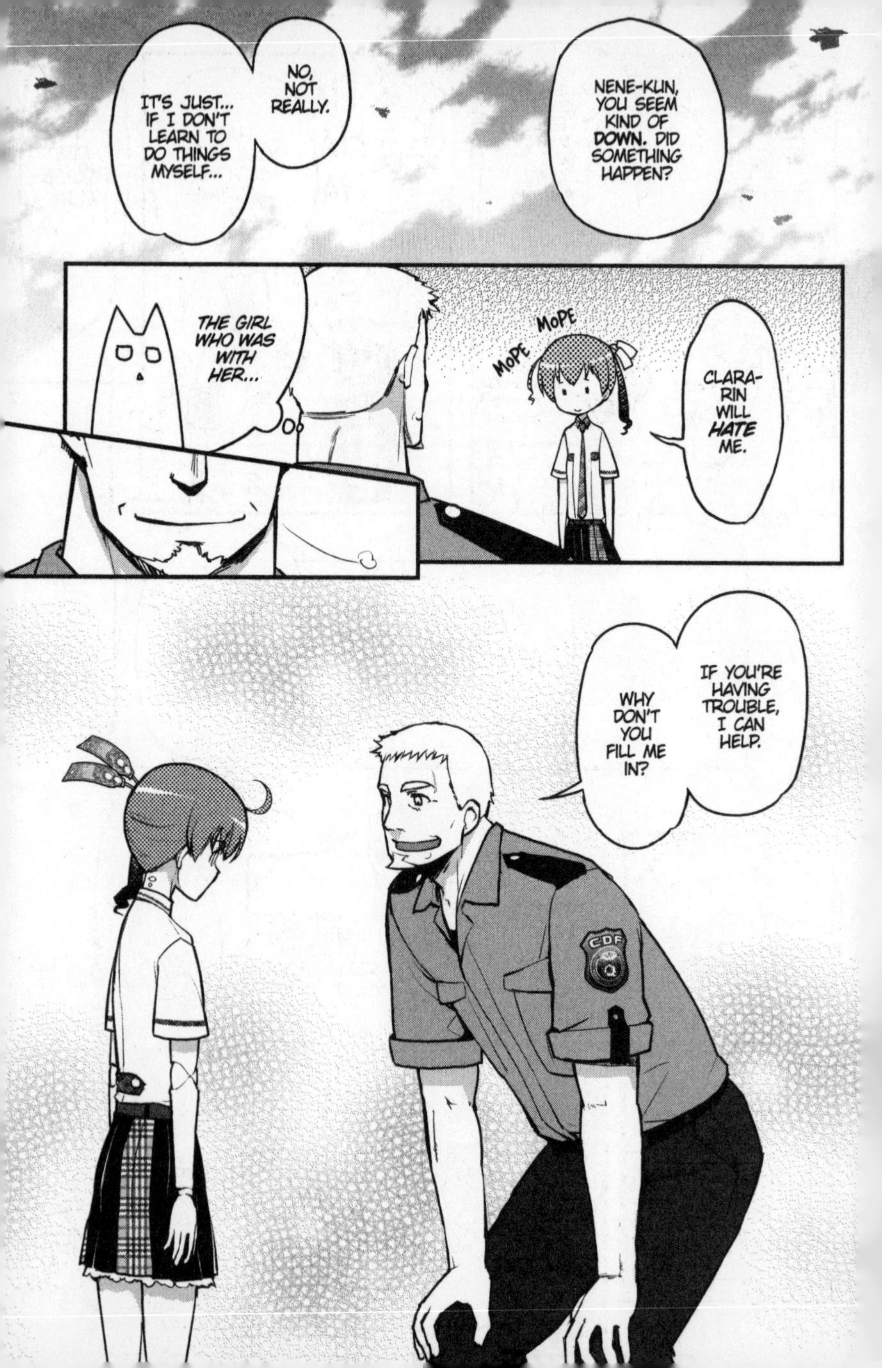
NENE-KUN, YOU SEEM KIND OF DOWN. DID SOMETHING HAPPEN?
NO, NOT REALLY.
IT'S JUST... IF I DON'T LEARN TO DO THINGS MYSELF...
CLARA-RIN WILL HATE ME.
MOPE MOPE
THE GIRL WHO WAS WITH HER...
IF YOU'RE HAVING TROUBLE, I CAN HELP.
WHY DON'T YOU FILL ME IN?

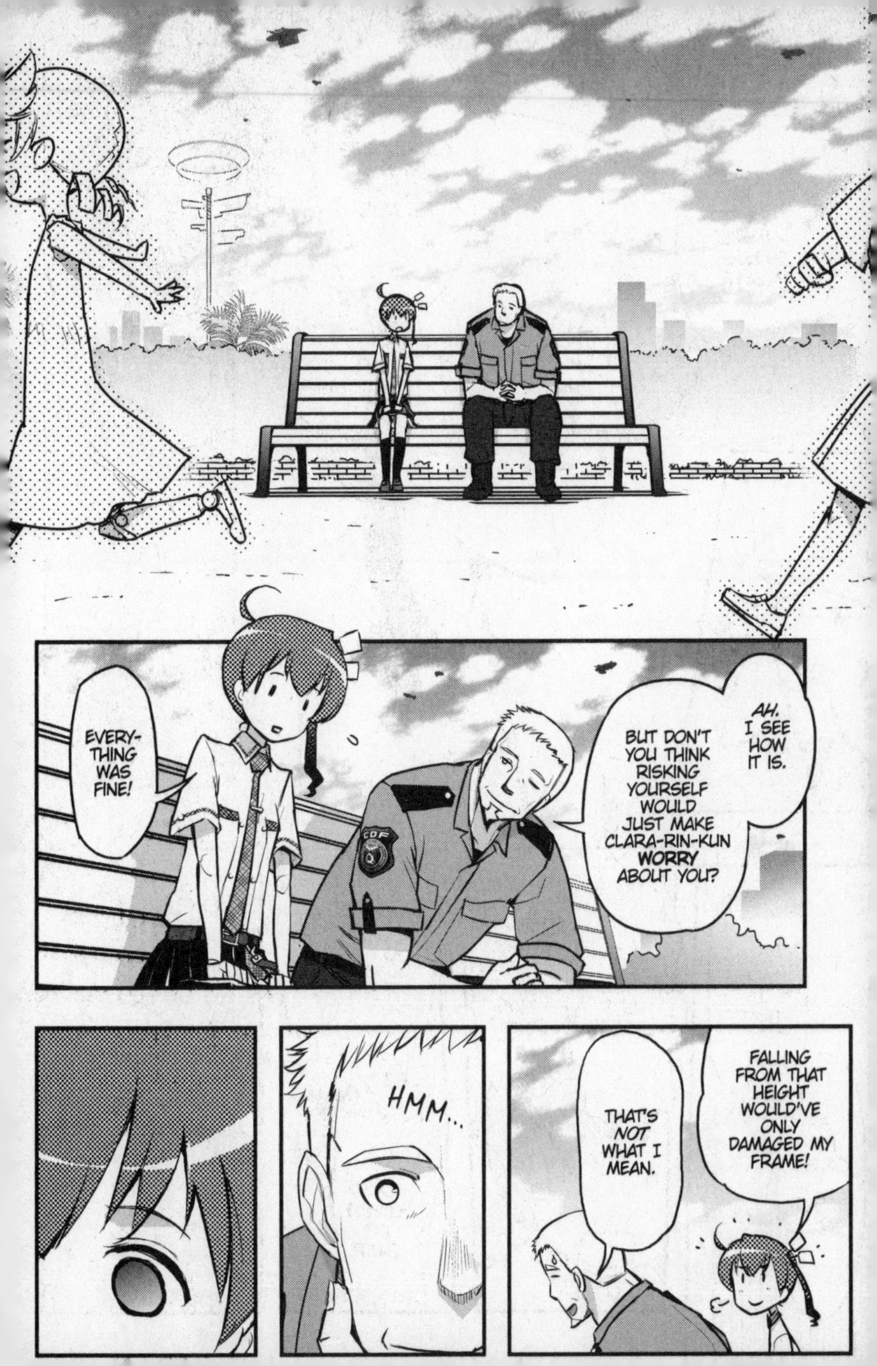
AH. I SEE HOW IT IS.
BUT DON'T YOU THINK RISKING YOURSELF WOULD JUST MAKE CLARA-RIN-KUN **WORRY** ABOUT YOU?
EVERYTHING WAS FINE!
FALLING FROM THAT HEIGHT WOULD'VE ONLY DAMAGED MY FRAME!
THAT'S *NOT* WHAT I MEAN.
HMM...

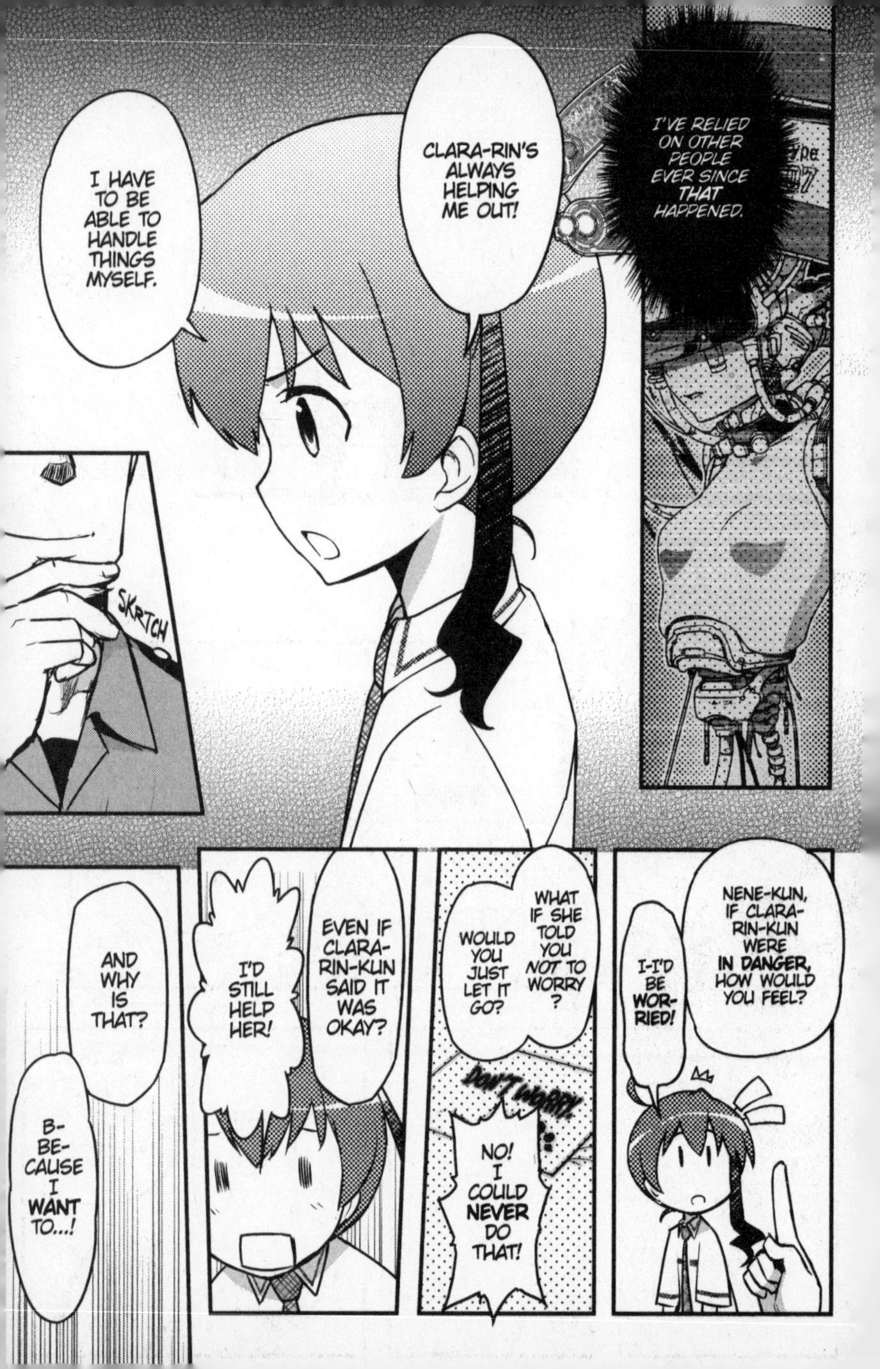
I'VE RELIED ON OTHER PEOPLE EVER SINCE THAT HAPPENED.
CLARA-RIN'S ALWAYS HELPING ME OUT!
I HAVE TO BE ABLE TO HANDLE THINGS MYSELF.
SKRTCH
NENE-KUN, IF CLARA-RIN-KUN WERE IN DANGER, HOW WOULD YOU FEEL?
I-I'D BE WORRIED!
WHAT IF SHE TOLD YOU NOT TO WORRY?
WOULD YOU JUST LET IT GO?
DON'T WORRY!
NO! I COULD NEVER DO THAT!
EVEN IF CLARA-RIN-KUN SAID IT WAS OKAY?
I'D STILL HELP HER!
AND WHY IS THAT?
B-BE-CAUSE I WANT TO...!

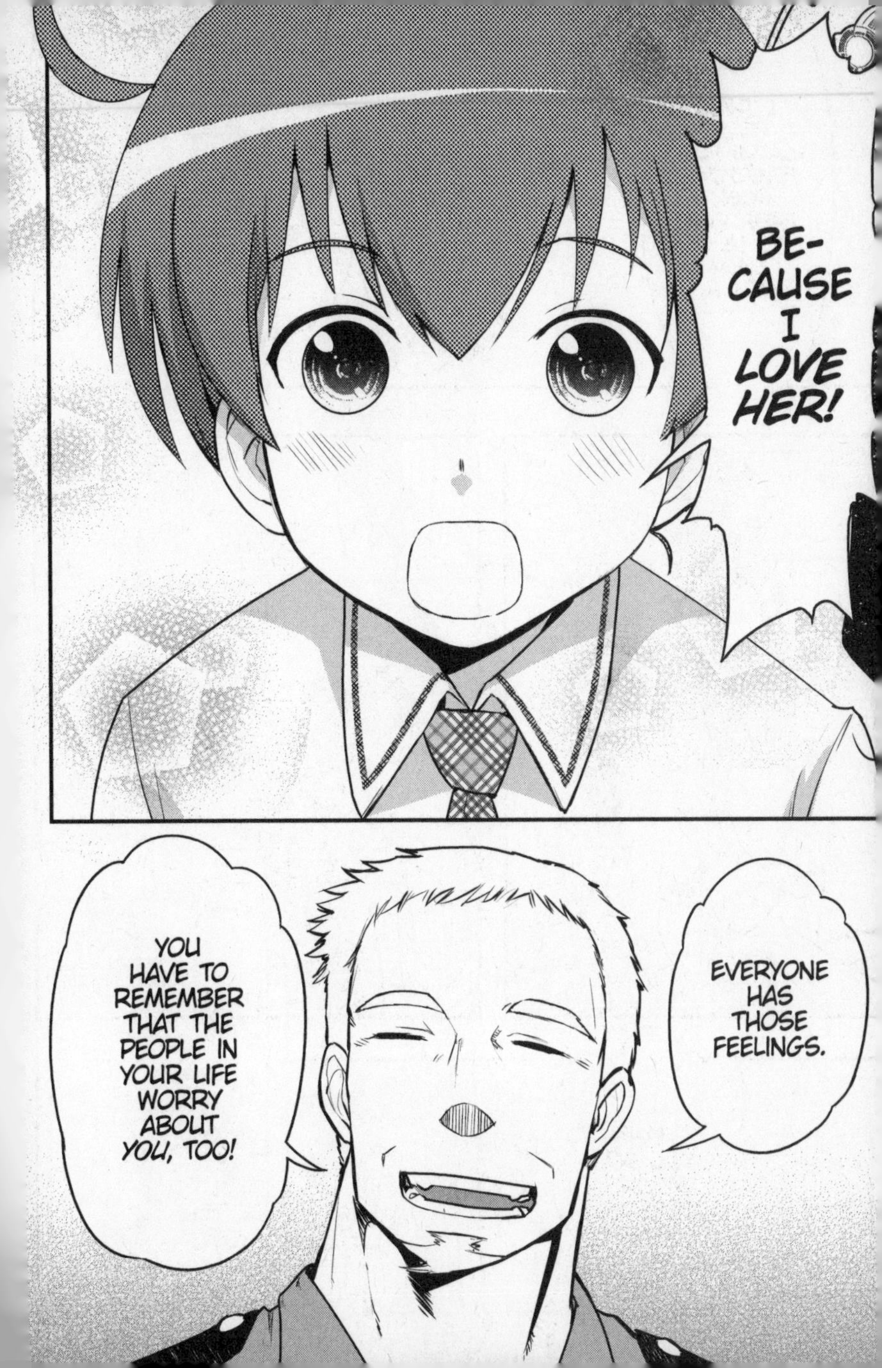
BE-CAUSE I LOVE HER!
EVERYONE HAS THOSE FEELINGS.
YOU HAVE TO REMEMBER THAT THE PEOPLE IN YOUR LIFE WORRY ABOUT YOU, TOO!

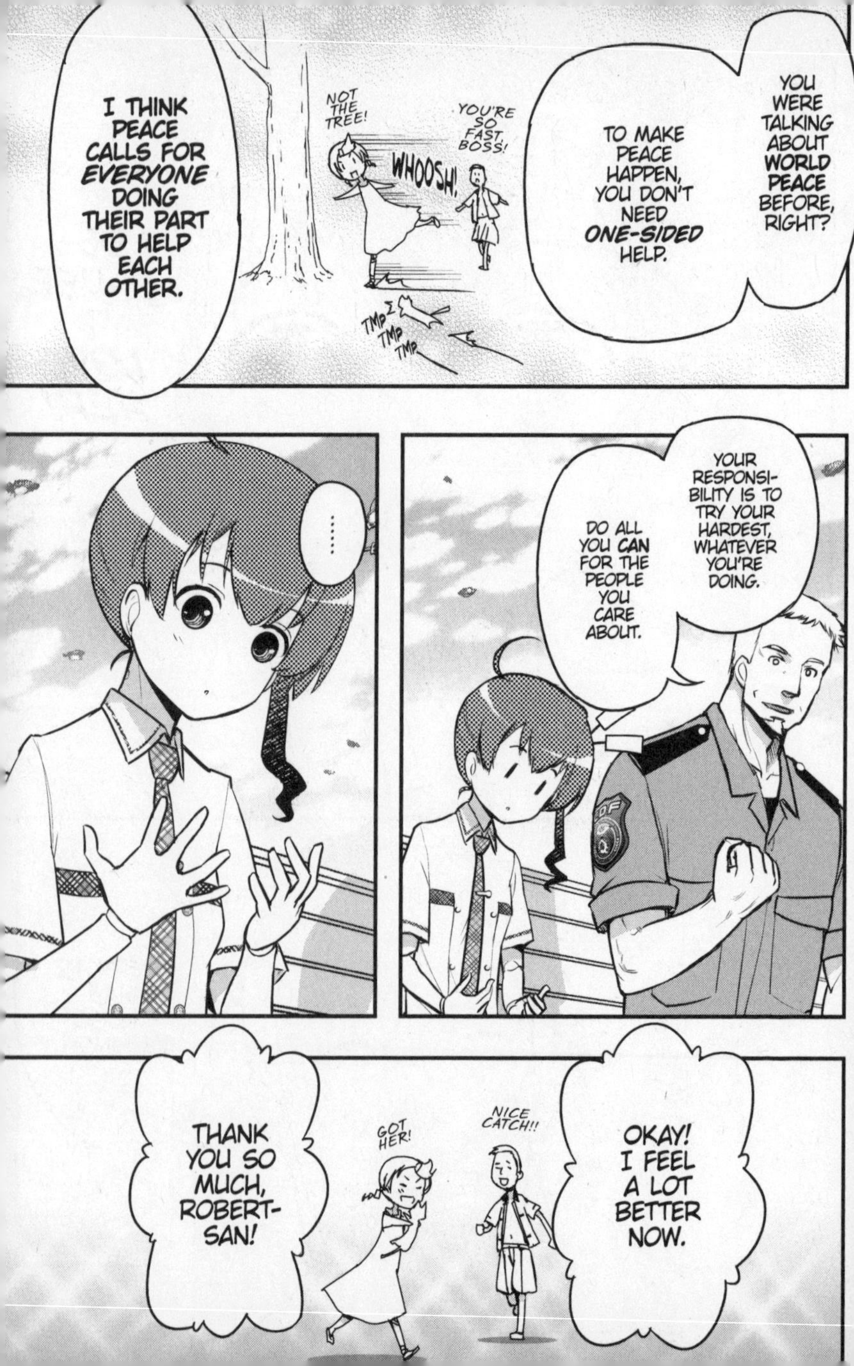
YOU WERE TALKING ABOUT WORLD PEACE BEFORE, RIGHT?
TO MAKE PEACE HAPPEN, YOU DON'T NEED ONE-SIDED HELP.
YOU'RE SO FAST, BOSS!
WHOOSH!
NOT THE TREE!
TMP TMP TMP TMP
I THINK PEACE CALLS FOR EVERYONE DOING THEIR PART TO HELP EACH OTHER.
YOUR RESPONSIBILITY IS TO TRY YOUR HARDEST, WHATEVER YOU'RE DOING.
DO ALL YOU CAN FOR THE PEOPLE YOU CARE ABOUT.
......
OKAY! I FEEL A LOT BETTER NOW.
NICE CATCH!!
GOT HER!
THANK YOU SO MUCH, ROBERT-SAN!

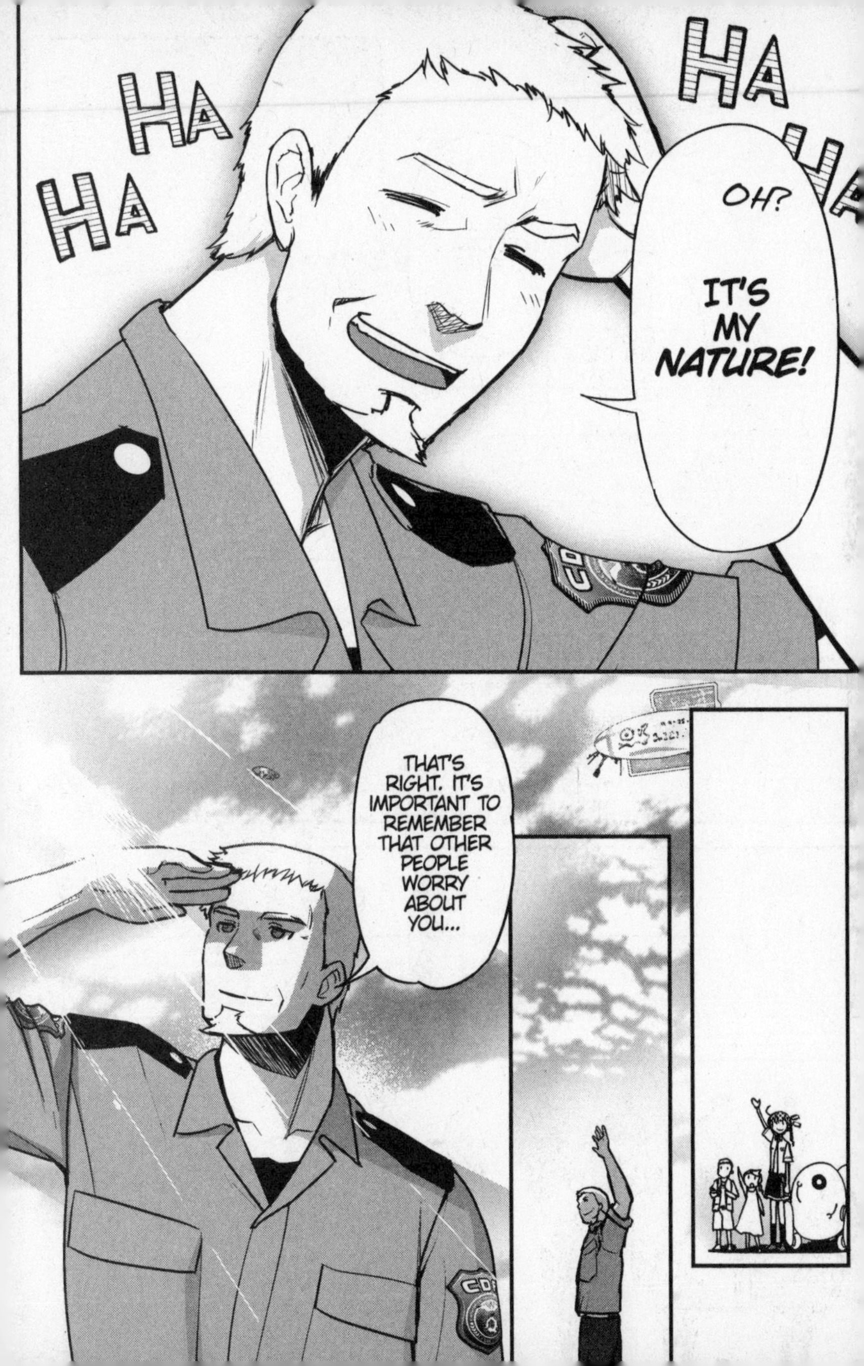
HA HA
OH? IT'S MY NATURE!
HA HA
THAT'S RIGHT. IT'S IMPORTANT TO REMEMBER THAT OTHER PEOPLE WORRY ABOUT YOU...

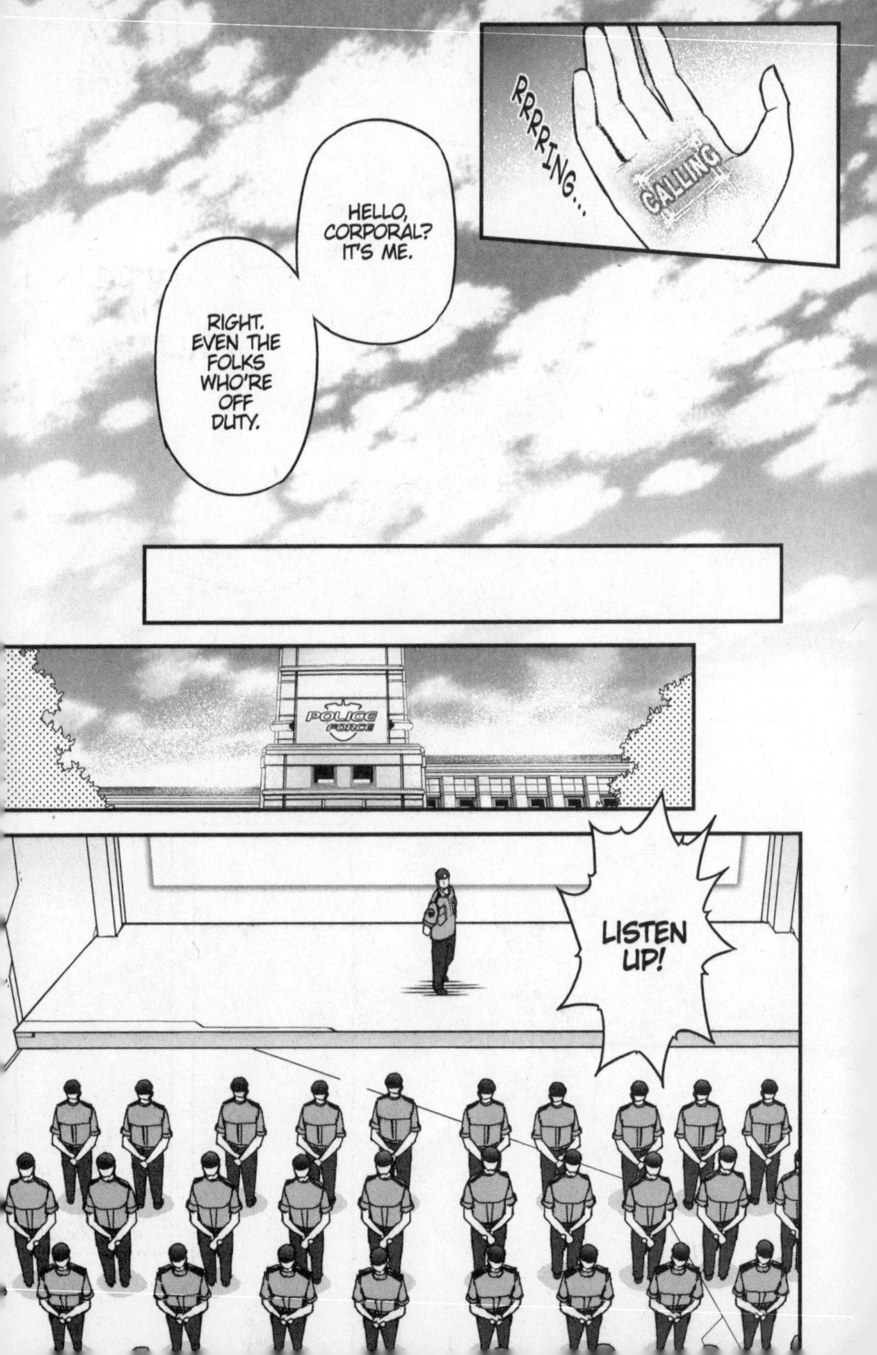
RRRRING...
CALLING
HELLO, CORPORAL? IT'S ME.
RIGHT. EVEN THE FOLKS WHO'RE OFF DUTY.
POLICE FORCE
LISTEN UP!

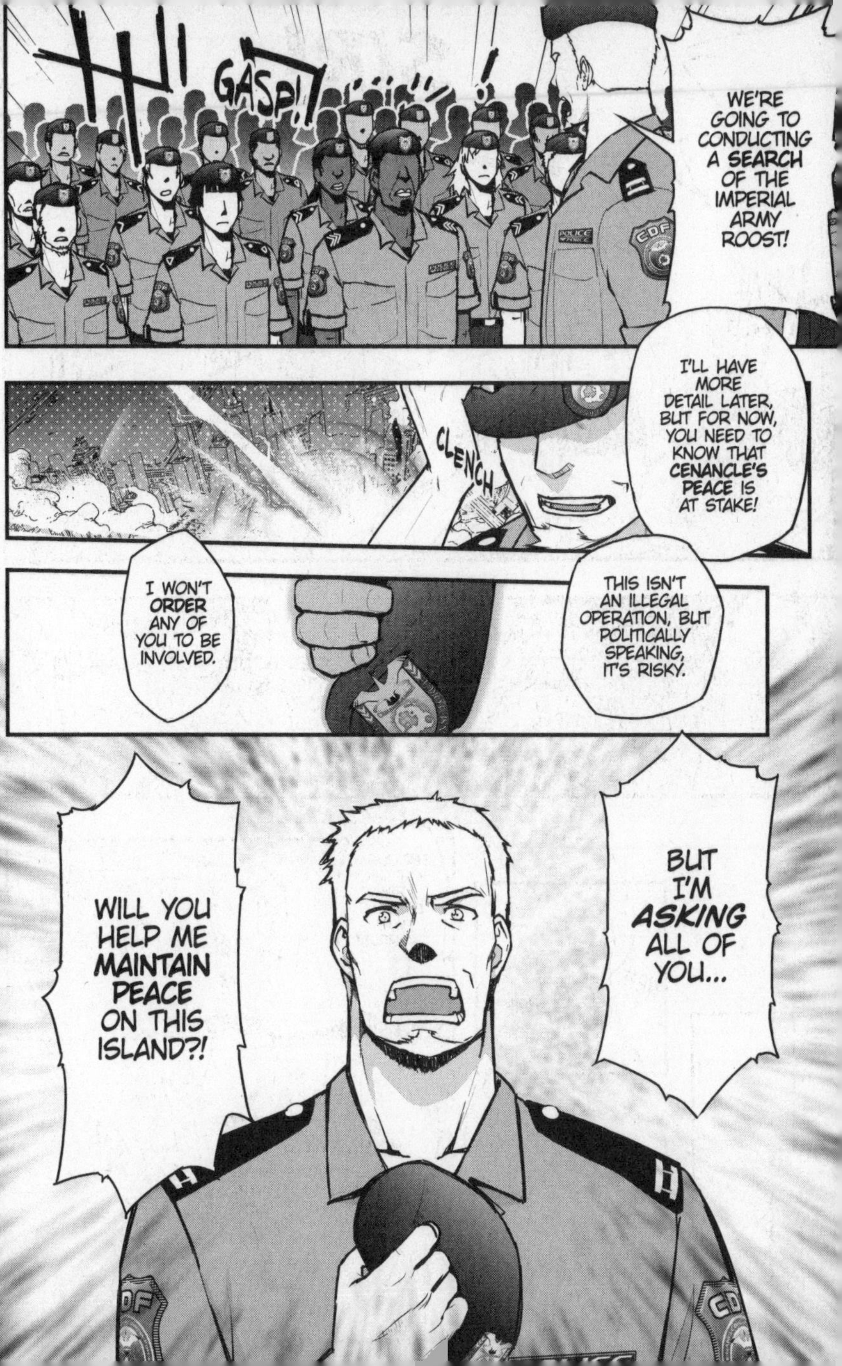
WE'RE GOING TO CONDUCTING A SEARCH OF THE IMPERIAL ARMY ROOST!
GASP!
I'LL HAVE MORE DETAIL LATER, BUT FOR NOW, YOU NEED TO KNOW THAT CENANCLE'S PEACE IS AT STAKE!
CLENCH
THIS ISN'T AN ILLEGAL OPERATION, BUT POLITICALLY SPEAKING, IT'S RISKY.
I WON'T ORDER ANY OF YOU TO BE INVOLVED.
BUT I'M ASKING ALL OF YOU...
WILL YOU HELP ME MAINTAIN PEACE ON THIS ISLAND?!

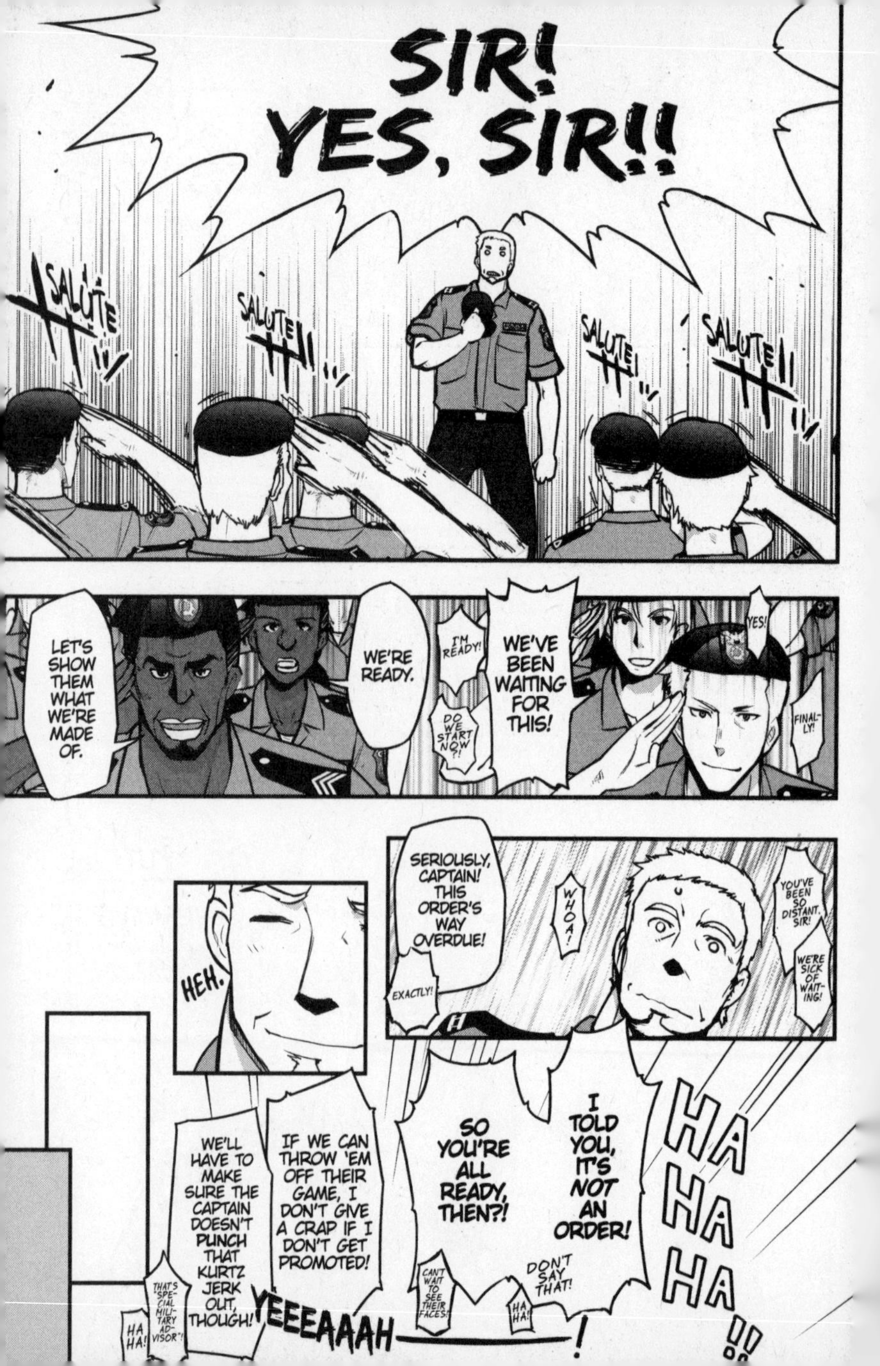
SIR! YES, SIR!!
SALUTE!!
SALUTE!!
SALUTE!!
SALUTE!!
YES!
FINAL-LY!
WE'VE BEEN WAITING FOR THIS!
I'M READY!
DO WE START NOW?!
WE'RE READY.
LET'S SHOW THEM WHAT WE'RE MADE OF.
YOU'VE BEEN SO DISTANT, SIR!
WE'RE SICK OF WAIT-ING!
WHOA!
SERIOUSLY, CAPTAIN! THIS ORDER'S WAY OVERDUE!
EXACTLY!
HEH.
HA HA HA HA!!
I TOLD YOU, IT'S NOT AN ORDER!
DON'T SAY THAT!
HA HA!
SO YOU'RE ALL READY, THEN?!
CAN'T WAIT TO SEE THEIR FACES!
IF WE CAN THROW 'EM OFF THEIR GAME, I DON'T GIVE A CRAP IF I DON'T GET PROMOTED!
WE'LL HAVE TO MAKE SURE THE CAPTAIN DOESN'T PUNCH THAT KURTZ JERK OUT, THOUGH!
THAT'S "SPE-CIAL MILI-TARY AD-VISOR"!
HA HA!
YEEEAAAH—!

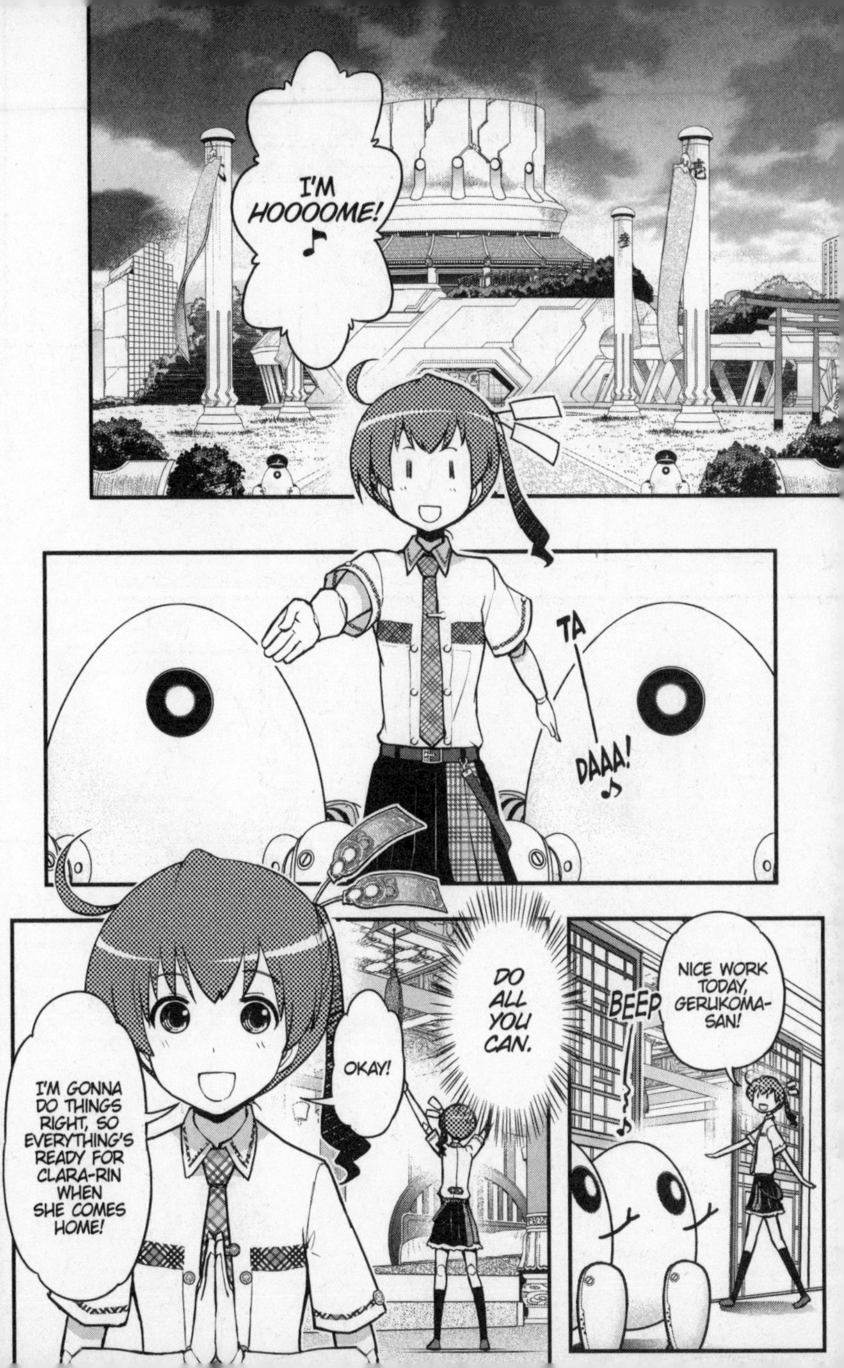
I'M HOOOOME! ♪
TA DAAA! ♪
BEEP ♪
NICE WORK TODAY, GERUKOMA-SAN!
DO ALL YOU CAN.
OKAY!
I'M GONNA DO THINGS RIGHT, SO EVERYTHING'S READY FOR CLARA-RIN WHEN SHE COMES HOME!

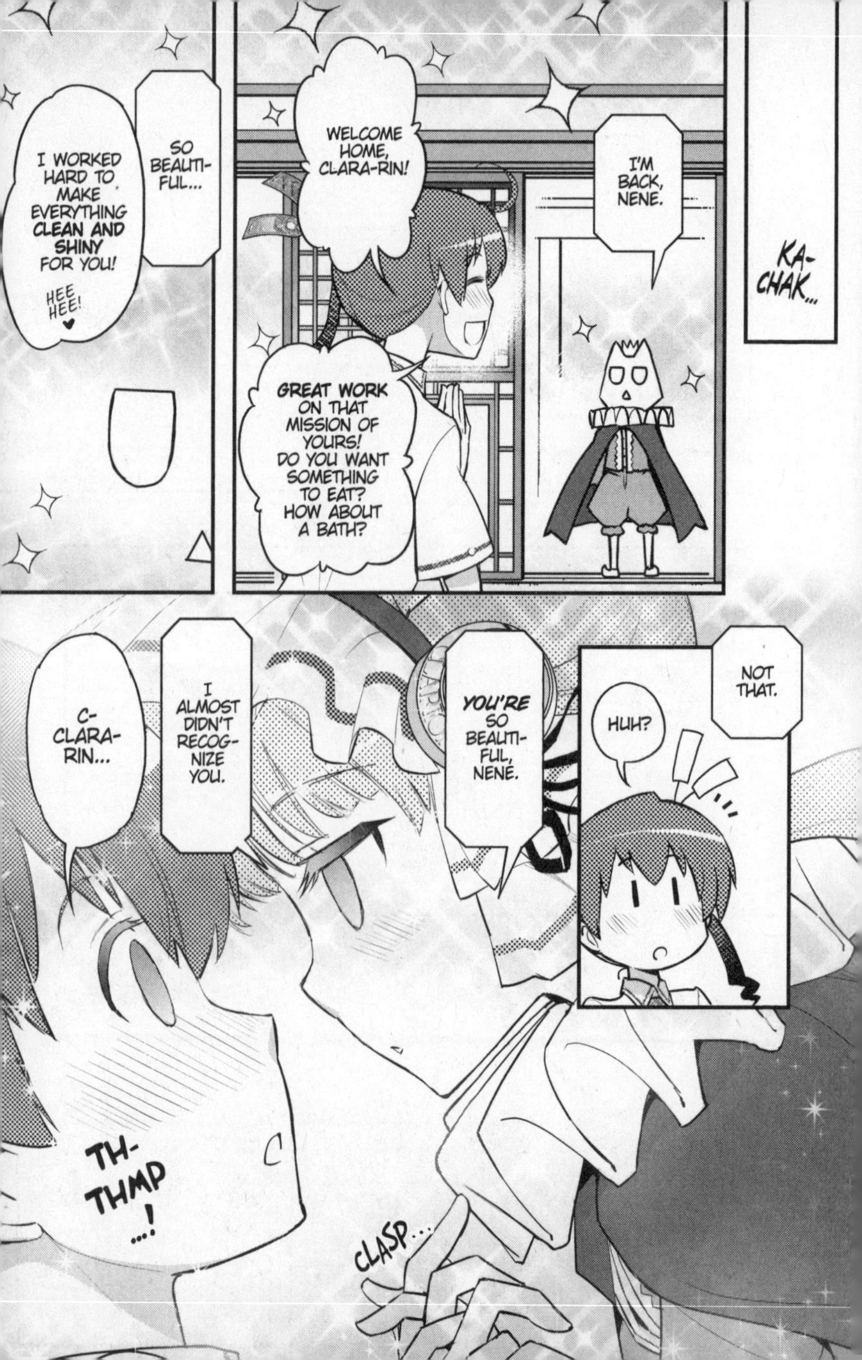
KA-CHAK...
I'M BACK, NENE.
WELCOME HOME, CLARA-RIN!
GREAT WORK ON THAT MISSION OF YOURS! DO YOU WANT SOMETHING TO EAT? HOW ABOUT A BATH?
SO BEAUTIFUL...
I WORKED HARD TO MAKE EVERYTHING CLEAN AND SHINY FOR YOU!
HEE HEE! ♥
NOT THAT.
HUH?
YOU'RE SO BEAUTIFUL, NENE.
I ALMOST DIDN'T RECOGNIZE YOU.
C-CLARA-RIN...
TH-THMP...!
CLASP...

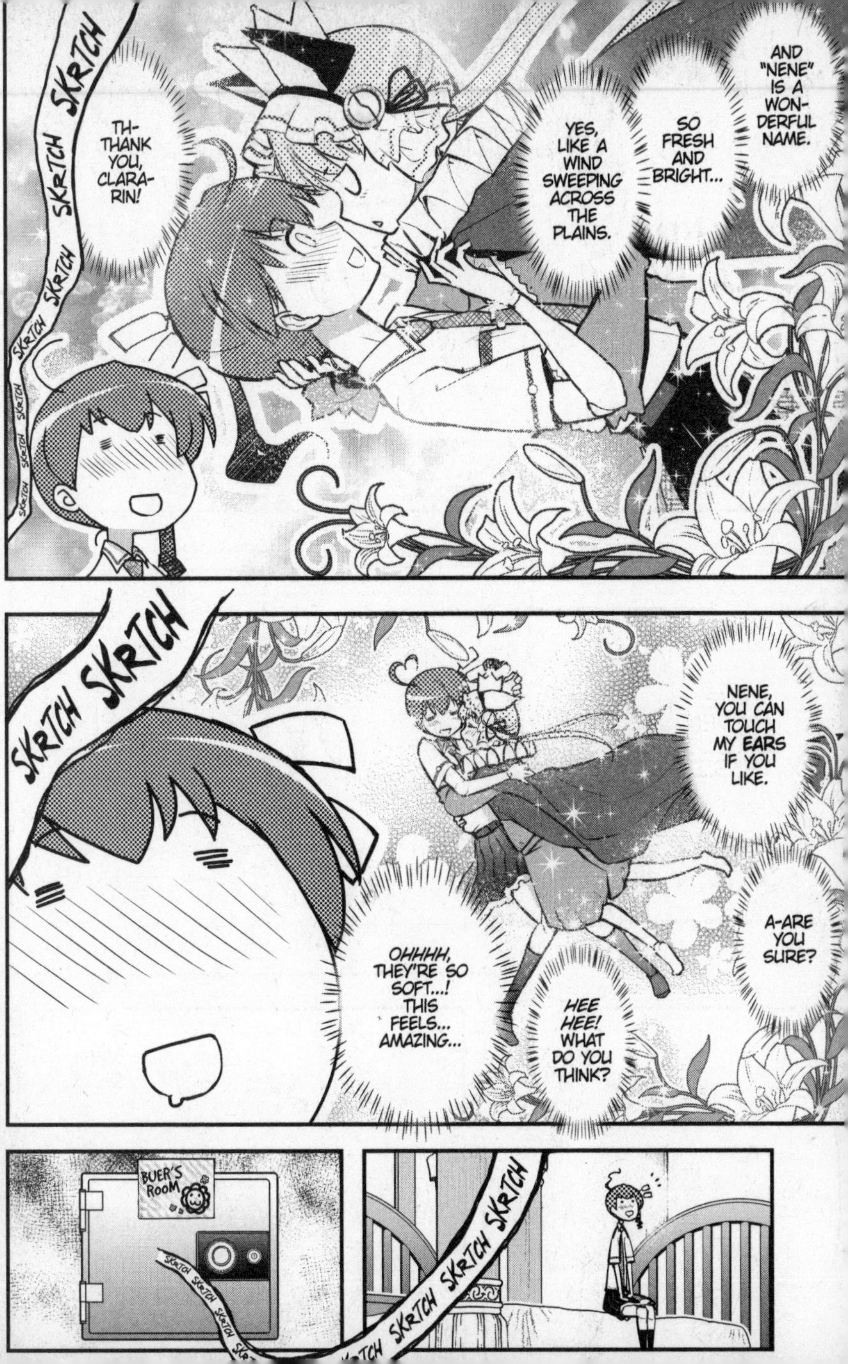
AND "NENE" IS A WON-DERFUL NAME.
SO FRESH AND BRIGHT...
YES, LIKE A WIND SWEEPING ACROSS THE PLAINS.
TH-THANK YOU, CLARA-RIN!
SKRTCH SKRTCH SKRTCH SKRTCH SKRTCH SKRTCH
NENE, YOU CAN TOUCH MY EARS IF YOU LIKE.
A-ARE YOU SURE?
HEE HEE! WHAT DO YOU THINK?
OHHHH, THEY'RE SO SOFT...! THIS FEELS... AMAZING...
SKRTCH SKRTCH
SKRTCH SKRTCH SKRTCH
BUER'S ROOM
SKRTCH SKRTCH SKRTCH

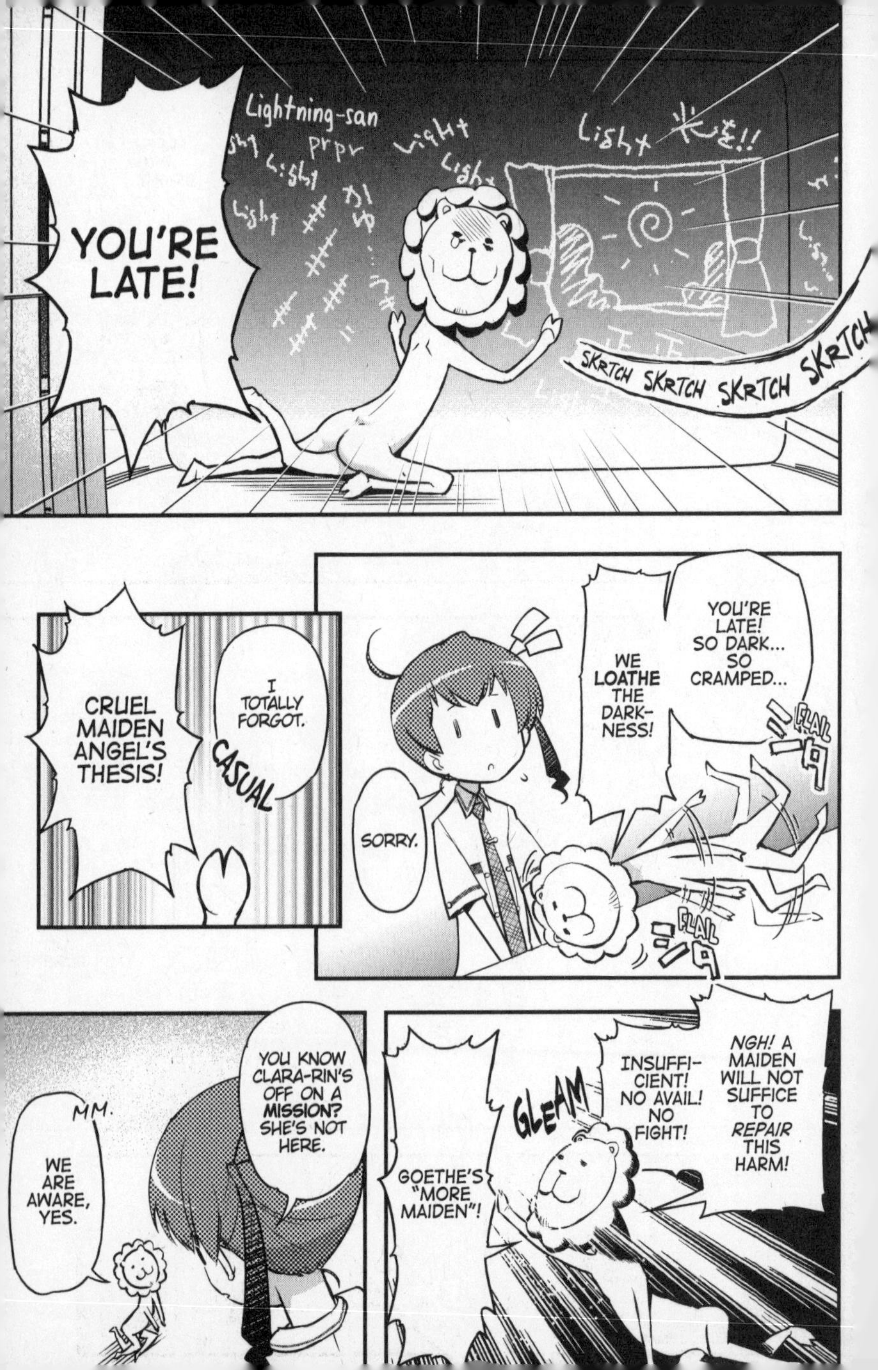
YOU'RE LATE!
Lightning-san
SKRTCH SKRTCH SKRTCH SKRTCH
YOU'RE LATE! SO DARK... SO CRAMPED...
WE LOATHE THE DARKNESS!
FLAIL
SORRY.
FLAIL
I TOTALLY FORGOT.
CASUAL
CRUEL MAIDEN ANGEL'S THESIS!
NGH! A MAIDEN WILL NOT SUFFICE TO REPAIR THIS HARM!
INSUFFICIENT! NO AVAIL! NO FIGHT!
GLEAM
GOETHE'S "MORE MAIDEN"!
YOU KNOW CLARA-RIN'S OFF ON A MISSION? SHE'S NOT HERE.
MM.
WE ARE AWARE, YES.

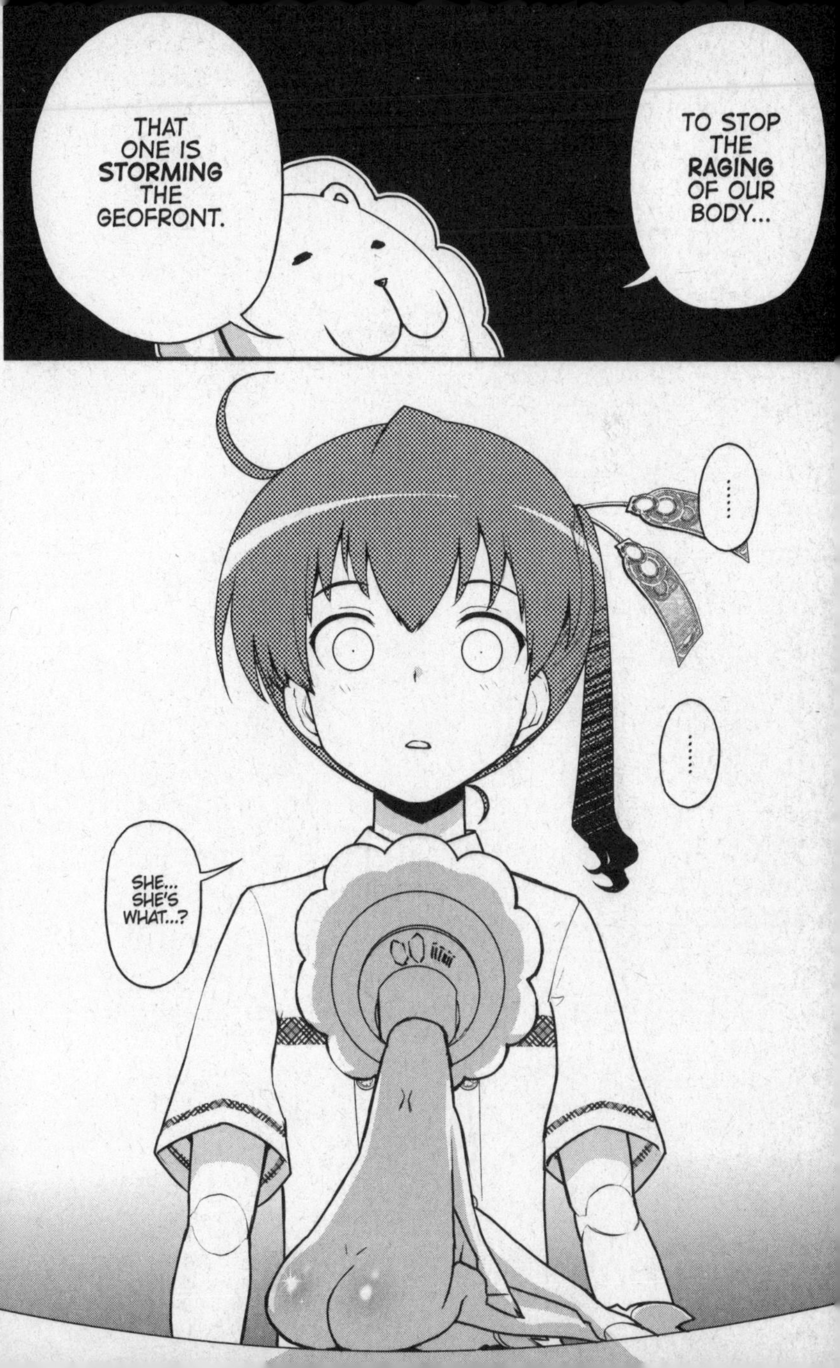
TO STOP THE RAGING OF OUR BODY...
THAT ONE IS STORMING THE GEOFRONT.
......
......
SHE... SHE'S WHAT...?

GHOST URN

GHOST URN

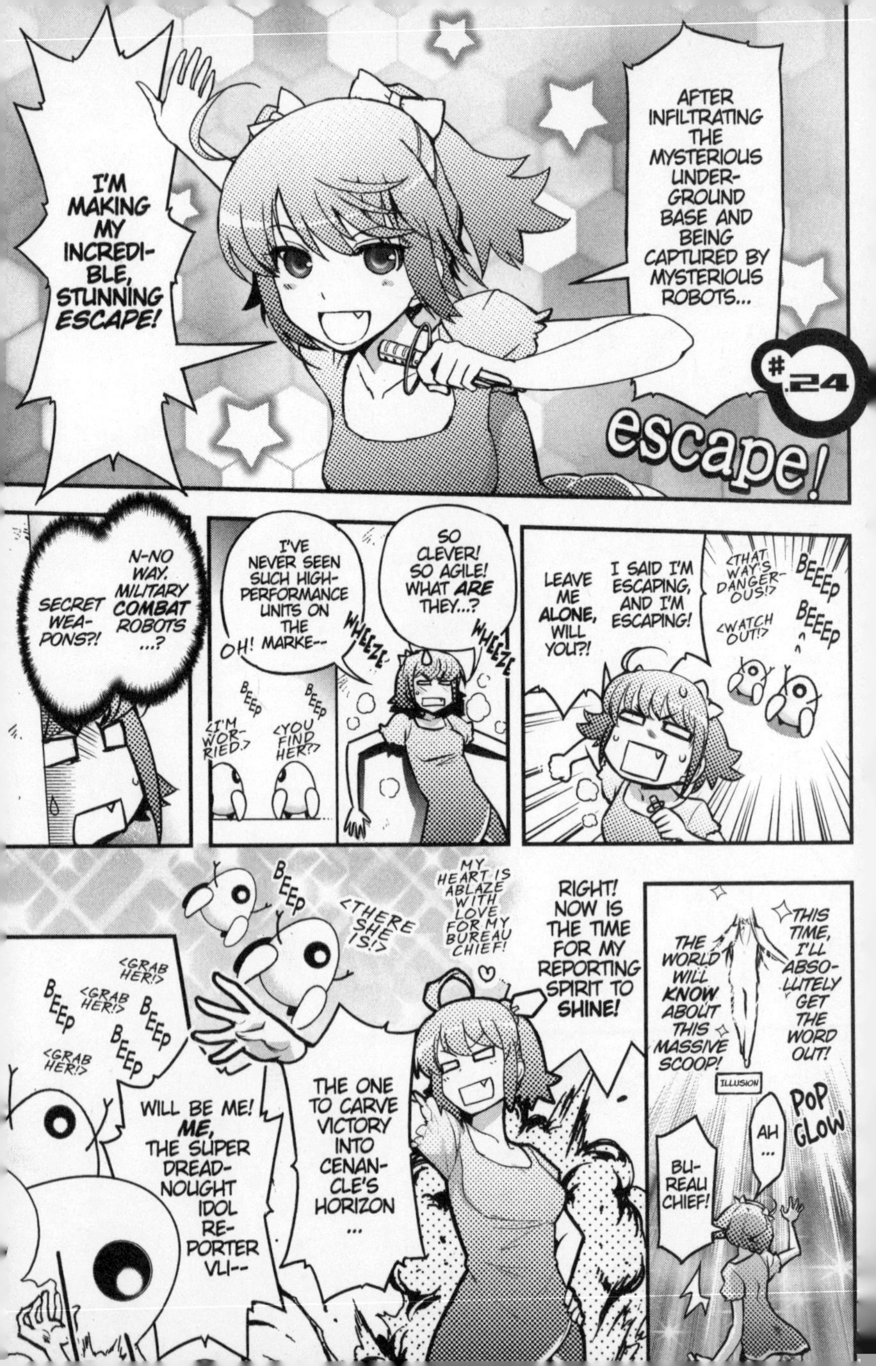
AFTER INFILTRATING THE MYSTERIOUS UNDER-GROUND BASE AND BEING CAPTURED BY MYSTERIOUS ROBOTS...
#.24
escape!
I'M MAKING MY INCREDI-BLE, STUNNING ESCAPE!
<THAT WAY'S DANGER-OUS!?>
BEEEP
<WATCH OUT!?>
BEEEP
I SAID I'M ESCAPING, AND I'M ESCAPING!
LEAVE ME ALONE, WILL YOU?!
SO CLEVER! SO AGILE! WHAT ARE THEY...?
WHEEZE
I'VE NEVER SEEN SUCH HIGH-PERFORMANCE UNITS ON THE MARKE--
OH!
WHEEZE
BEEP
<YOU FIND HER?>
BEEP
<I'M WOR-RIED.>
N-NO WAY. MILITARY COMBAT ROBOTS ...?
SECRET WEA-PONS?!
THIS TIME, I'LL ABSO-LUTELY GET THE WORD OUT!
THE WORLD WILL KNOW ABOUT THIS MASSIVE SCOOP!
ILLUSION
POP
GLOW
AH ...
BU-REAU CHIEF!
RIGHT! NOW IS THE TIME FOR MY REPORTING SPIRIT TO SHINE!
MY HEART IS ABLAZE WITH LOVE FOR MY BUREAU CHIEF!
<THERE SHE IS!>
BEEP
THE ONE TO CARVE VICTORY INTO CENAN-CLE'S HORIZON ...
WILL BE ME! ME, THE SUPER DREAD-NOUGHT IDOL RE-PORTER VLI--
<GRAB HER!>
BEEP
<GRAB HER!>
BEEP
BEEP
<GRAB HER!>

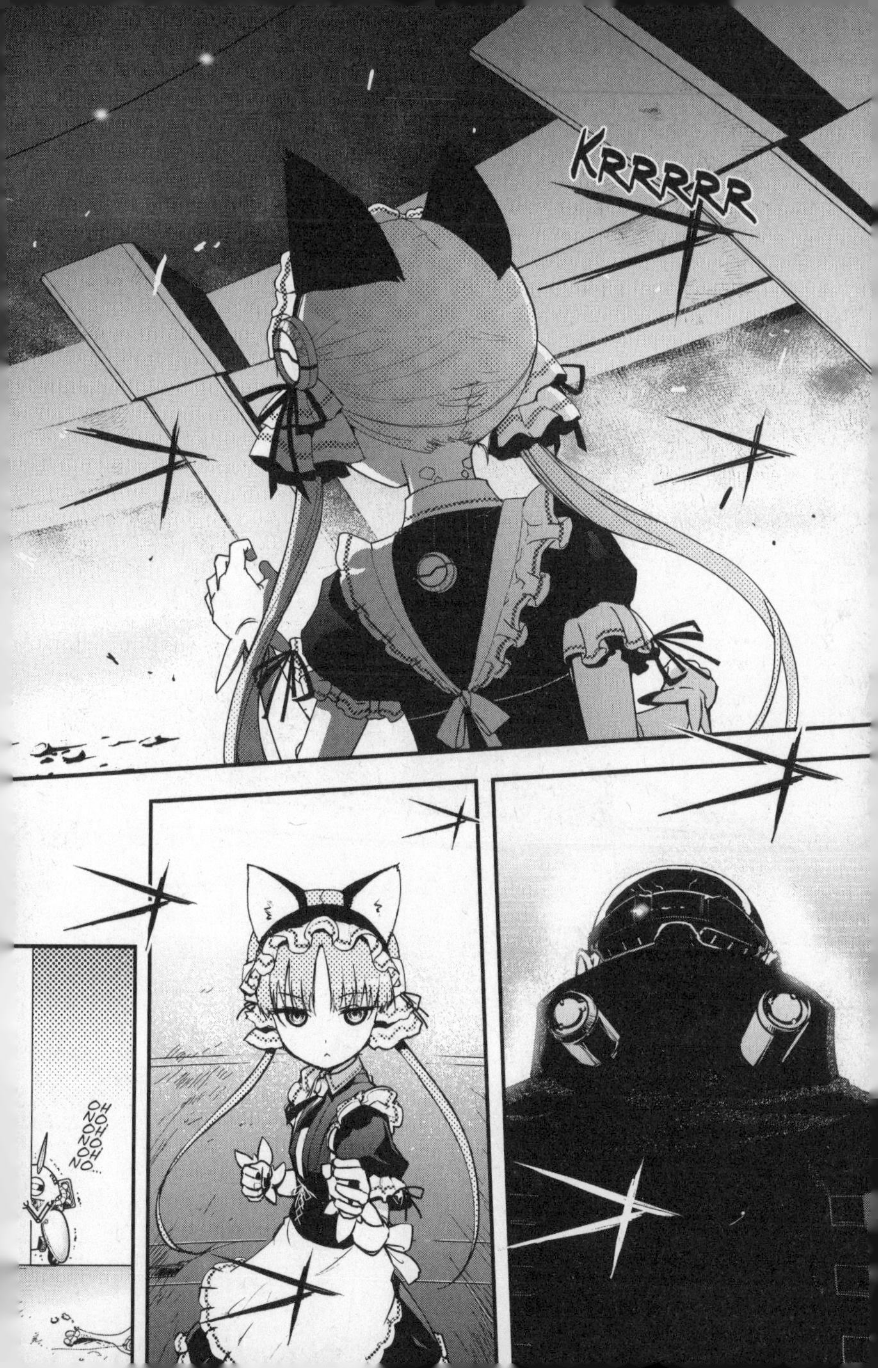
KRRRRRR
OHNOHNOHNO...

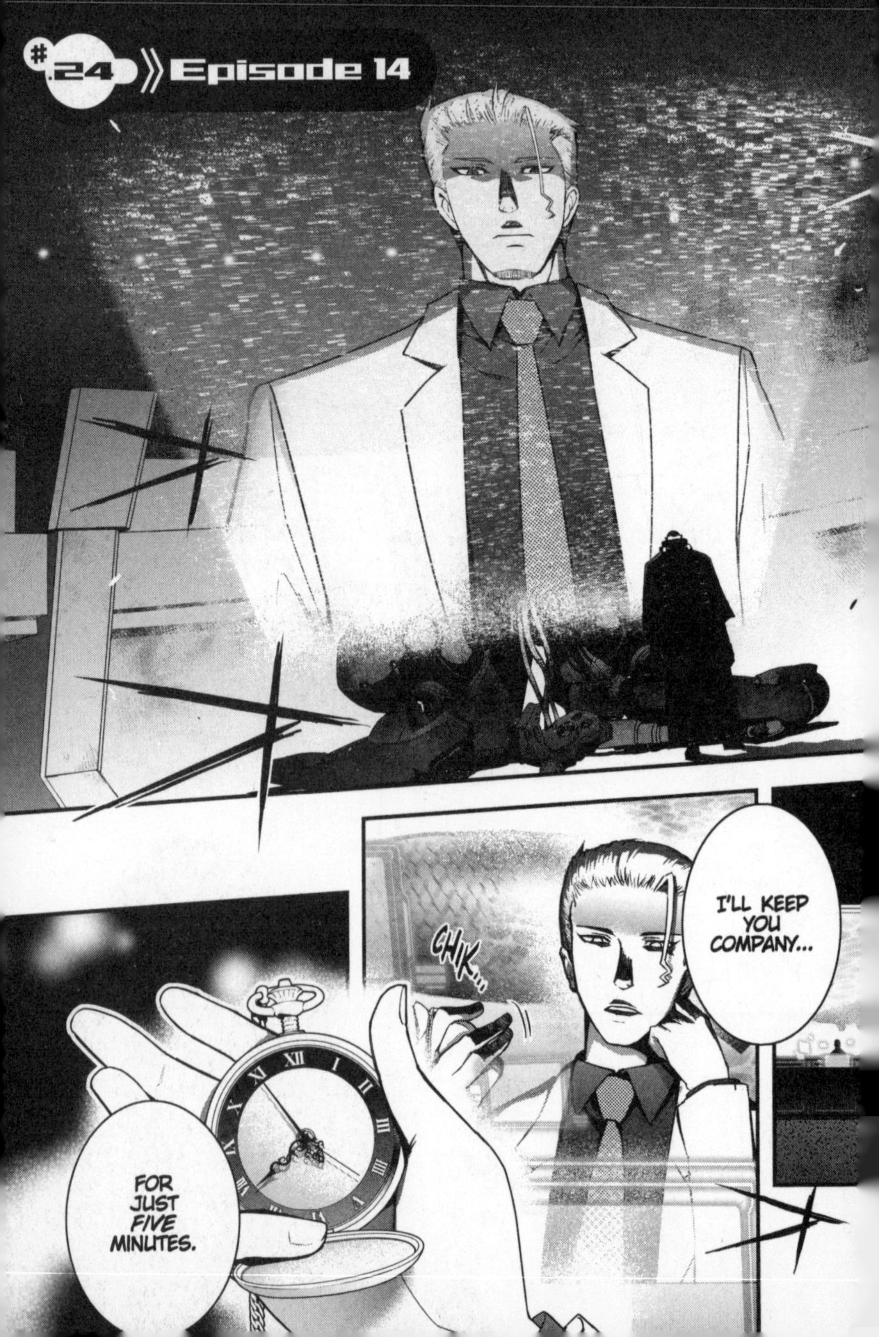
#.24 》Episode 14
I'LL KEEP YOU COMPANY...
CHIK...
FOR JUST *FIVE* MINUTES.

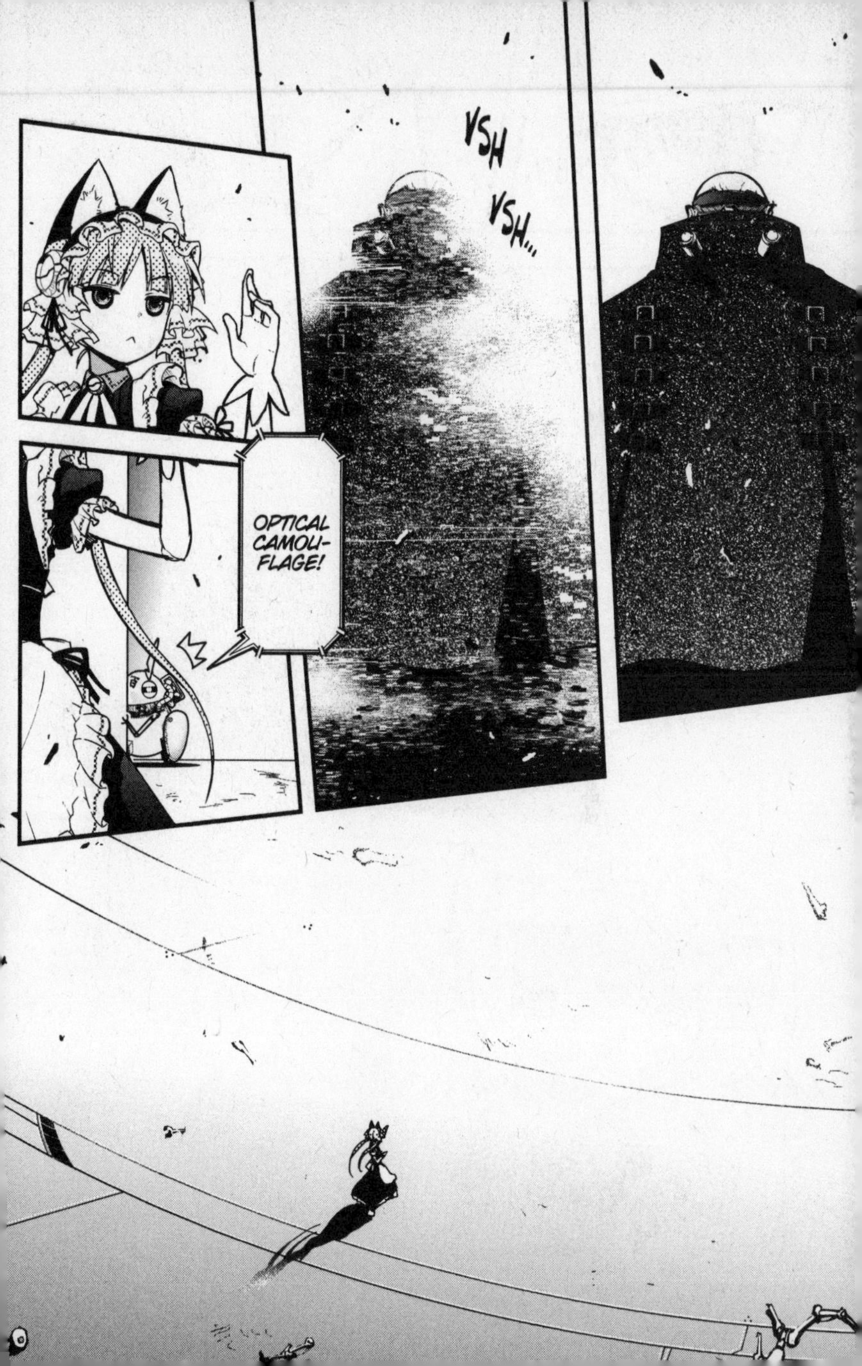
VSH
VSH...
OPTICAL CAMOU-FLAGE!

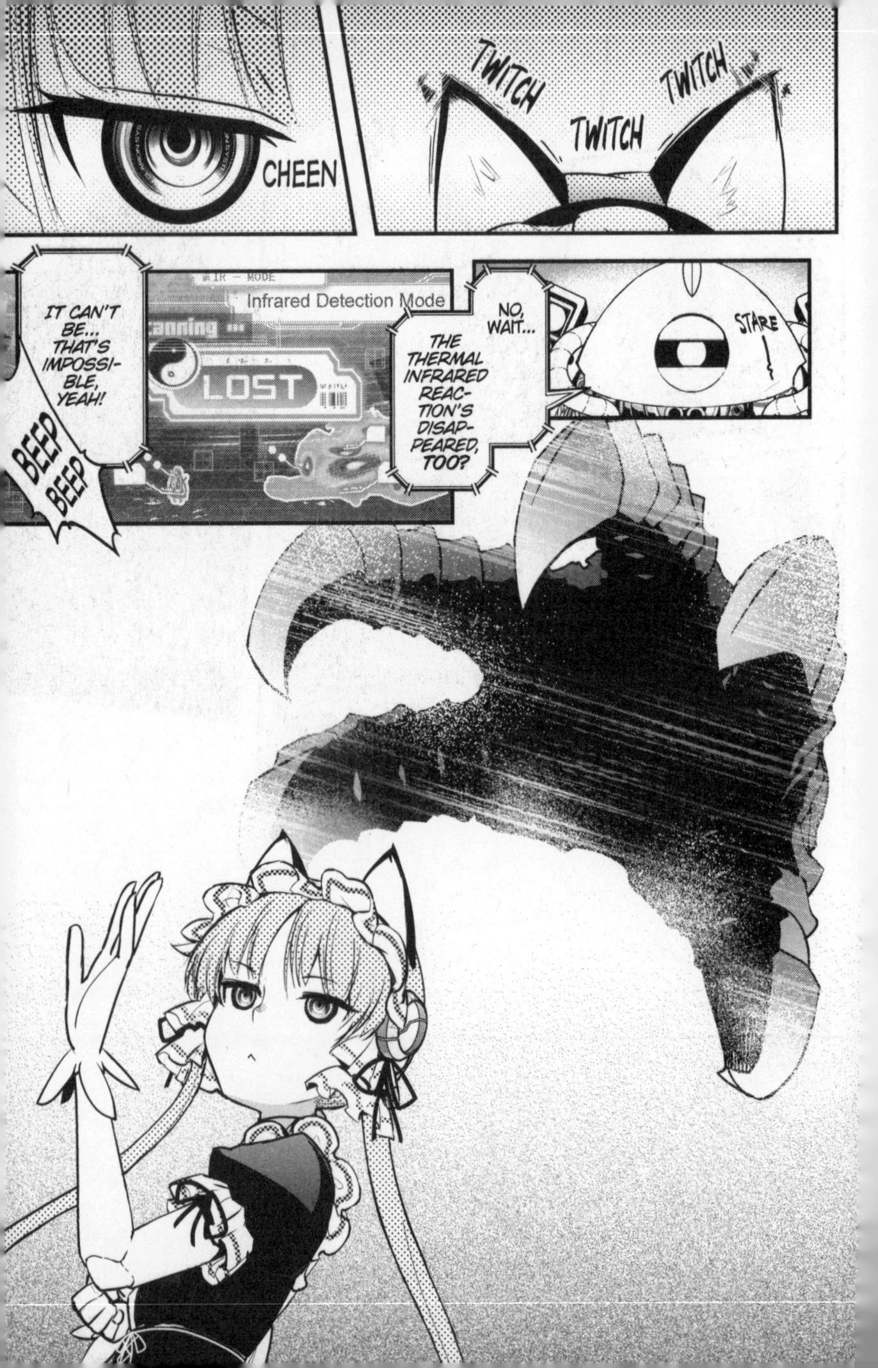
TWITCH
TWITCH
TWITCH
CHEEN
STARE
NO, WAIT...
THE THERMAL INFRARED REACTION'S DISAPPEARED, TOO?
Infrared Detection Mode
LOST
IT CAN'T BE... THAT'S IMPOSSIBLE, YEAH!
BEEP BEEP

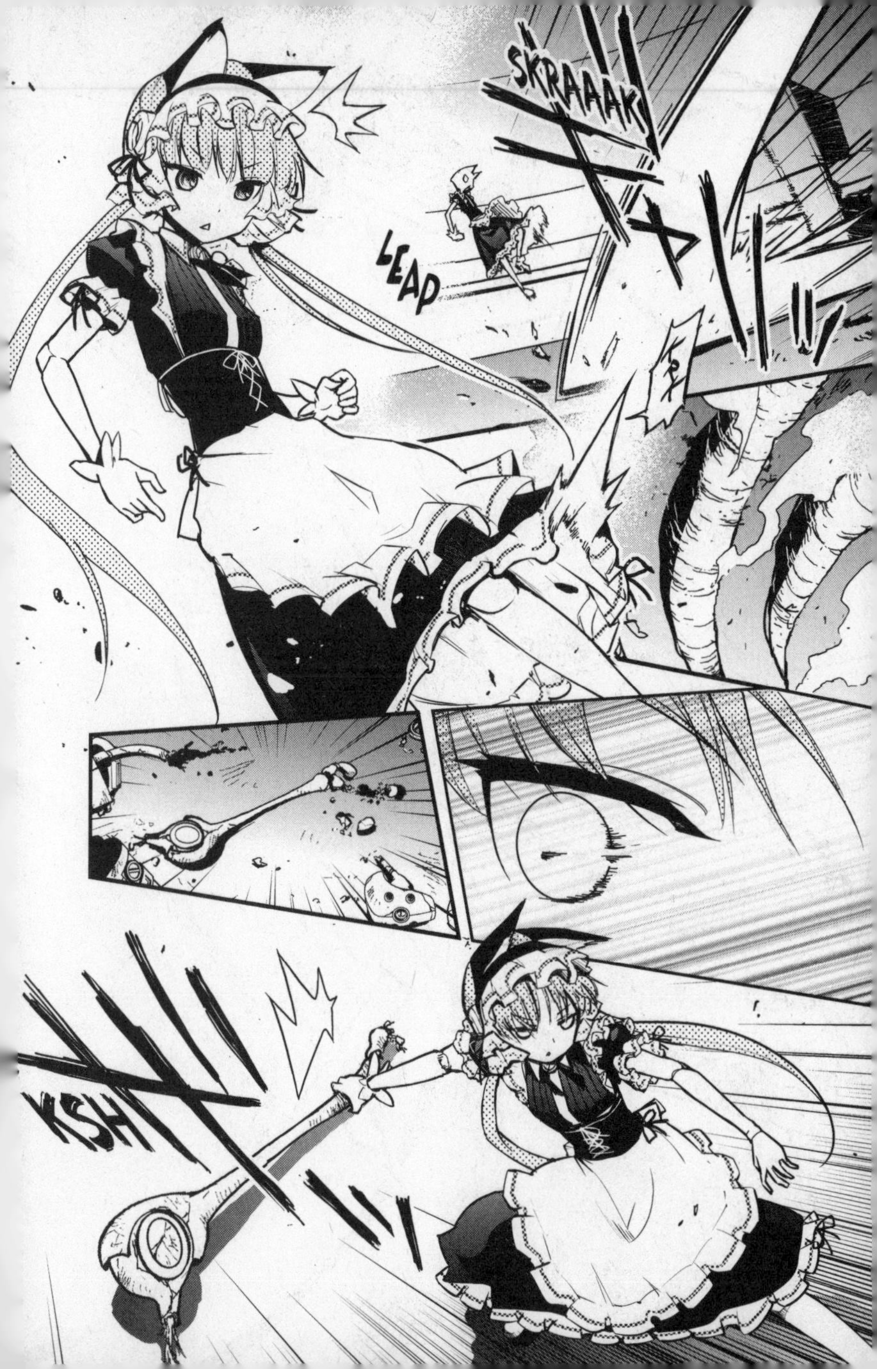
SKRAAAK
LEAP
KSH

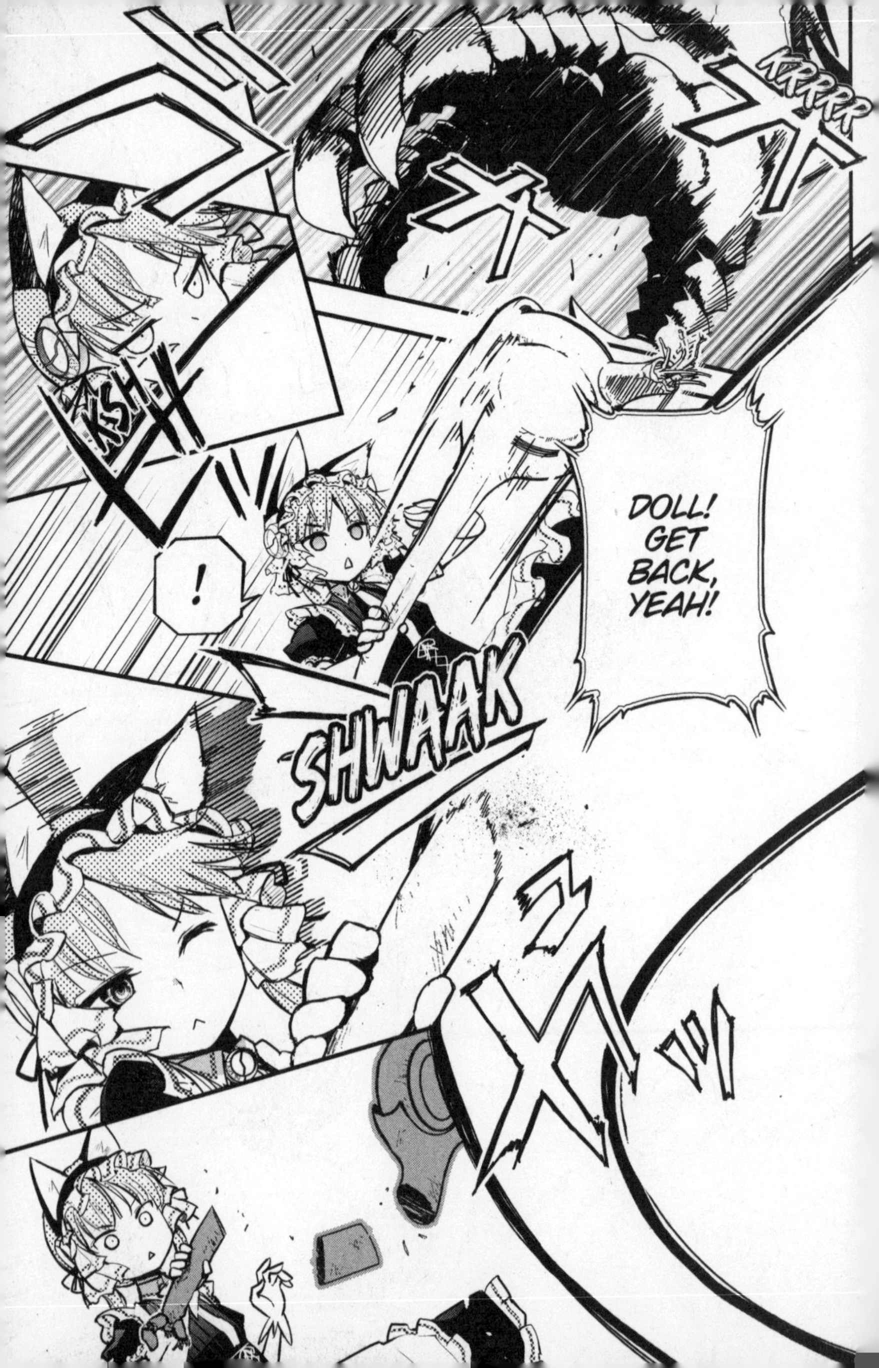
KRRRR
KSH
DOLL! GET BACK, YEAH!
!
SHWAAK

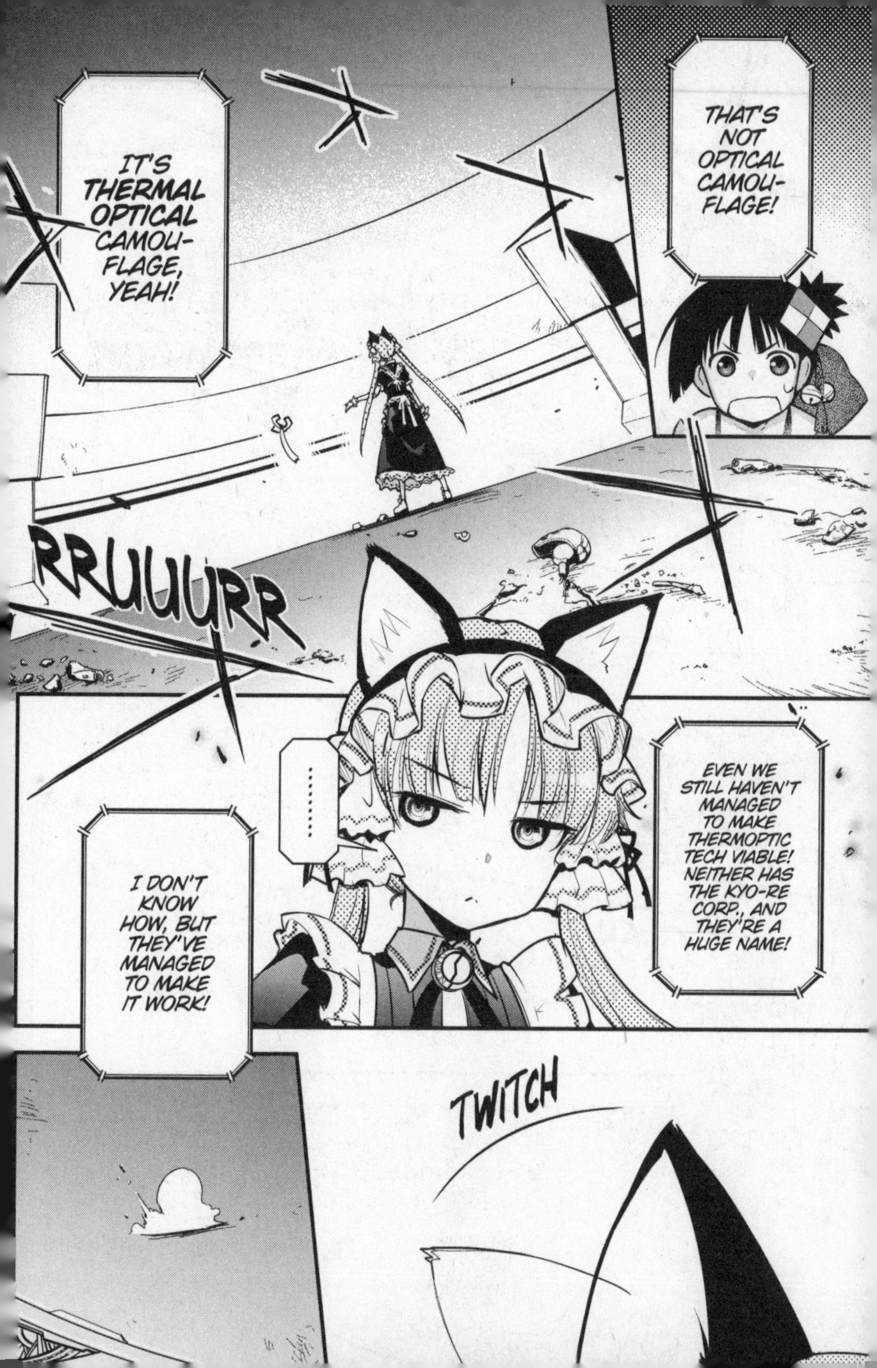
THAT'S NOT OPTICAL CAMOU-FLAGE!
IT'S THERMAL OPTICAL CAMOU-FLAGE, YEAH!
RRUUURR
EVEN WE STILL HAVEN'T MANAGED TO MAKE THERMOPTIC TECH VIABLE! NEITHER HAS THE KYO-RE CORP., AND THEY'RE A HUGE NAME!
......
I DON'T KNOW HOW, BUT THEY'VE MANAGED TO MAKE IT WORK!
TWITCH

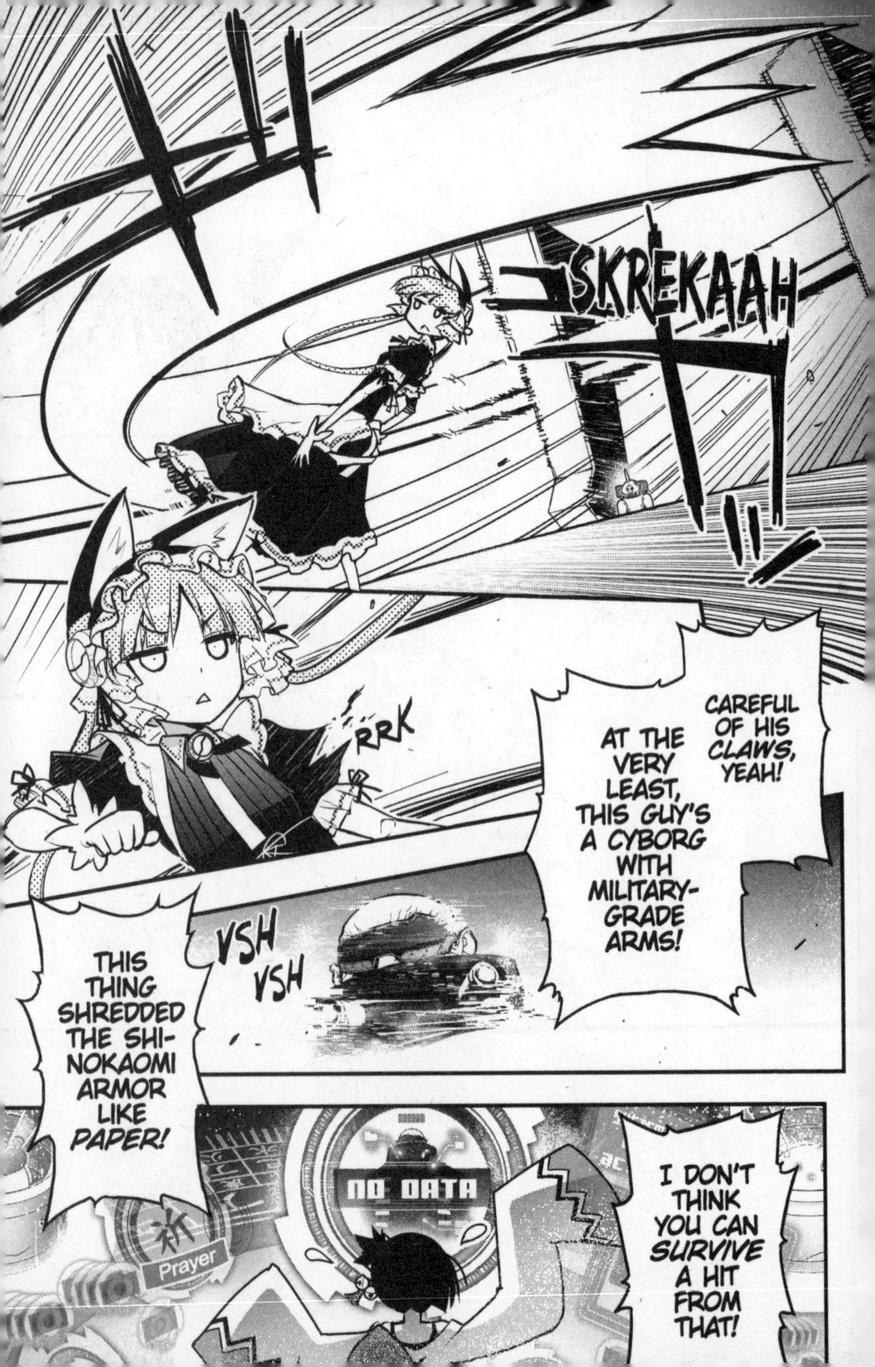
SKREKAAH
!!
CAREFUL OF HIS *CLAWS*, YEAH!
AT THE VERY LEAST, THIS GUY'S A CYBORG WITH MILITARY-GRADE ARMS!
RRK
VSH VSH
THIS THING SHREDDED THE SHI-NOKAOMI ARMOR LIKE *PAPER!*
I DON'T THINK YOU CAN *SURVIVE* A HIT FROM THAT!
NO DATA
Prayer

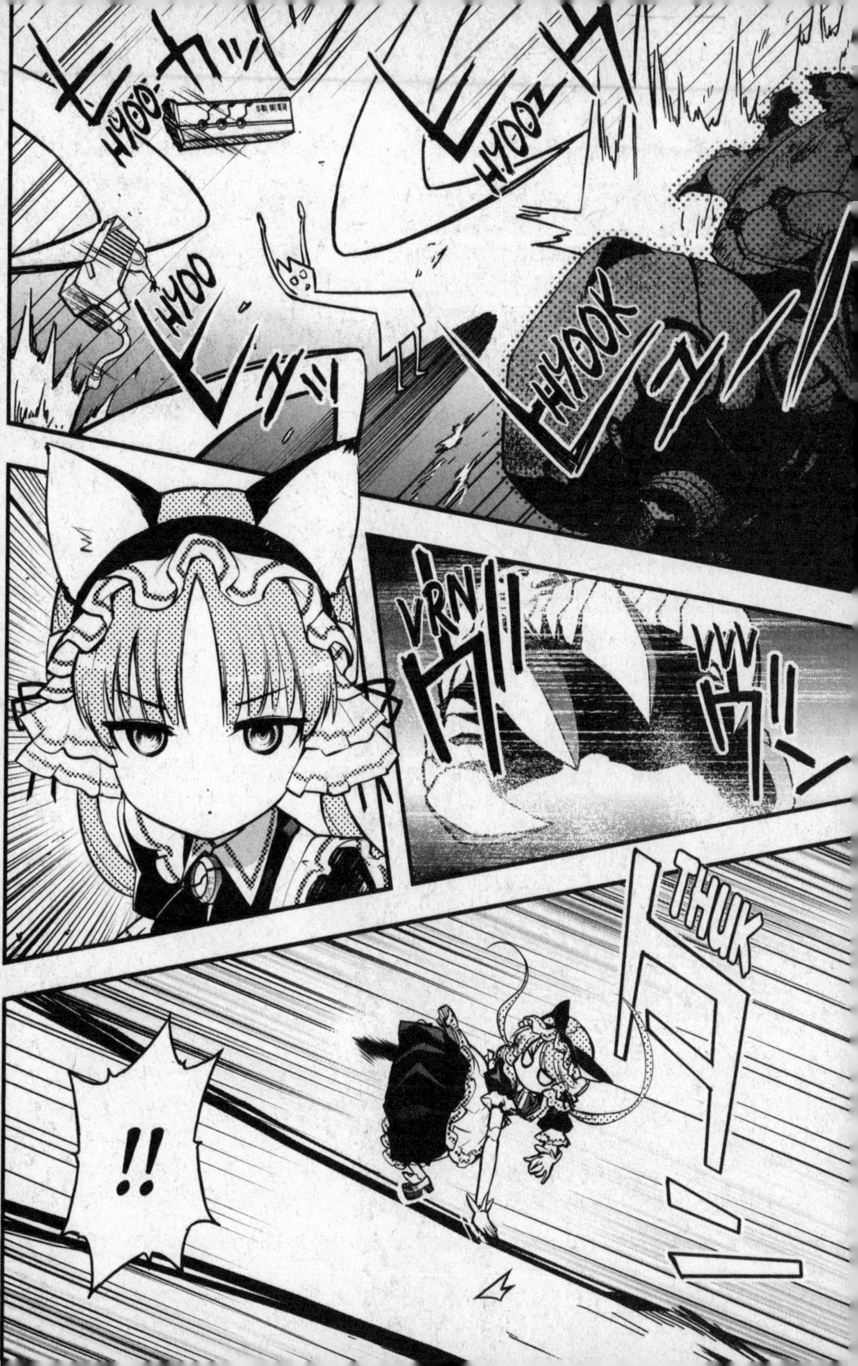
HYOOZ
HYOO
HYOOK
HYOO
VVV
VRN
THUK
!!

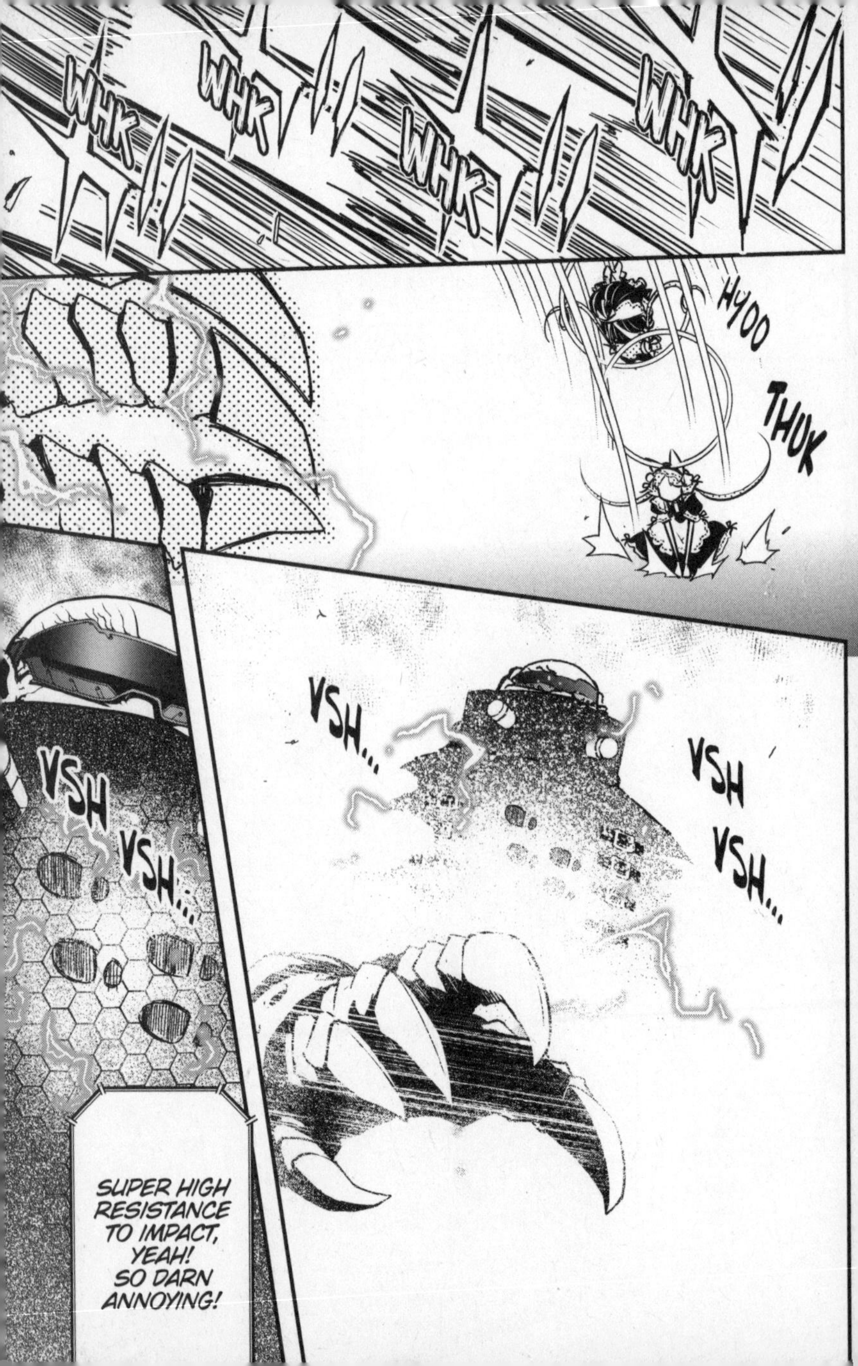
WHK
WHK
WHK
WHK
HYOO
THUK
VSH...
VSH
VSH...
VSH
VSH...
SUPER HIGH RESISTANCE TO IMPACT, YEAH! SO DARN ANNOYING!

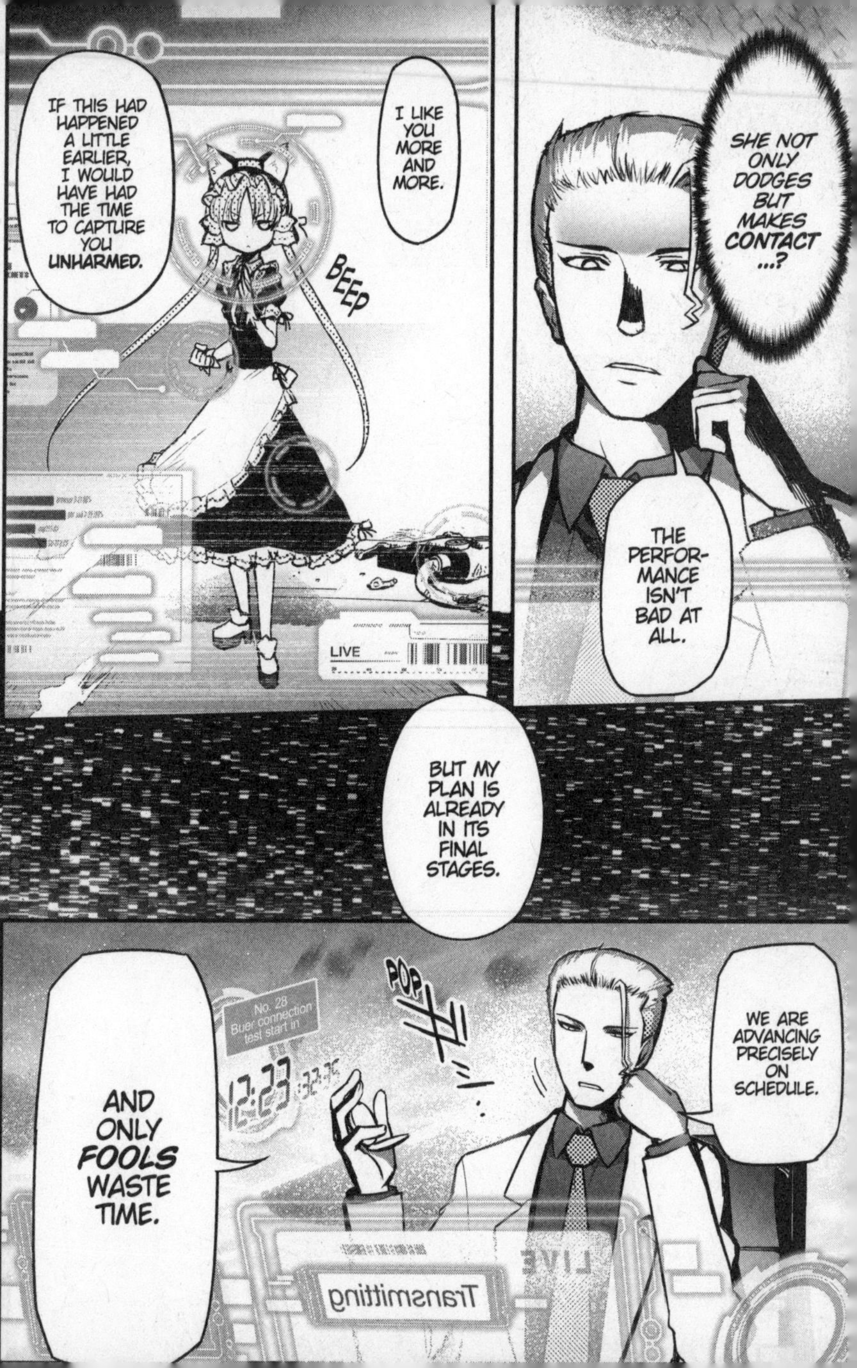
SHE NOT ONLY DODGES BUT MAKES CONTACT ...?
THE PERFORMANCE ISN'T BAD AT ALL.
I LIKE YOU MORE AND MORE.
IF THIS HAD HAPPENED A LITTLE EARLIER, I WOULD HAVE HAD THE TIME TO CAPTURE YOU UNHARMED.
BEEP
LIVE
BUT MY PLAN IS ALREADY IN ITS FINAL STAGES.
WE ARE ADVANCING PRECISELY ON SCHEDULE.
POP
No. 28 Buer connection test start in
AND ONLY FOOLS WASTE TIME.
LIVE
Transmitting

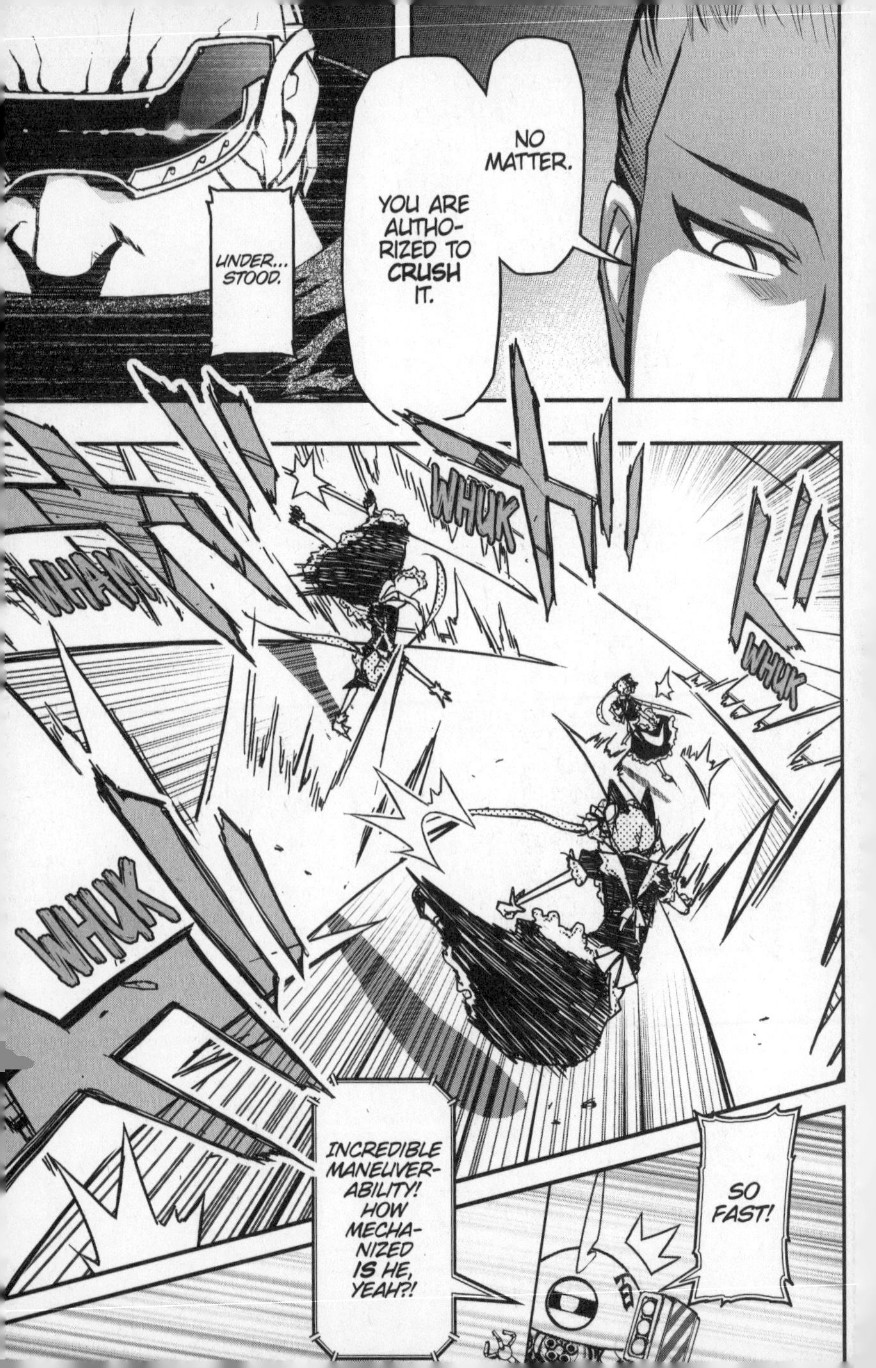
NO MATTER.
YOU ARE AUTHO-RIZED TO CRUSH IT.
UNDER... STOOD.
WHUK
WHUK
WHAM
WHUK
SO FAST!
INCREDIBLE MANEUVER-ABILITY! HOW MECHA-NIZED IS HE, YEAH?!

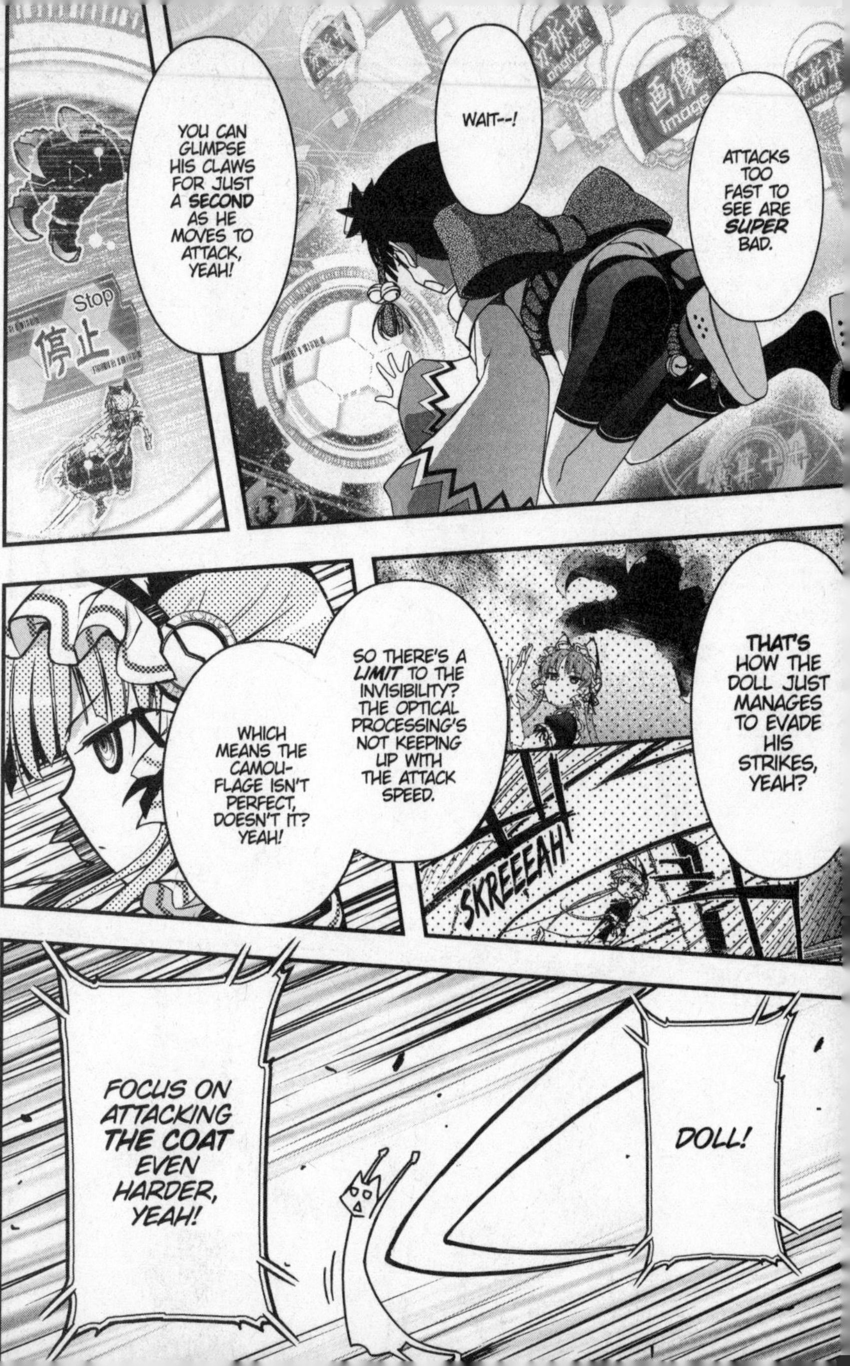
画像
Image
ATTACKS TOO FAST TO SEE ARE SUPER BAD.
WAIT--!
YOU CAN GLIMPSE HIS CLAWS FOR JUST A SECOND AS HE MOVES TO ATTACK, YEAH!
Stop
停止
THAT'S HOW THE DOLL JUST MANAGES TO EVADE HIS STRIKES, YEAH?
SKREEEAH
SO THERE'S A LIMIT TO THE INVISIBILITY? THE OPTICAL PROCESSING'S NOT KEEPING UP WITH THE ATTACK SPEED.
WHICH MEANS THE CAMOU-FLAGE ISN'T PERFECT, DOESN'T IT? YEAH!
DOLL!
FOCUS ON ATTACKING THE COAT EVEN HARDER, YEAH!

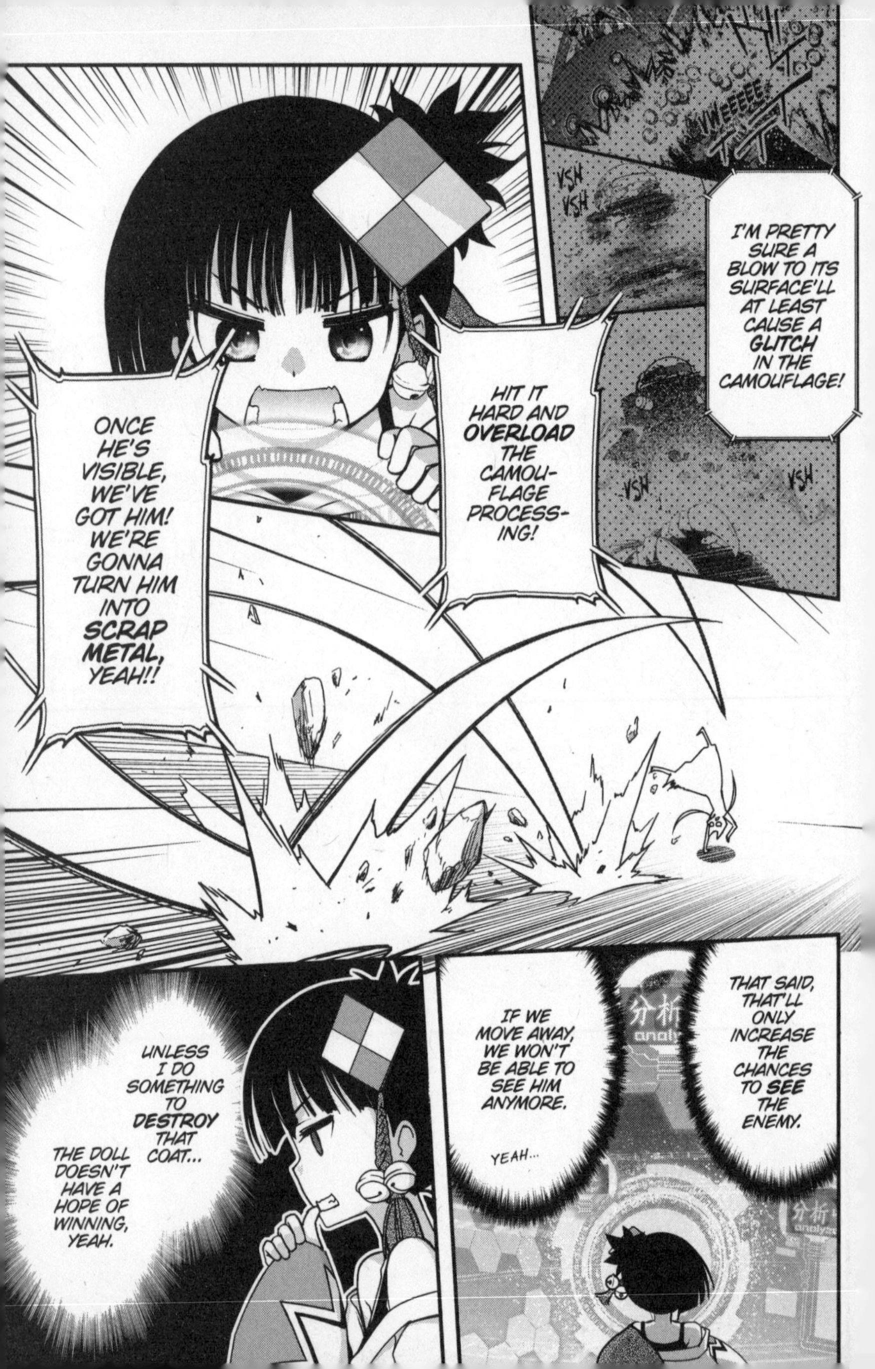

VSH VSH
I'M PRETTY SURE A BLOW TO ITS SURFACE'LL AT LEAST CAUSE A GLITCH IN THE CAMOUFLAGE!
VSH
VSH
HIT IT HARD AND OVERLOAD THE CAMOU-FLAGE PROCESS-ING!
ONCE HE'S VISIBLE, WE'VE GOT HIM! WE'RE GONNA TURN HIM INTO SCRAP METAL, YEAH!!
THAT SAID, THAT'LL ONLY INCREASE THE CHANCES TO SEE THE ENEMY.
分析
IF WE MOVE AWAY, WE WON'T BE ABLE TO SEE HIM ANYMORE.
YEAH...
UNLESS I DO SOMETHING TO DESTROY THAT COAT...
THE DOLL DOESN'T HAVE A HOPE OF WINNING, YEAH.

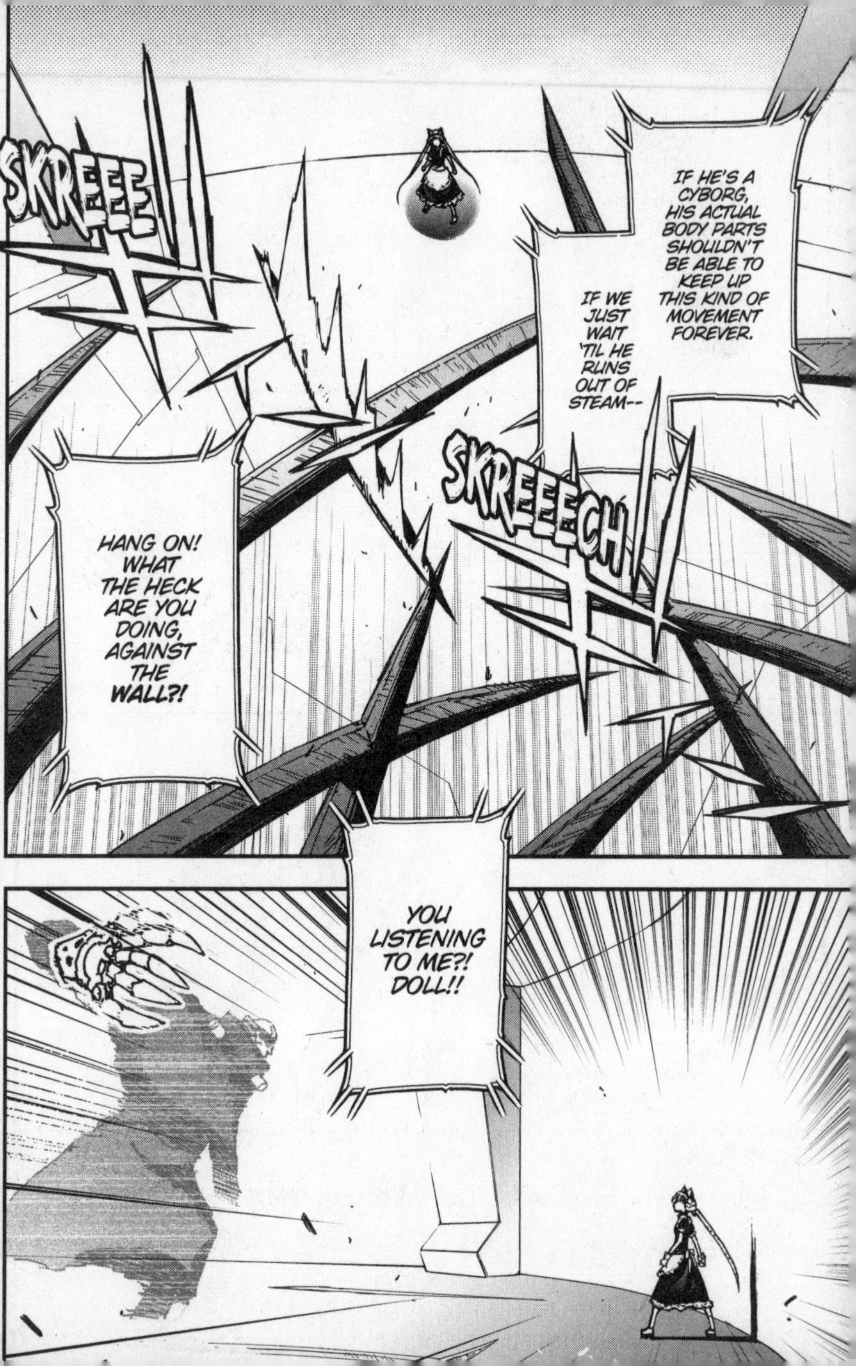
IF HE'S A CYBORG, HIS ACTUAL BODY PARTS SHOULDN'T BE ABLE TO KEEP UP THIS KIND OF MOVEMENT FOREVER.
IF WE JUST WAIT 'TIL HE RUNS OUT OF STEAM--
SKREEE
SKREEECH
HANG ON! WHAT THE HECK ARE YOU DOING, AGAINST THE WALL?!
YOU LISTENING TO ME?! DOLL!!

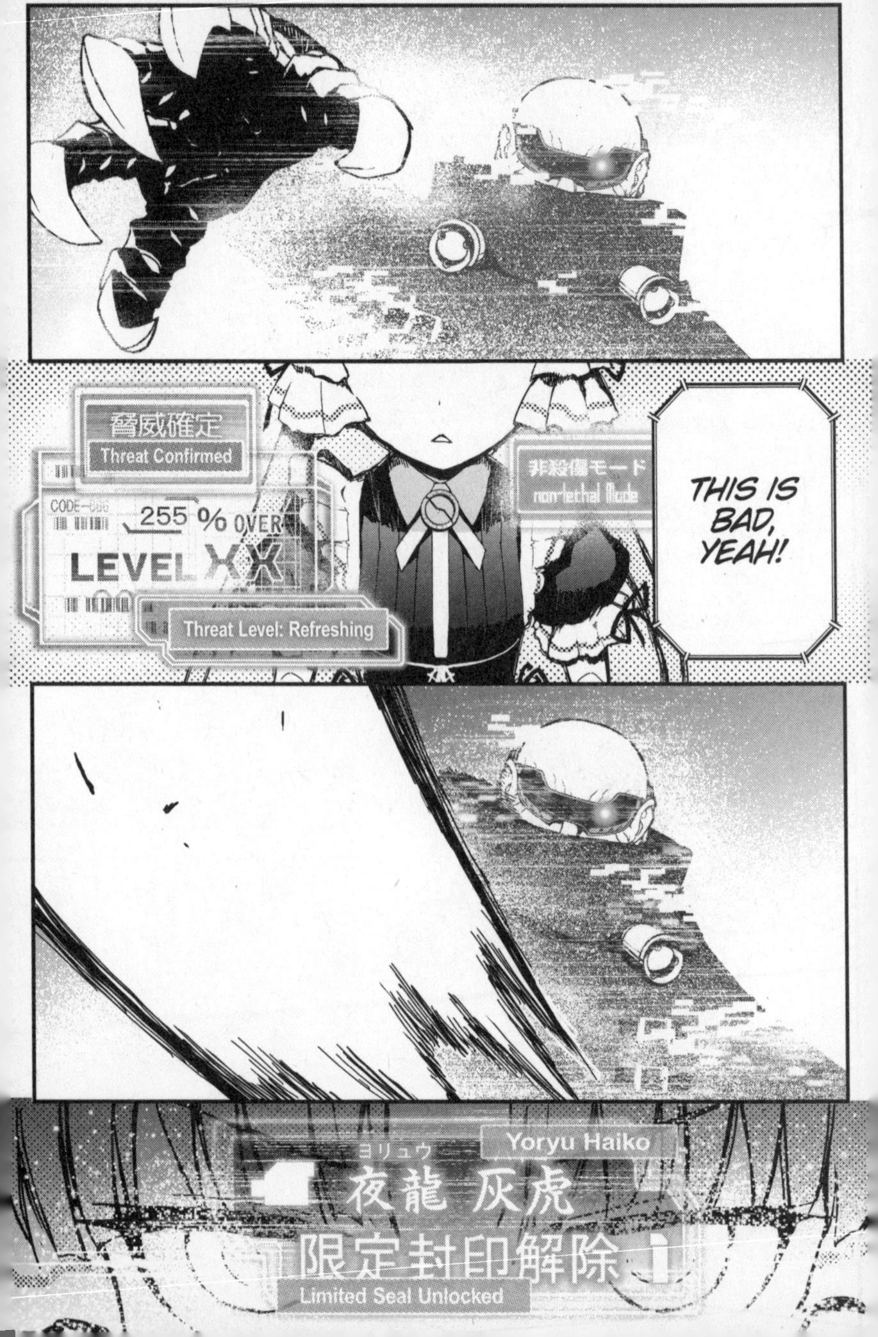
THIS IS BAD, YEAH!
非殺傷モード
non-lethal Mode
脅威確定
Threat Confirmed
255 % OVER
LEVEL XX
Threat Level: Refreshing
Yoryu Haiko
ヨリュウ
夜龍 灰虎
限定封印解除
Limited Seal Unlocked

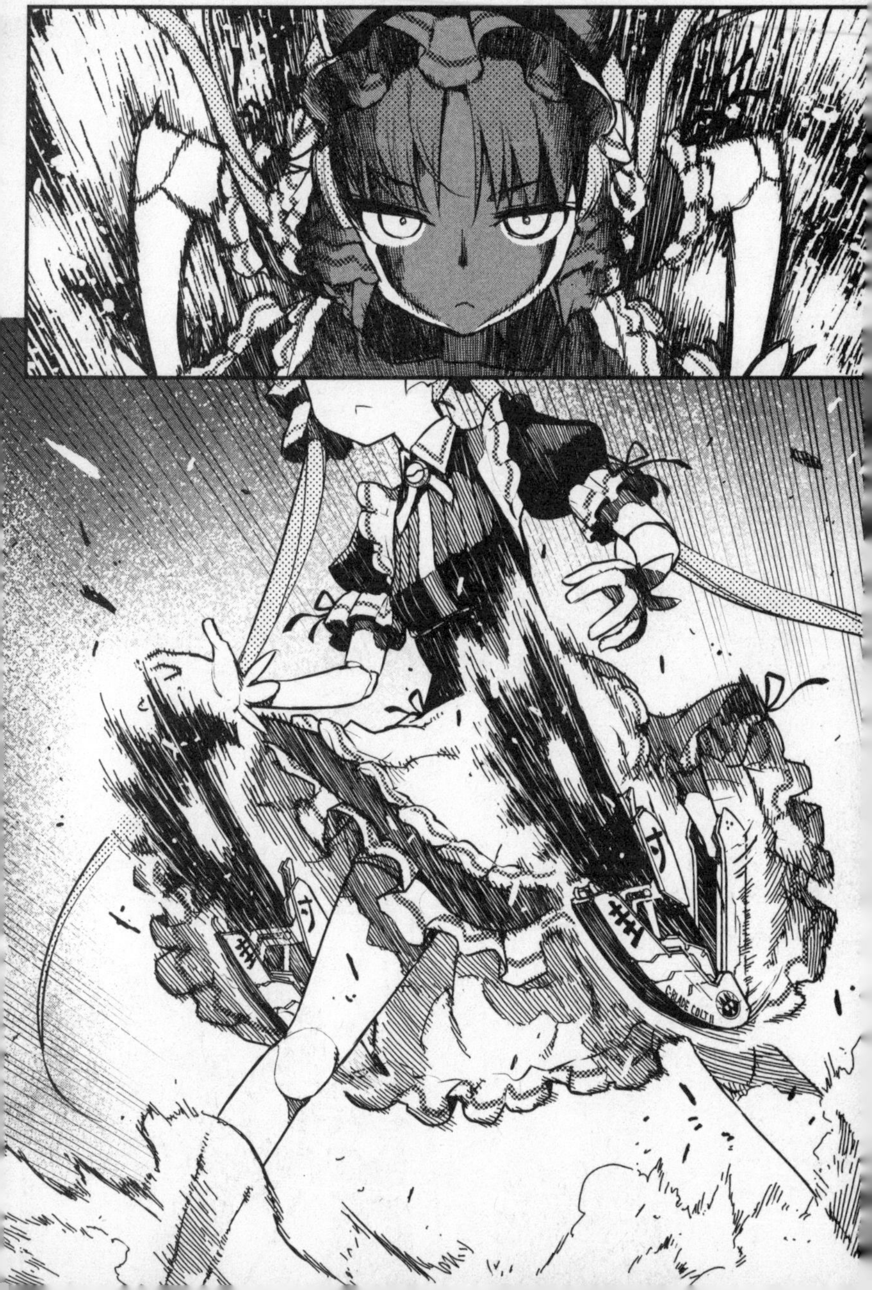
す
す
C-BLADE COLT II

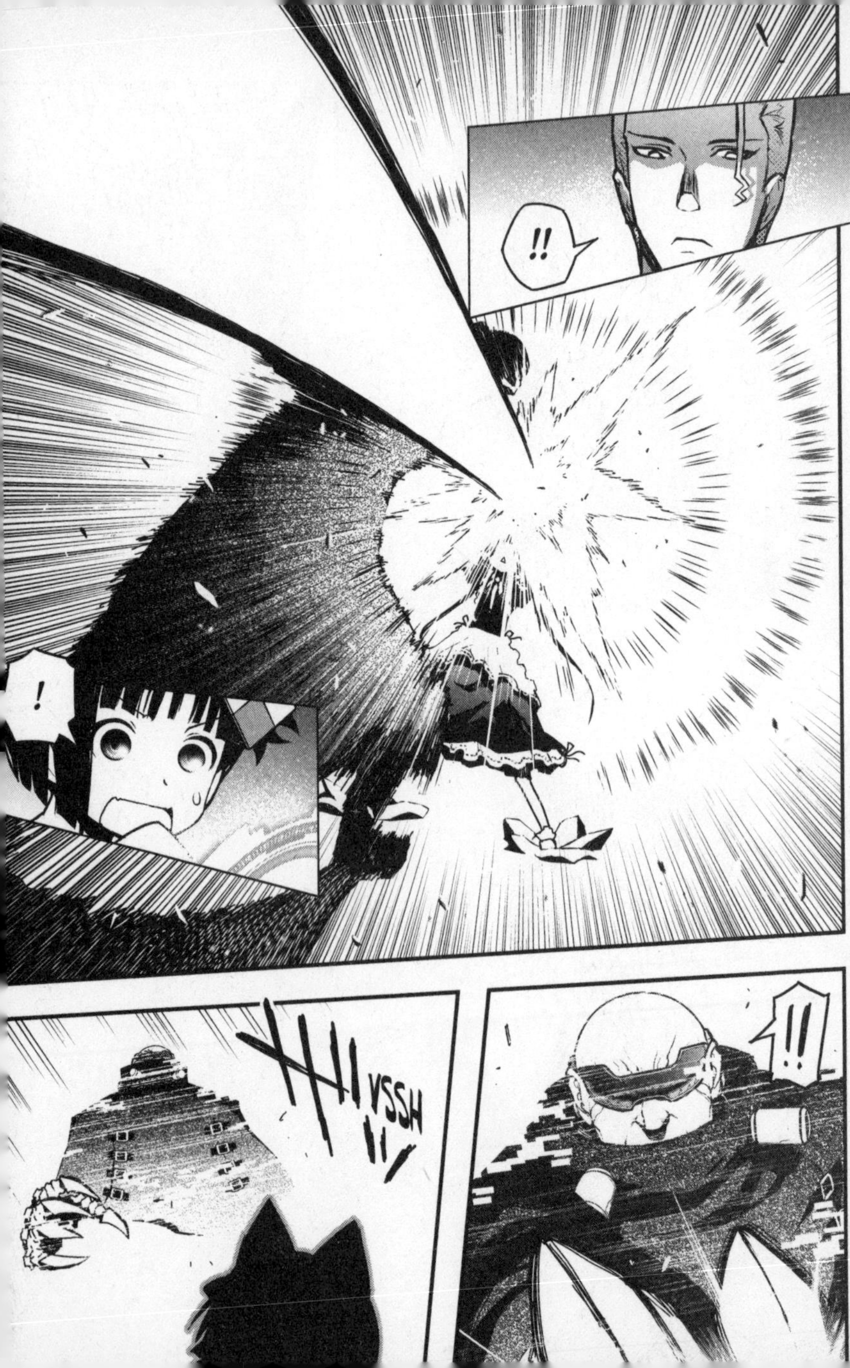
!!
!
!!
VSSH

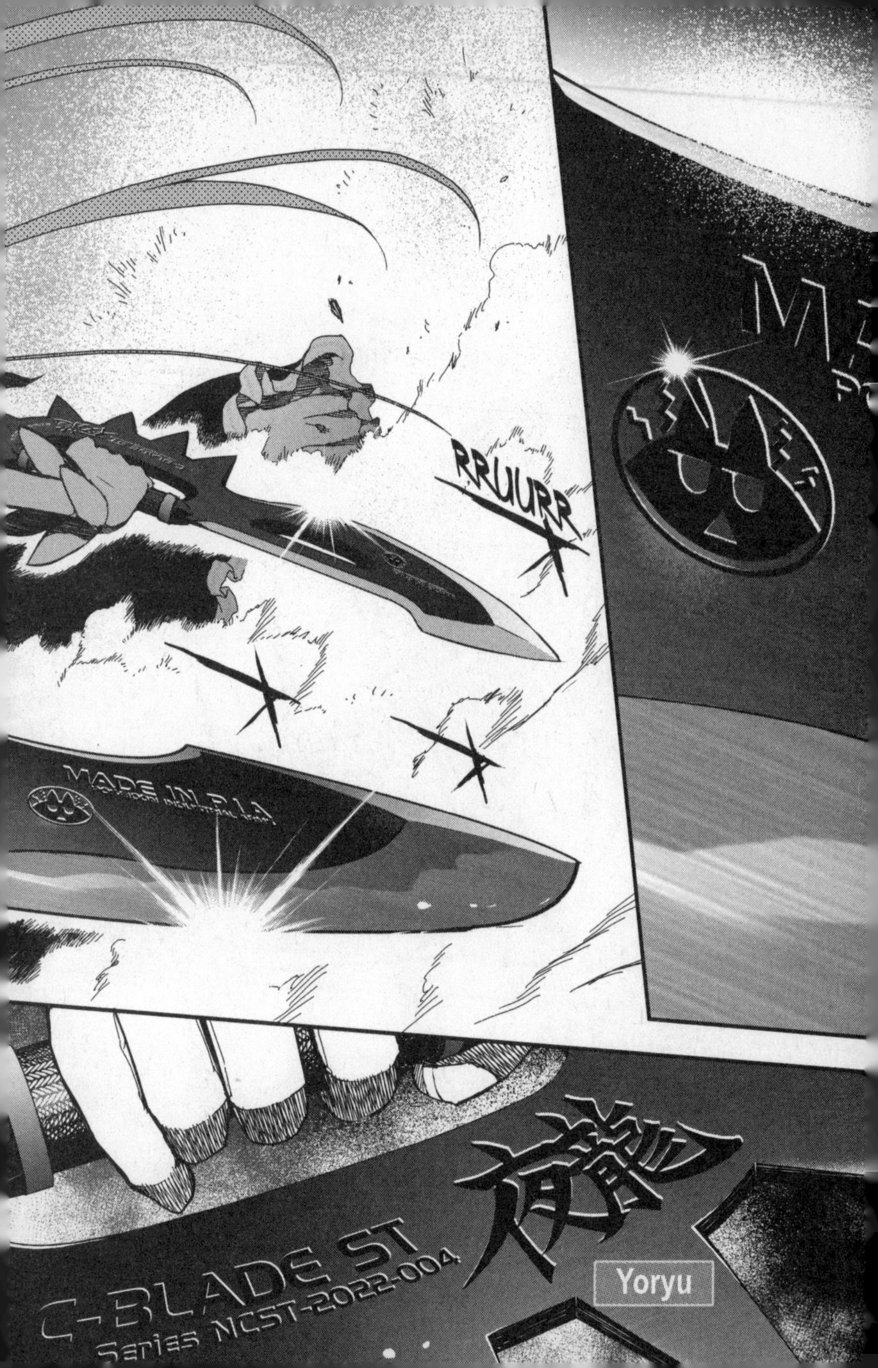
RRUUURR
MADE IN P.I.A
C-BLADE ST
Series NCST-2022-004
Yoryu

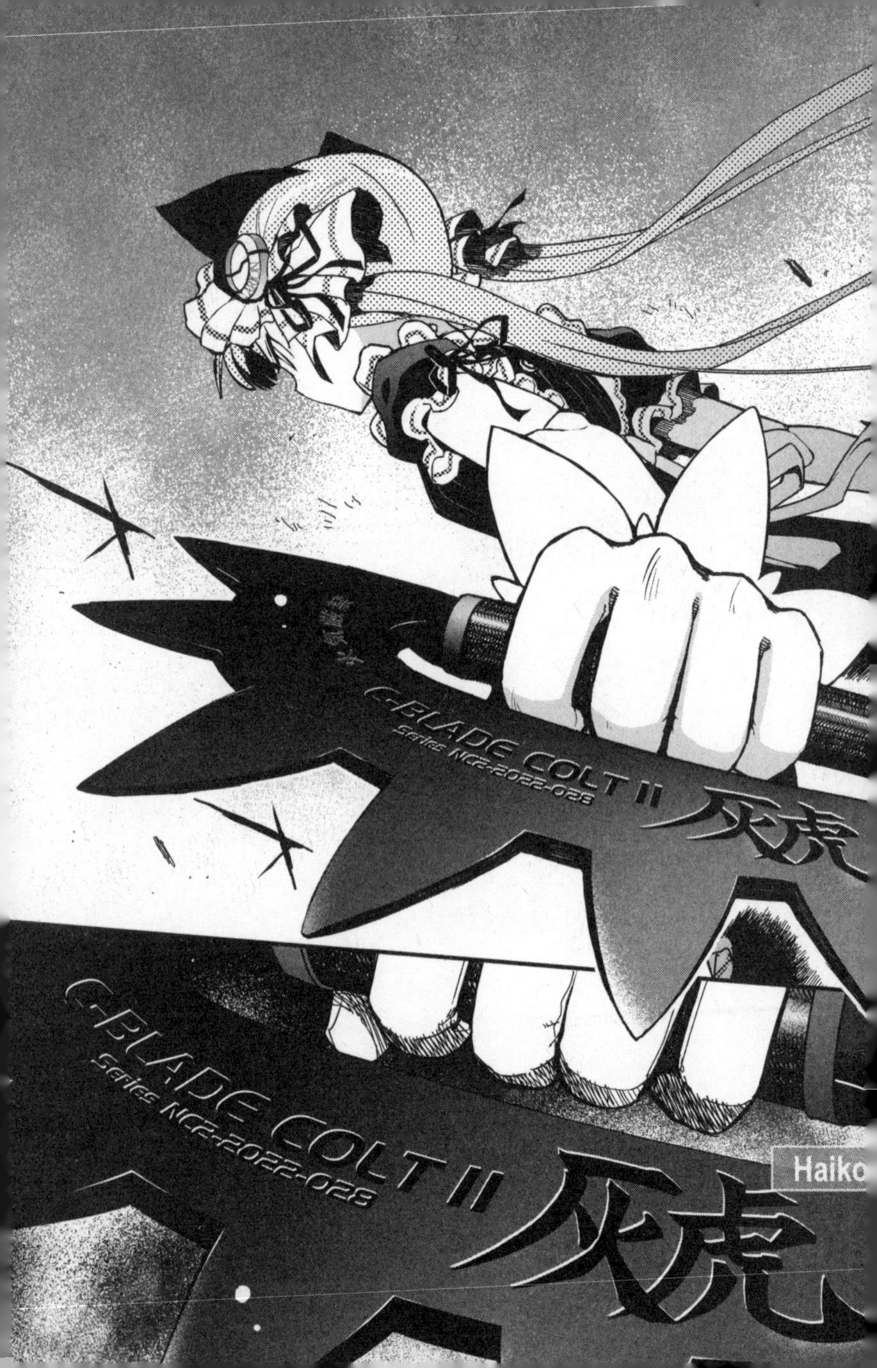
Haiko
C-BLADE COLT II
Series NC2-2022-028
灰虎
C-BLADE COLT II
Series NC2-2022-028
灰虎

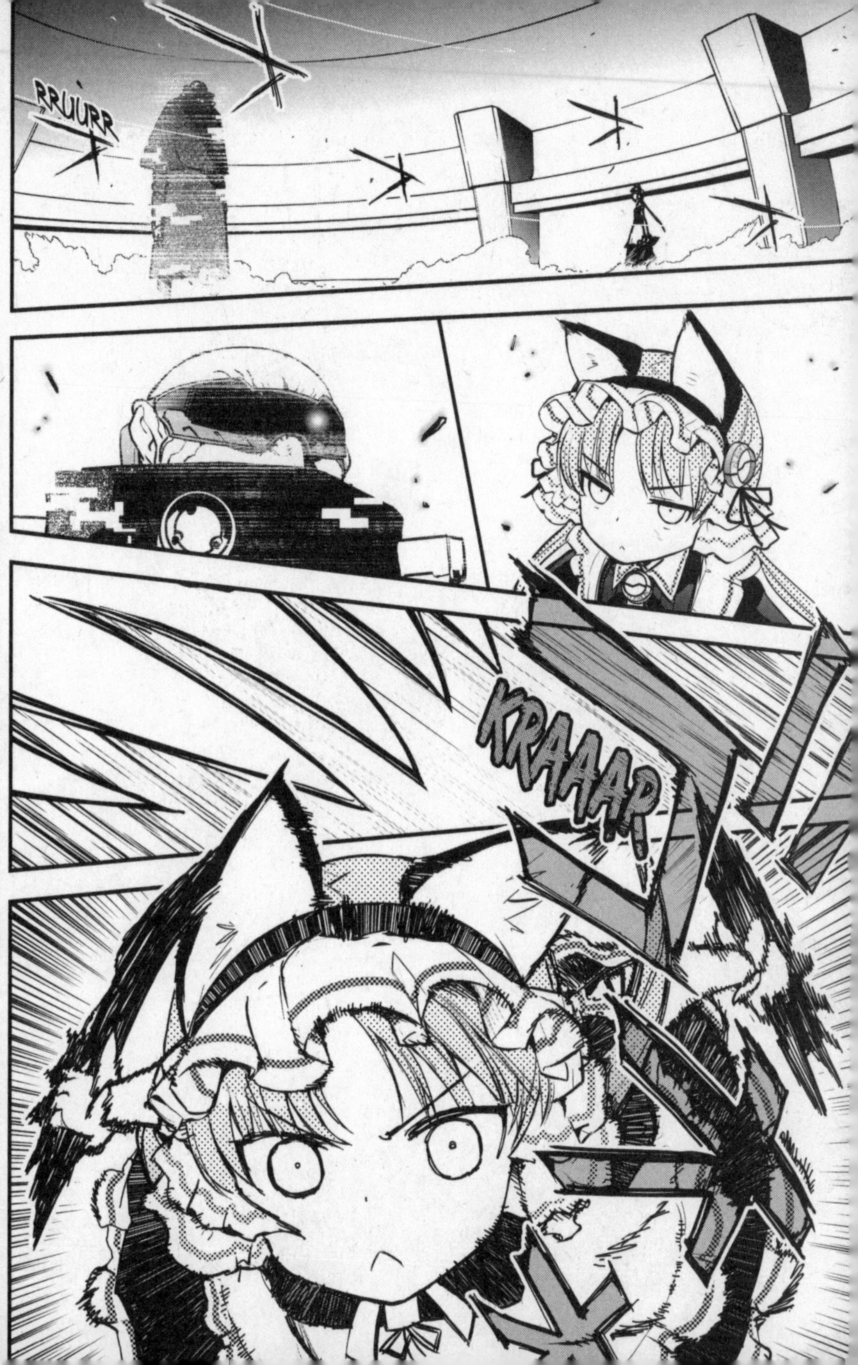
RRUURR
KRAAAR

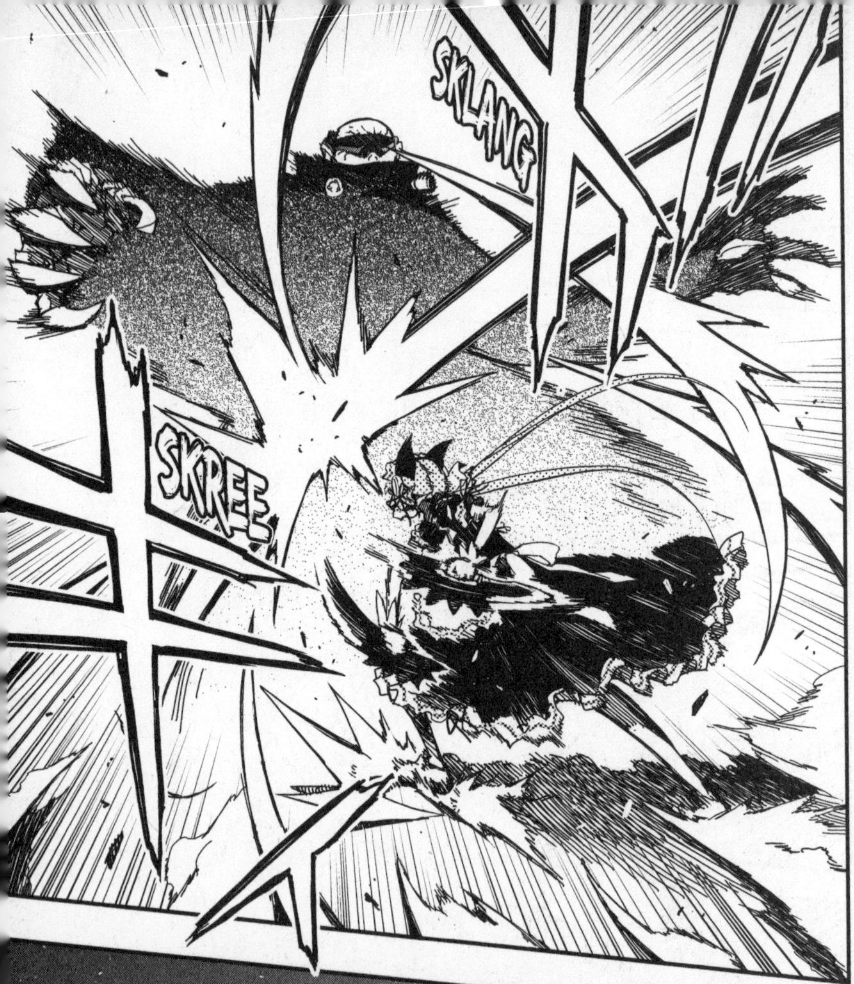
SKLANG
SKREE
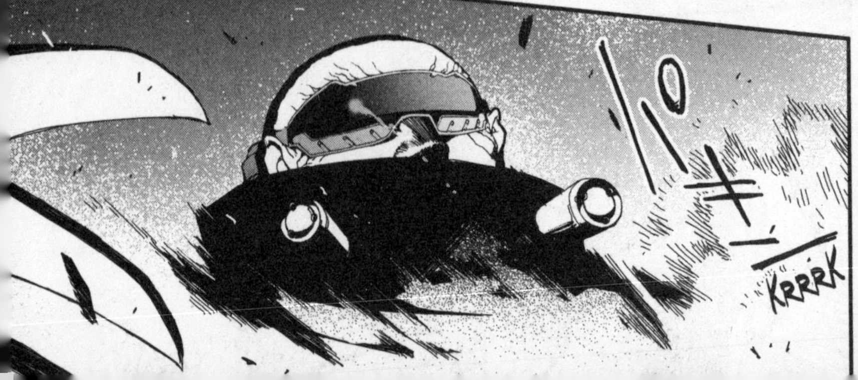
KRRRK

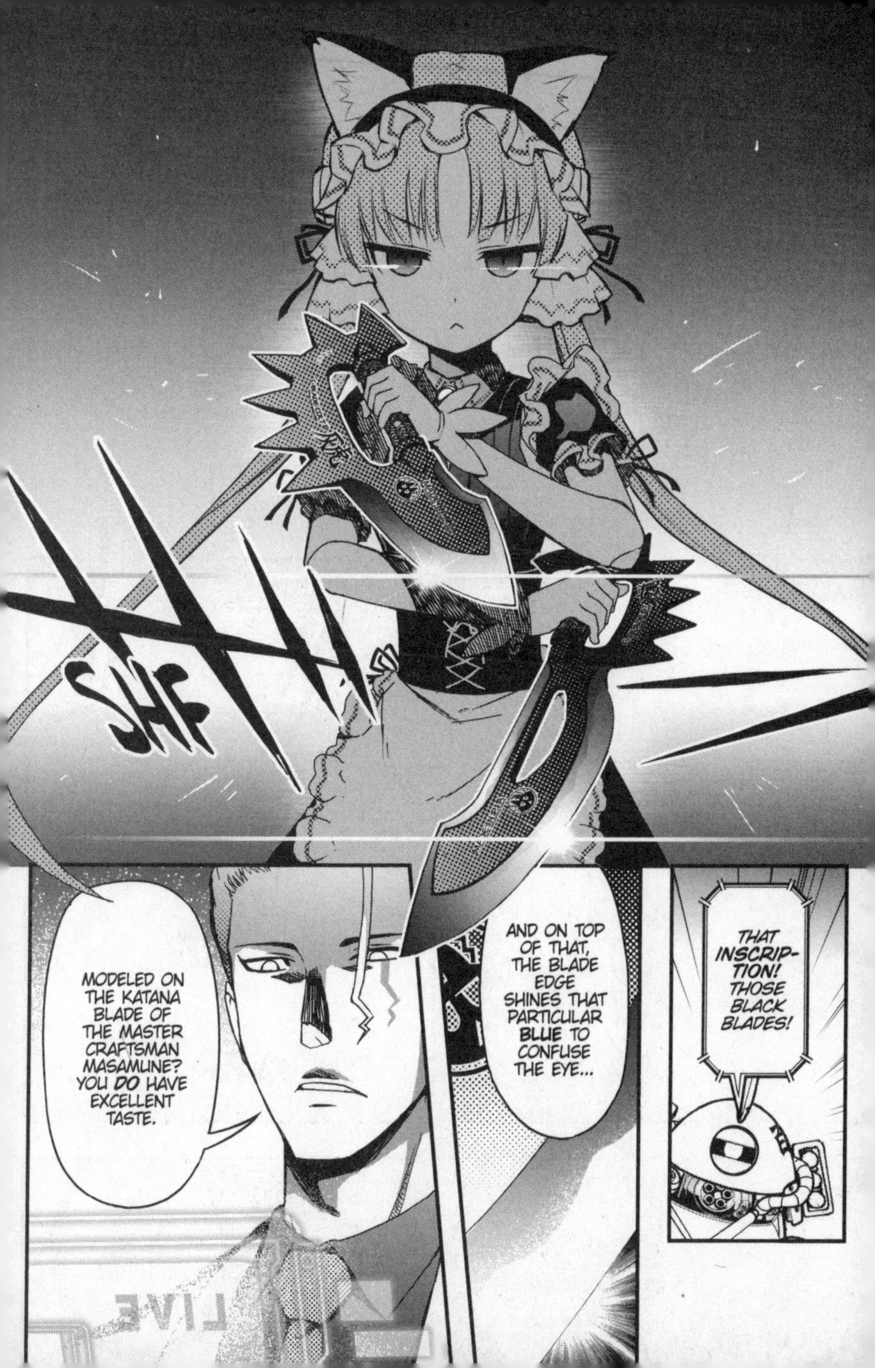
SHF
THAT INSCRIPTION! THOSE BLACK BLADES!
MODELED ON THE KATANA BLADE OF THE MASTER CRAFTSMAN MASAMUNE? YOU *DO* HAVE EXCELLENT TASTE.
AND ON TOP OF THAT, THE BLADE EDGE SHINES THAT PARTICULAR **BLUE** TO CONFUSE THE EYE...

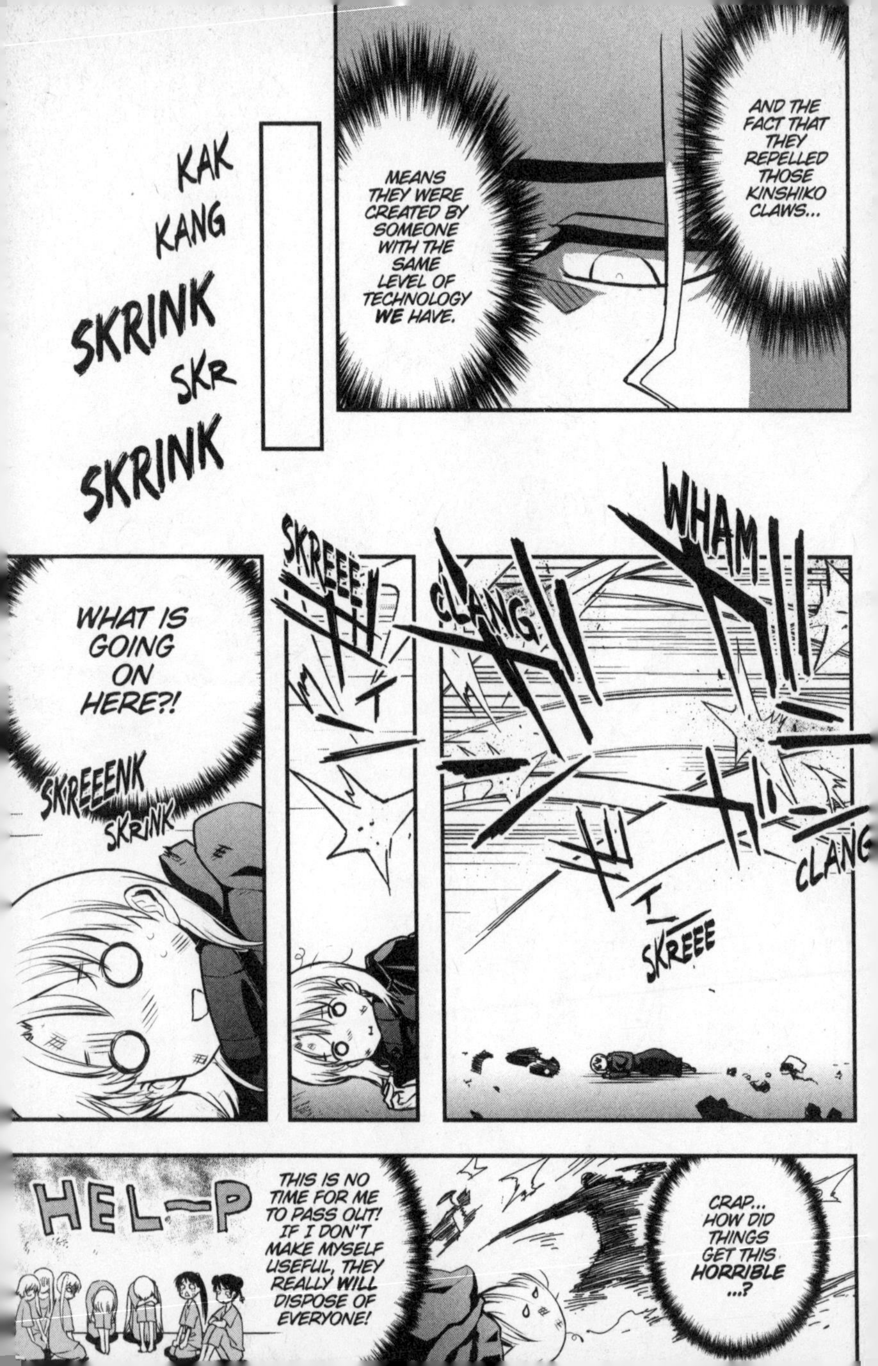
AND THE FACT THAT THEY REPELLED THOSE KINSHIKO CLAWS...
MEANS THEY WERE CREATED BY SOMEONE WITH THE SAME LEVEL OF TECHNOLOGY WE HAVE.
KAK
KANG
SKRINK
SKR
SKRINK
WHAM
CLANG
CLANG
SKREEE
SKREEE
WHAT IS GOING ON HERE?!
SKREEENK
SKRINK
CRAP... HOW DID THINGS GET THIS HORRIBLE ...?
THIS IS NO TIME FOR ME TO PASS OUT! IF I DON'T MAKE MYSELF USEFUL, THEY REALLY WILL DISPOSE OF EVERYONE!
HEL-P

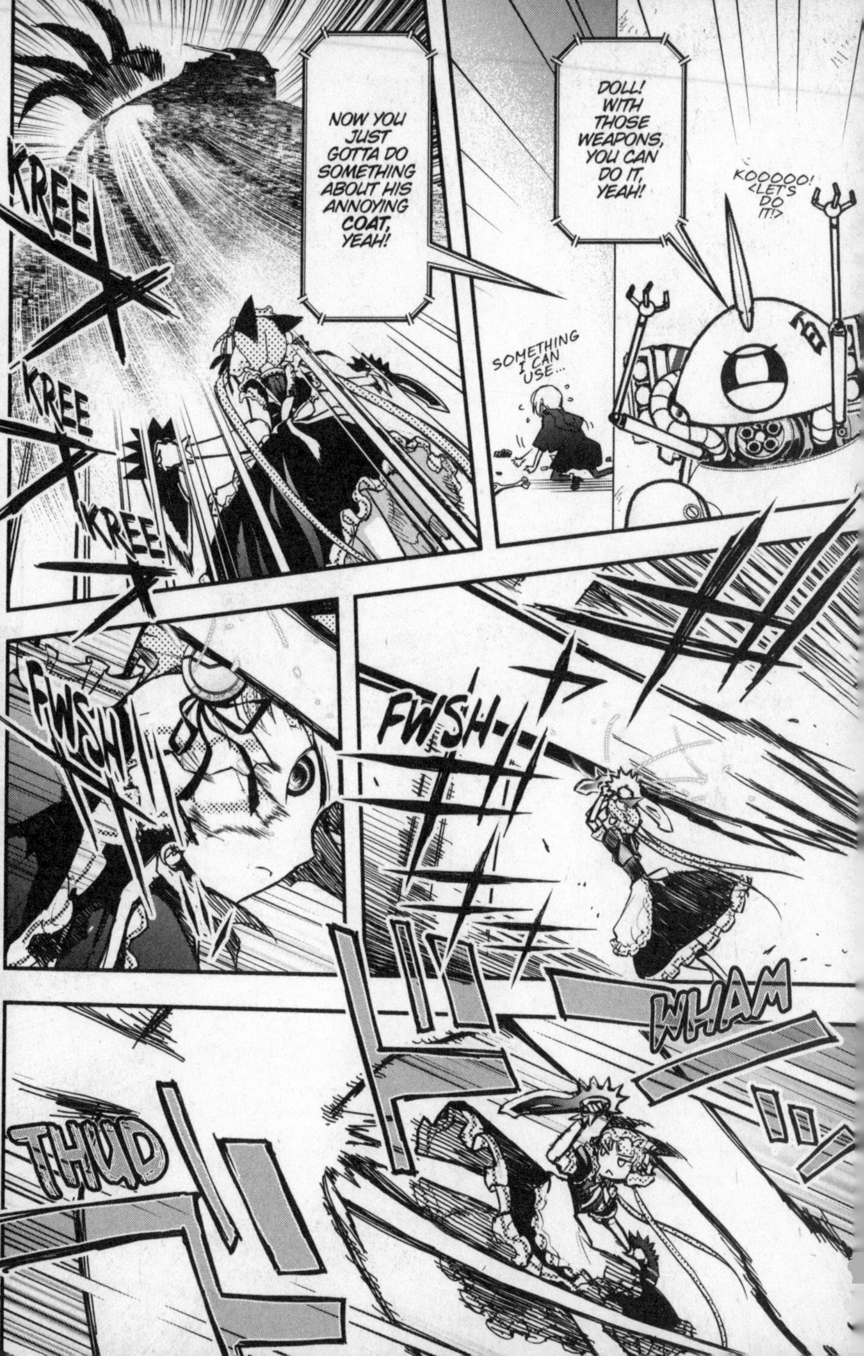
DOLL! WITH THOSE WEAPONS, YOU CAN DO IT, YEAH!
KOOOOO! <LET'S DO IT!>
SOMETHING I CAN USE...
NOW YOU JUST GOTTA DO SOMETHING ABOUT HIS ANNOYING COAT, YEAH!
KREE
KREE
KREE
FWSH-...
FWSH!
WHAM
THUD

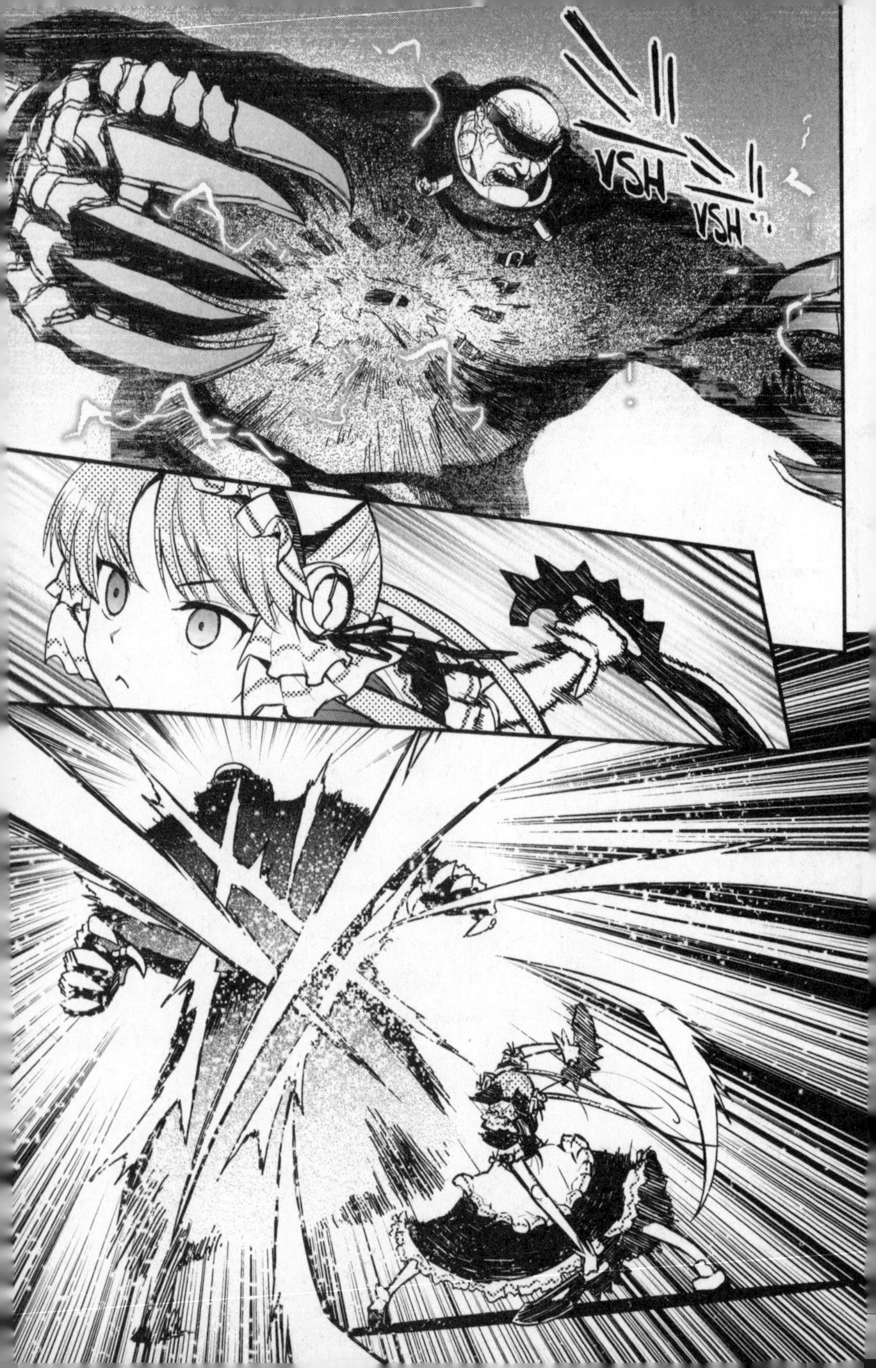
VSH
VSH

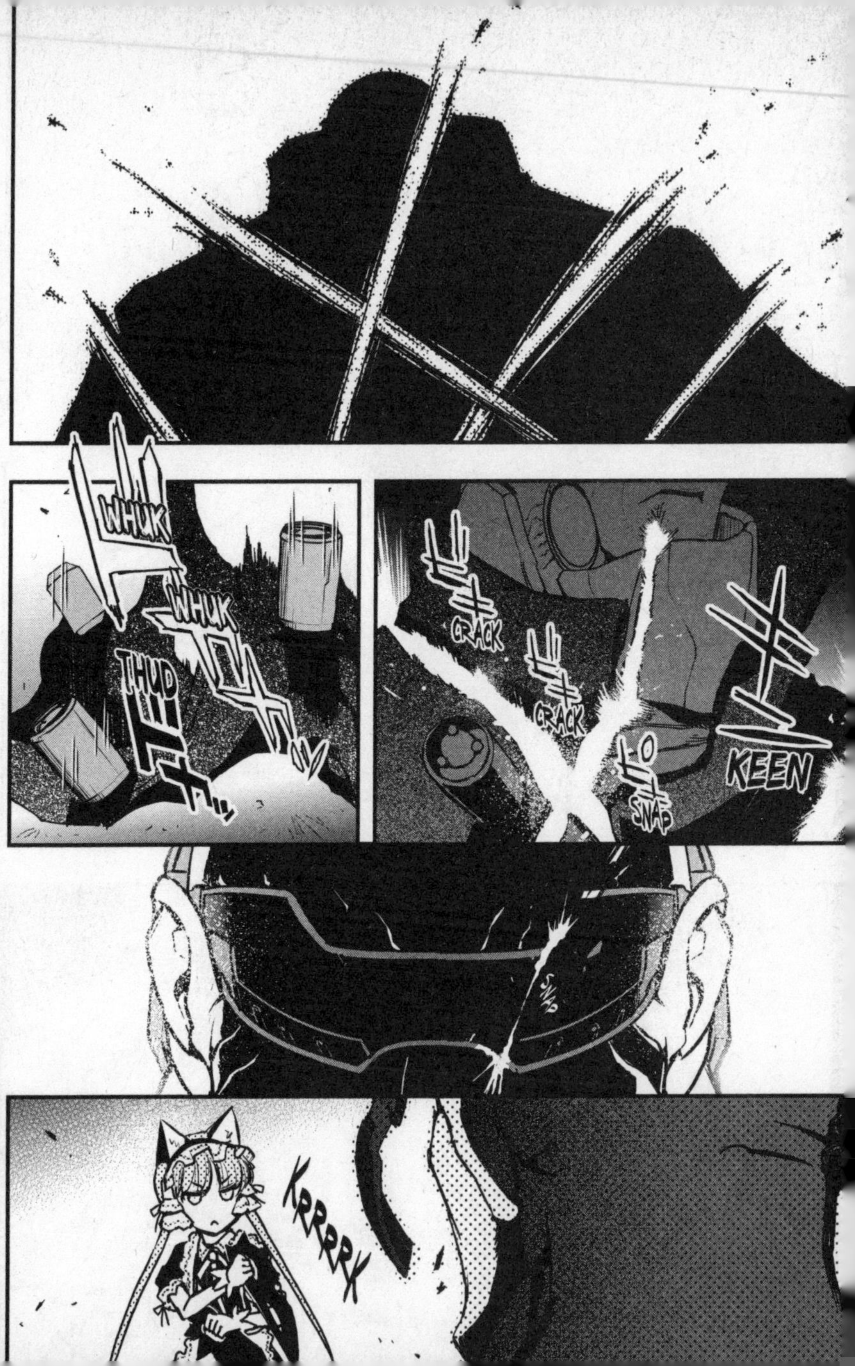
CRACK
CRACK
SNAP
KEEN
WHUK
WHUK
THUD
SNAP
KRRRRK

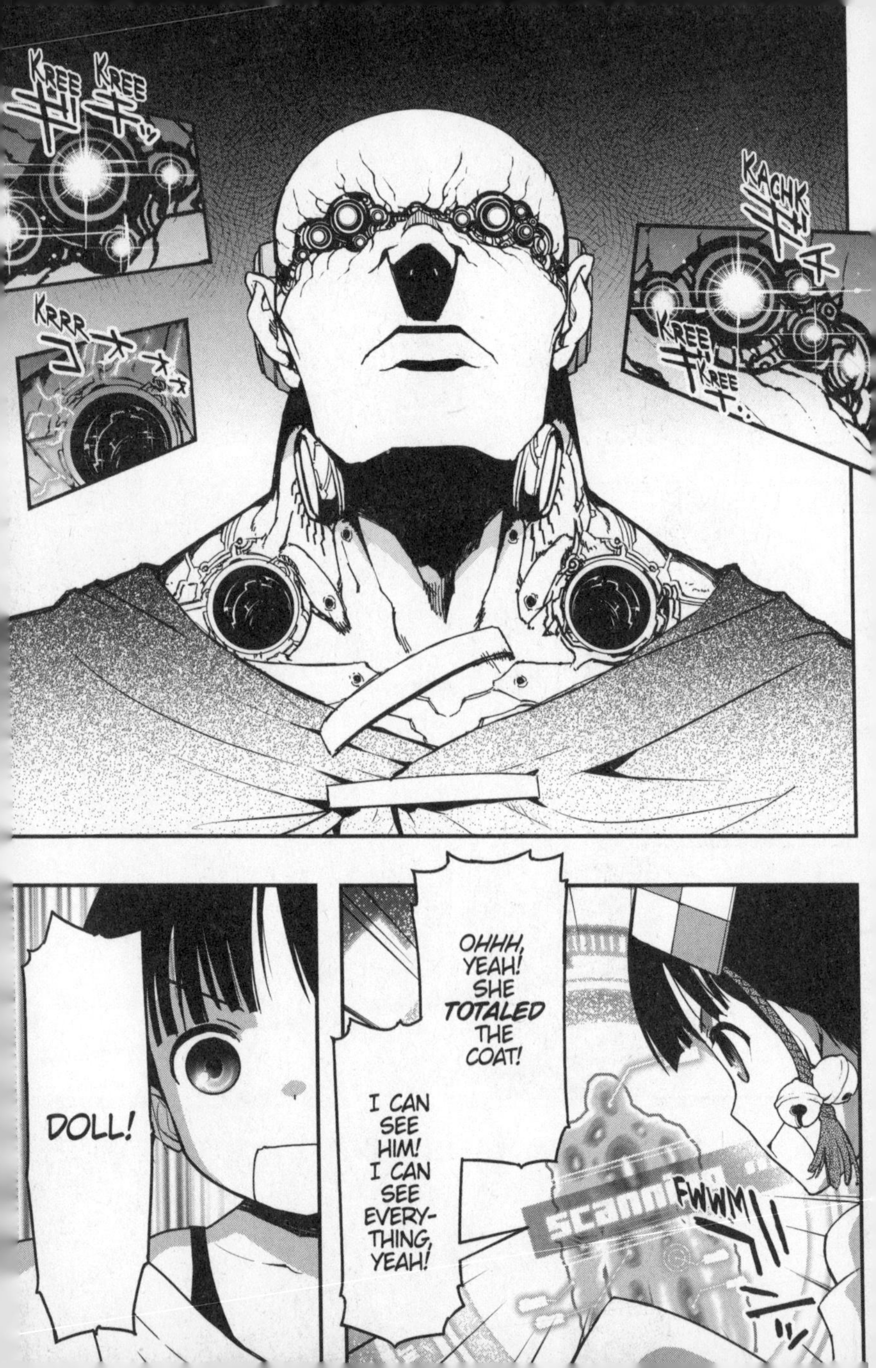
KACHK
KREE KREE
KREE KREE
KRRR
OHHH, YEAH! SHE TOTALED THE COAT!
I CAN SEE HIM! I CAN SEE EVERY-THING, YEAH!
FWWM
DOLL!

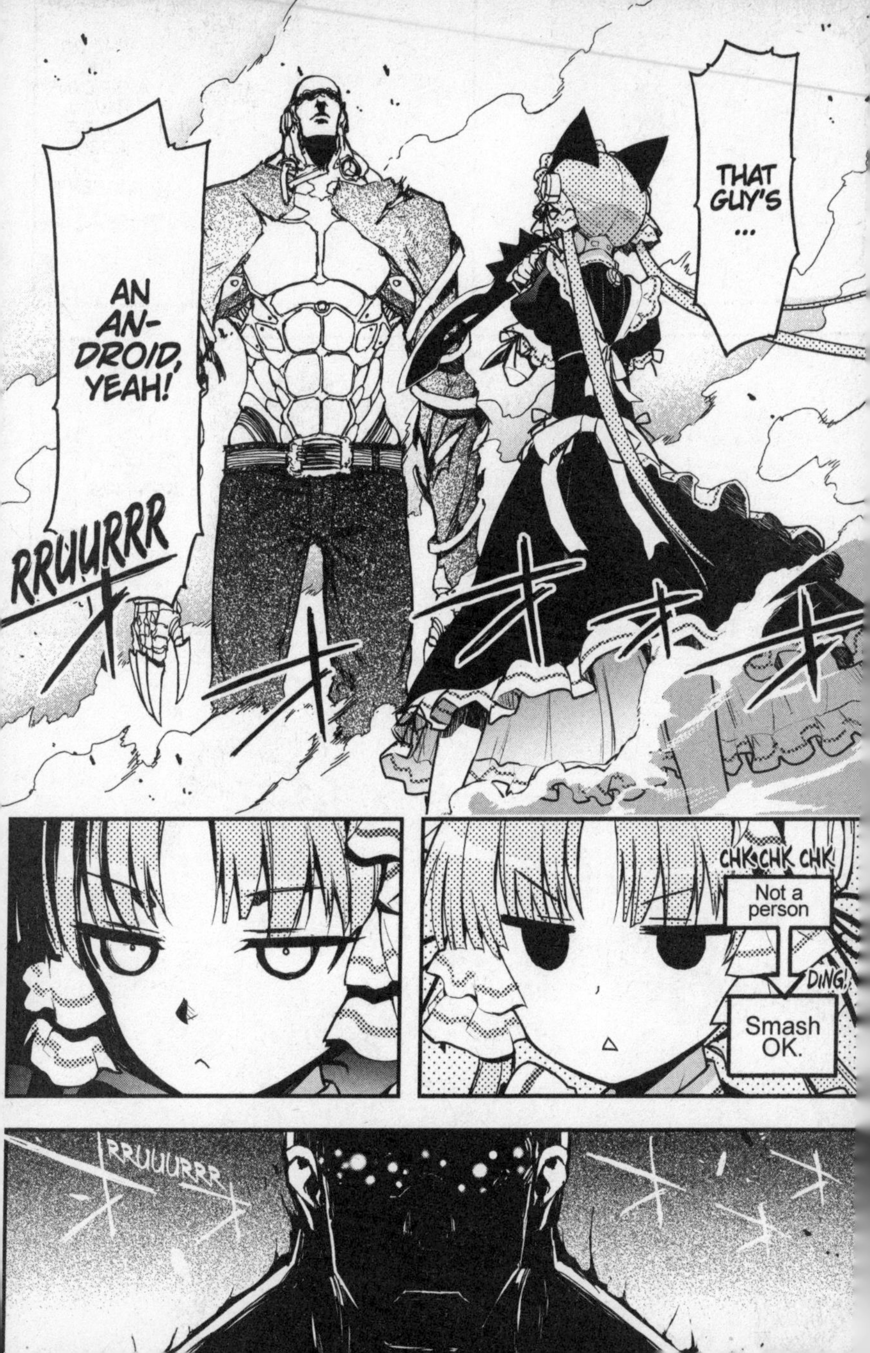
THAT GUY'S ...
AN AN-DROID, YEAH!
RRUURRR
CHK CHK CHK
Not a person
DING!
Smash OK.
RRUUURRR

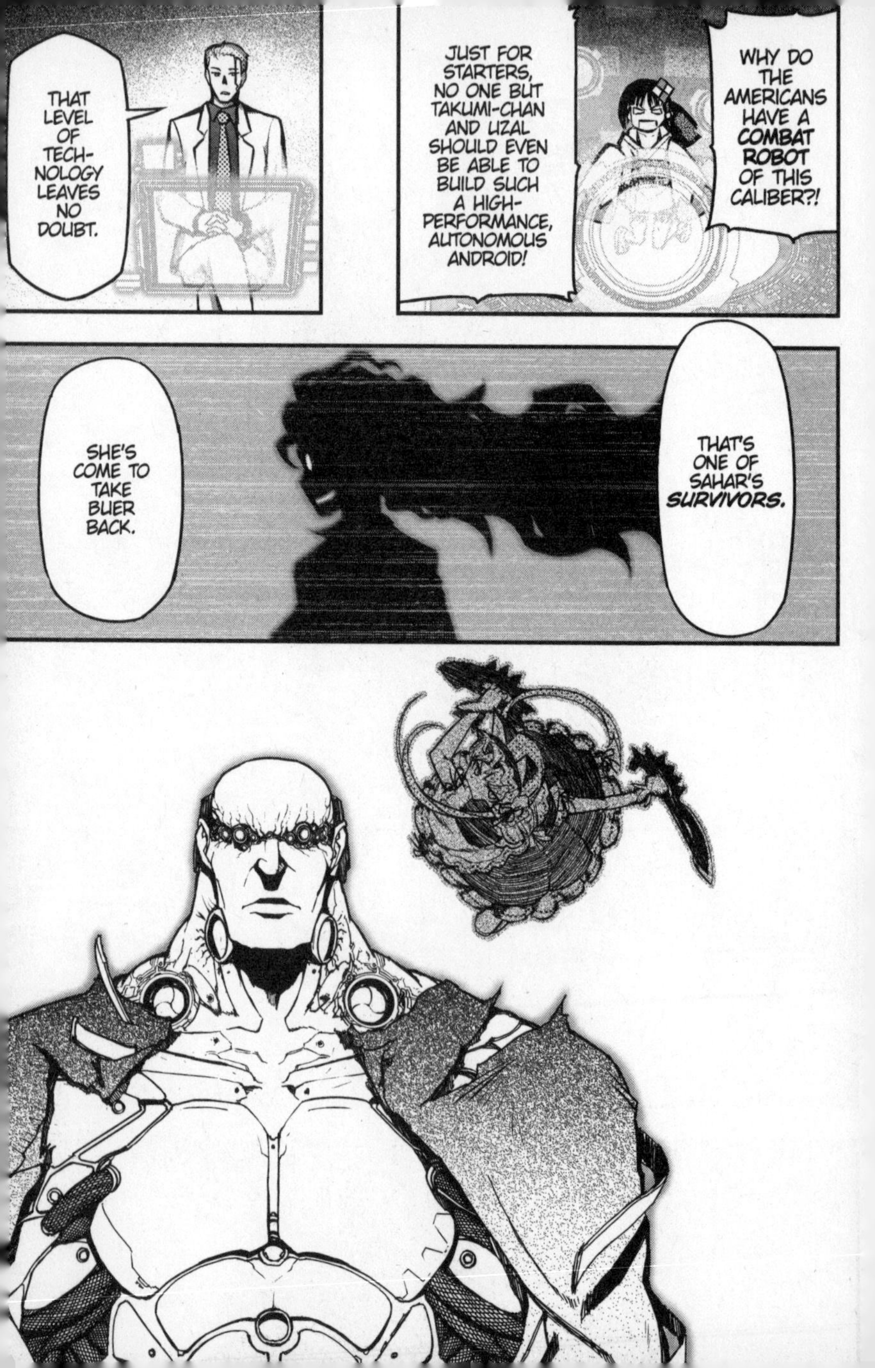
WHY DO THE AMERICANS HAVE A COMBAT ROBOT OF THIS CALIBER?!
JUST FOR STARTERS, NO ONE BUT TAKUMI-CHAN AND UZAL SHOULD EVEN BE ABLE TO BUILD SUCH A HIGH-PERFORMANCE, AUTONOMOUS ANDROID!
THAT LEVEL OF TECHNOLOGY LEAVES NO DOUBT.
THAT'S ONE OF SAHAR'S SURVIVORS.
SHE'S COME TO TAKE BUER BACK.

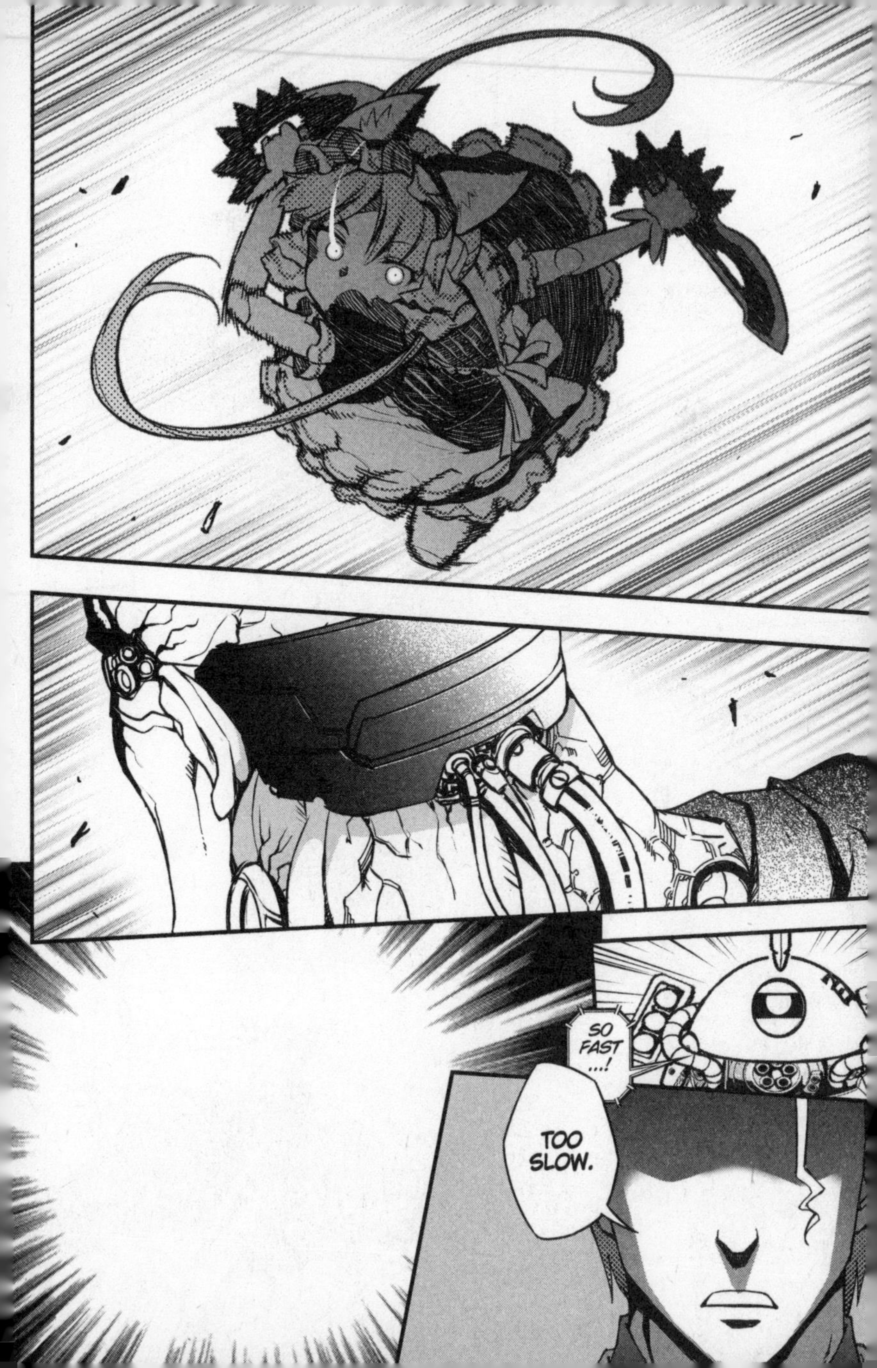
SO FAST ...!
TOO SLOW.

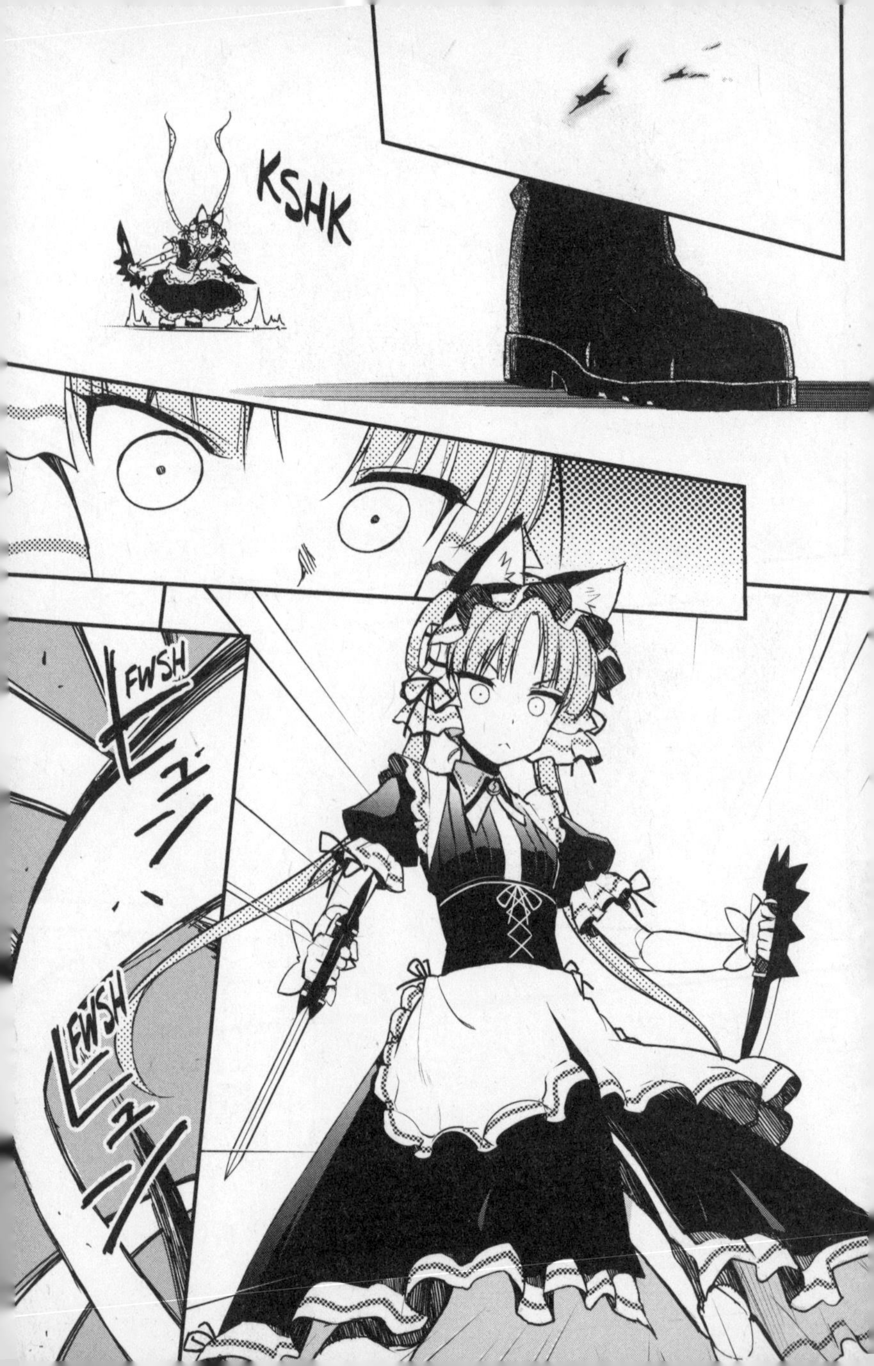
KSHK
FWSH
FWSH

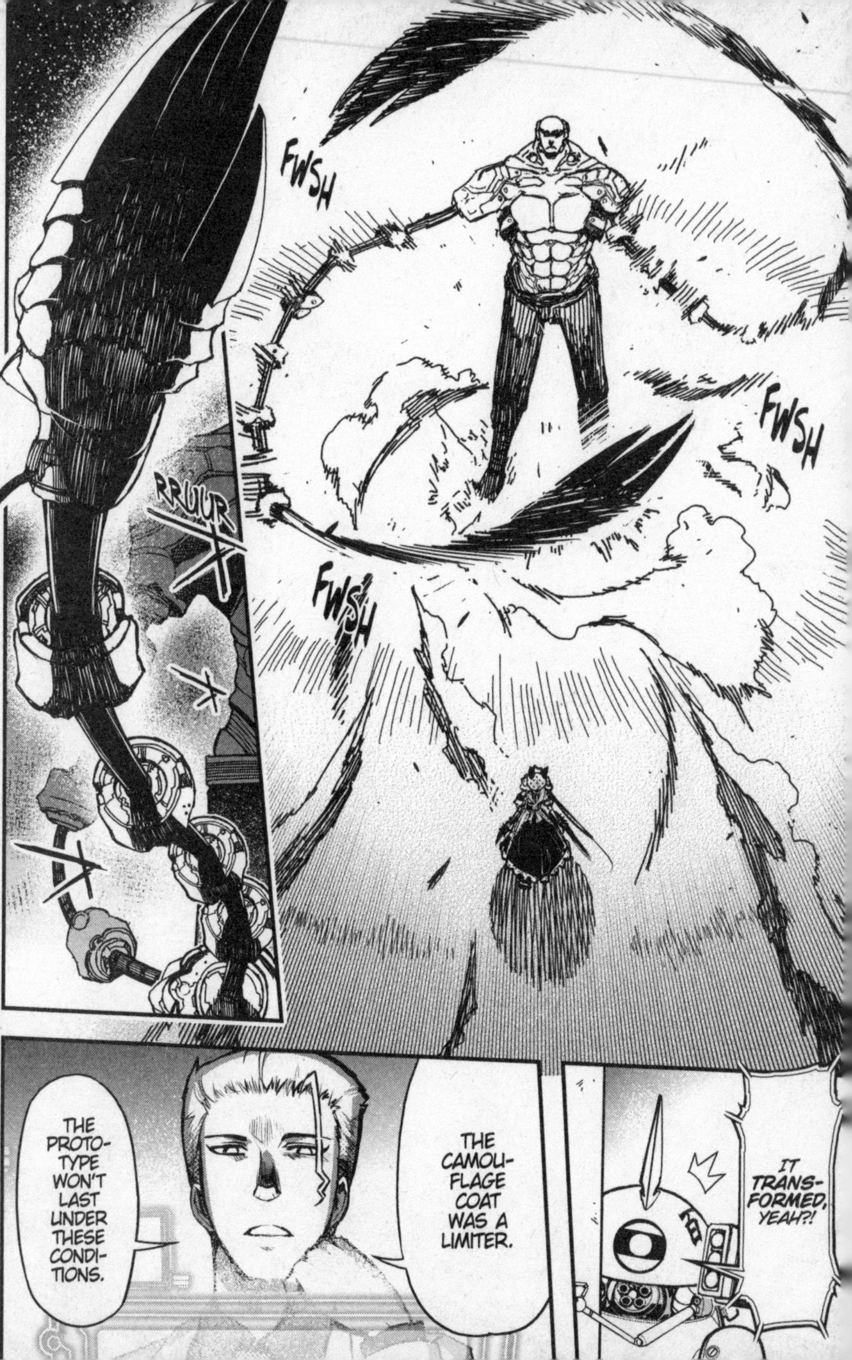
FWSH
FWSH
FWSH
RRUUR
IT TRANSFORMED, YEAH?!
THE CAMOUFLAGE COAT WAS A LIMITER.
THE PROTOTYPE WON'T LAST UNDER THESE CONDITIONS.

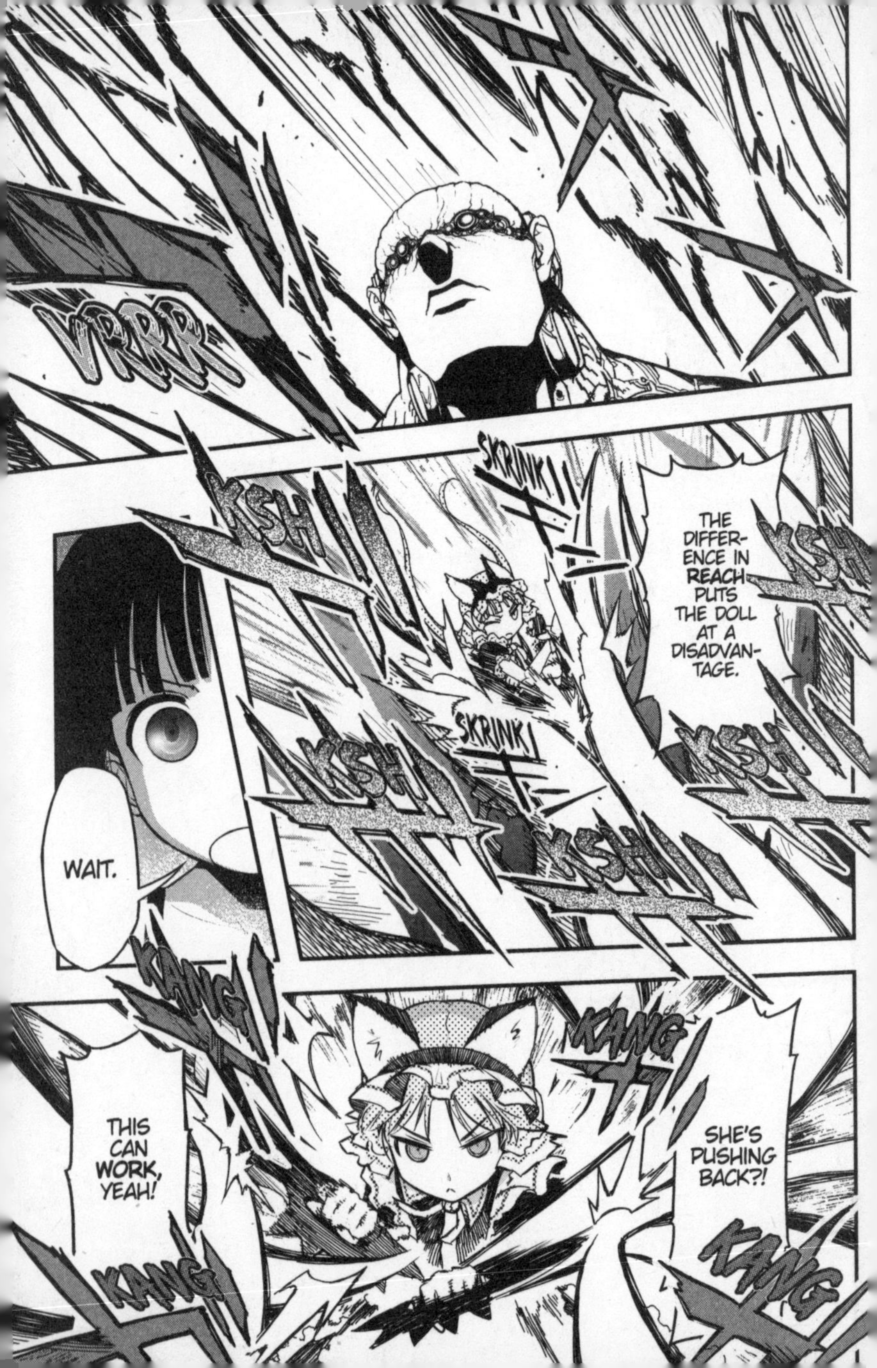
VRRR
SKRINK
KSH
THE DIFFERENCE IN REACH PUTS THE DOLL AT A DISADVANTAGE.
KSH
KSH
SKRINK
KSH
KSH
WAIT.
KANG
SHE'S PUSHING BACK?!
KANG
KANG
THIS CAN WORK, YEAH!
KANG

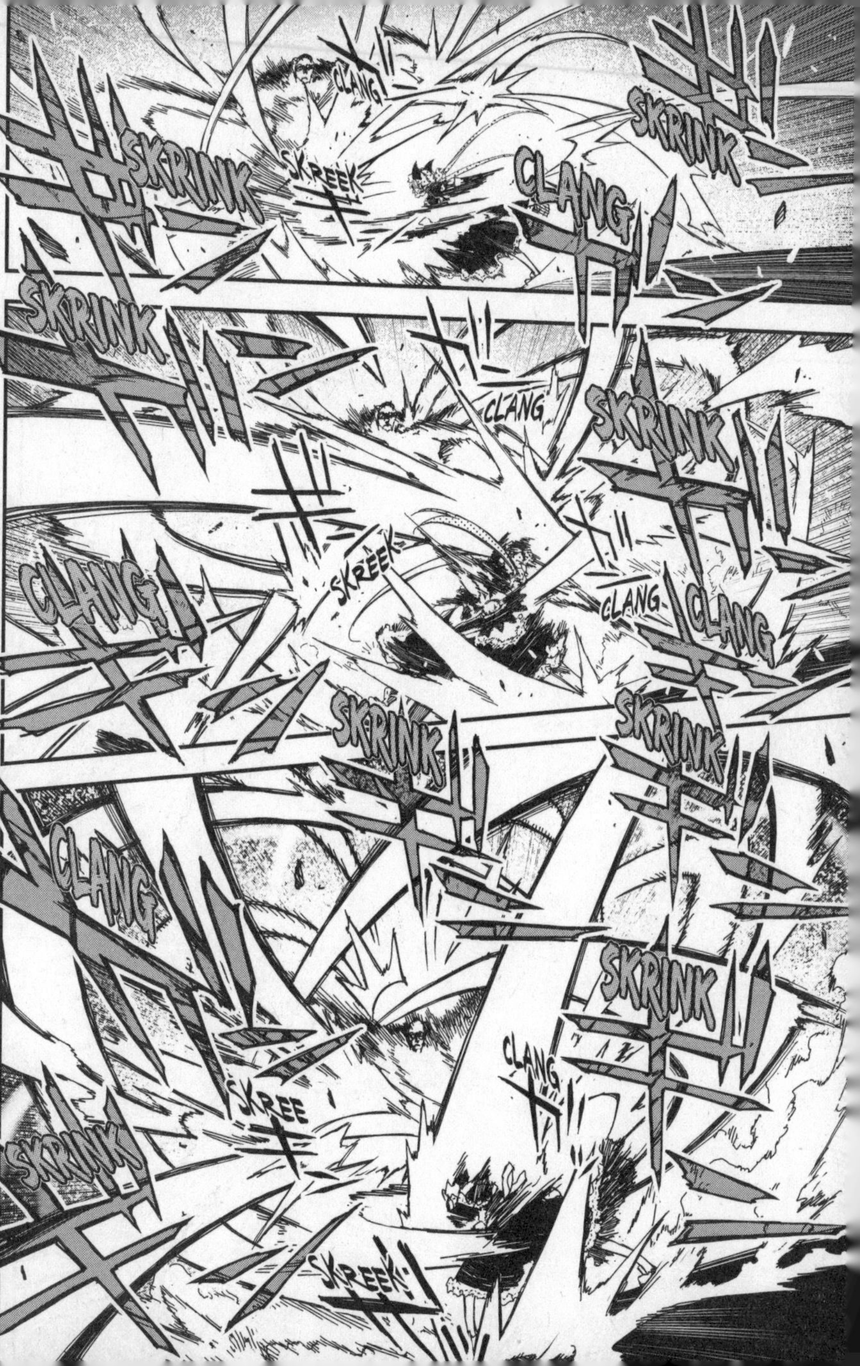
SKRINK
CLANG
CLANG
SKREEK
SKRINK
SKRINK
CLANG
SKRINK
CLANG
CLANG
SKREEK
CLANG
SKRINK
SKRINK
SKRINK
CLANG
CLANG
SKREE
SKRINK
SKREEK!

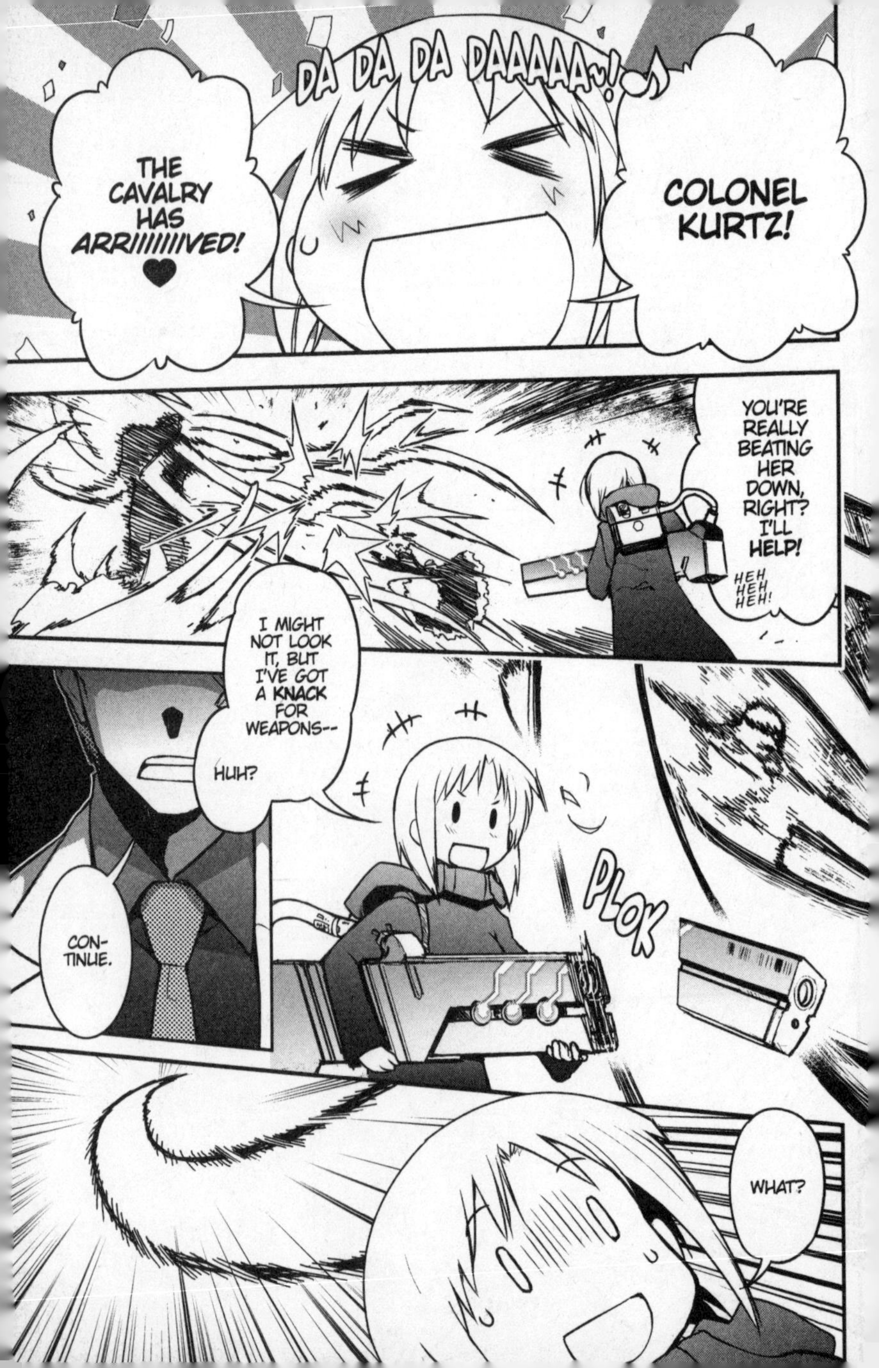
DA DA DA DAAAAA~!♪
COLONEL KURTZ!
THE CAVALRY HAS ARRIIIIIIIVED! ♥
YOU'RE REALLY BEATING HER DOWN, RIGHT? I'LL HELP!
HEH HEH HEH!
I MIGHT NOT LOOK IT, BUT I'VE GOT A KNACK FOR WEAPONS--
PLOK
HUH?
CON-TINUE.
WHAT?

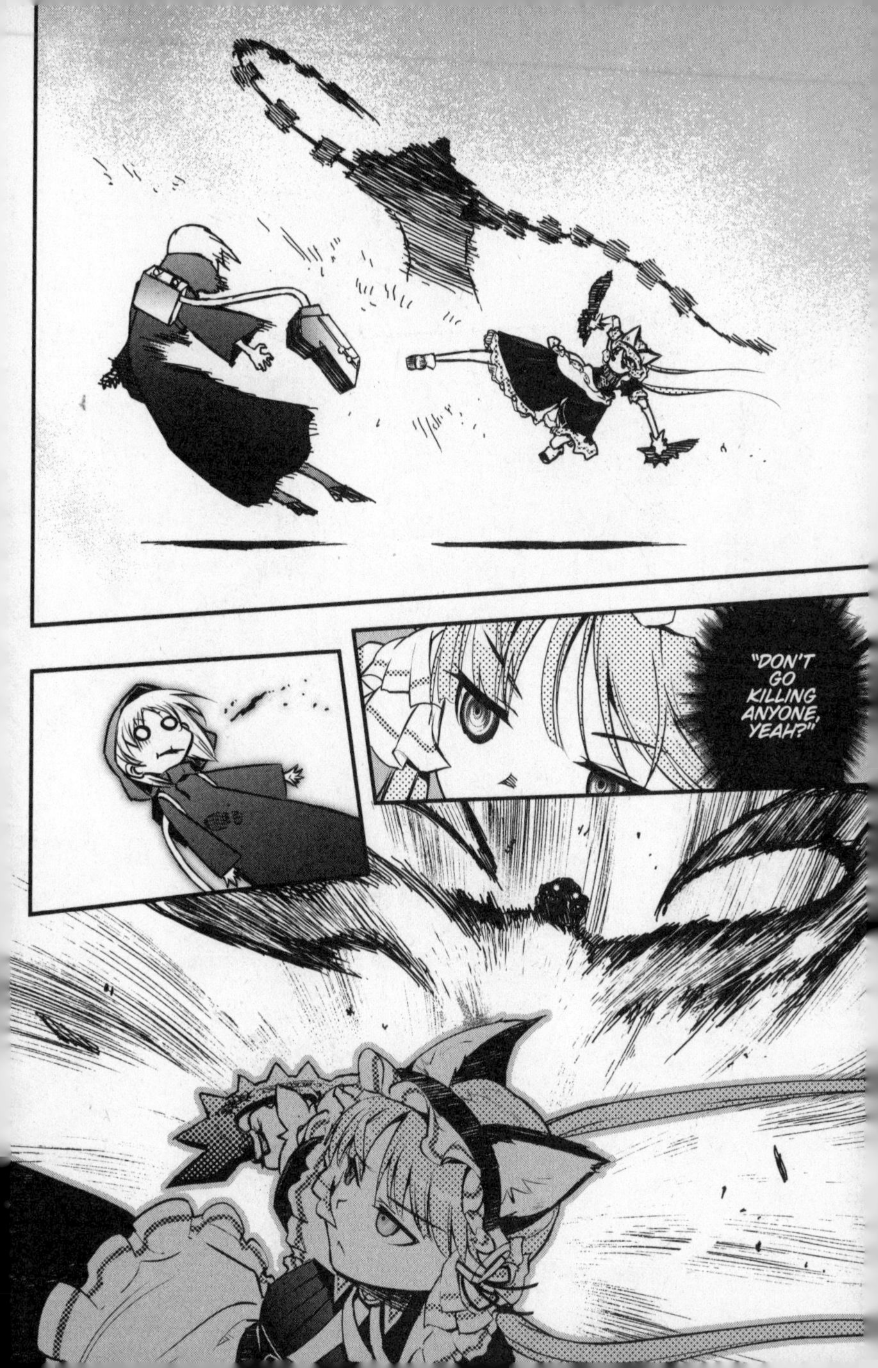
"DON'T GO KILLING ANYONE, YEAH?"

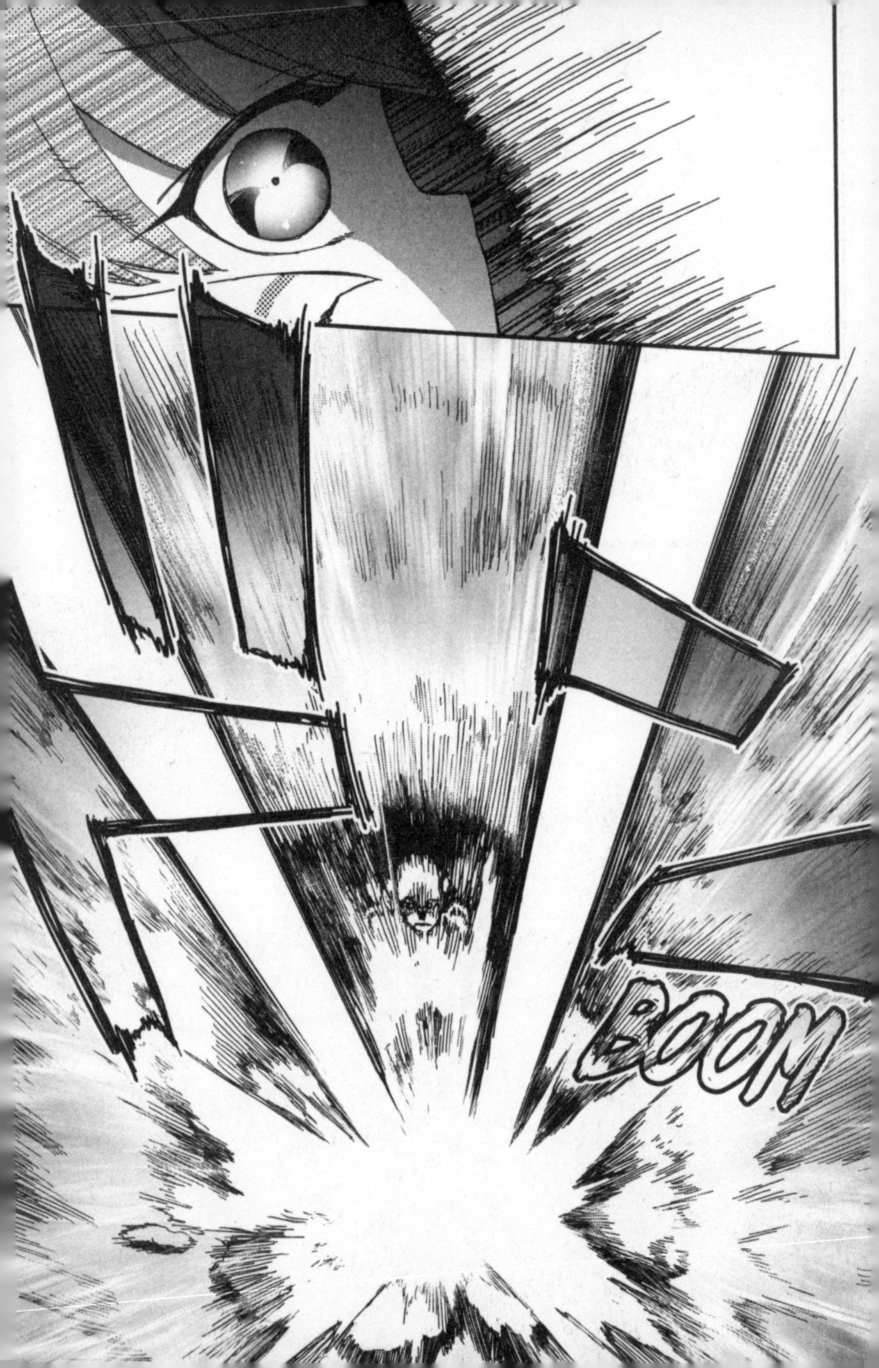
BOOM

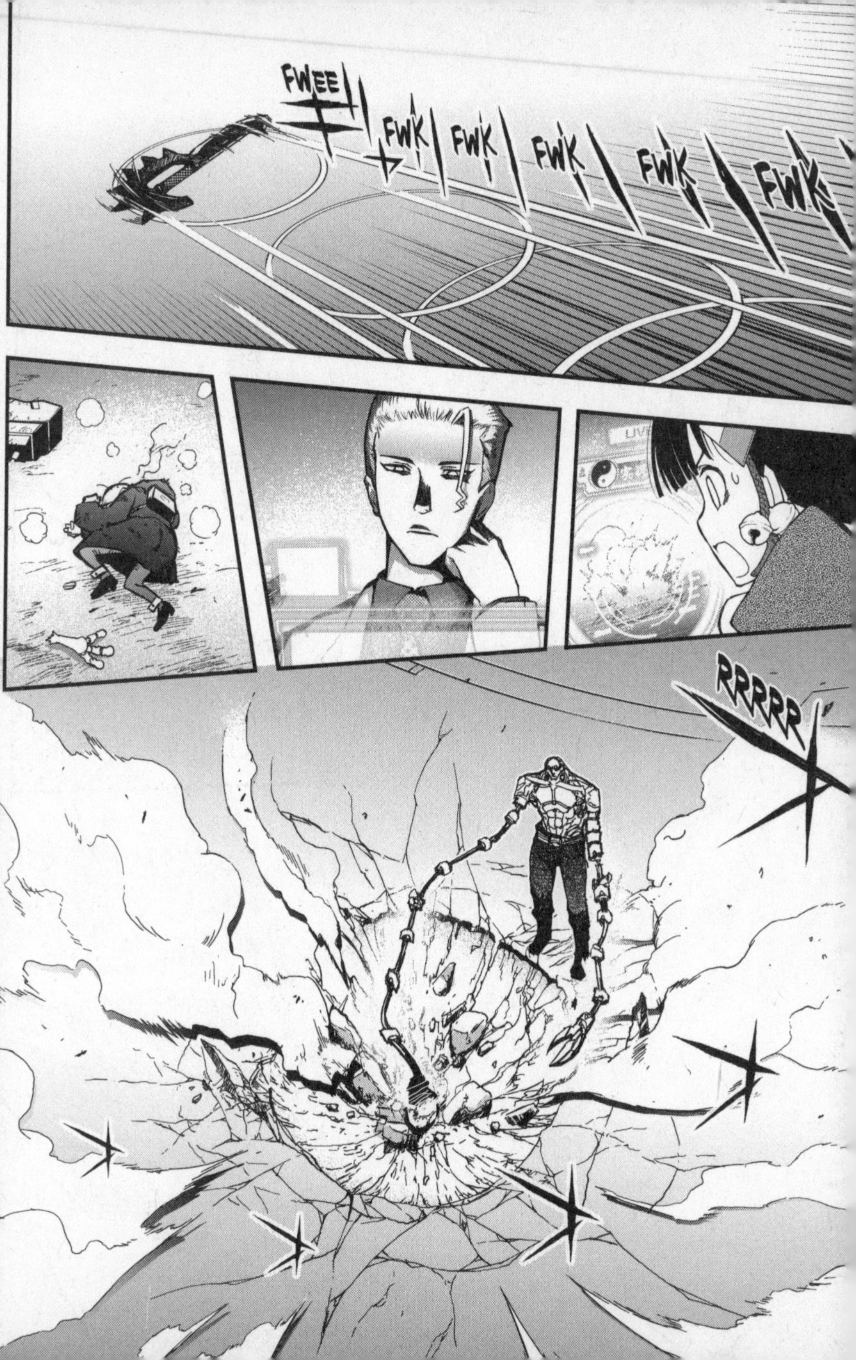
FWEE
FWK
FWK
FWK
FWK
FWK
RRRRR

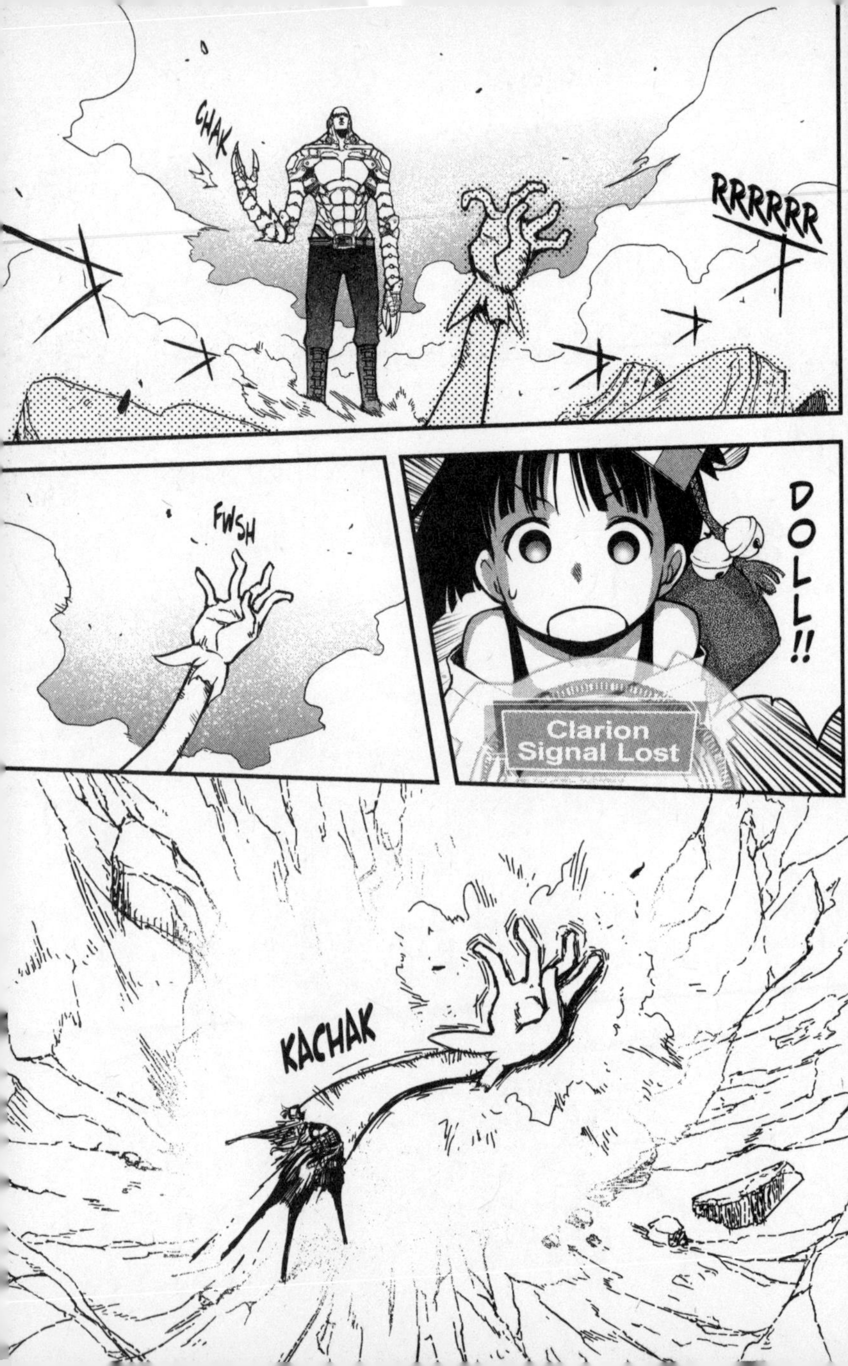
RRRRRR
CHAK
DOLL!!
Clarion Signal Lost
FWSH
KACHAK

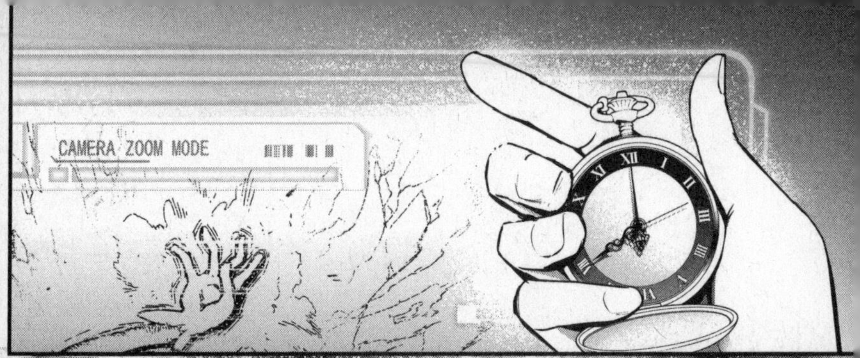
CAMERA ZOOM MODE
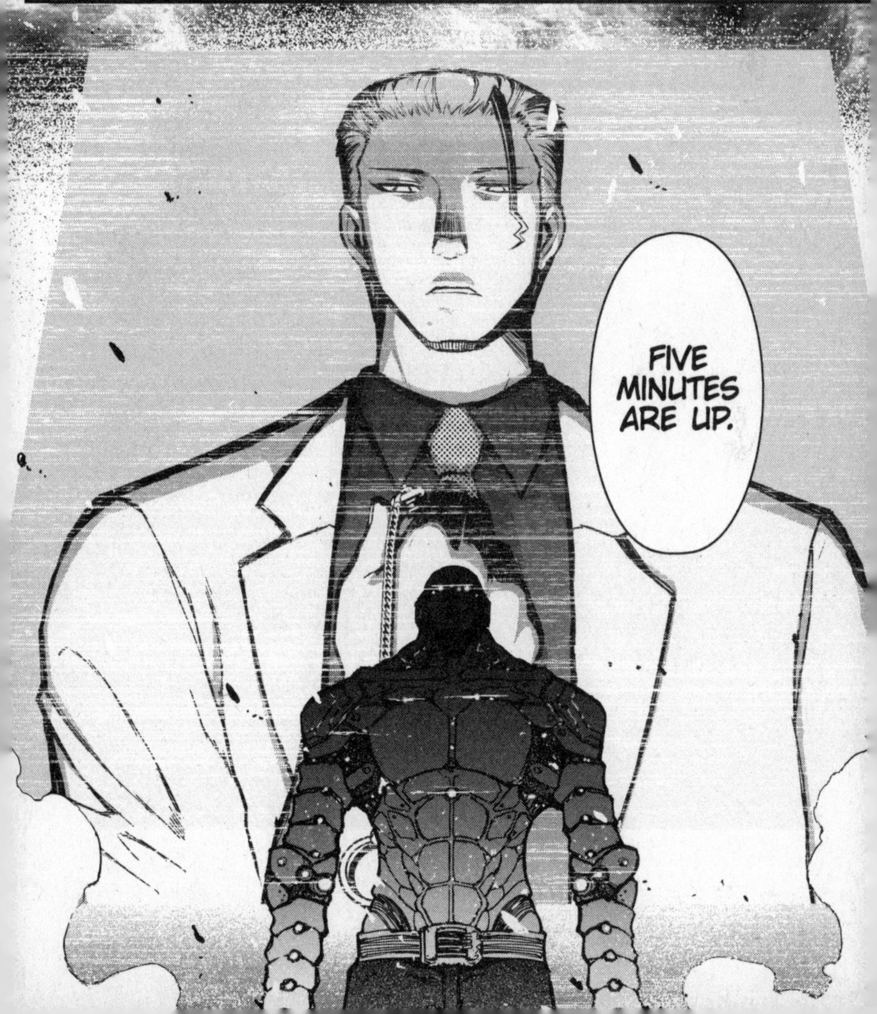
FIVE MINUTES ARE UP.

GHOST URN

GHOST URN

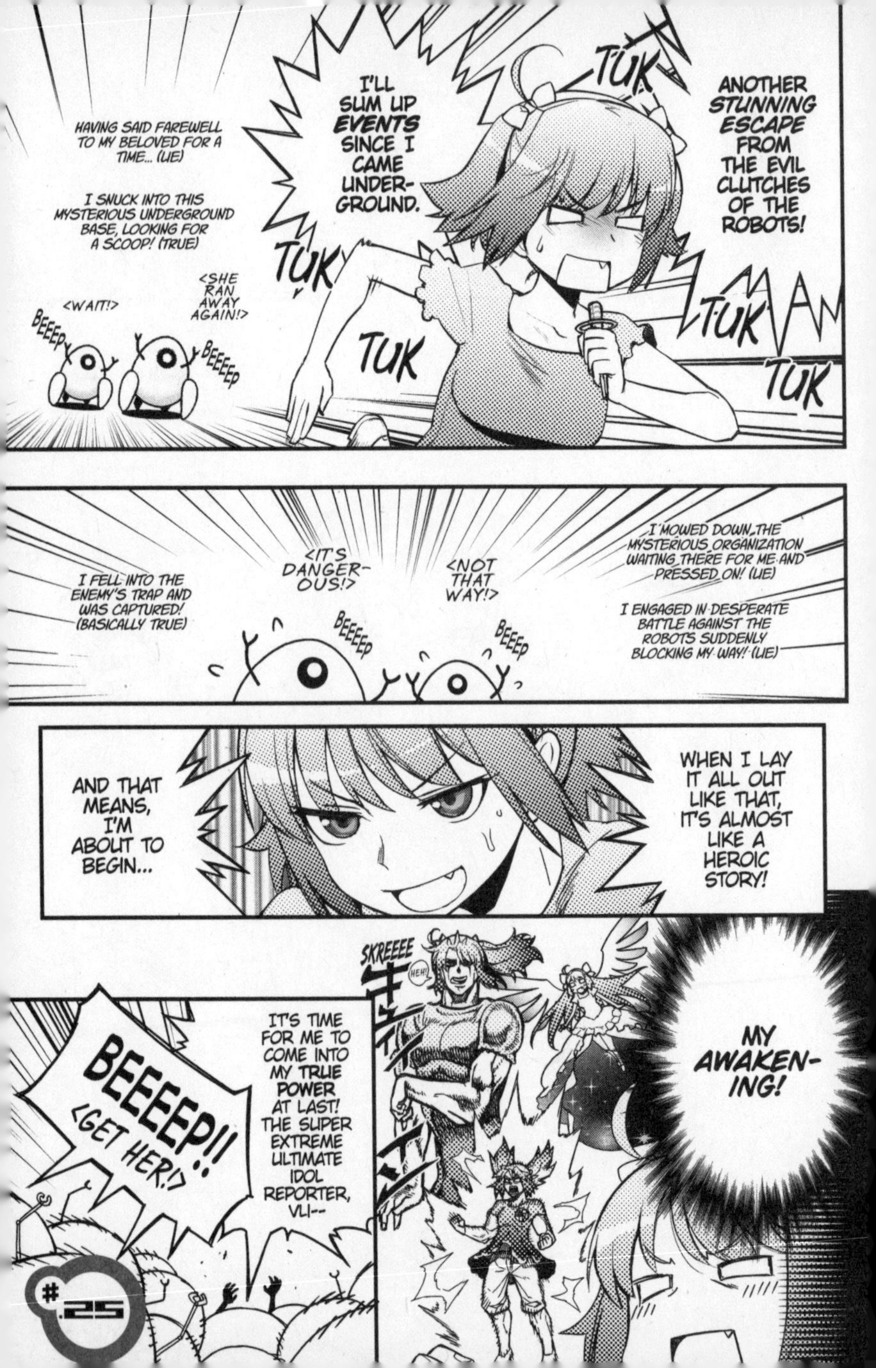

ANOTHER STUNNING ESCAPE FROM THE EVIL CLUTCHES OF THE ROBOTS!
TUK
T-UK
TUK
I'LL SUM UP EVENTS SINCE I CAME UNDERGROUND.
TUK
TUK
HAVING SAID FAREWELL TO MY BELOVED FOR A TIME... (LIE)
I SNUCK INTO THIS MYSTERIOUS UNDERGROUND BASE, LOOKING FOR A SCOOP! (TRUE)
<SHE RAN AWAY AGAIN!>
BEEEEP
<WAIT!>
BEEEP
I MOWED DOWN THE MYSTERIOUS ORGANIZATION WAITING THERE FOR ME AND PRESSED ON! (LIE)
I ENGAGED IN DESPERATE BATTLE AGAINST THE ROBOTS SUDDENLY BLOCKING MY WAY! (LIE)
<NOT THAT WAY!>
BEEEP
<IT'S DANGEROUS!>
BEEEEP
I FELL INTO THE ENEMY'S TRAP AND WAS CAPTURED! (BASICALLY TRUE)
WHEN I LAY IT ALL OUT LIKE THAT, IT'S ALMOST LIKE A HEROIC STORY!
AND THAT MEANS, I'M ABOUT TO BEGIN...
MY AWAKENING!
SKREEEE
HEH!
IT'S TIME FOR ME TO COME INTO MY TRUE POWER AT LAST! THE SUPER EXTREME ULTIMATE IDOL REPORTER, VLI--
BEEEEEP!! <GET HER!>
#.25

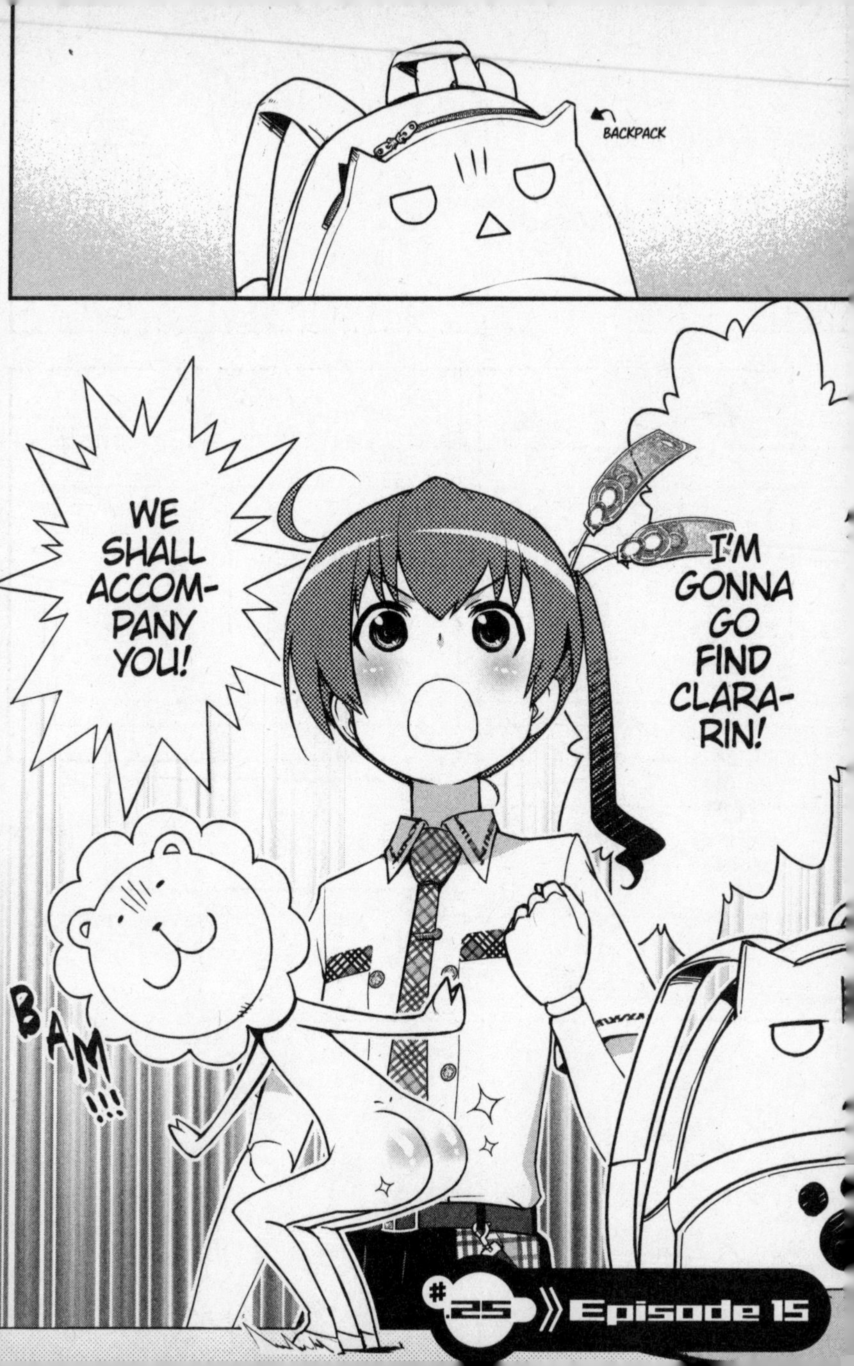
BACKPACK
I'M GONNA GO FIND CLARA-RIN!
WE SHALL ACCOMPANY YOU!
BAM!!!
#.25 Episode 15

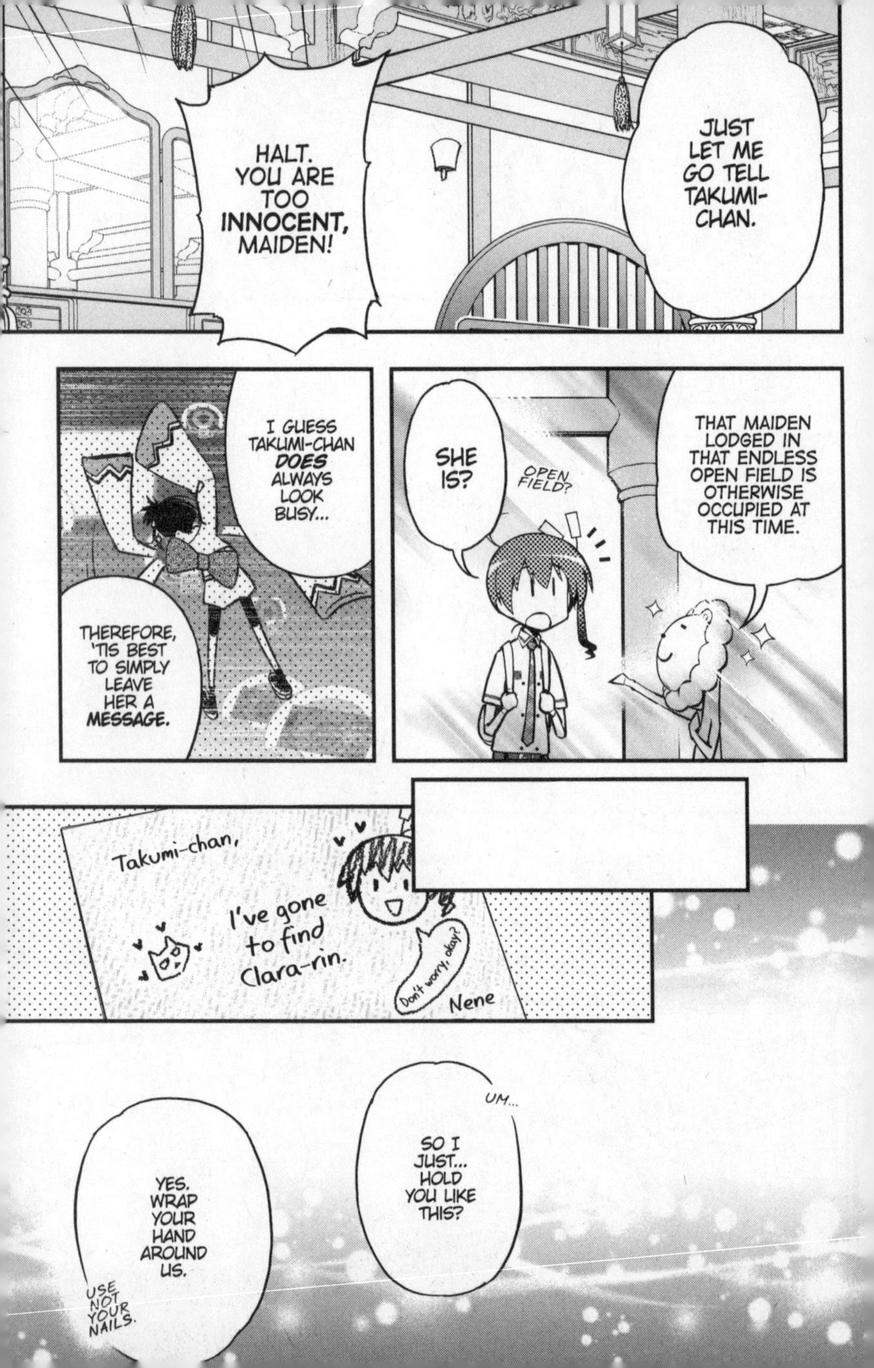
JUST LET ME GO TELL TAKUMI-CHAN.
HALT. YOU ARE TOO INNOCENT, MAIDEN!
THAT MAIDEN LODGED IN THAT ENDLESS OPEN FIELD IS OTHERWISE OCCUPIED AT THIS TIME.
SHE IS?
OPEN FIELD?
I GUESS TAKUMI-CHAN DOES ALWAYS LOOK BUSY...
THEREFORE, 'TIS BEST TO SIMPLY LEAVE HER A MESSAGE.
Takumi-chan,
I've gone to find Clara-rin.
Don't worry, okay?
Nene
UM...
SO I JUST... HOLD YOU LIKE THIS?
YES. WRAP YOUR HAND AROUND US.
USE NOT YOUR NAILS.

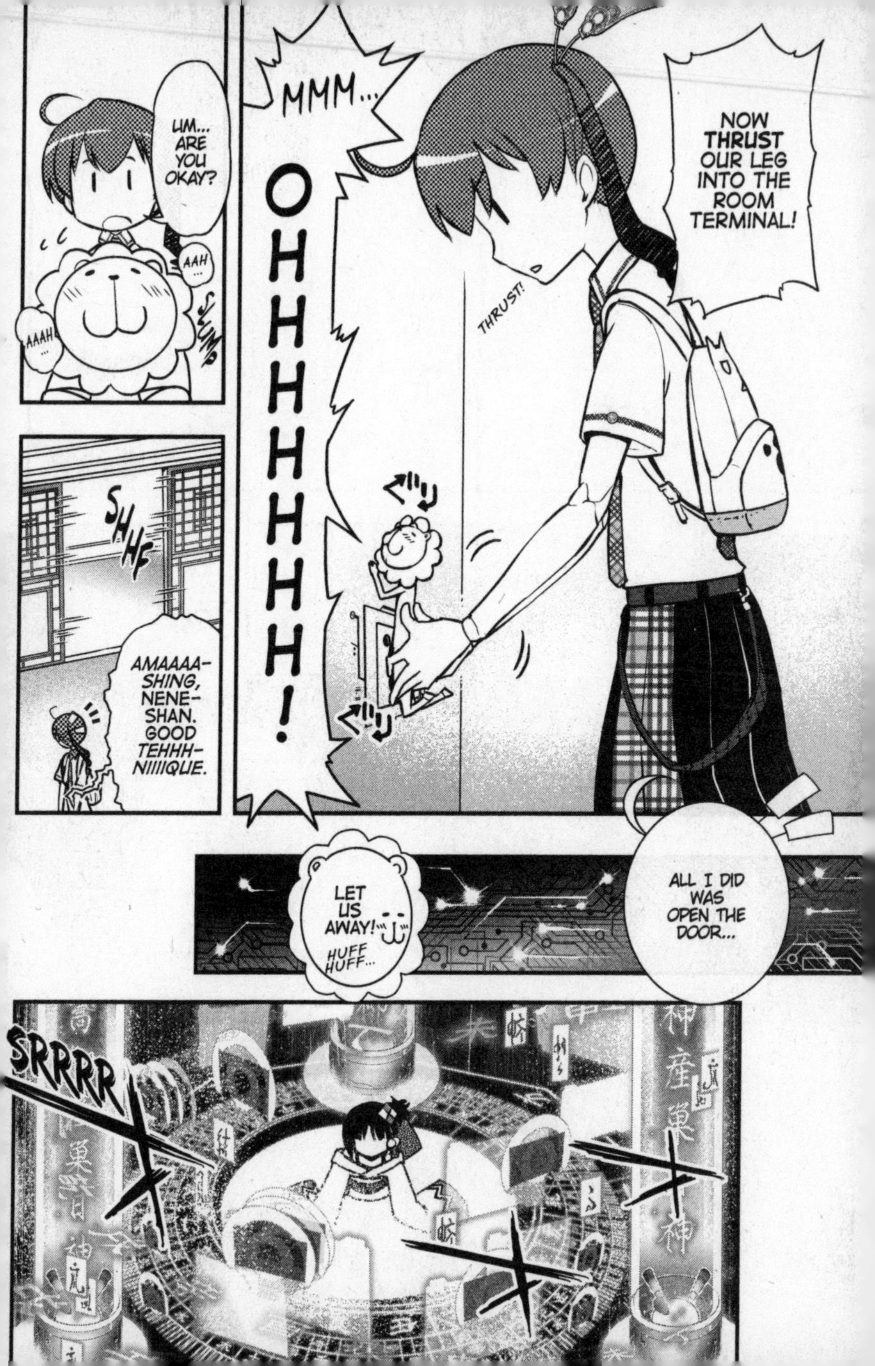
NOW THRUST OUR LEG INTO THE ROOM TERMINAL!
THRUST!
MMM...
OHHHHHHH!
UM... ARE YOU OKAY?
AAH...
SLUMP
AAAH...
SHHF
AMAAAA-SHING, NENE-SHAN. GOOD TEHHH-NIIIIQUE.
ALL I DID WAS OPEN THE DOOR...
LET US AWAY!
HUFF HUFF...
SRRRR

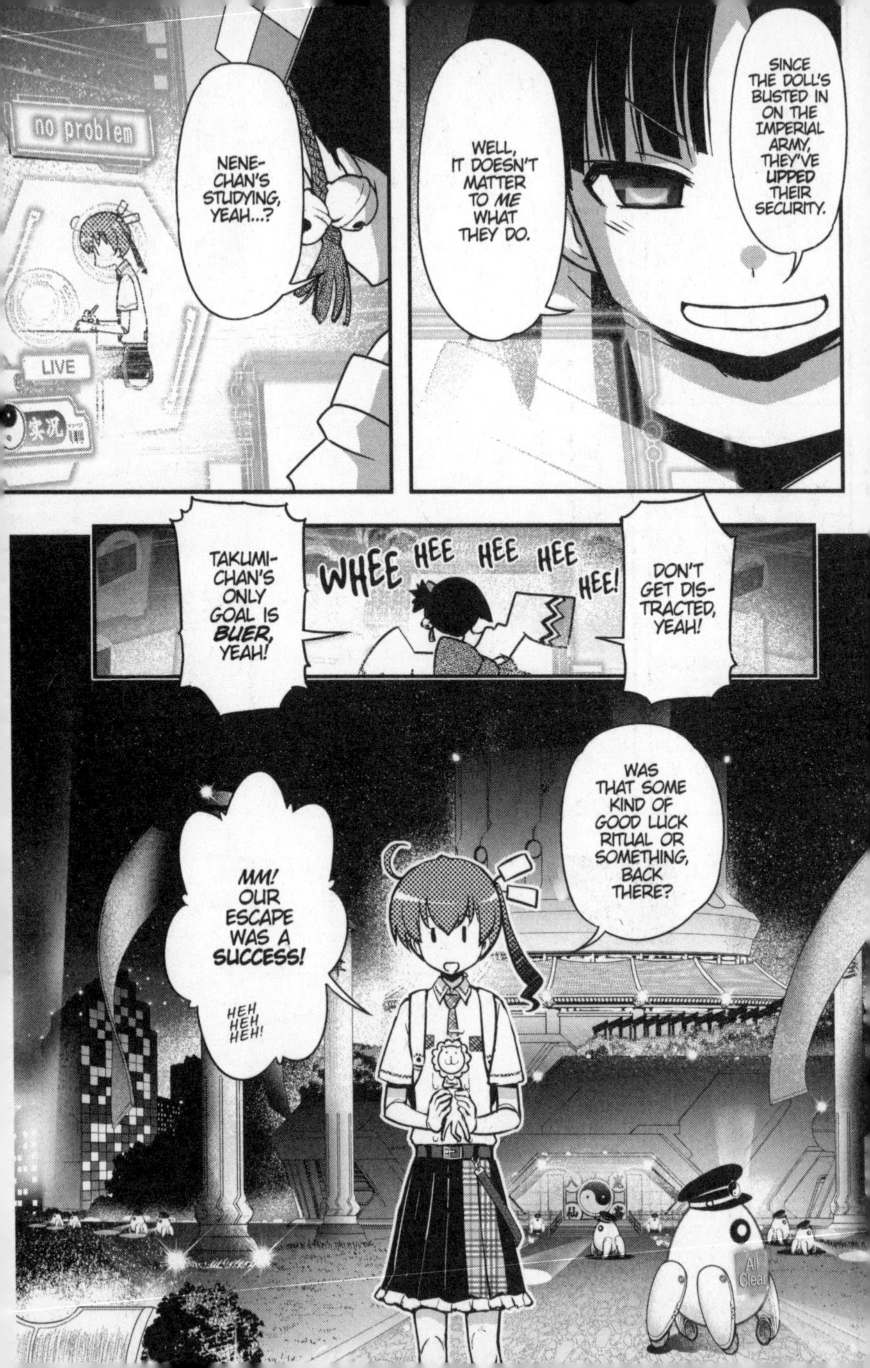
SINCE THE DOLL'S BUSTED IN ON THE IMPERIAL ARMY, THEY'VE UPPED THEIR SECURITY.
WELL, IT DOESN'T MATTER TO *ME* WHAT THEY DO.
no problem
NENE-CHAN'S STUDYING, YEAH...?
LIVE
实况
DON'T GET DIS-TRACTED, YEAH!
WHEE HEE HEE HEE HEE!
TAKUMI-CHAN'S ONLY GOAL IS ***BUER***, YEAH!
WAS THAT SOME KIND OF GOOD LUCK RITUAL OR SOMETHING, BACK THERE?
MM! OUR ESCAPE WAS A **SUCCESS!**
HEH HEH HEH!
All Clear

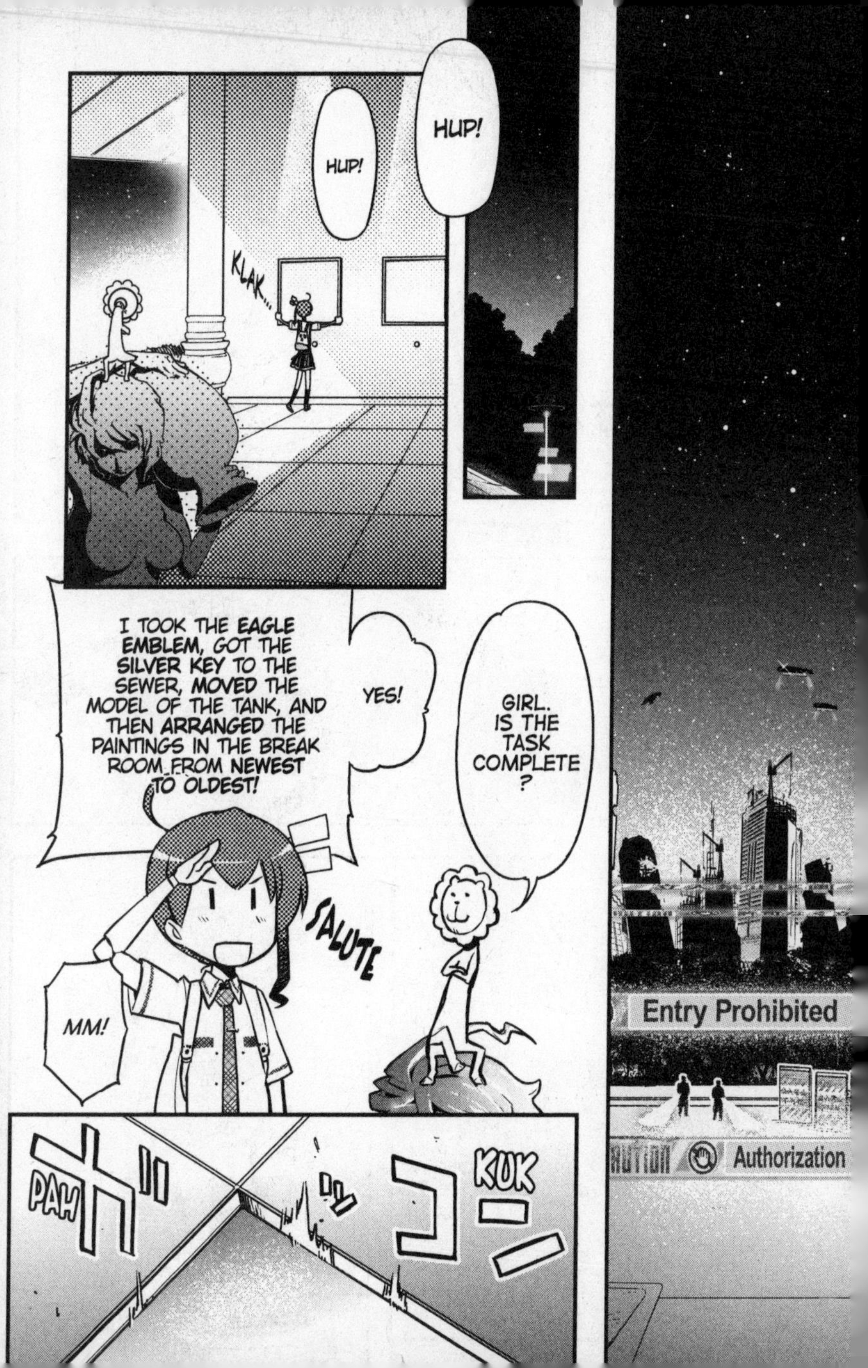
Entry Prohibited
Authorization
HUP!
HUP!
KLAK...
GIRL. IS THE TASK COMPLETE?
YES!
I TOOK THE EAGLE EMBLEM, GOT THE SILVER KEY TO THE SEWER, MOVED THE MODEL OF THE TANK, AND THEN ARRANGED THE PAINTINGS IN THE BREAK ROOM FROM NEWEST TO OLDEST!
SALUTE
MM!
KUK
コーン
ガッ
PAH

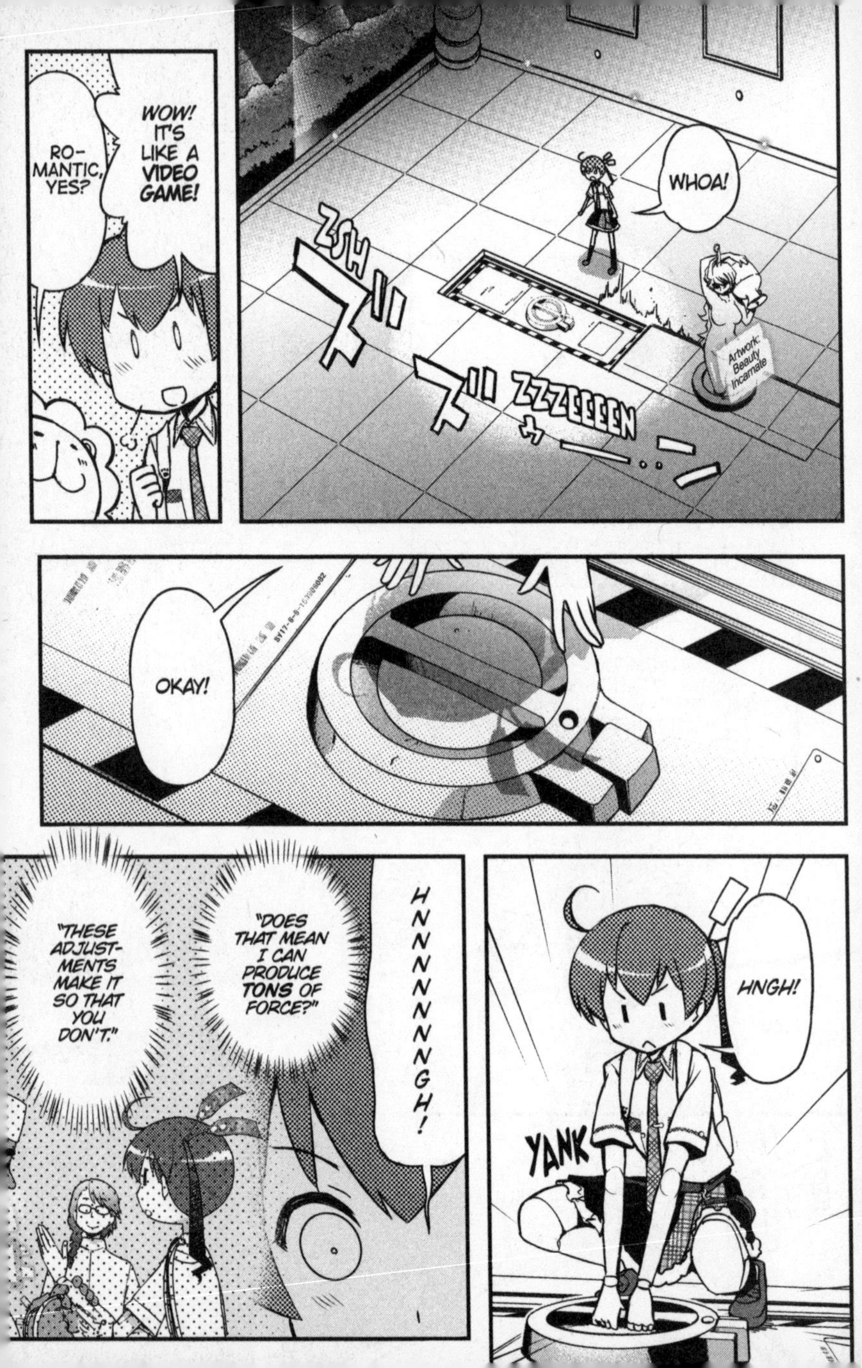
WHOA!
ZSH
ZZZEEEEN
Artwork: Beauty Incarnate
WOW! IT'S LIKE A VIDEO GAME!
RO-MANTIC, YES?
OKAY!
HNGH!
YANK
HNNNNNNNGH!
"DOES THAT MEAN I CAN PRODUCE TONS OF FORCE?"
"THESE ADJUST-MENTS MAKE IT SO THAT YOU DON'T."

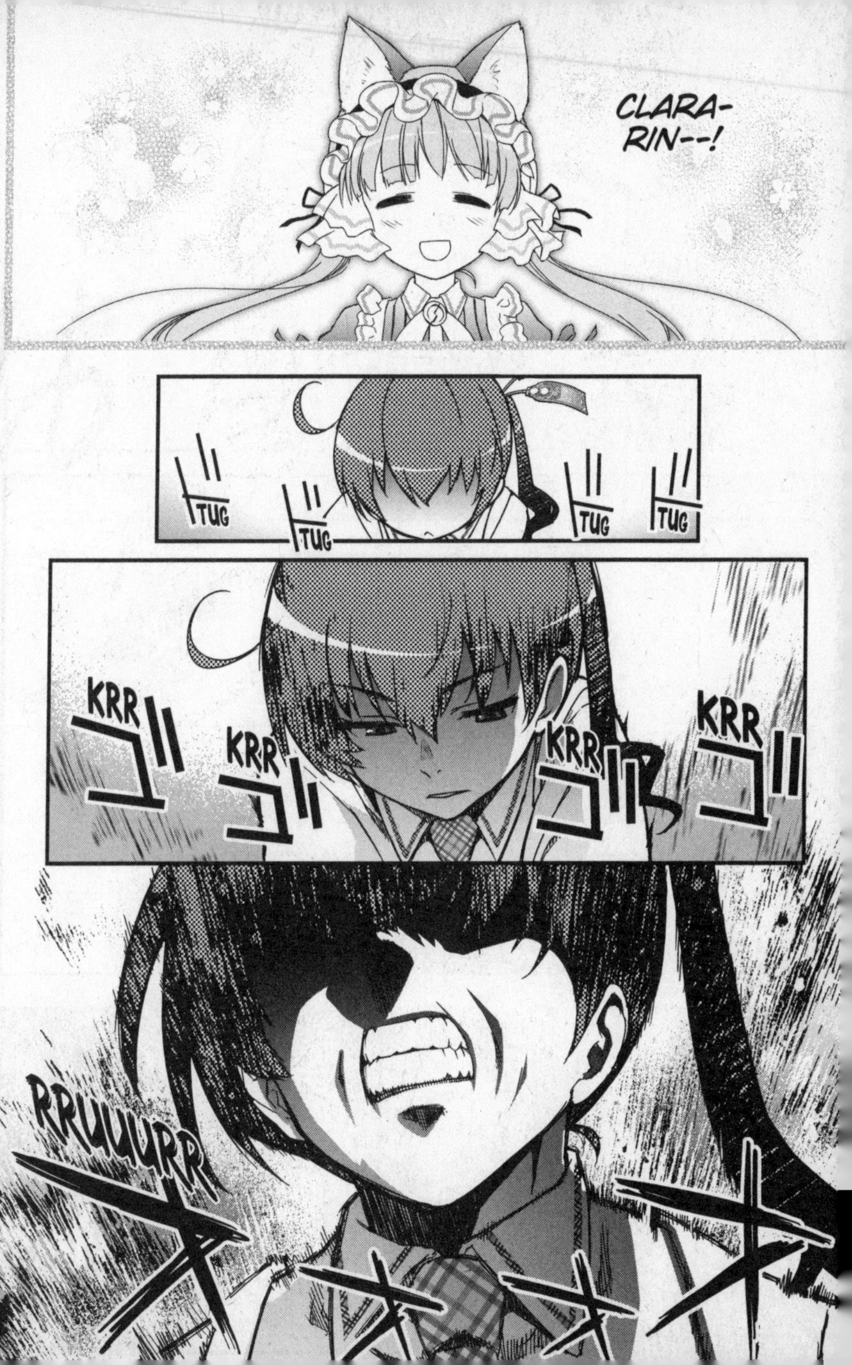
CLARA-RIN--!
TUG
TUG
TUG
TUG
KRR
KRR
KRR
KRR
RRUUUURR

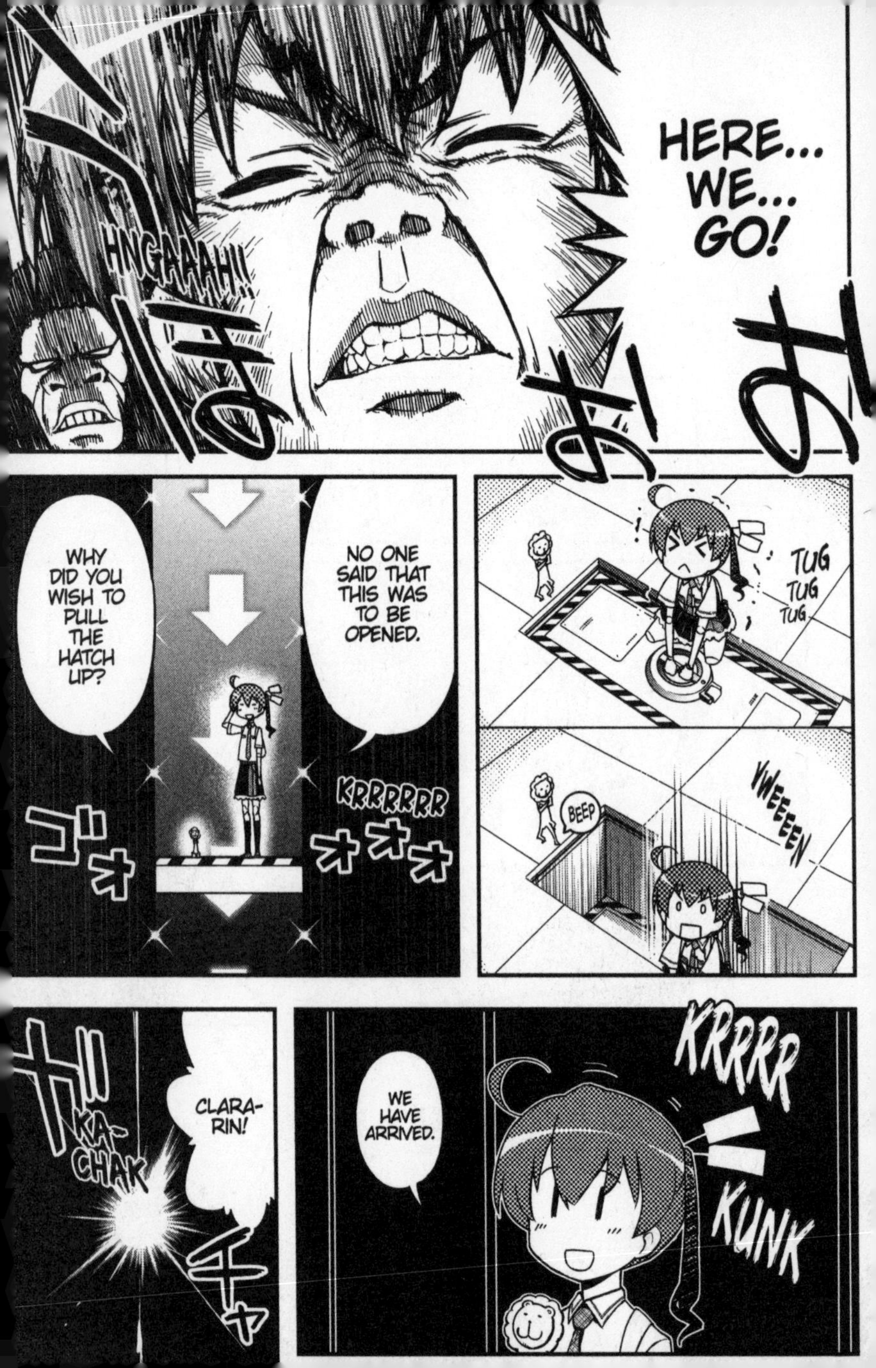
HERE... WE... GO!
HNGAAAH!!
TUG
TUG
TUG
BEEP
VWEEEEEN
NO ONE SAID THAT THIS WAS TO BE OPENED.
KRRRRRRR
オオオ
WHY DID YOU WISH TO PULL THE HATCH UP?
ゴオ
KRRRR
KUNK
WE HAVE ARRIVED.
CLARA-RIN!
KA-CHAK
ガチャ

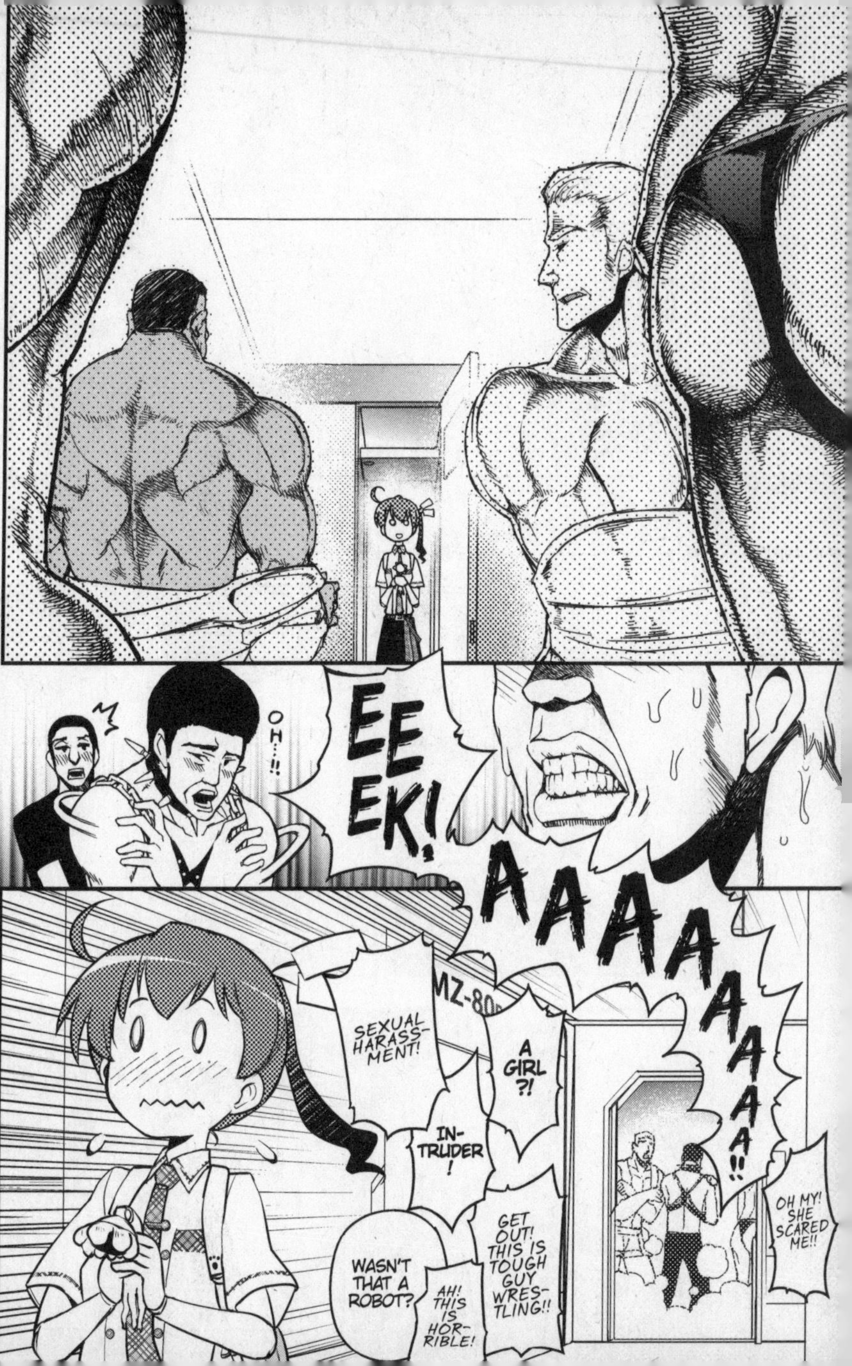
AAAAAAAAAA!!
EEEEK!
OH...!!
OH MY! SHE SCARED ME!!
A GIRL?!
SEXUAL HARASS-MENT!
MZ-80
INTRUDER!
GET OUT! THIS IS TOUGH GUY WRES-TLING!!
AH! THIS IS HOR-RIBLE!
WASN'T THAT A ROBOT?

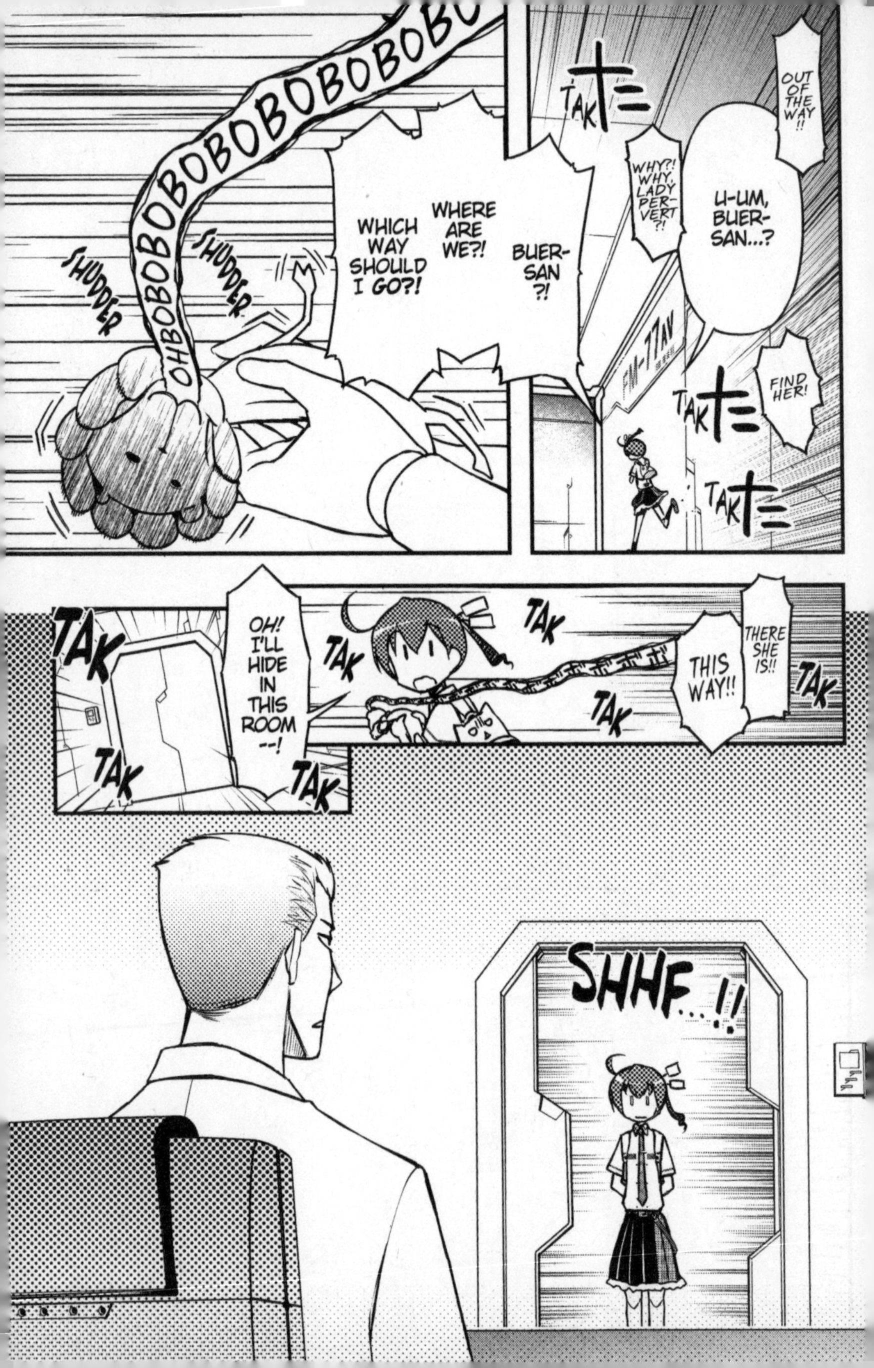
OUT OF THE WAY!!
U-UM, BUER-SAN...?
WHY?! WHY, LADY PERVERT?!
TAK
FIND HER!
TAK
TAK
BUER-SAN?!
WHERE ARE WE?!
WHICH WAY SHOULD I GO?!
OHBOBOBOBOBOBOBOBOBOBOBOBOBO
SHUDDER
SHUDDER
THERE SHE IS!!
THIS WAY!!
TAK
TAK
TAK
TAK
OH! I'LL HIDE IN THIS ROOM--!
TAK
TAK
TAK
SHHF...!!

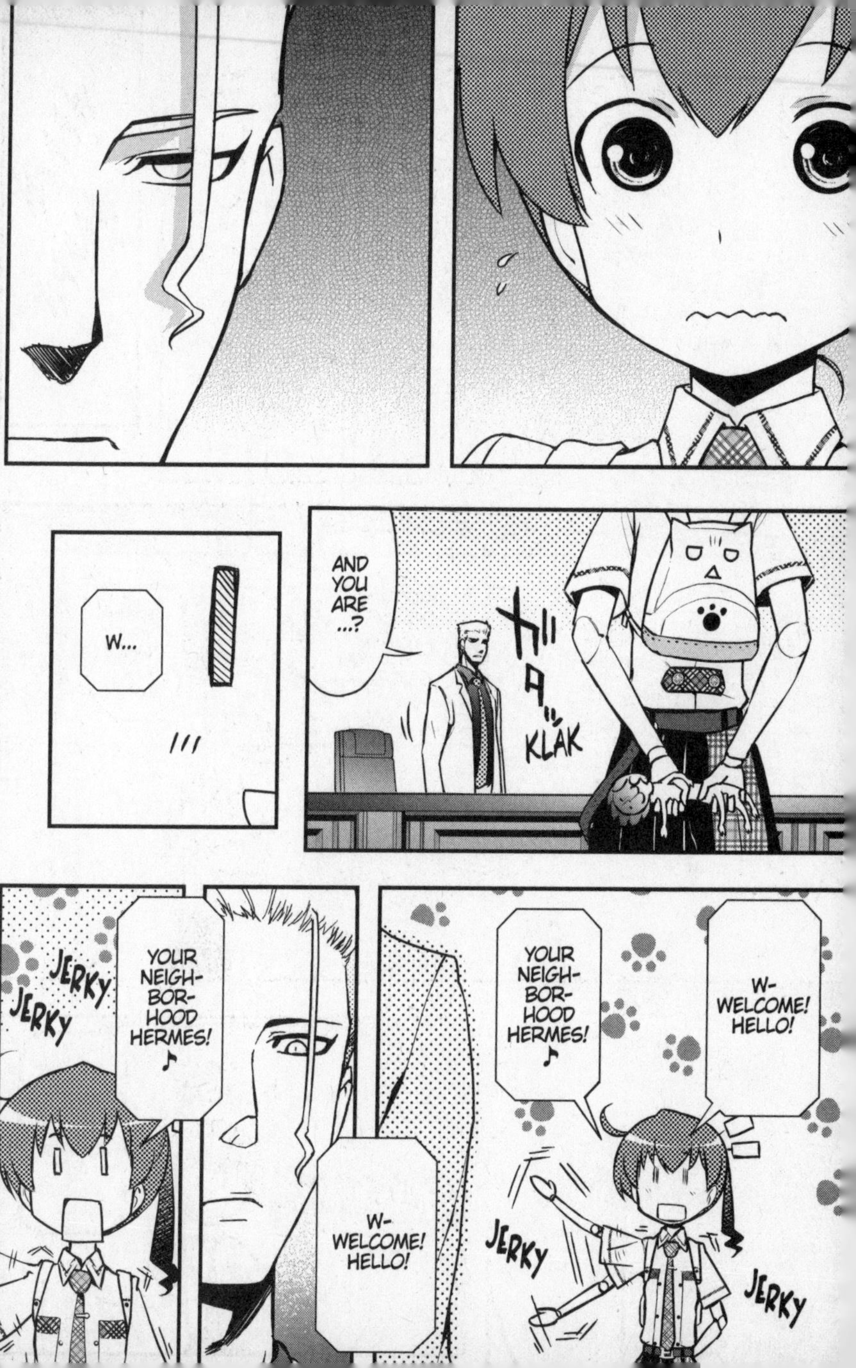
AND YOU ARE ...?
KLAK
W...
!
W- WELCOME! HELLO!
YOUR NEIGH- BOR- HOOD HERMES! ♪
JERKY
JERKY
W- WELCOME! HELLO!
YOUR NEIGH- BOR- HOOD HERMES! ♪
JERKY
JERKY

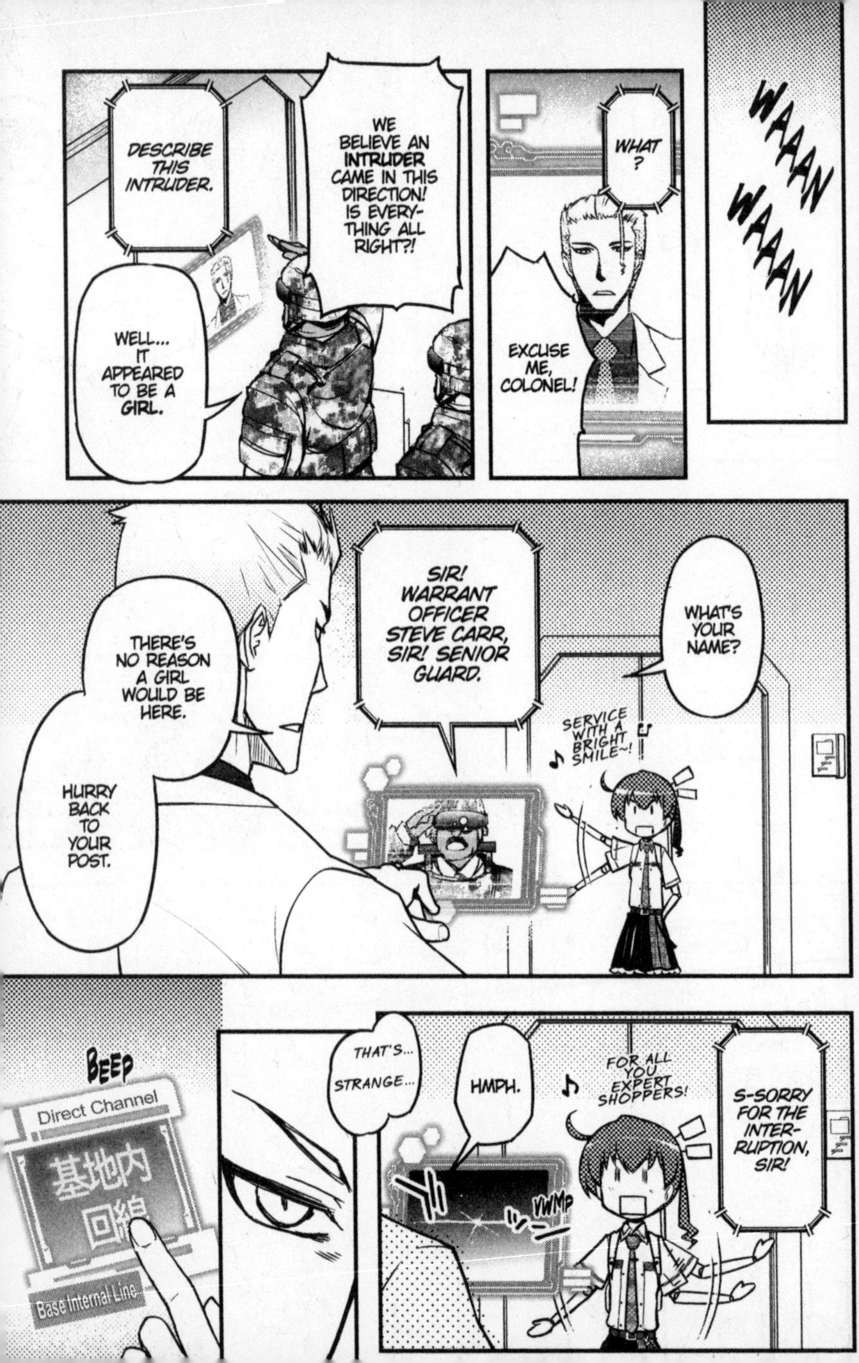

WAAAN WAAAN WAAAN
WHAT?
EXCUSE ME, COLONEL!
WE BELIEVE AN INTRUDER CAME IN THIS DIRECTION! IS EVERYTHING ALL RIGHT?!
DESCRIBE THIS INTRUDER.
WELL... IT APPEARED TO BE A GIRL.
WHAT'S YOUR NAME?
SERVICE WITH A BRIGHT SMILE~!
SIR! WARRANT OFFICER STEVE CARR, SIR! SENIOR GUARD.
THERE'S NO REASON A GIRL WOULD BE HERE.
HURRY BACK TO YOUR POST.
S-SORRY FOR THE INTERRUPTION, SIR!
FOR ALL YOU EXPERT SHOPPERS!
HMPH.
VWMP
THAT'S... STRANGE...
BEEP
Direct Channel
基地内回線
Base Internal Line

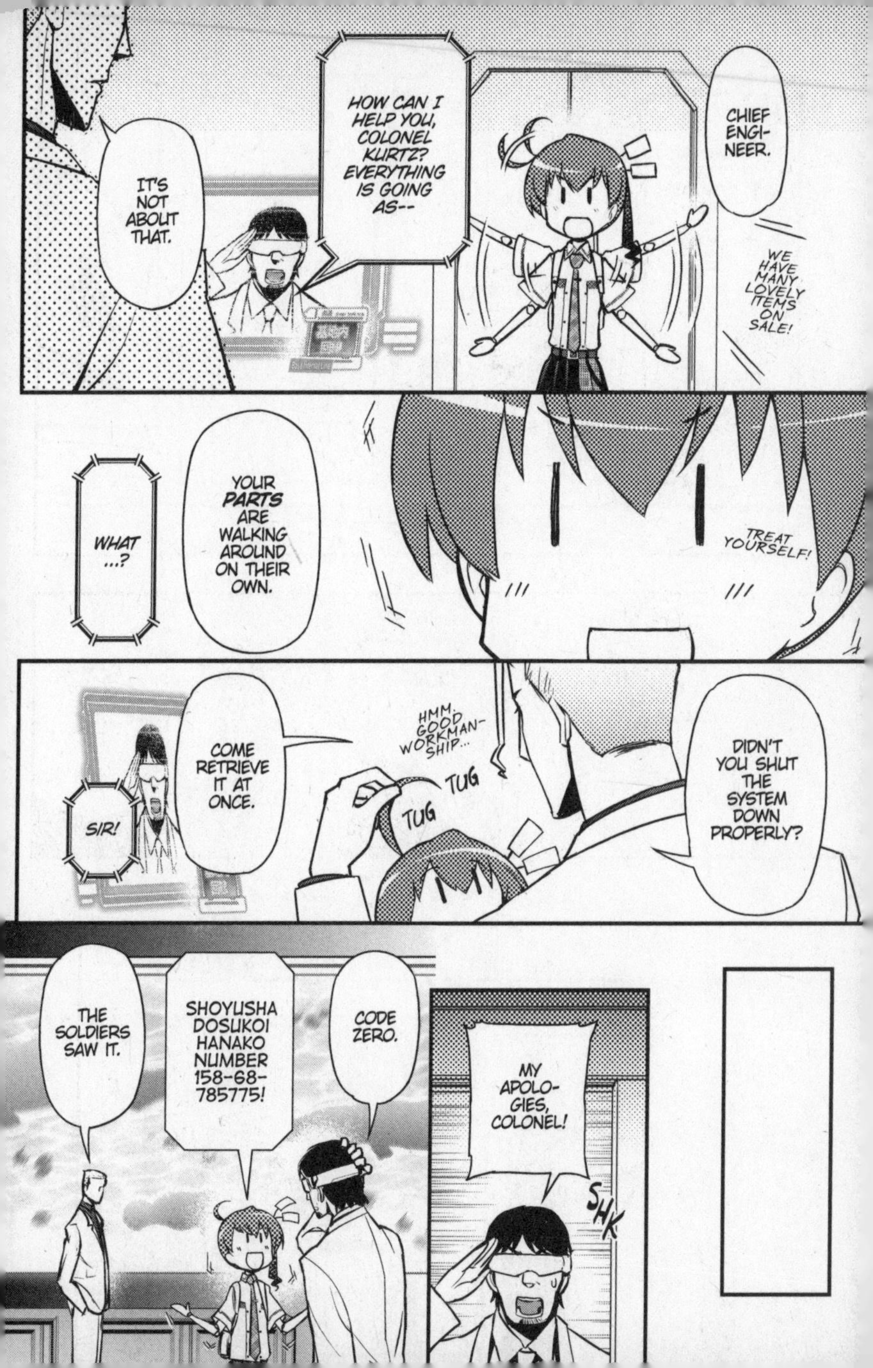
CHIEF ENGINEER.
WE HAVE MANY LOVELY ITEMS ON SALE!
HOW CAN I HELP YOU, COLONEL KURTZ? EVERYTHING IS GOING AS--
IT'S NOT ABOUT THAT.
TREAT YOURSELF!
YOUR PARTS ARE WALKING AROUND ON THEIR OWN.
WHAT...?
DIDN'T YOU SHUT THE SYSTEM DOWN PROPERLY?
TUG
TUG
HMM, GOOD WORKMANSHIP...
COME RETRIEVE IT AT ONCE.
SIR!
MY APOLOGIES, COLONEL!
SHK
CODE ZERO.
SHOYUSHA DOSUKOI HANAKO NUMBER 158-68-785775!
THE SOLDIERS SAW IT.

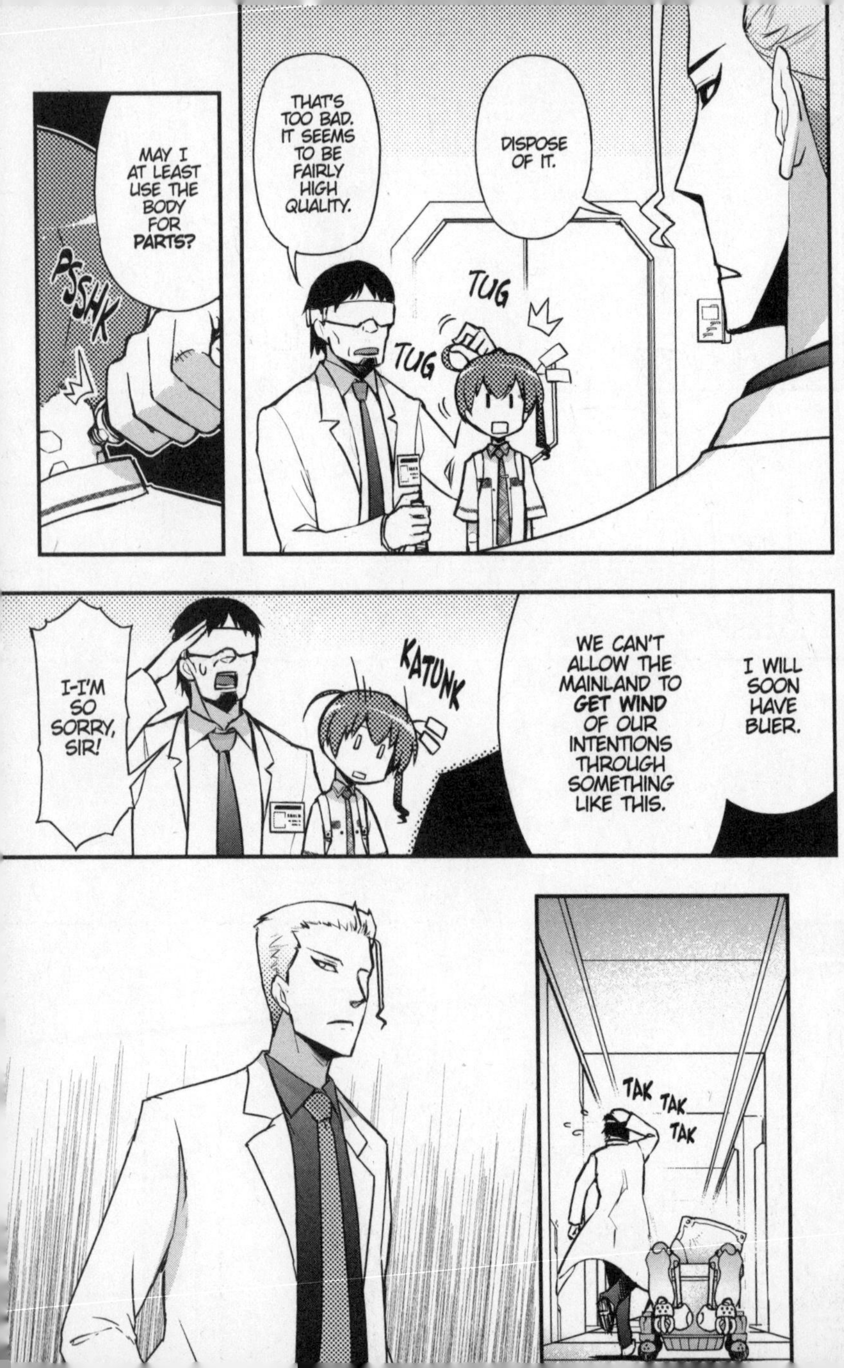
DISPOSE OF IT.
THAT'S TOO BAD. IT SEEMS TO BE FAIRLY HIGH QUALITY.
TUG
TUG
MAY I AT LEAST USE THE BODY FOR PARTS?
PSSHK
I WILL SOON HAVE BUER.
WE CAN'T ALLOW THE MAINLAND TO GET WIND OF OUR INTENTIONS THROUGH SOMETHING LIKE THIS.
KATUNK
I-I'M SO SORRY, SIR!
TAK TAK TAK

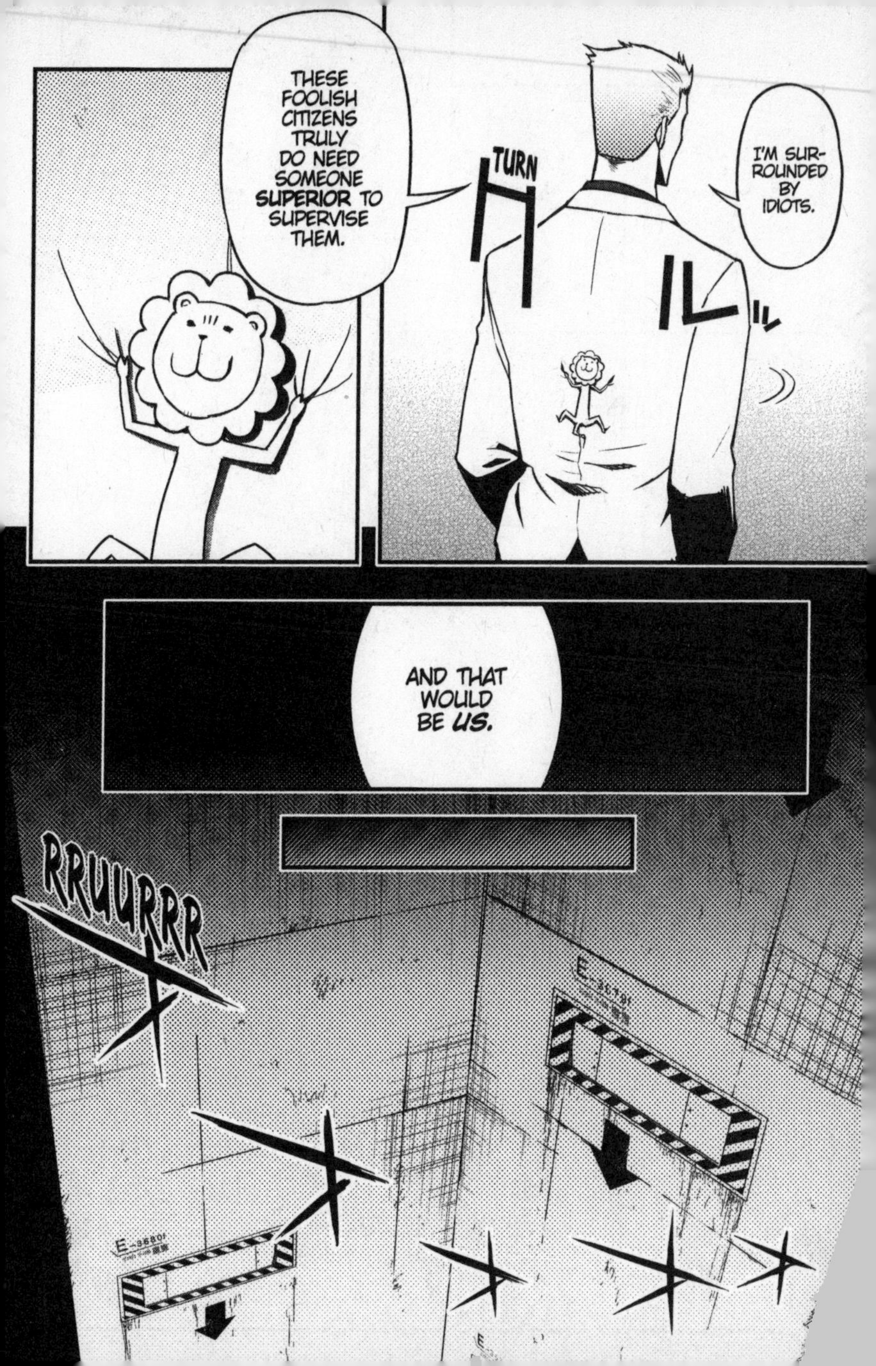
I'M SURROUNDED BY IDIOTS.
TURN
THESE FOOLISH CITIZENS TRULY DO NEED SOMEONE SUPERIOR TO SUPERVISE THEM.
AND THAT WOULD BE US.
RRUURRR

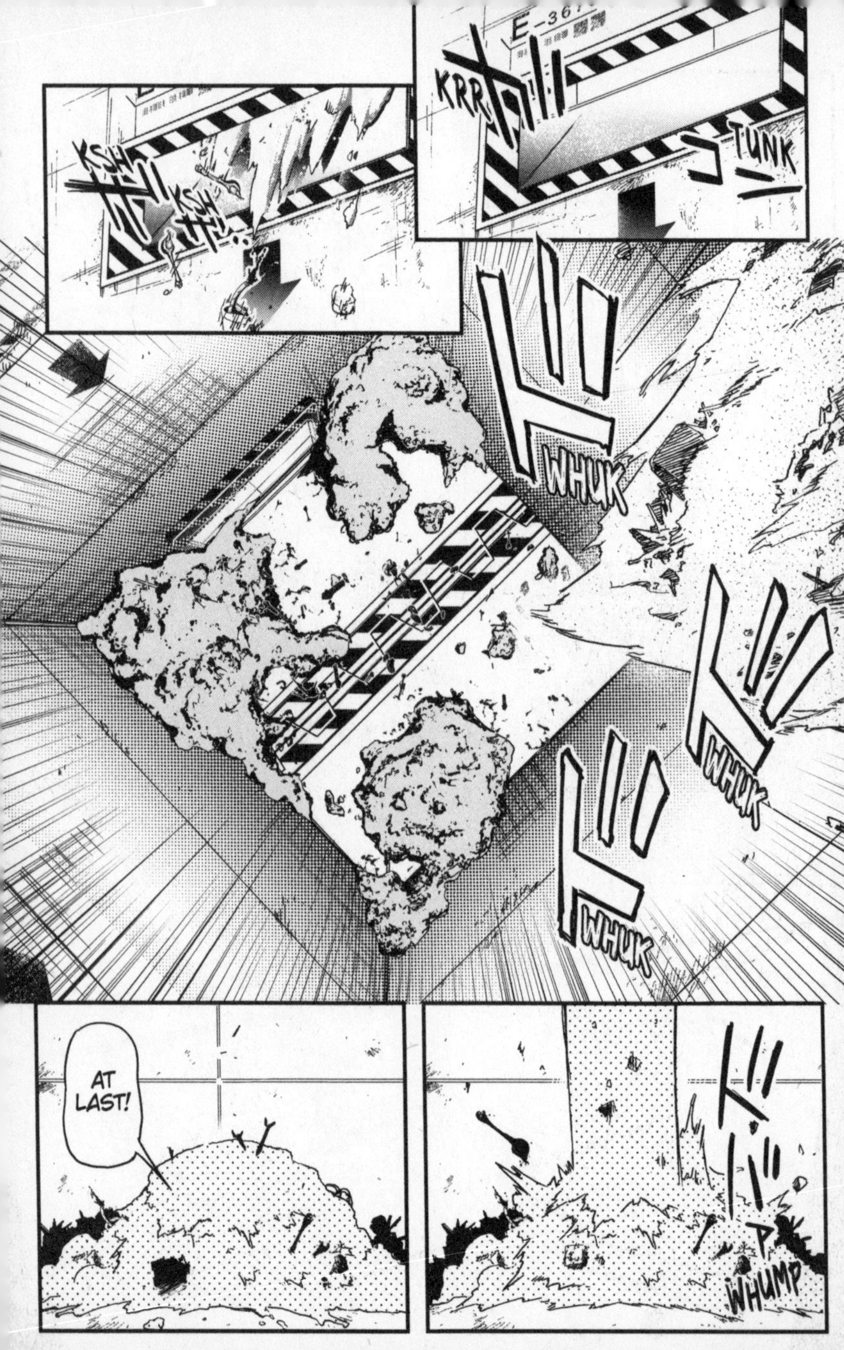
KRR
TUNK
KSH
KSH
WHUK
WHUK
WHUK
WHUMP
AT LAST!

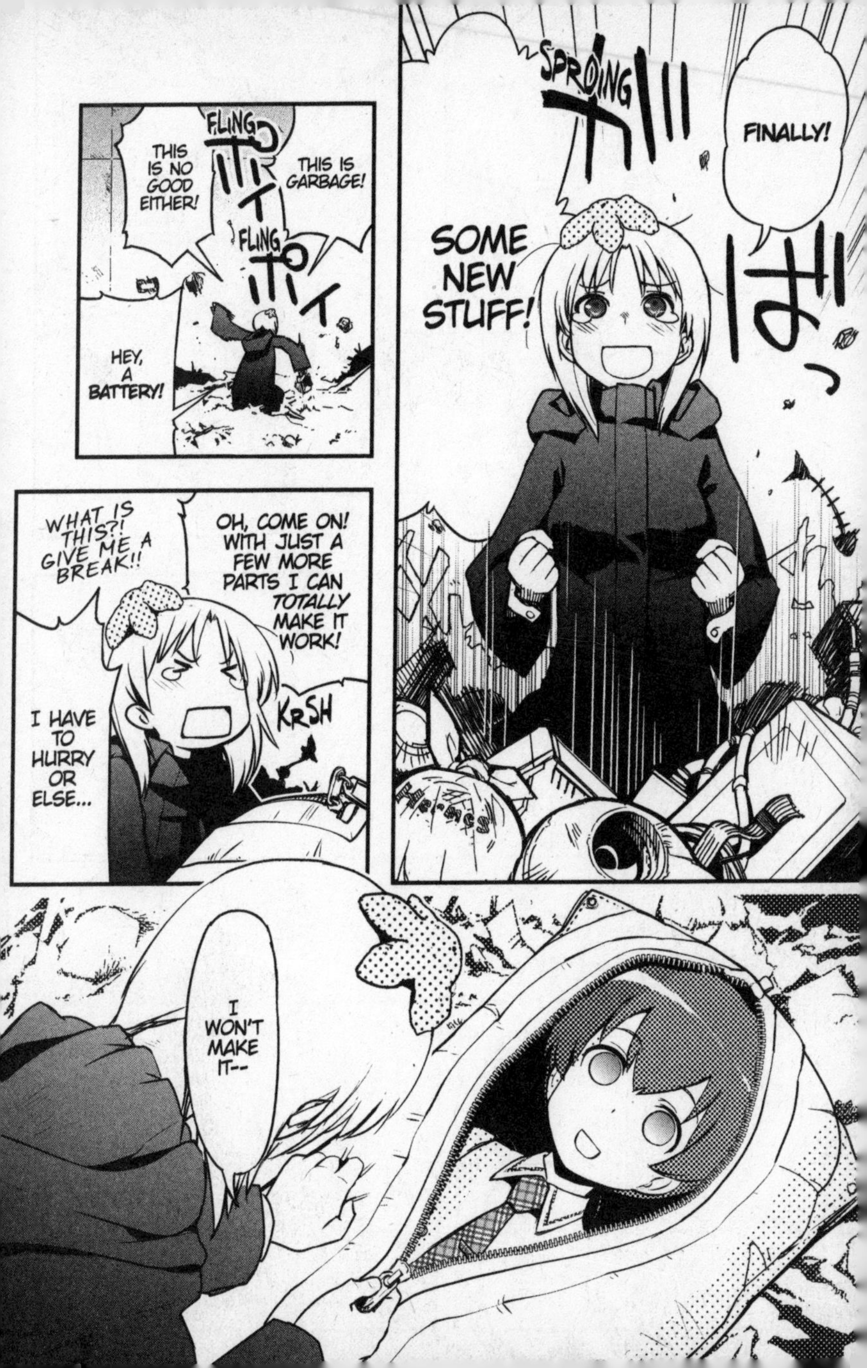
SPROING
FINALLY!
SOME NEW STUFF!
FLING
THIS IS GARBAGE!
THIS IS NO GOOD EITHER!
FLING
HEY, A BATTERY!
OH, COME ON! WITH JUST A FEW MORE PARTS I CAN TOTALLY MAKE IT WORK!
WHAT IS THIS?! GIVE ME A BREAK!!
KRSH
I HAVE TO HURRY OR ELSE...
I WON'T MAKE IT--

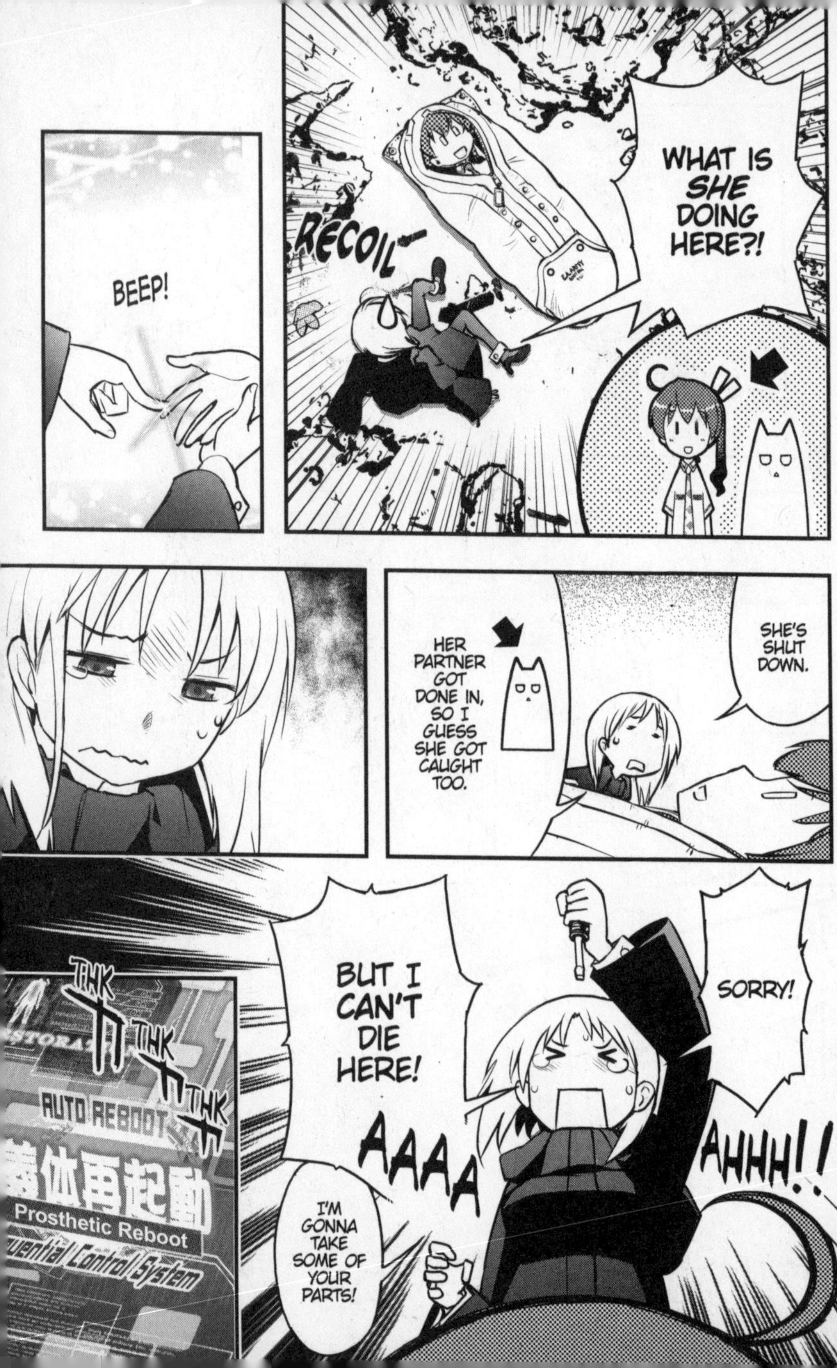
WHAT IS SHE DOING HERE?!
RECOIL
BEEP!
SHE'S SHUT DOWN.
HER PARTNER GOT DONE IN, SO I GUESS SHE GOT CAUGHT TOO.
SORRY!
BUT I CAN'T DIE HERE!
AAAAAHHH!!
I'M GONNA TAKE SOME OF YOUR PARTS!
THK
THK
THK
AUTO REBOOT
義体再起動
Prosthetic Reboot
Control System

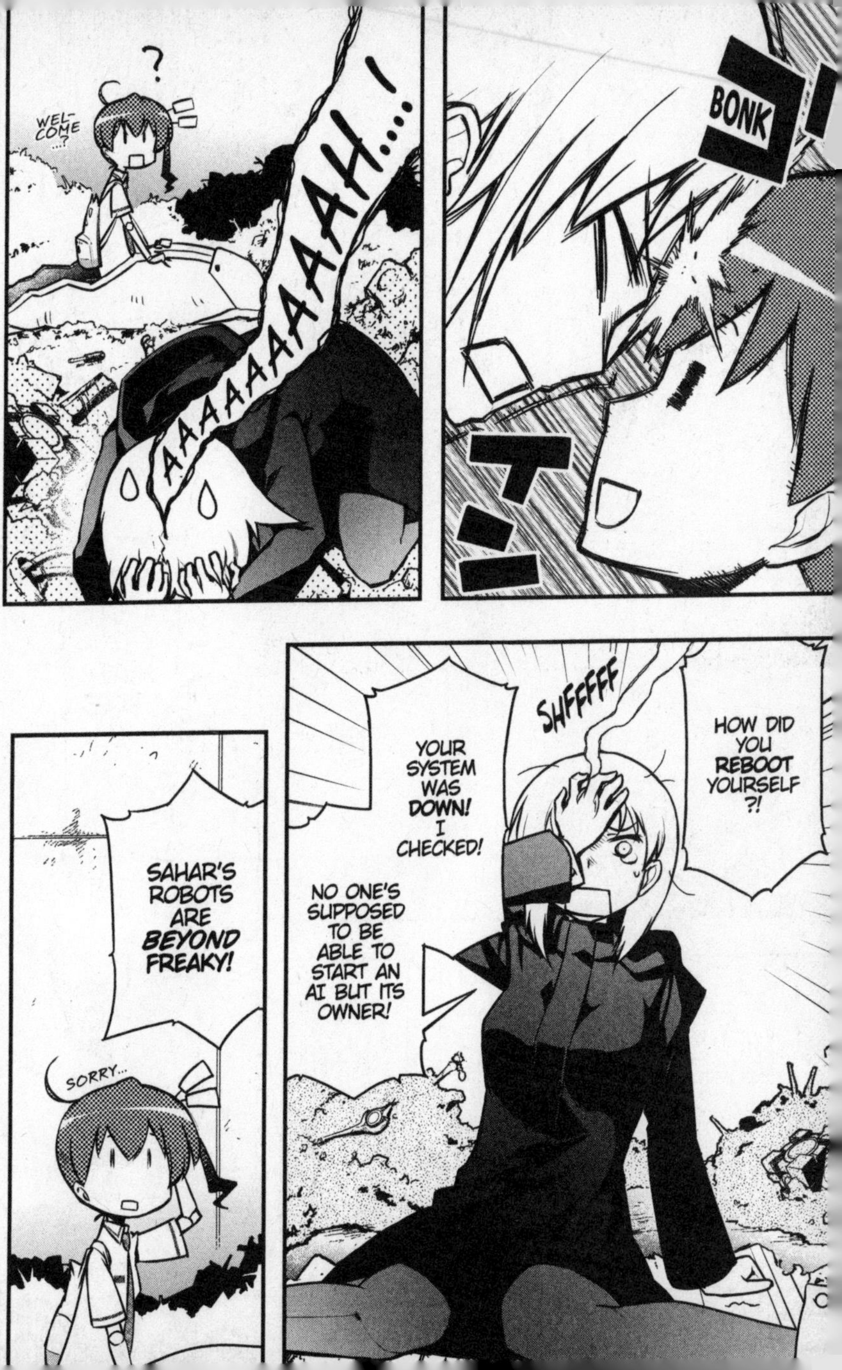
BONK
?
WEL-COME ...?
AAAAAAAAAH...!
SHFFFFF
HOW DID YOU REBOOT YOURSELF?!
YOUR SYSTEM WAS DOWN! I CHECKED!
NO ONE'S SUPPOSED TO BE ABLE TO START AN AI BUT ITS OWNER!
SAHAR'S ROBOTS ARE BEYOND FREAKY!
SORRY...

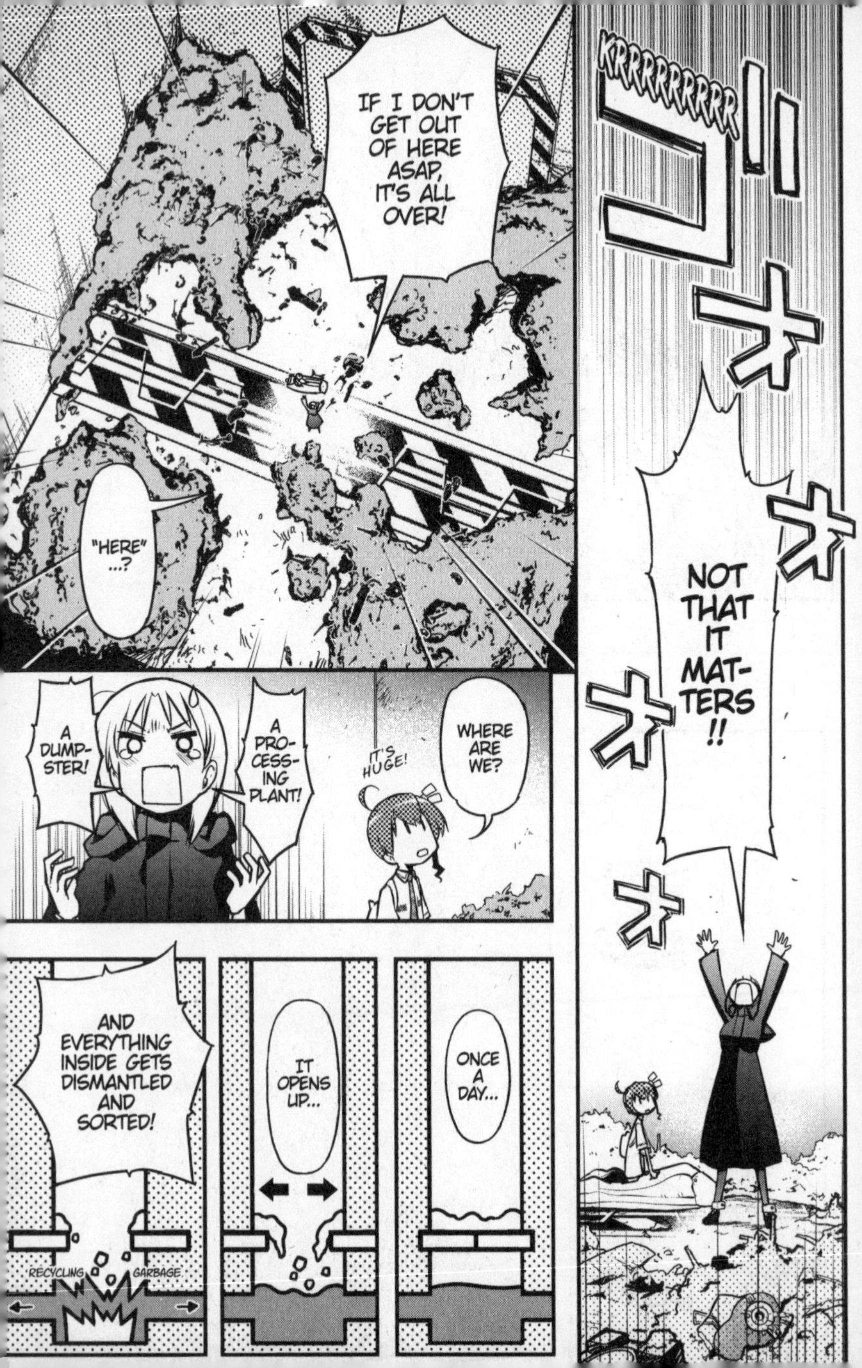
KRRRRRRRRR
NOT THAT IT MATTERS!!
IF I DON'T GET OUT OF HERE ASAP, IT'S ALL OVER!
"HERE"...?
WHERE ARE WE?
IT'S HUGE!
A PROCESSING PLANT!
A DUMPSTER!
ONCE A DAY...
IT OPENS UP...
AND EVERYTHING INSIDE GETS DISMANTLED AND SORTED!
RECYCLING
GARBAGE

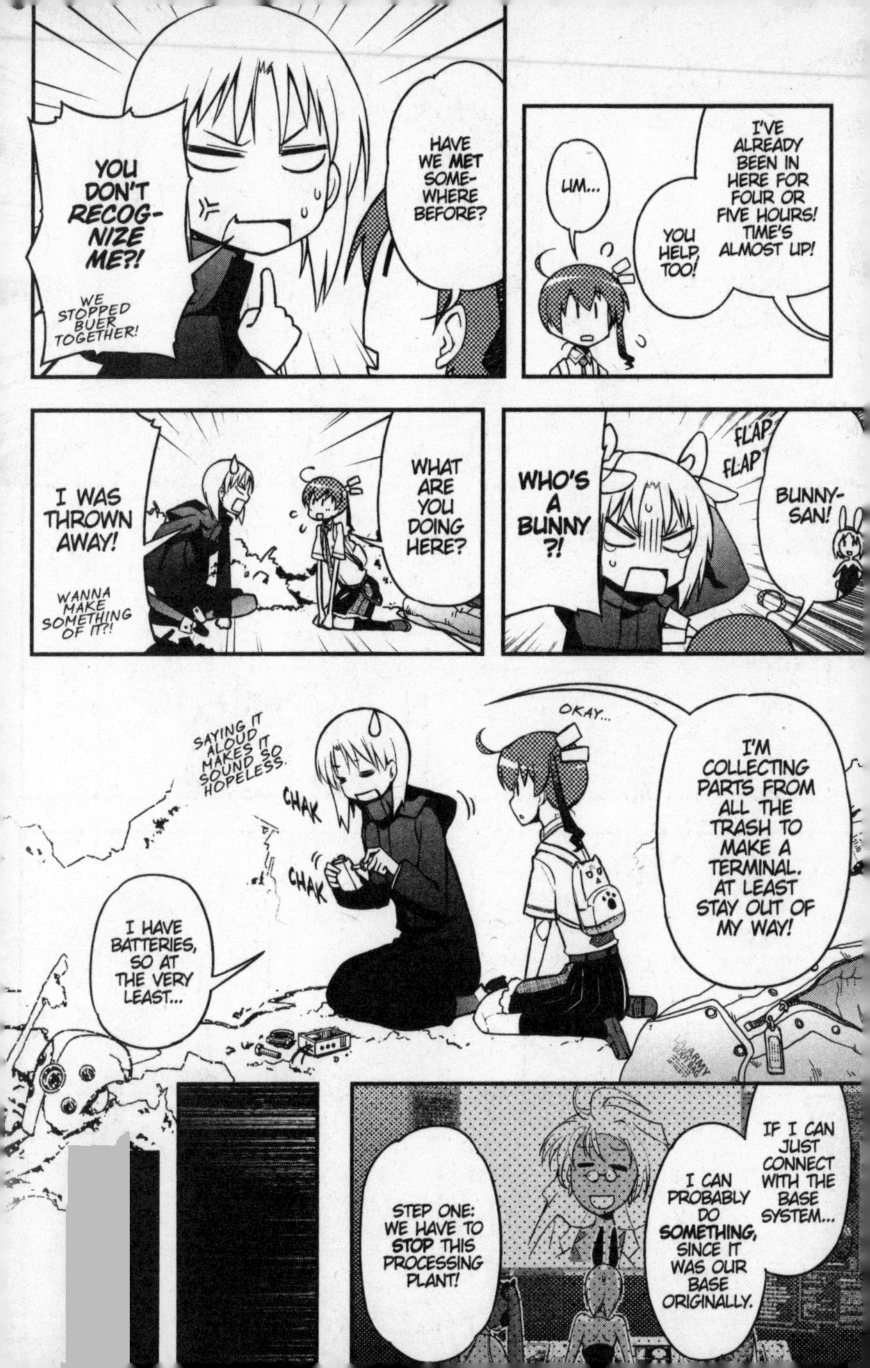
I'VE ALREADY BEEN IN HERE FOR FOUR OR FIVE HOURS! TIME'S ALMOST UP!
YOU HELP, TOO!
UM...
HAVE WE MET SOME-WHERE BEFORE?
YOU DON'T RECOG-NIZE ME?!
WE STOPPED BUER TOGETHER!
FLAP
FLAP
BUNNY-SAN!
WHO'S A BUNNY?!
WHAT ARE YOU DOING HERE?
I WAS THROWN AWAY!
WANNA MAKE SOMETHING OF IT?!
OKAY...
I'M COLLECTING PARTS FROM ALL THE TRASH TO MAKE A TERMINAL. AT LEAST STAY OUT OF MY WAY!
SAYING IT ALOUD MAKES IT SOUND SO HOPELESS.
CHAK
CHAK
I HAVE BATTERIES, SO AT THE VERY LEAST...
IF I CAN JUST CONNECT WITH THE BASE SYSTEM...
I CAN PROBABLY DO SOMETHING, SINCE IT WAS OUR BASE ORIGINALLY.
STEP ONE: WE HAVE TO STOP THIS PROCESSING PLANT!

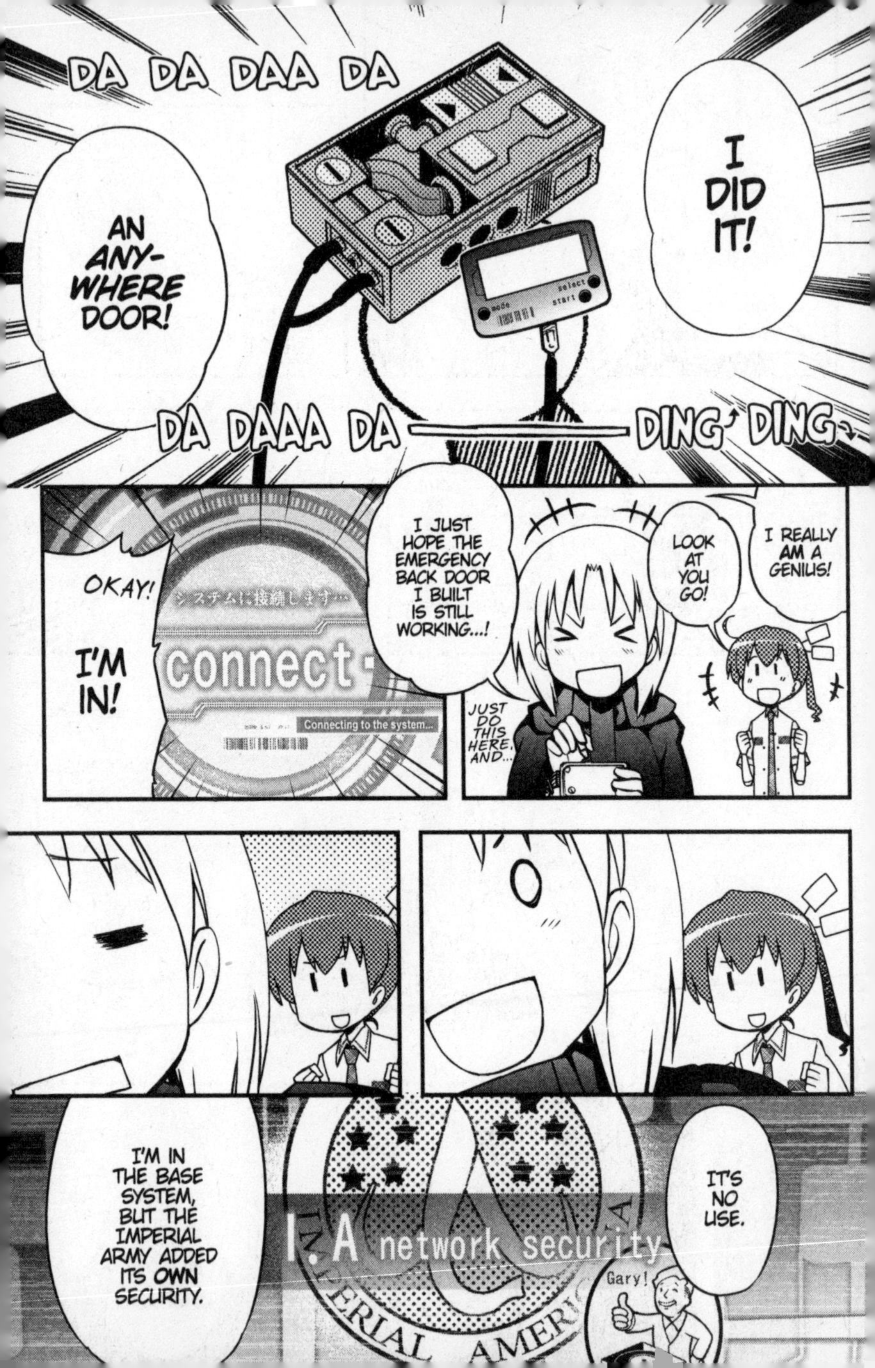
I DID IT!
DA DA DAA DA
AN ANY-WHERE DOOR!
DING DING
DA DAAA DA
I REALLY AM A GENIUS!
LOOK AT YOU GO!
I JUST HOPE THE EMERGENCY BACK DOOR I BUILT IS STILL WORKING...!
JUST DO THIS HERE, AND...
OKAY!
システムに接続します…
connect
Connecting to the system...
I'M IN!
IT'S NO USE.
Gary!
I.A network security
I'M IN THE BASE SYSTEM, BUT THE IMPERIAL ARMY ADDED ITS OWN SECURITY.

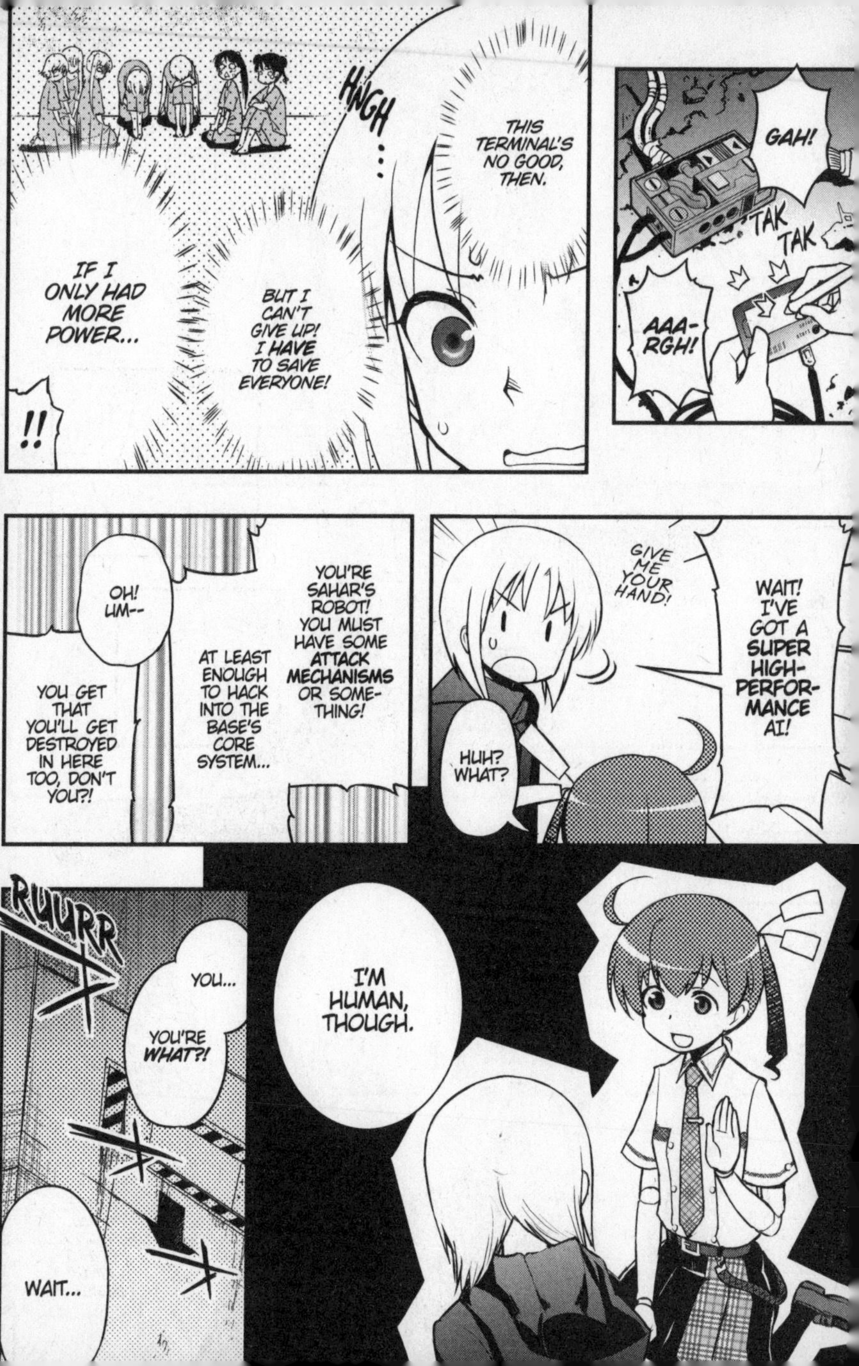
GAH!
TAK TAK
AAAA-RGH!
HNGH...
THIS TERMINAL'S NO GOOD, THEN.
BUT I CAN'T GIVE UP! I HAVE TO SAVE EVERYONE!
IF I ONLY HAD MORE POWER...
!!
WAIT! I'VE GOT A SUPER HIGH-PERFORMANCE AI!
GIVE ME YOUR HAND!
HUH? WHAT?
YOU'RE SAHAR'S ROBOT! YOU MUST HAVE SOME ATTACK MECHANISMS OR SOME-THING!
AT LEAST ENOUGH TO HACK INTO THE BASE'S CORE SYSTEM...
OH! UM--
YOU GET THAT YOU'LL GET DESTROYED IN HERE TOO, DON'T YOU?!
I'M HUMAN, THOUGH.
RUURR
YOU...
YOU'RE WHAT?!
WAIT...

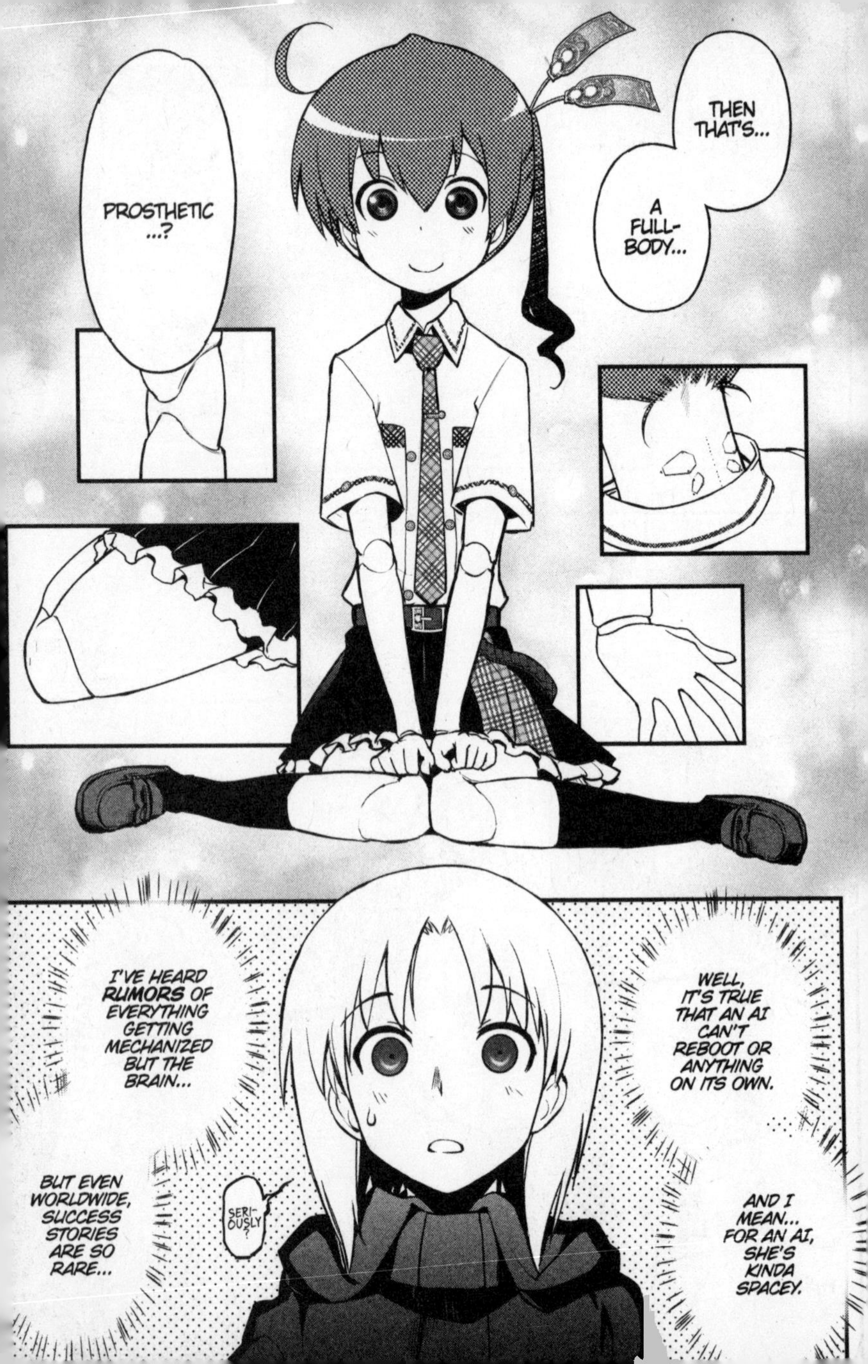
THEN THAT'S...
A FULL-BODY...
PROSTHETIC ...?
WELL, IT'S TRUE THAT AN AI CAN'T REBOOT OR ANYTHING ON ITS OWN.
AND I MEAN... FOR AN AI, SHE'S KINDA SPACEY.
SERI-OUSLY?
I'VE HEARD **RUMORS** OF EVERYTHING GETTING MECHANIZED BUT THE BRAIN...
BUT EVEN WORLDWIDE, SUCCESS STORIES ARE SO RARE...

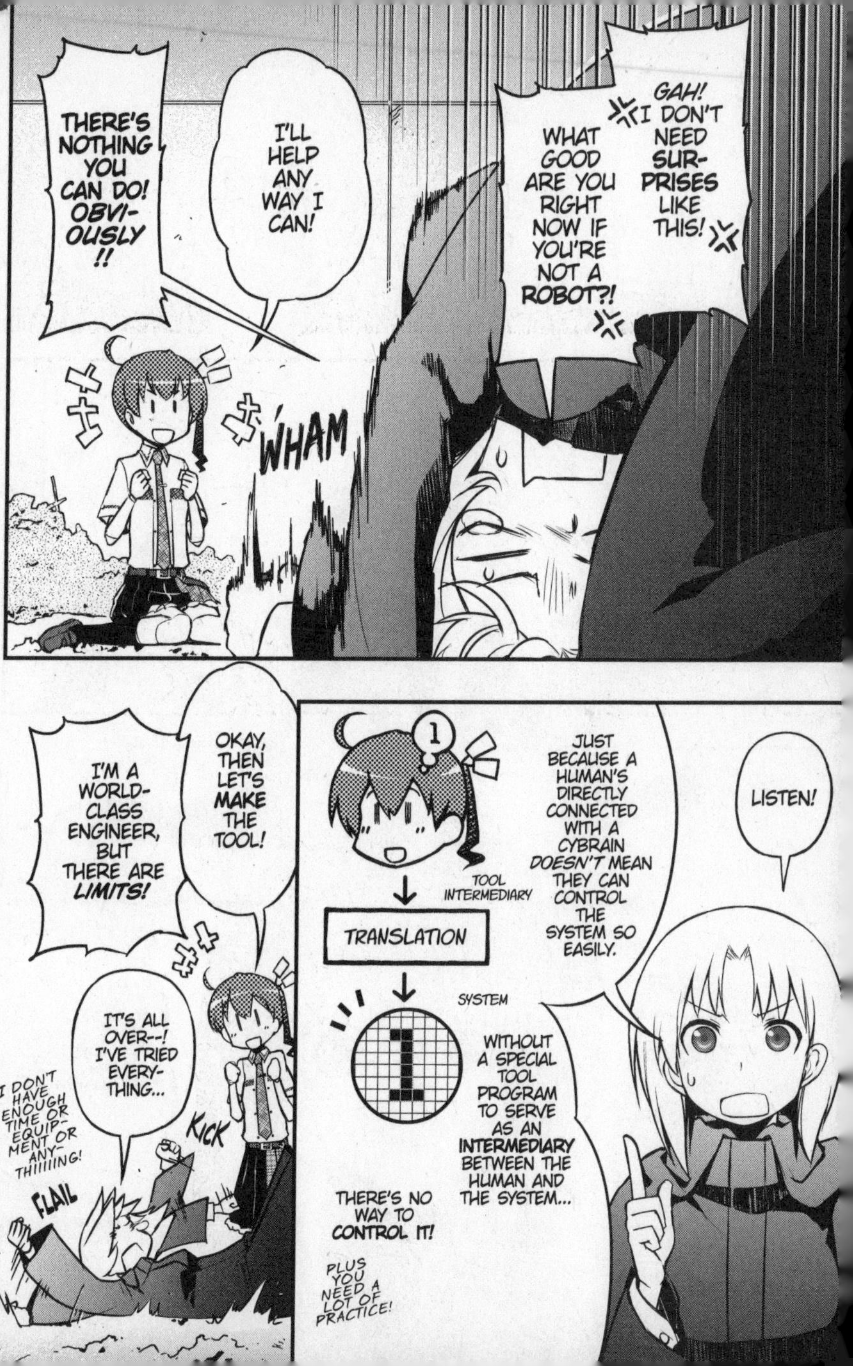
GAH! I DON'T NEED SURPRISES LIKE THIS!
WHAT GOOD ARE YOU RIGHT NOW IF YOU'RE NOT A ROBOT?!
I'LL HELP ANY WAY I CAN!
THERE'S NOTHING YOU CAN DO! OBVIOUSLY!!
WHAM
LISTEN!
JUST BECAUSE A HUMAN'S DIRECTLY CONNECTED WITH A CYBRAIN DOESN'T MEAN THEY CAN CONTROL THE SYSTEM SO EASILY.
TOOL INTERMEDIARY
TRANSLATION
SYSTEM
WITHOUT A SPECIAL TOOL PROGRAM TO SERVE AS AN INTERMEDIARY BETWEEN THE HUMAN AND THE SYSTEM...
THERE'S NO WAY TO CONTROL IT!
PLUS YOU NEED A LOT OF PRACTICE!
OKAY, THEN LET'S MAKE THE TOOL!
I'M A WORLD-CLASS ENGINEER, BUT THERE ARE LIMITS!
IT'S ALL OVER--! I'VE TRIED EVERYTHING...
I DON'T HAVE ENOUGH TIME OR EQUIPMENT OR ANYTHIIIIING!
KICK
FLAIL

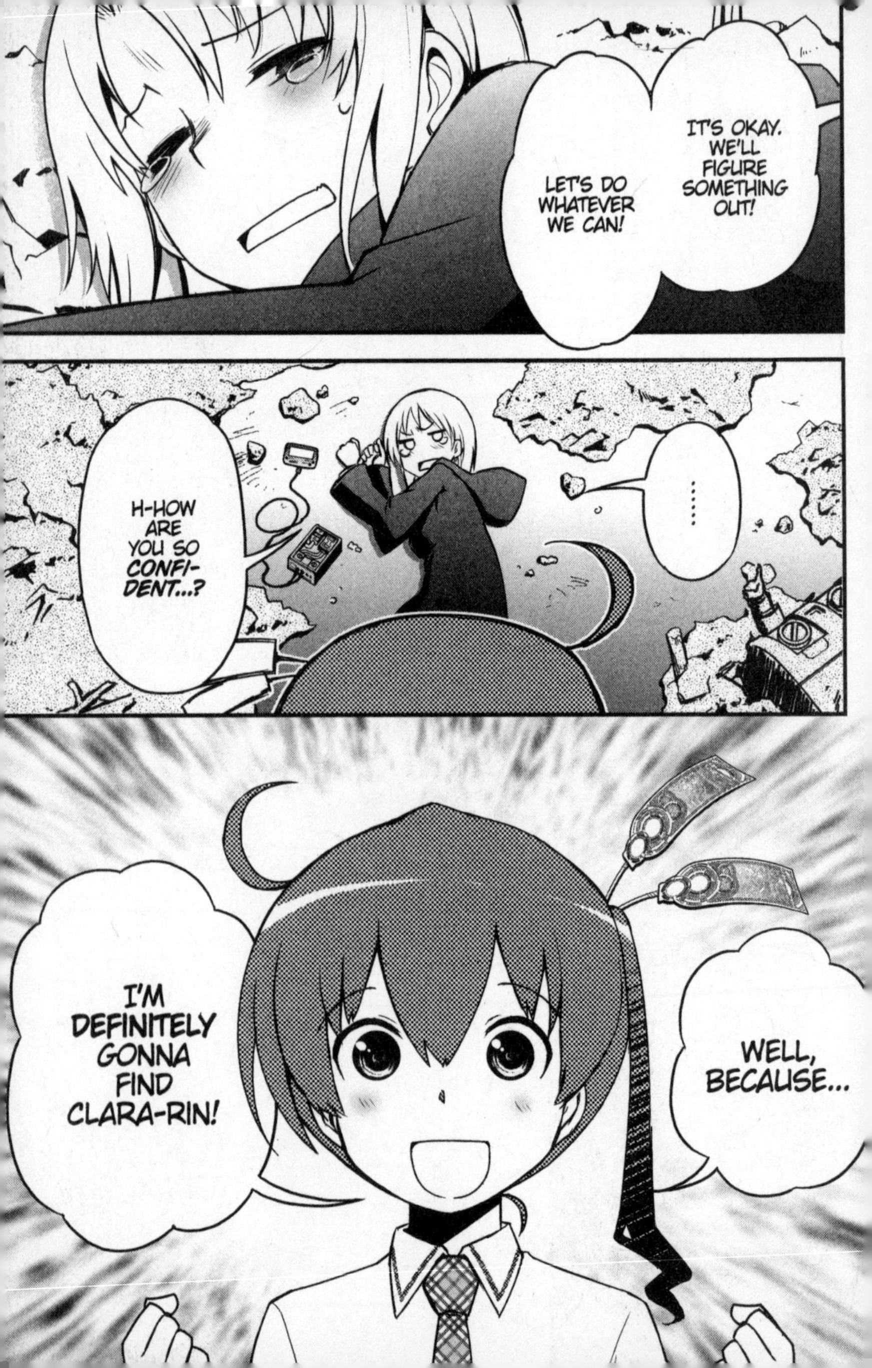
IT'S OKAY. WE'LL FIGURE SOMETHING OUT!
LET'S DO WHATEVER WE CAN!
......
H-HOW ARE YOU SO CONFIDENT...?
WELL, BECAUSE...
I'M DEFINITELY GONNA FIND CLARA-RIN!

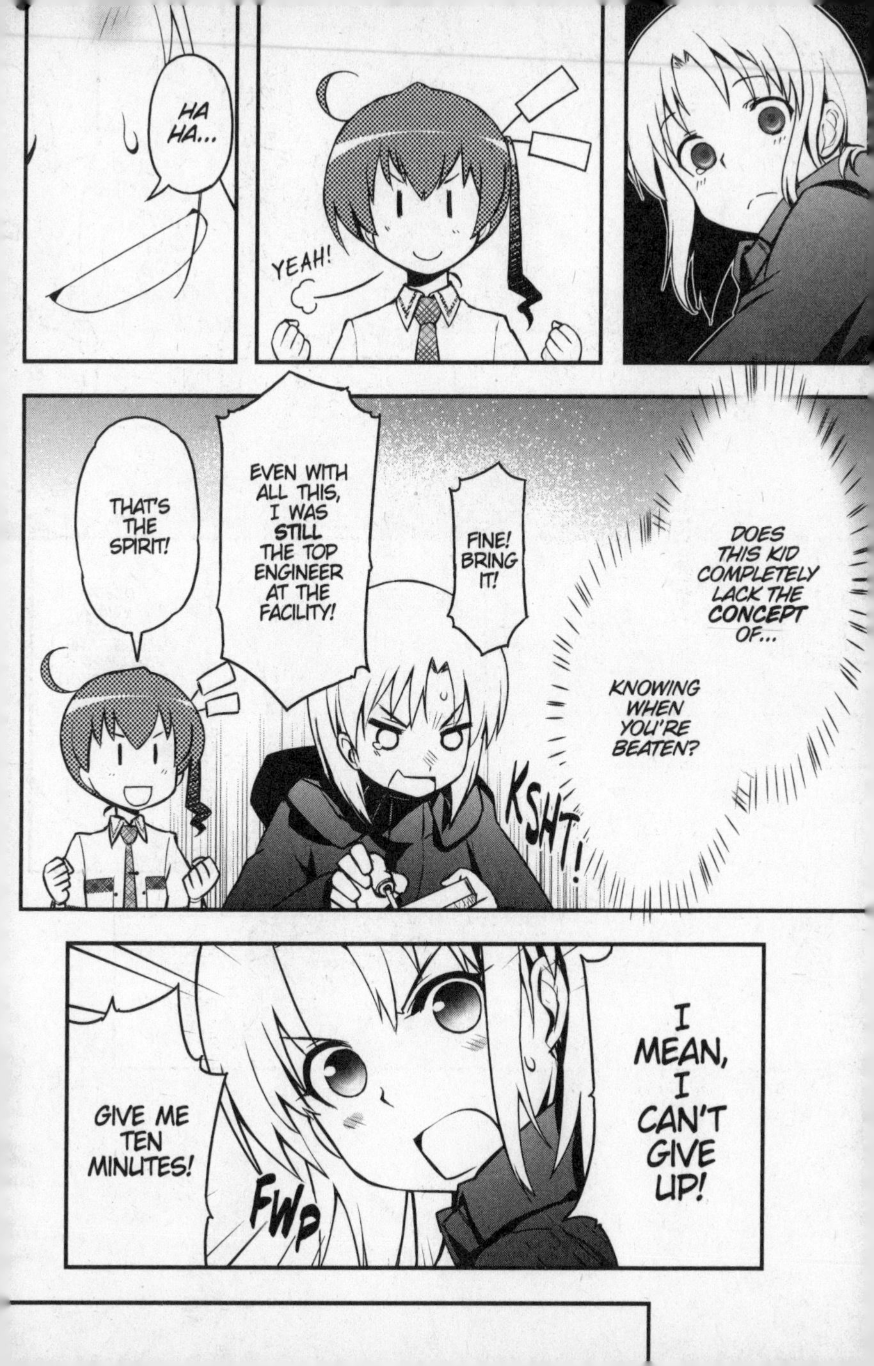
YEAH!
HA HA...
DOES THIS KID COMPLETELY LACK THE CONCEPT OF...
KNOWING WHEN YOU'RE BEATEN?
KSHT!
FINE! BRING IT!
EVEN WITH ALL THIS, I WAS STILL THE TOP ENGINEER AT THE FACILITY!
THAT'S THE SPIRIT!
I MEAN, I CAN'T GIVE UP!
GIVE ME TEN MINUTES!
FWP

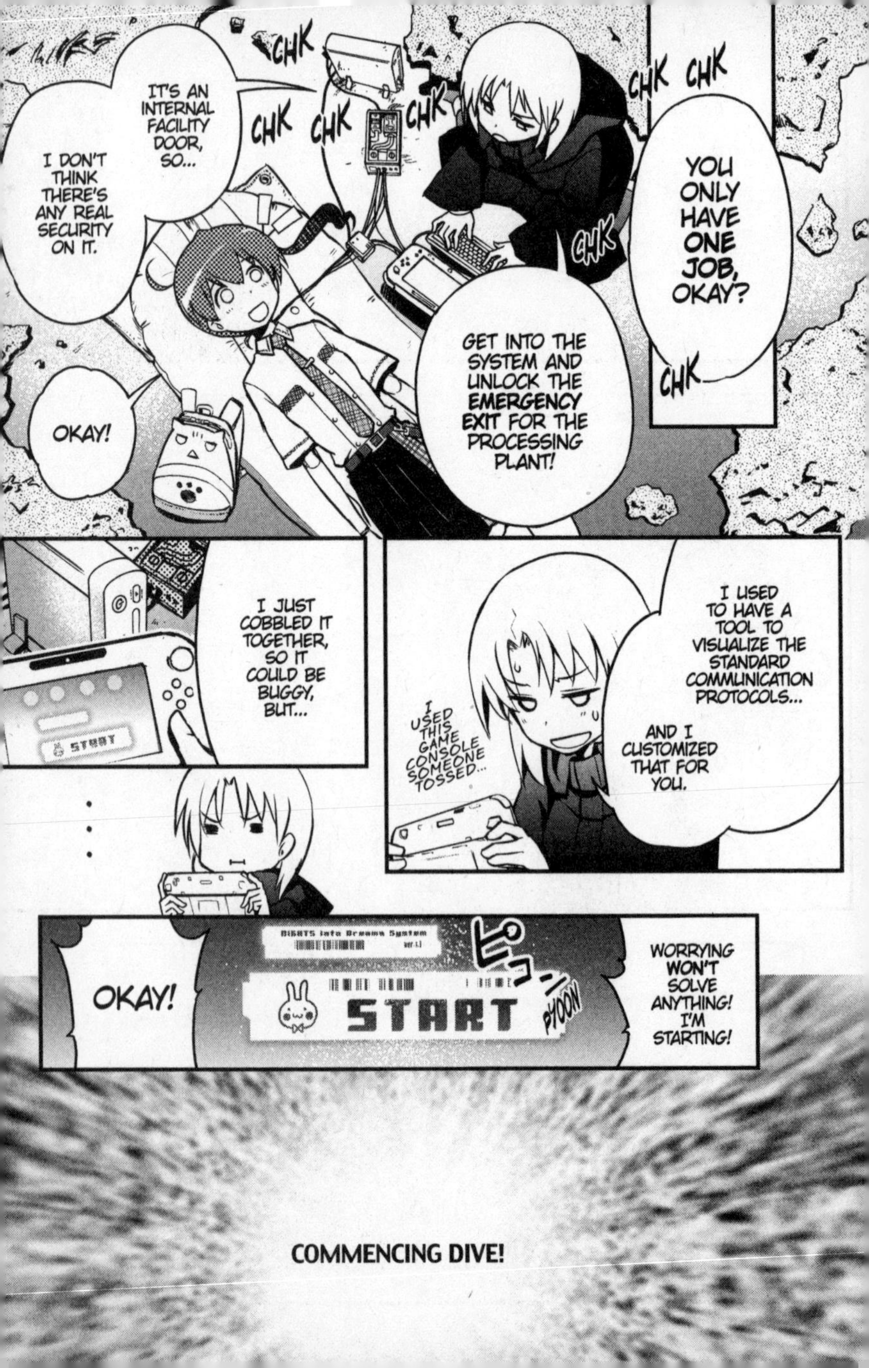
CHK
CHK
CHK
CHK
CHK CHK
CHK
CHK
YOU ONLY HAVE ONE JOB, OKAY?
GET INTO THE SYSTEM AND UNLOCK THE **EMERGENCY EXIT** FOR THE PROCESSING PLANT!
IT'S AN INTERNAL FACILITY DOOR, SO...
I DON'T THINK THERE'S ANY REAL SECURITY ON IT.
OKAY!
I USED TO HAVE A TOOL TO VISUALIZE THE STANDARD COMMUNICATION PROTOCOLS...
AND I CUSTOMIZED THAT FOR YOU.
I USED THIS GAME CONSOLE SOMEONE TOSSED...
I JUST COBBLED IT TOGETHER, SO IT COULD BE BUGGY, BUT...
START
WORRYING WON'T SOLVE ANYTHING! I'M STARTING!
PYOON
START
OKAY!
COMMENCING DIVE!

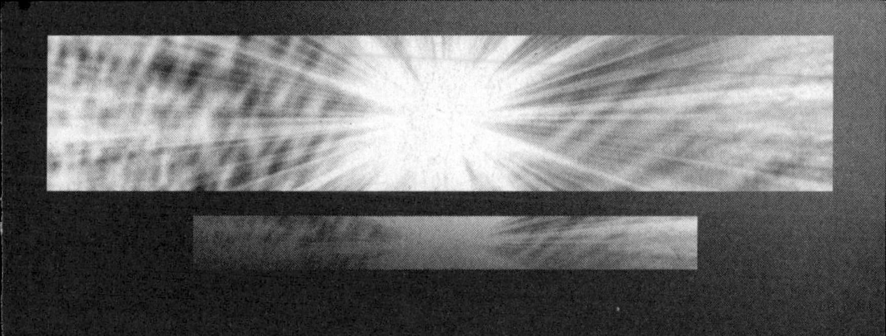

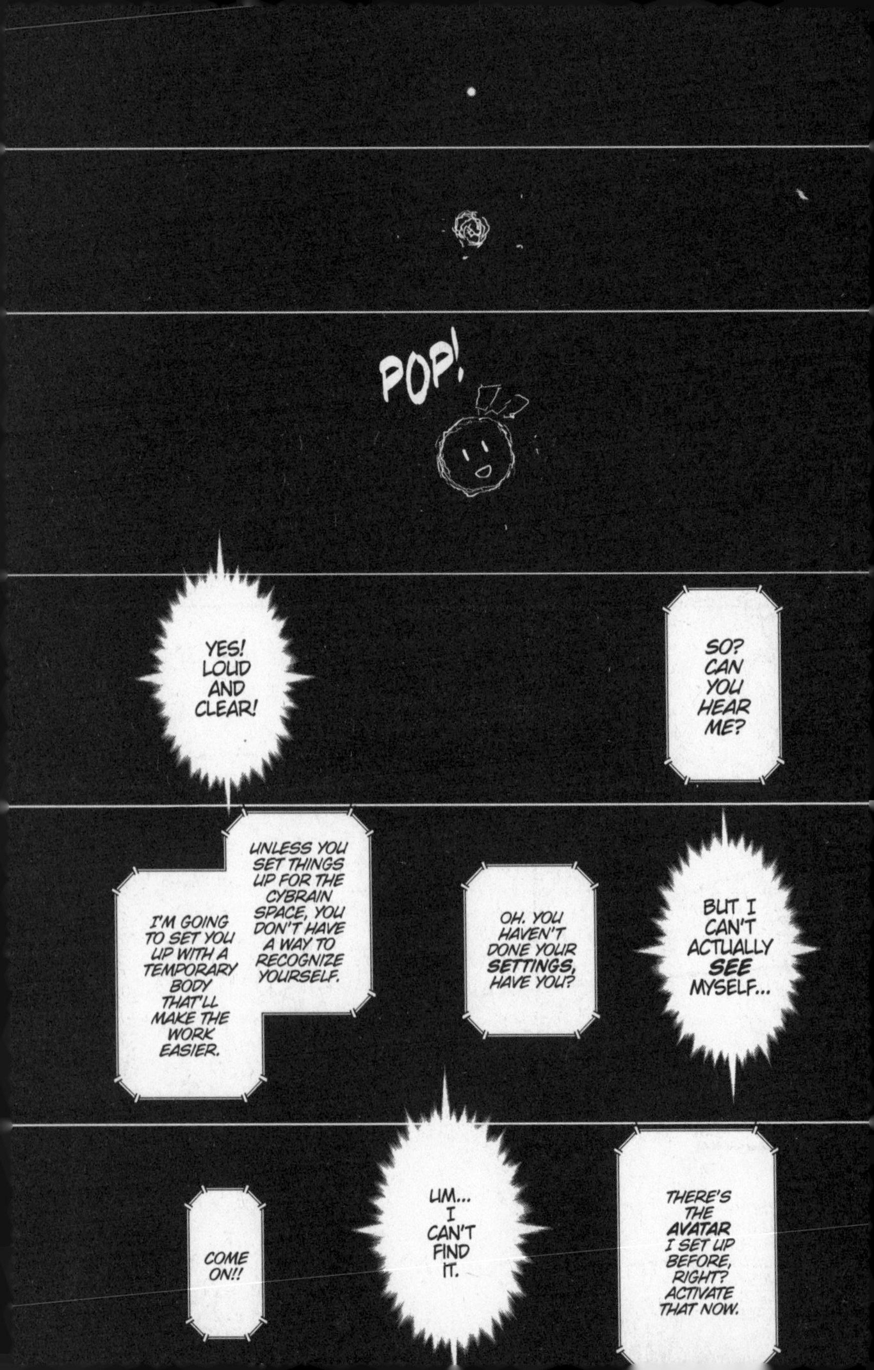
POP!
SO? CAN YOU HEAR ME?
YES! LOUD AND CLEAR!
BUT I CAN'T ACTUALLY SEE MYSELF...
OH. YOU HAVEN'T DONE YOUR SETTINGS, HAVE YOU?
UNLESS YOU SET THINGS UP FOR THE CYBRAIN SPACE, YOU DON'T HAVE A WAY TO RECOGNIZE YOURSELF.
I'M GOING TO SET YOU UP WITH A TEMPORARY BODY THAT'LL MAKE THE WORK EASIER.
THERE'S THE AVATAR I SET UP BEFORE, RIGHT? ACTIVATE THAT NOW.
UM... I CAN'T FIND IT.
COME ON!!

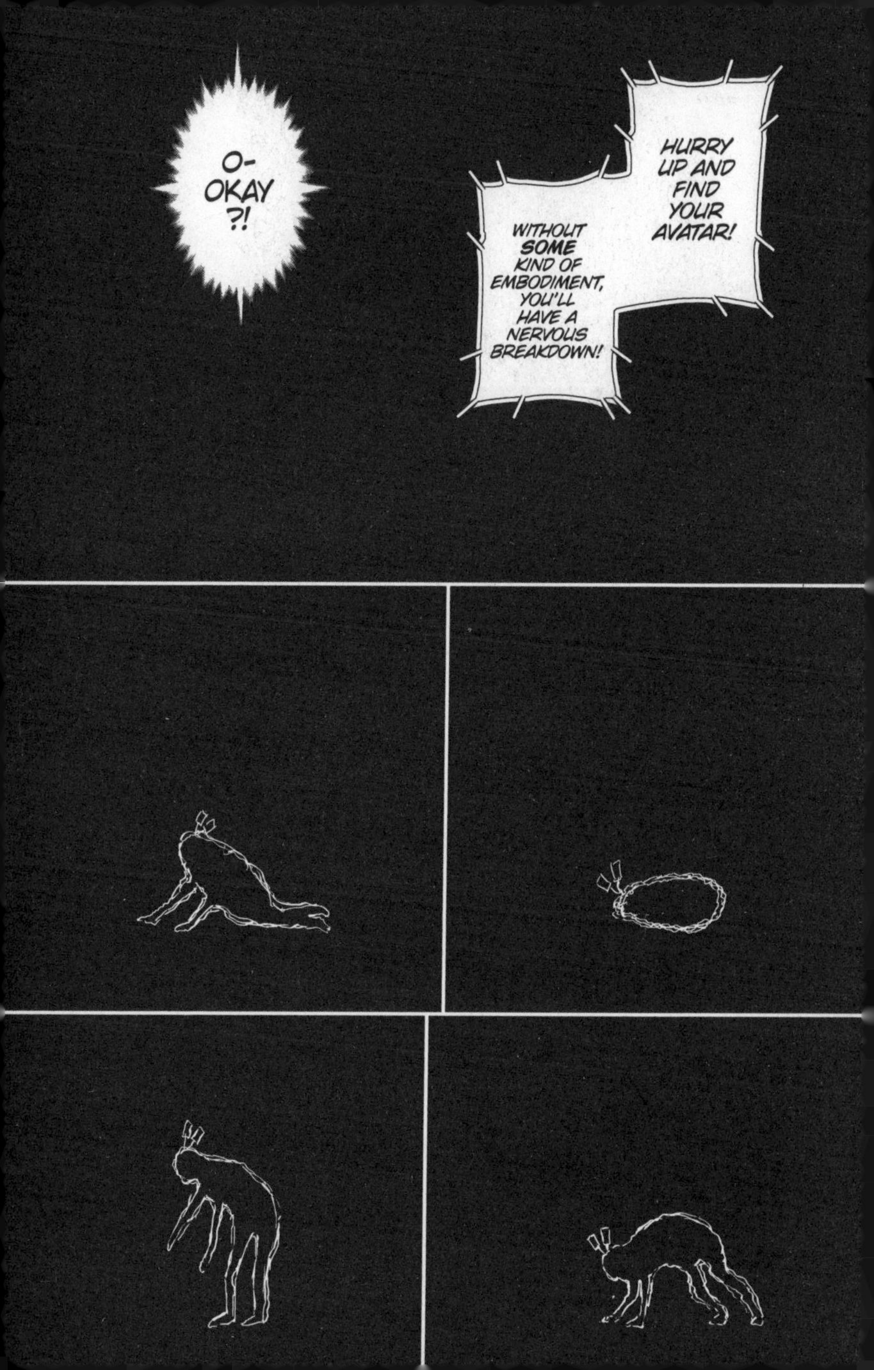
HURRY UP AND FIND YOUR AVATAR!
WITHOUT SOME KIND OF EMBODIMENT, YOU'LL HAVE A NERVOUS BREAKDOWN!
O-OKAY?!

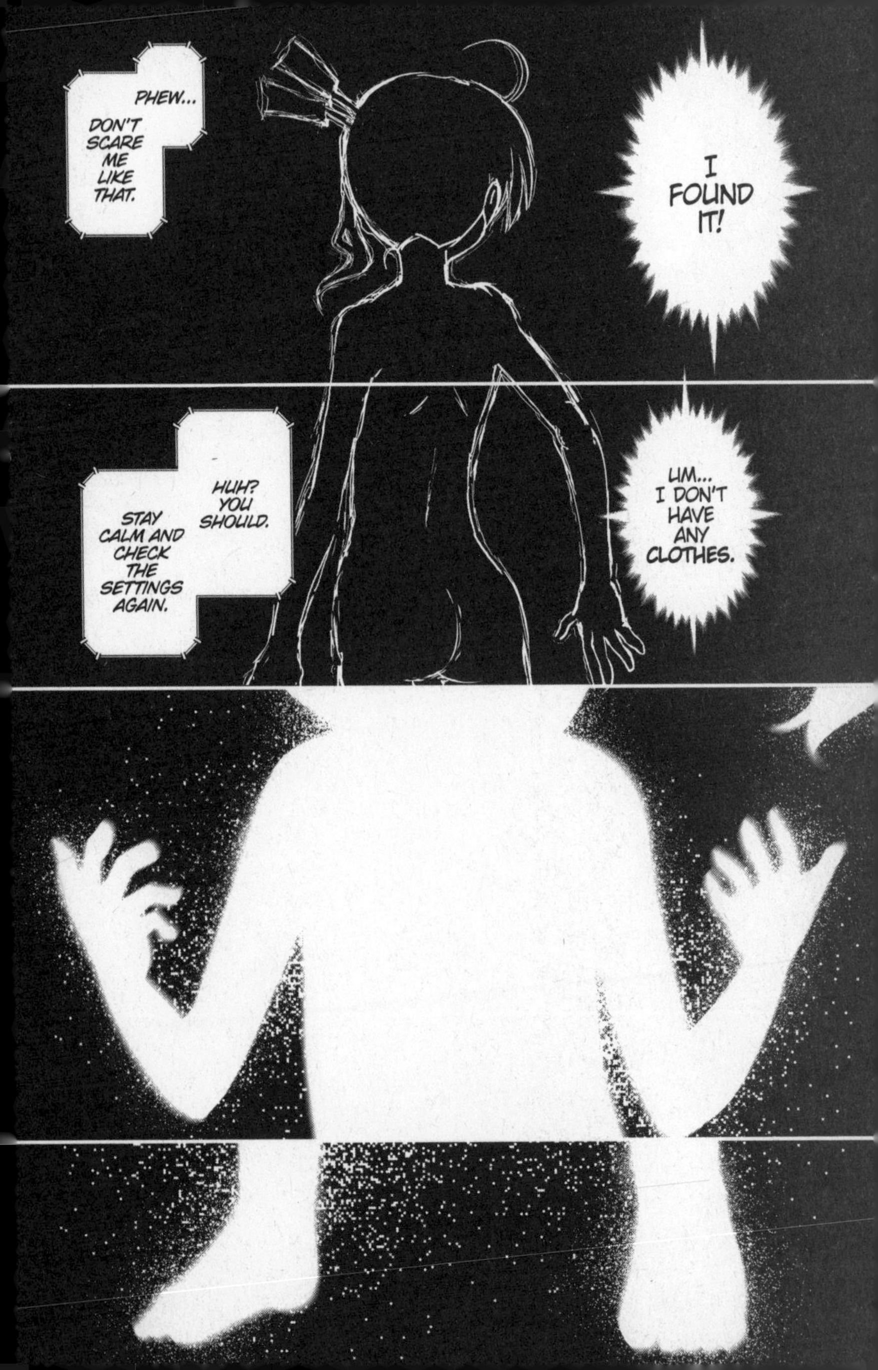
I FOUND IT!
PHEW... DON'T SCARE ME LIKE THAT.
UM... I DON'T HAVE ANY CLOTHES.
HUH? YOU SHOULD.
STAY CALM AND CHECK THE SETTINGS AGAIN.

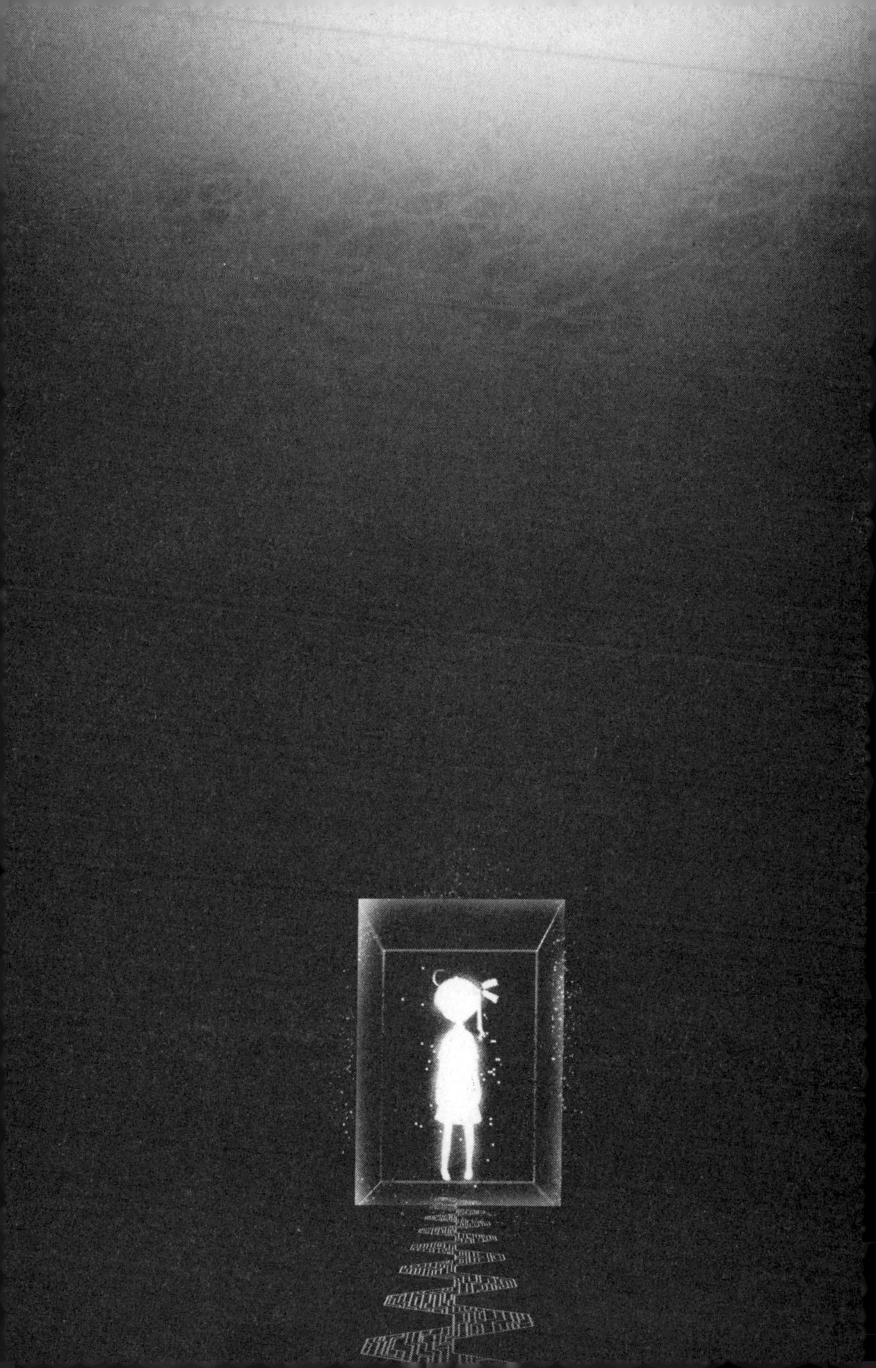

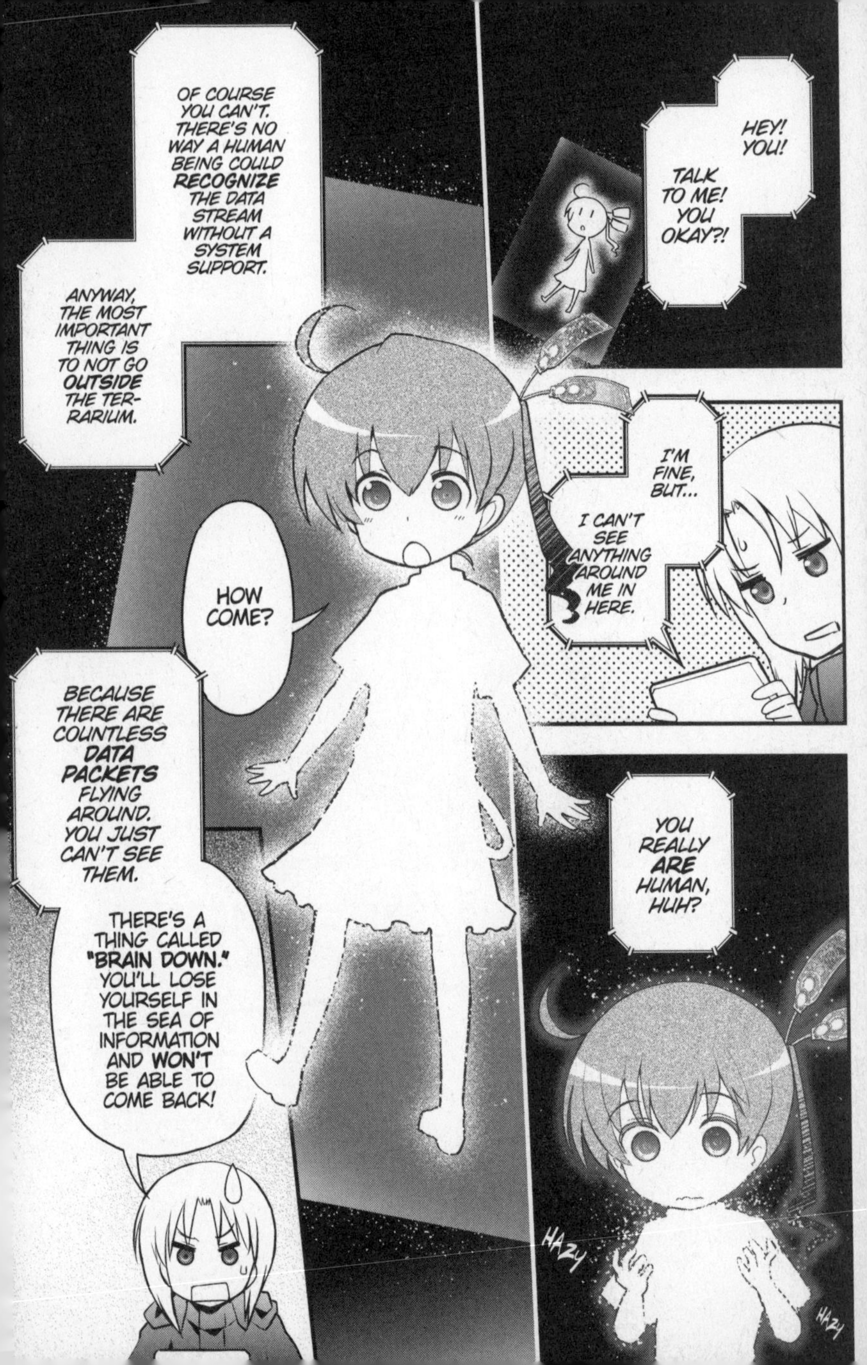
HEY! YOU!
TALK TO ME! YOU OKAY?!
I'M FINE, BUT...
I CAN'T SEE ANYTHING AROUND ME IN HERE.
YOU REALLY ARE HUMAN, HUH?
HAZY
HAZY
OF COURSE YOU CAN'T. THERE'S NO WAY A HUMAN BEING COULD RECOGNIZE THE DATA STREAM WITHOUT A SYSTEM SUPPORT.
ANYWAY, THE MOST IMPORTANT THING IS TO NOT GO OUTSIDE THE TER-RARIUM.
HOW COME?
BECAUSE THERE ARE COUNTLESS DATA PACKETS FLYING AROUND. YOU JUST CAN'T SEE THEM.
THERE'S A THING CALLED "BRAIN DOWN." YOU'LL LOSE YOURSELF IN THE SEA OF INFORMATION AND WON'T BE ABLE TO COME BACK!

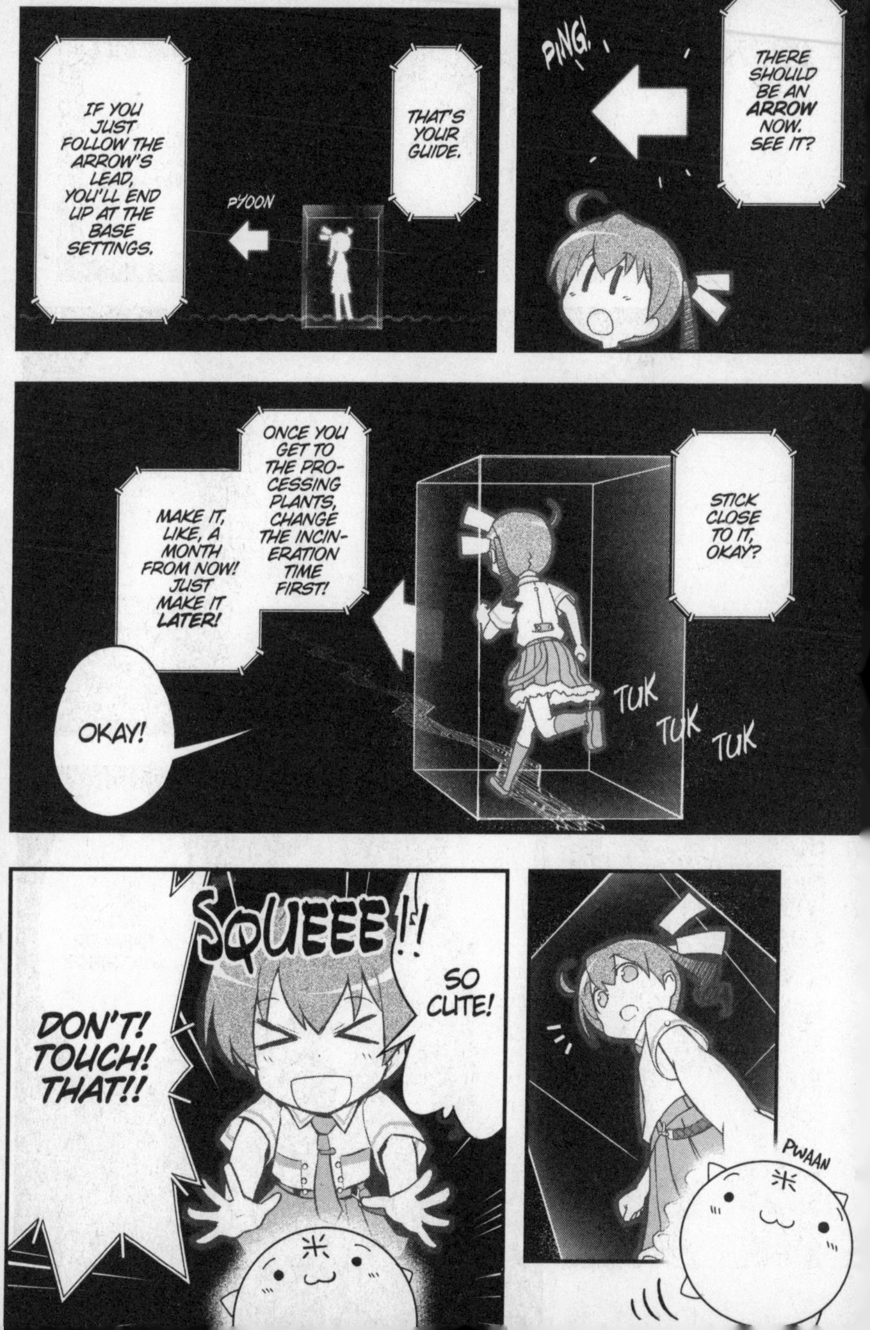
PING!
THERE SHOULD BE AN ARROW NOW. SEE IT?
THAT'S YOUR GUIDE.
PYOON
IF YOU JUST FOLLOW THE ARROW'S LEAD, YOU'LL END UP AT THE BASE SETTINGS.
STICK CLOSE TO IT, OKAY?
ONCE YOU GET TO THE PROCESSING PLANTS, CHANGE THE INCINERATION TIME FIRST!
MAKE IT, LIKE, A MONTH FROM NOW! JUST MAKE IT LATER!
TUK TUK TUK
OKAY!
PWAAN
SQUEEE!!
SO CUTE!
DON'T! TOUCH! THAT!!

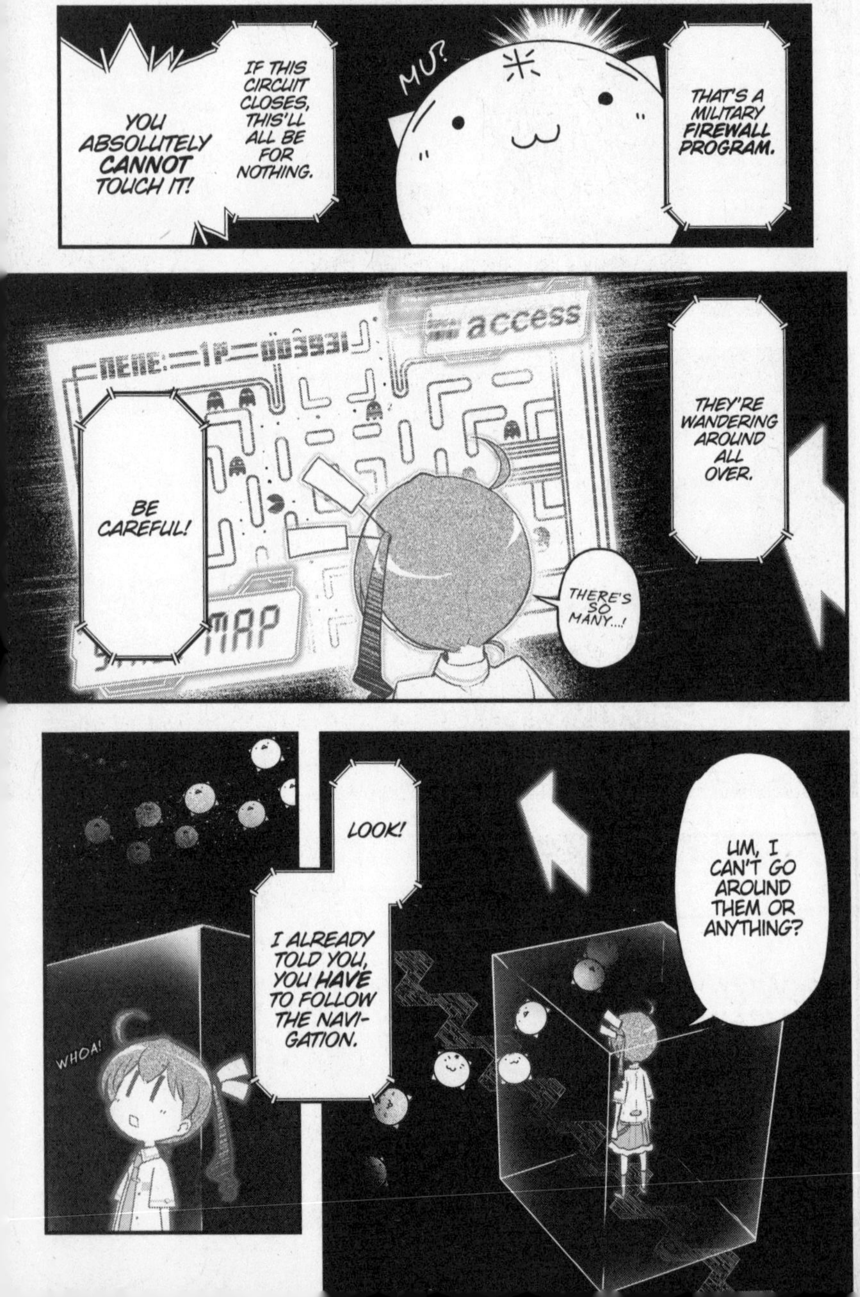
THAT'S A MILITARY FIREWALL PROGRAM.
MU?
IF THIS CIRCUIT CLOSES, THIS'LL ALL BE FOR NOTHING.
YOU ABSOLUTELY CANNOT TOUCH IT!
THEY'RE WANDERING AROUND ALL OVER.
access
THERE'S SO MANY...!
BE CAREFUL!
MAP
UM, I CAN'T GO AROUND THEM OR ANYTHING?
LOOK!
I ALREADY TOLD YOU, YOU HAVE TO FOLLOW THE NAVI-GATION.
WHOA!

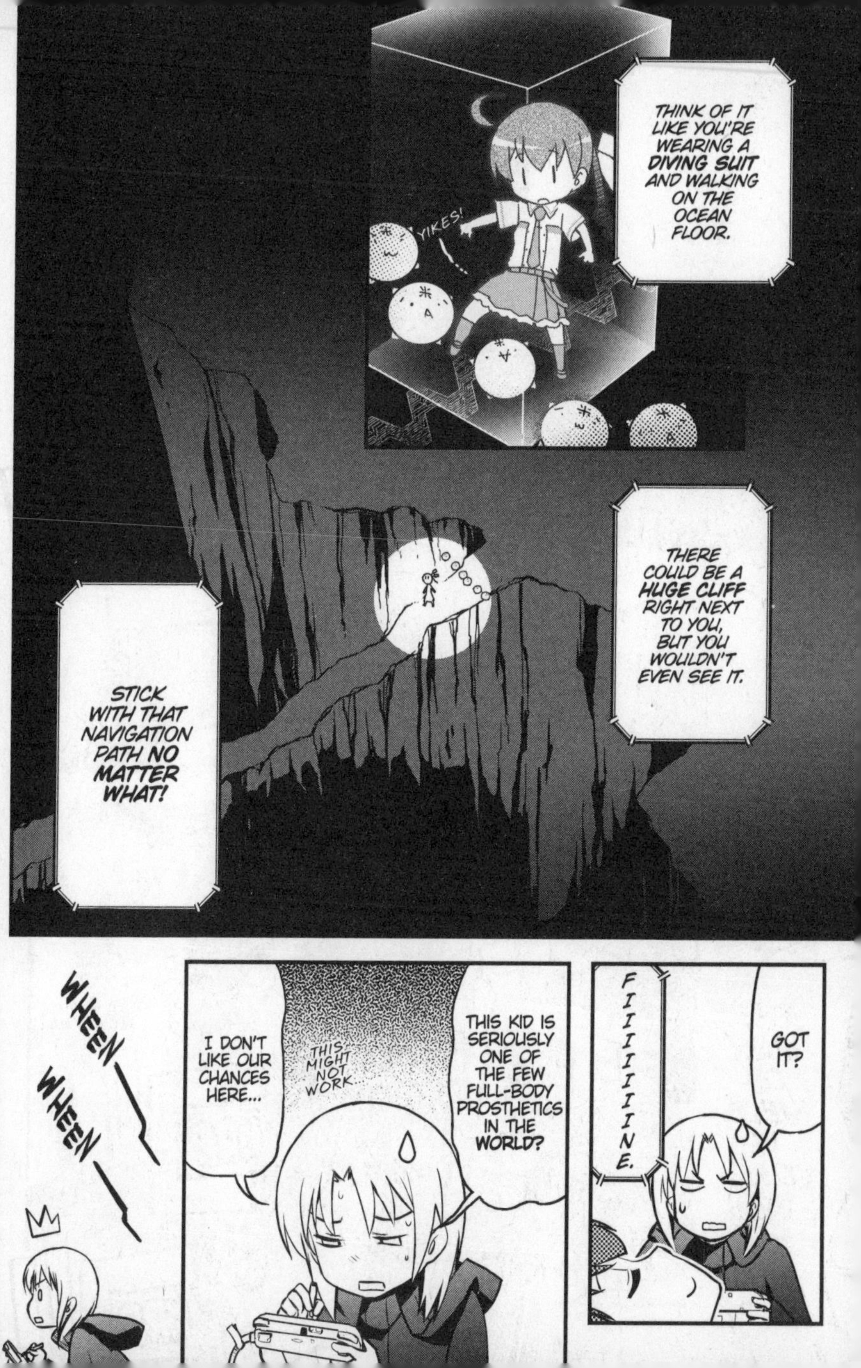
THINK OF IT LIKE YOU'RE WEARING A **DIVING SUIT** AND WALKING ON THE OCEAN FLOOR.
YIKES!
THERE COULD BE A **HUGE CLIFF** RIGHT NEXT TO YOU, BUT YOU WOULDN'T EVEN SEE IT.
STICK WITH THAT NAVIGATION PATH **NO MATTER WHAT!**
GOT IT?
FIIIIIIINE.
THIS KID IS SERIOUSLY ONE OF THE FEW FULL-BODY PROSTHETICS IN THE **WORLD?**
THIS MIGHT NOT WORK...
I DON'T LIKE OUR CHANCES HERE...
WHEEN—
WHEEN—

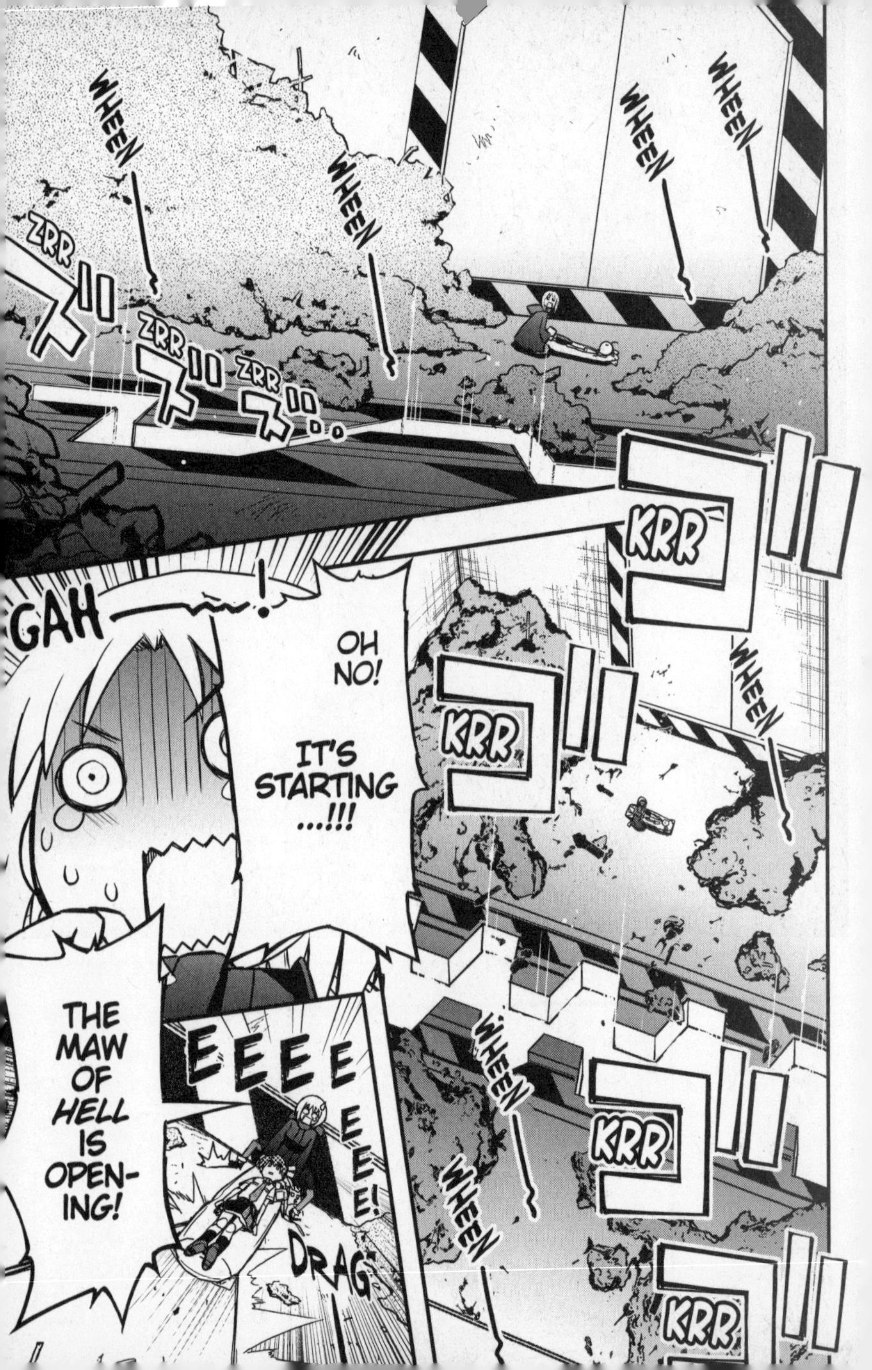
WHEEN
WHEEN
WHEEN
WHEEN
ZRR
ZRR
ZRR
KRR
WHEEN
KRR
WHEEN
KRR
WHEEN
KRR
GAH
OH NO!
IT'S STARTING ...!!!
THE MAW OF HELL IS OPEN-ING!
EEEEEEEE!
DRAG

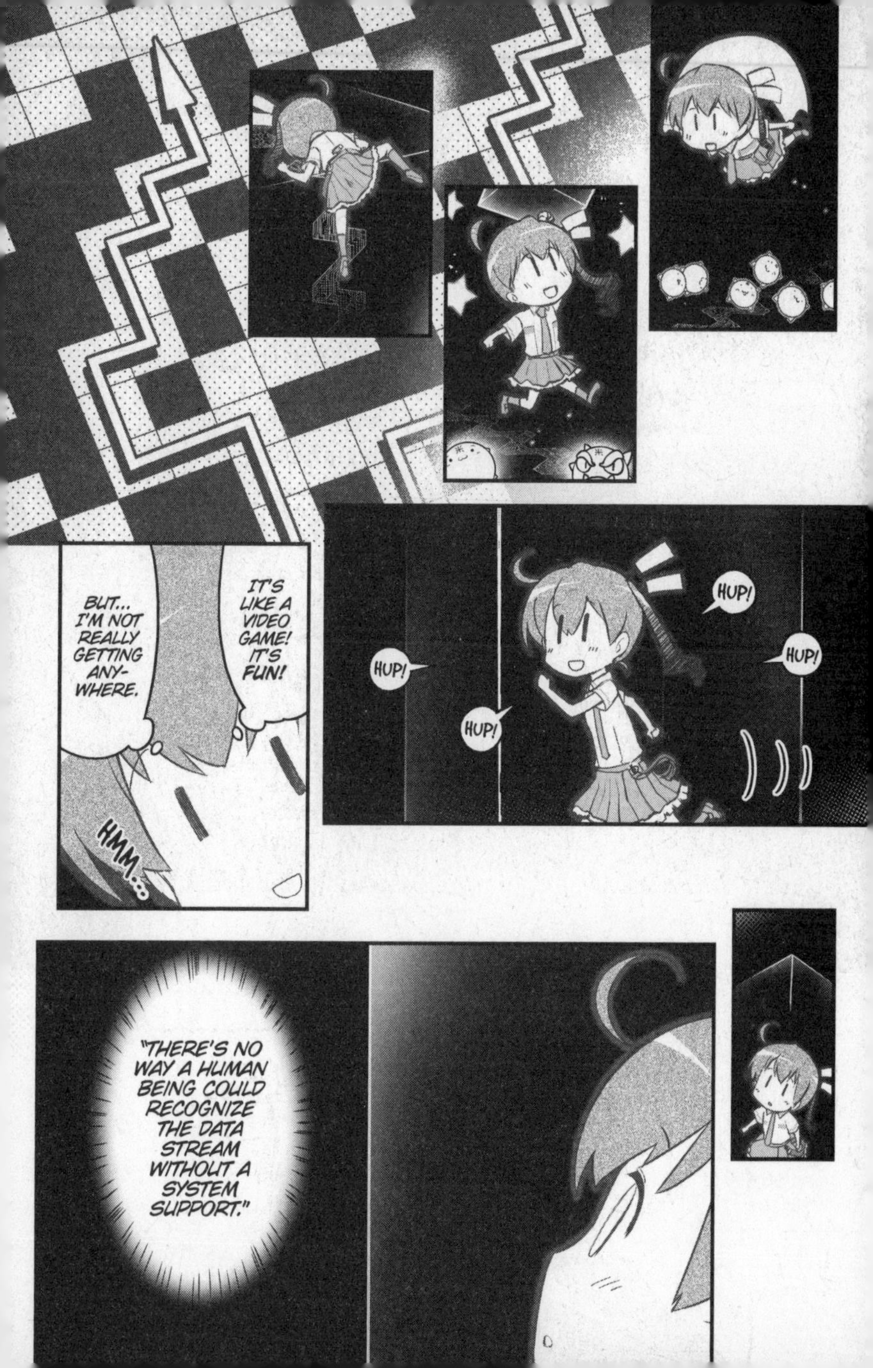
HUP!
HUP!
HUP!
HUP!
IT'S LIKE A VIDEO GAME! IT'S FUN!
BUT... I'M NOT REALLY GETTING ANY-WHERE.
HMM...
"THERE'S NO WAY A HUMAN BEING COULD RECOGNIZE THE DATA STREAM WITHOUT A SYSTEM SUPPORT."

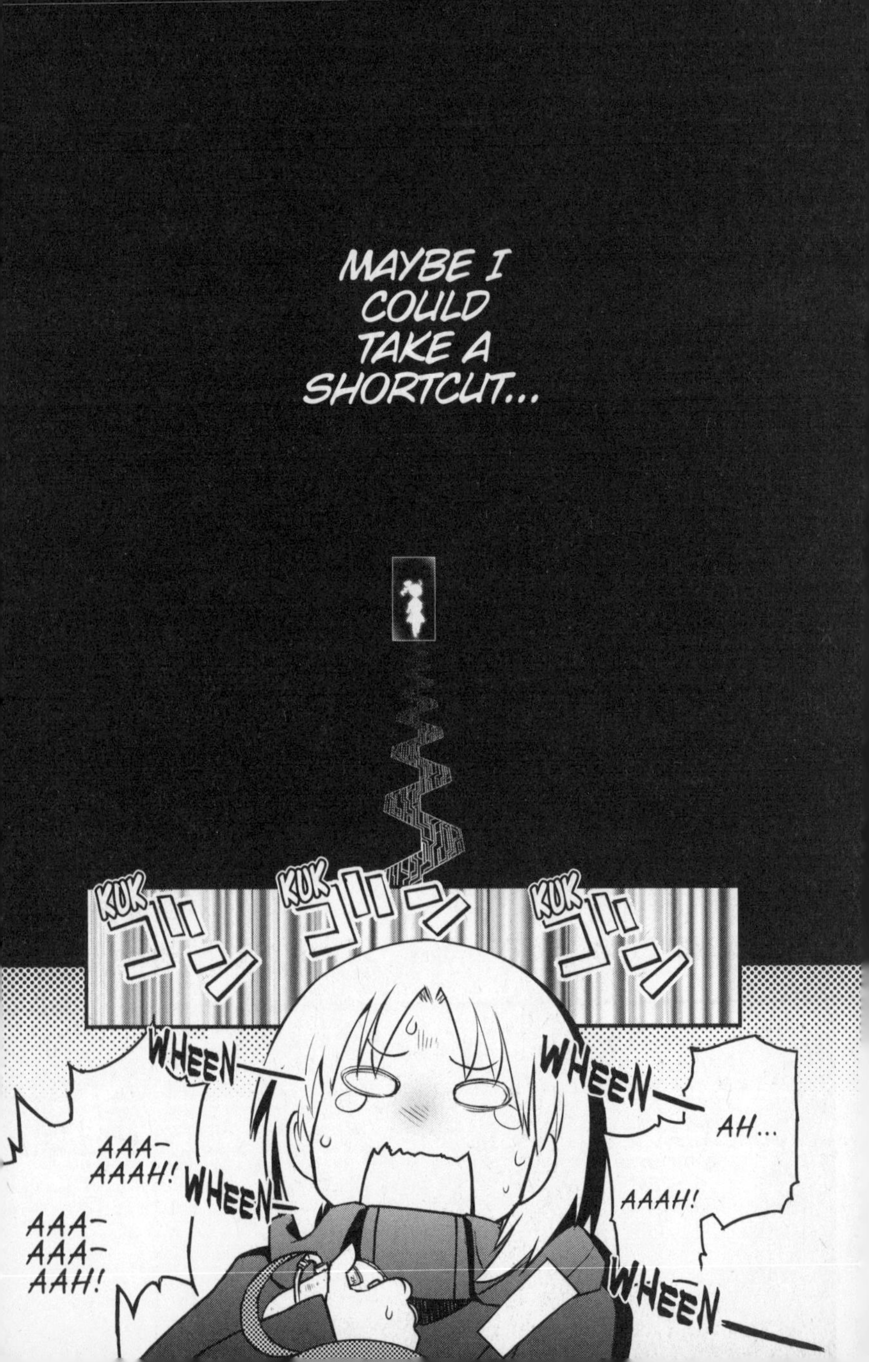

MAYBE I COULD TAKE A SHORTCUT...
KUK
KUK
KUK
WHEEN—
AH... AAAH!
WHEEN—
AAA-AAAH!
WHEEN—
WHEEN—
AAA-AAA-AAA-AAH!

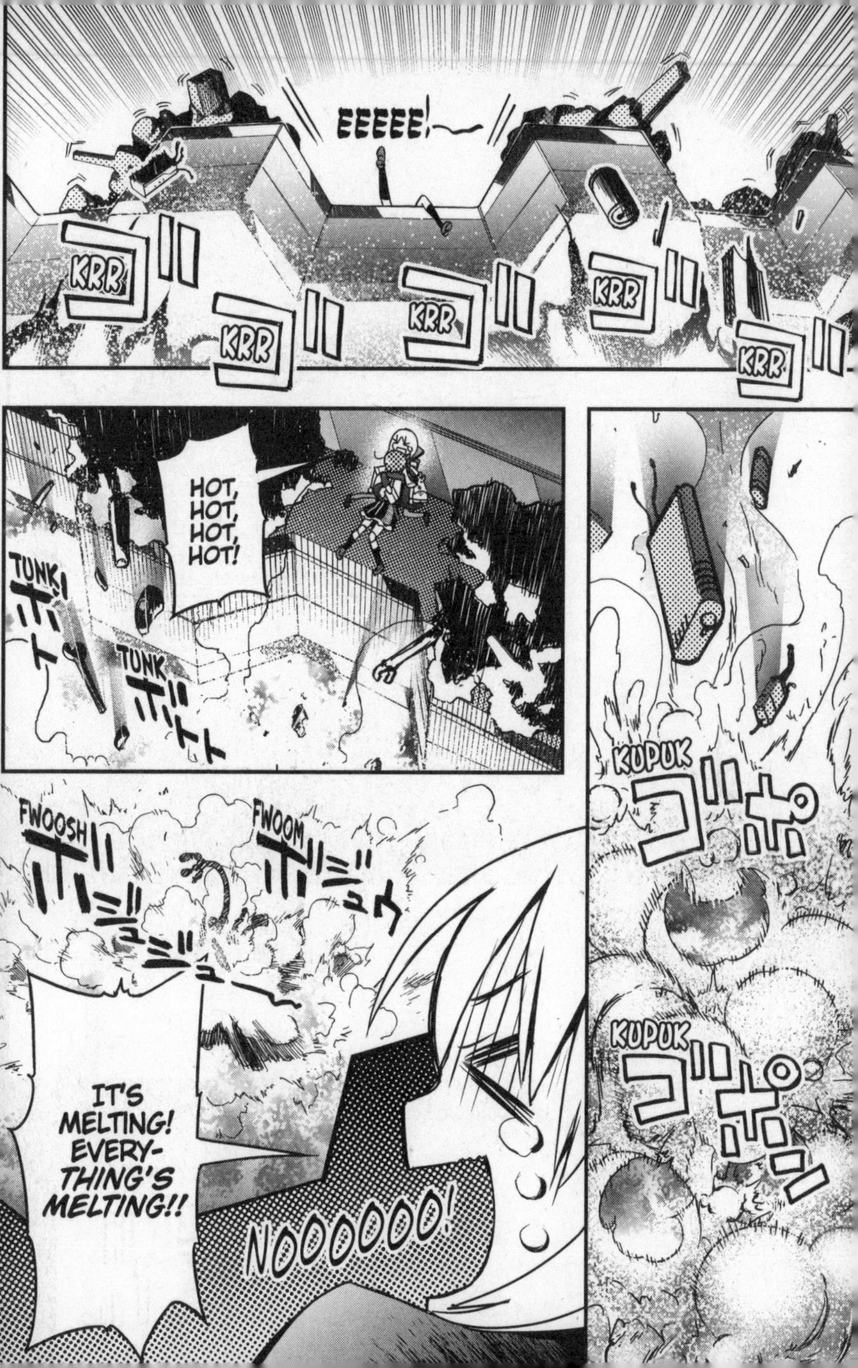
EEEEE!~
KRR
KRR
KRR
KRR
KRR
HOT, HOT, HOT, HOT!
TUNK!
TUNK
KUPUK
KUPUK
FWOOSH
FWOOM
IT'S MELTING! EVERY-THING'S MELTING!!
NOOOOOO!

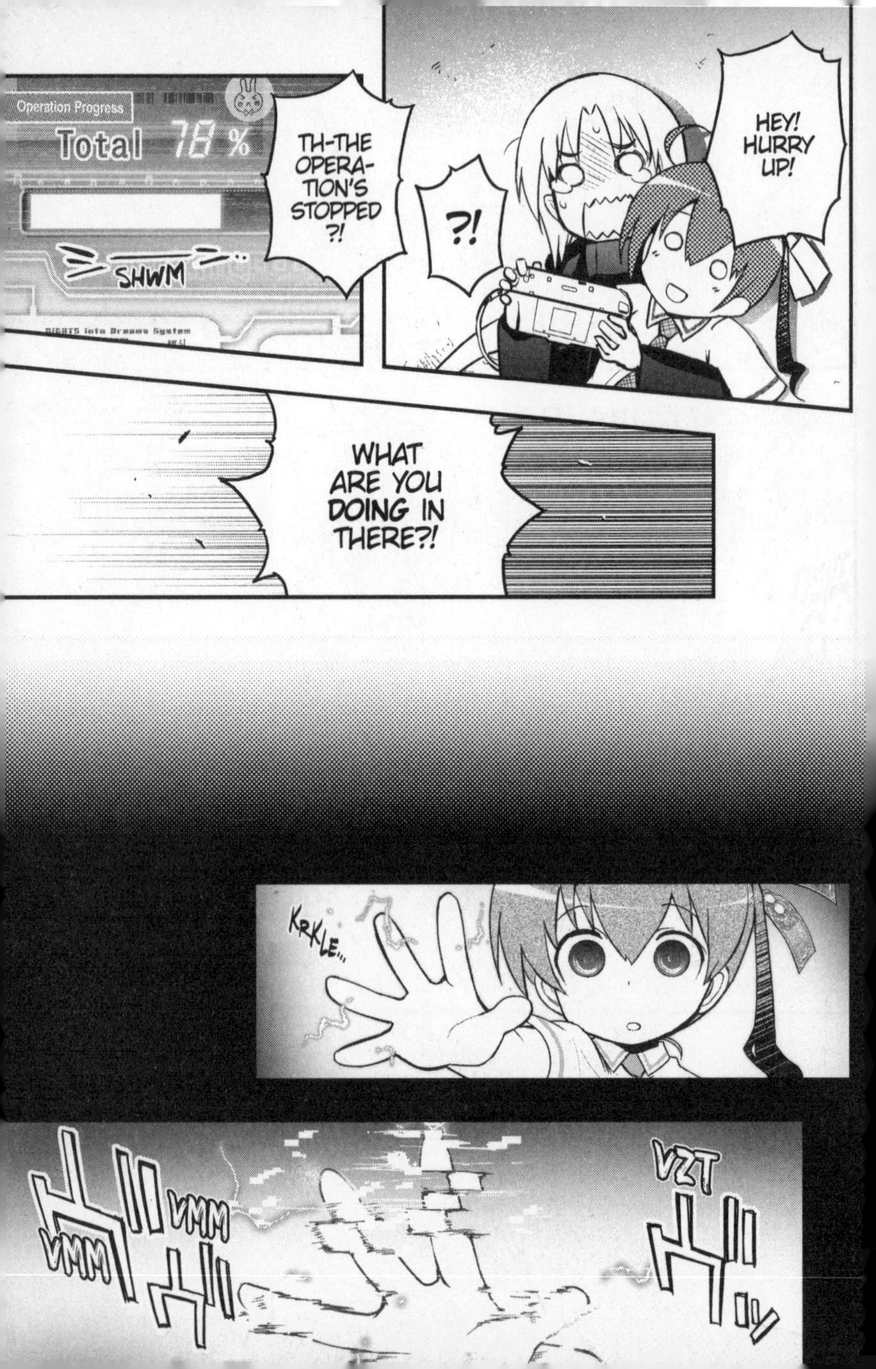
HEY! HURRY UP!
?!
TH-THE OPERATION'S STOPPED?!
Operation Progress
Total
SHWM
WHAT ARE YOU DOING IN THERE?!
KRKLE...
VZT
VMM
VMM

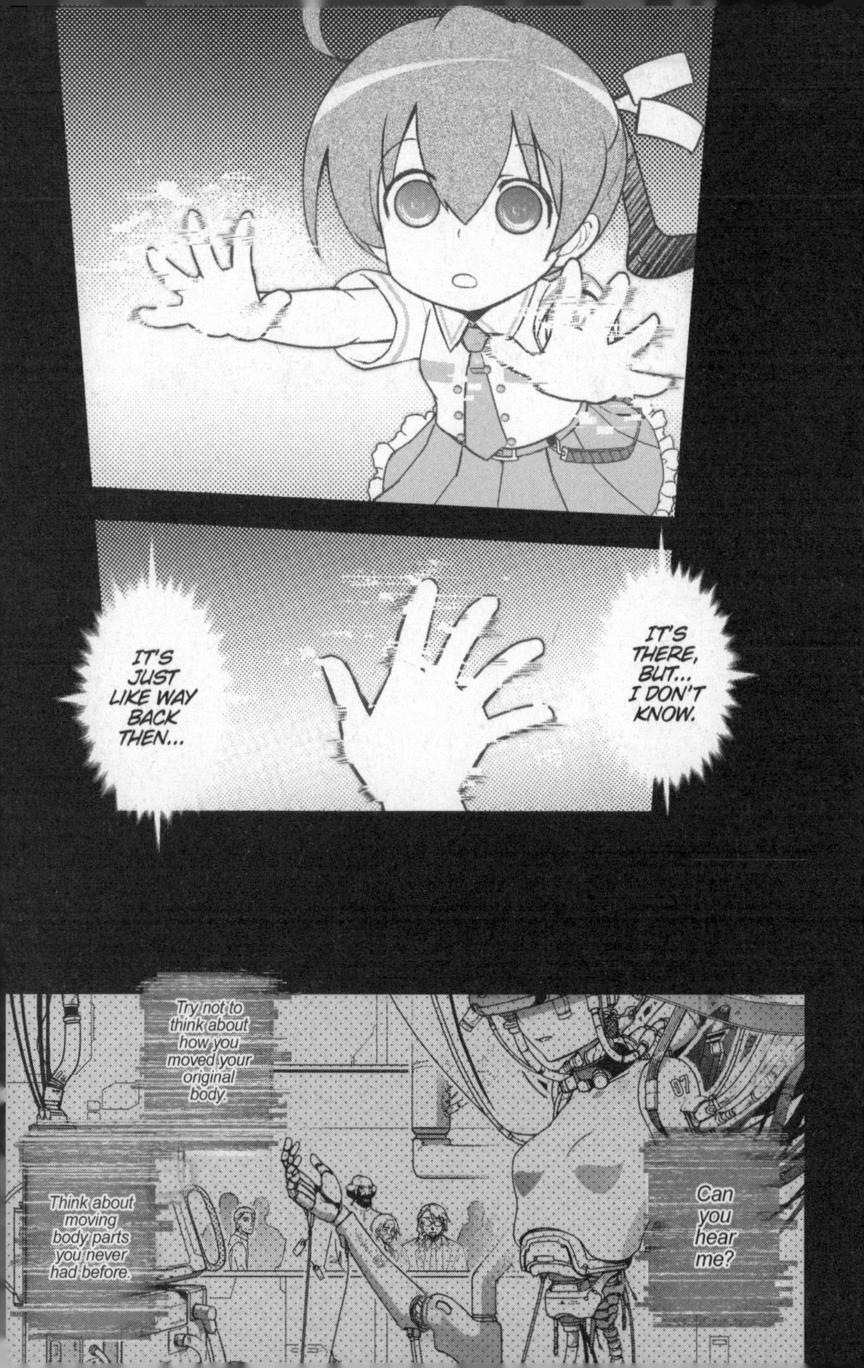
IT'S THERE, BUT... I DON'T KNOW.
IT'S JUST LIKE WAY BACK THEN...
Can you hear me?
Try not to think about how you moved your original body.
Think about moving body parts you never had before.

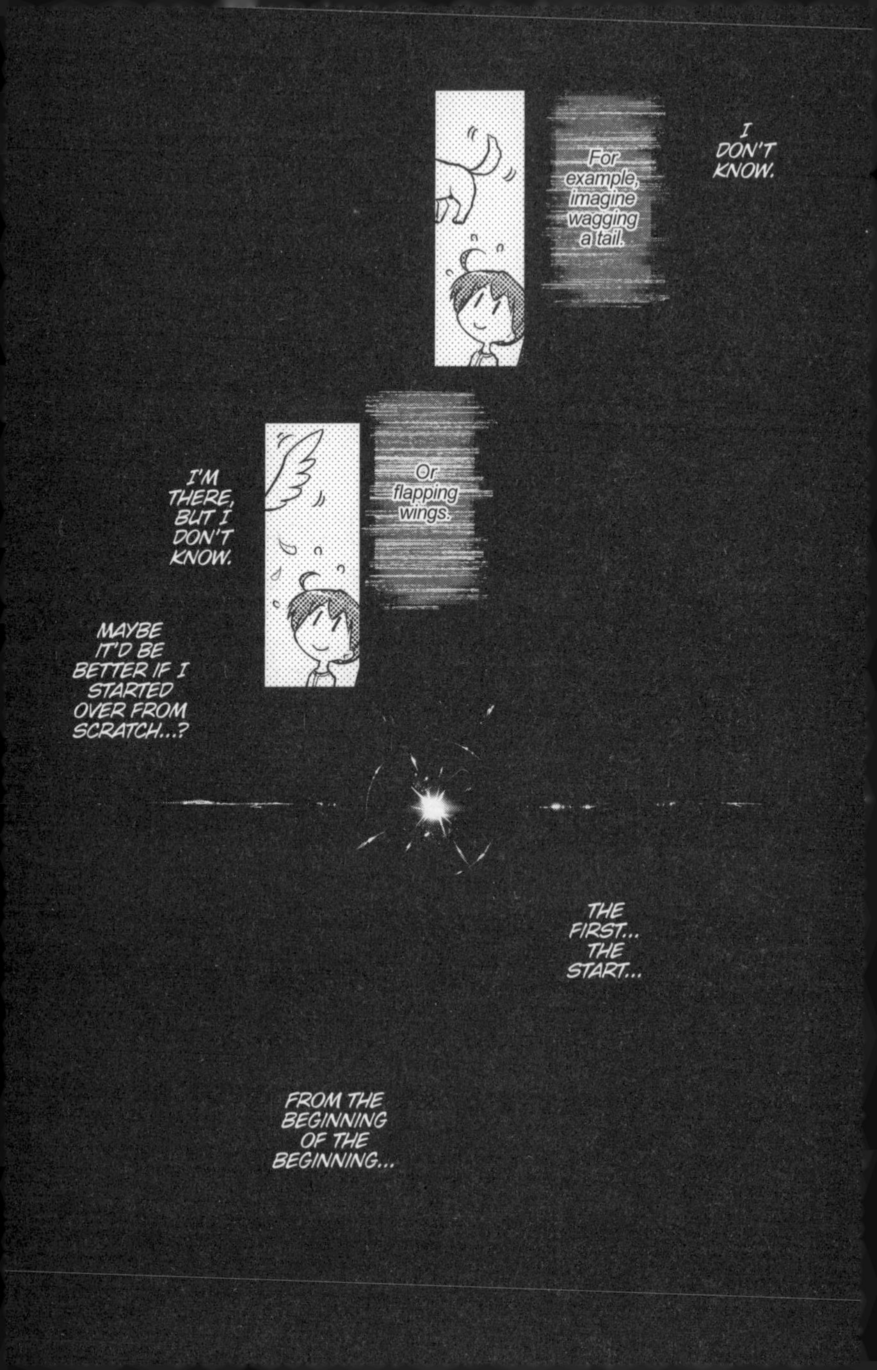
I DON'T KNOW.
For example, imagine wagging a tail.
Or flapping wings.
I'M THERE, BUT I DON'T KNOW.
MAYBE IT'D BE BETTER IF I STARTED OVER FROM SCRATCH...?
THE FIRST... THE START...
FROM THE BEGINNING OF THE BEGINNING...

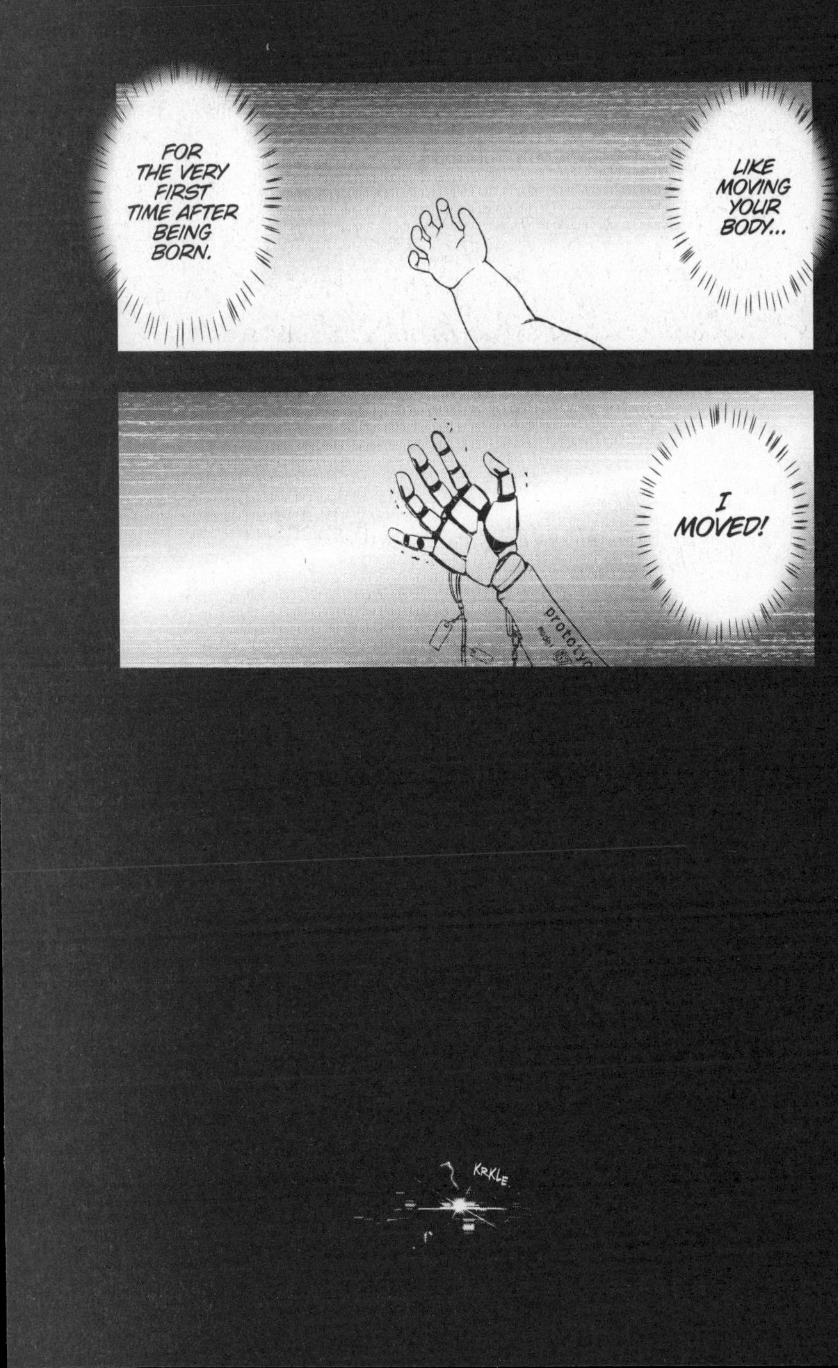
LIKE MOVING YOUR BODY...
FOR THE VERY FIRST TIME AFTER BEING BORN.
I MOVED!
KRKLE

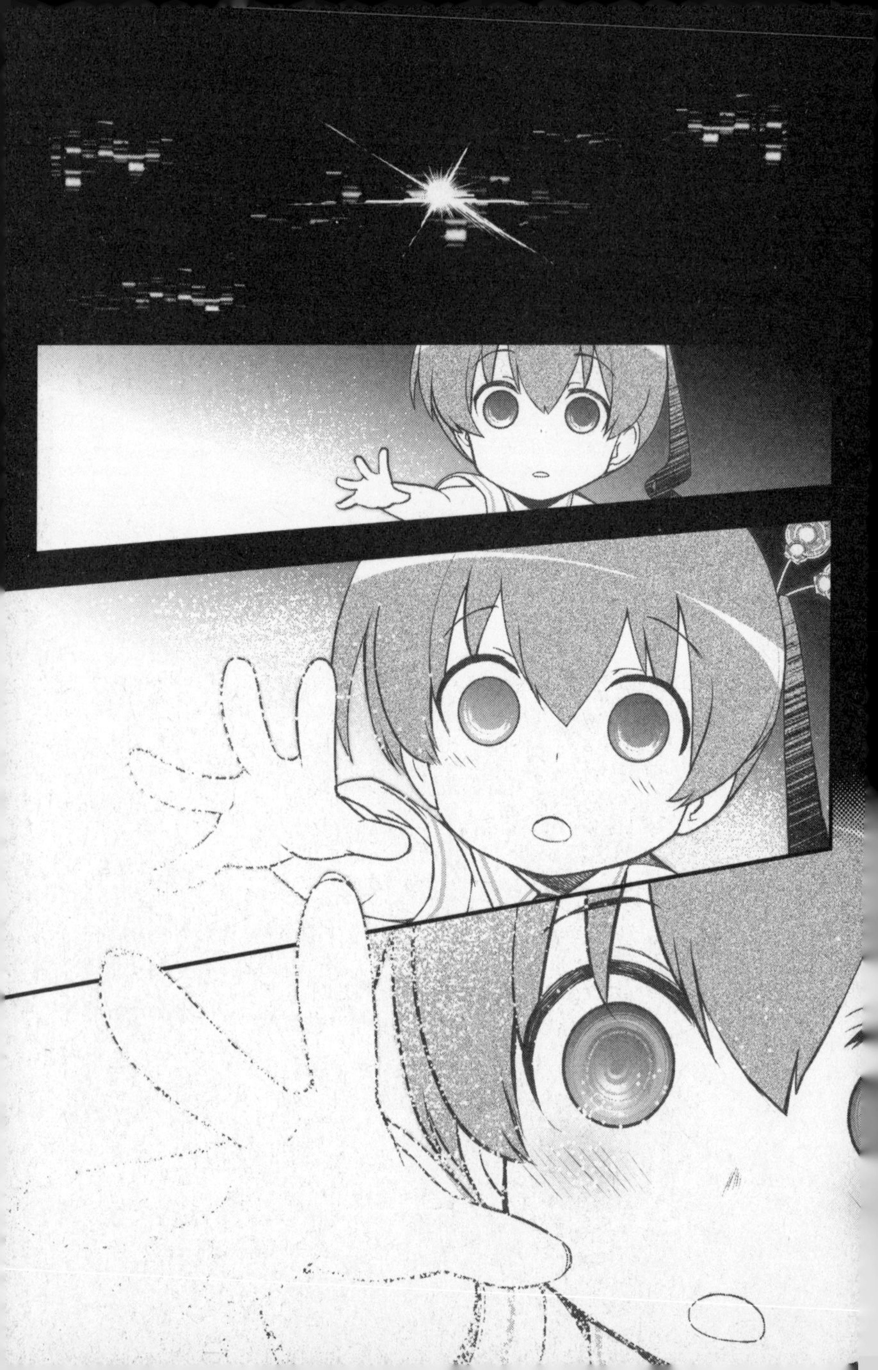

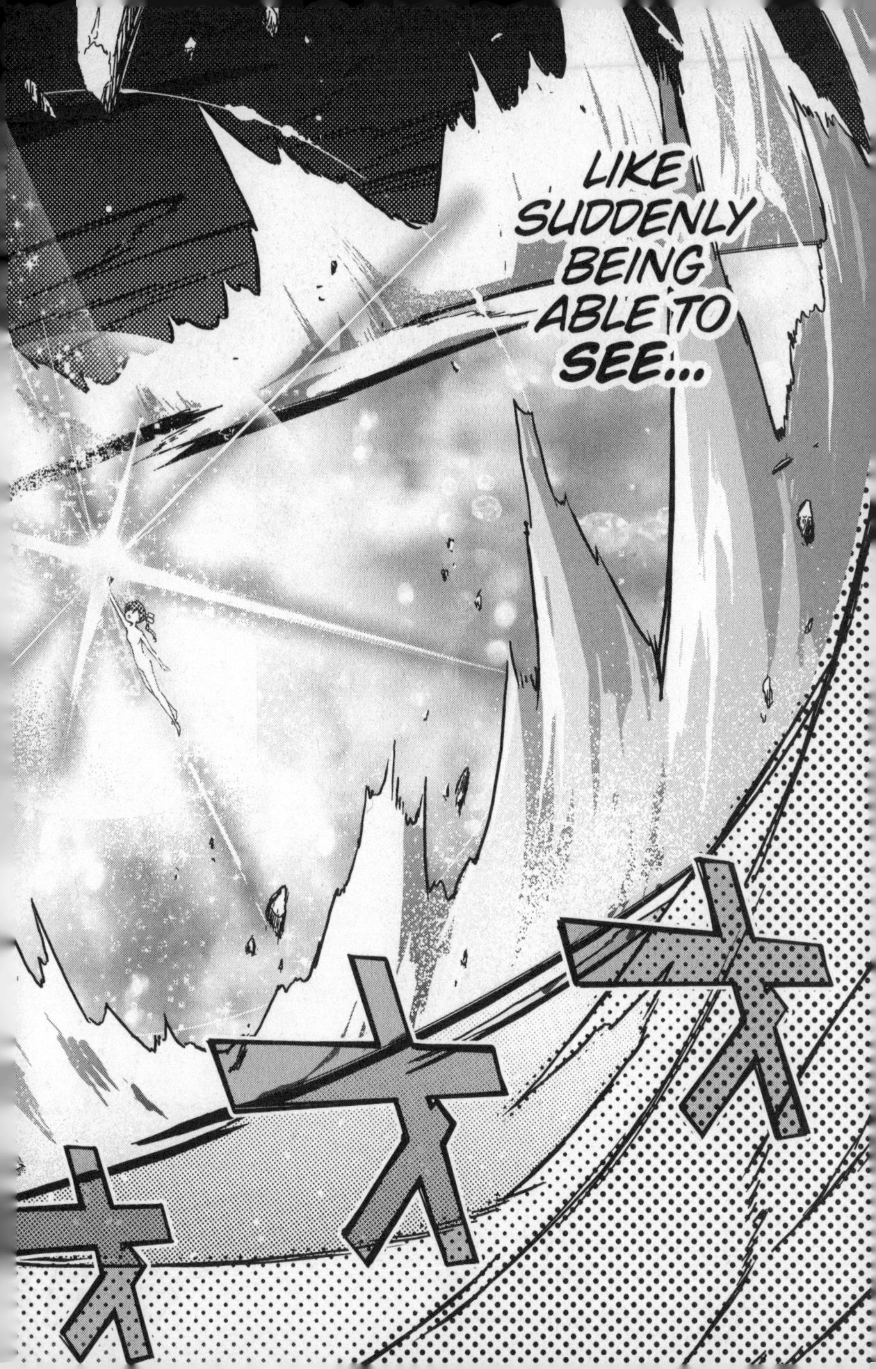
LIKE SUDDENLY BEING ABLE TO SEE...

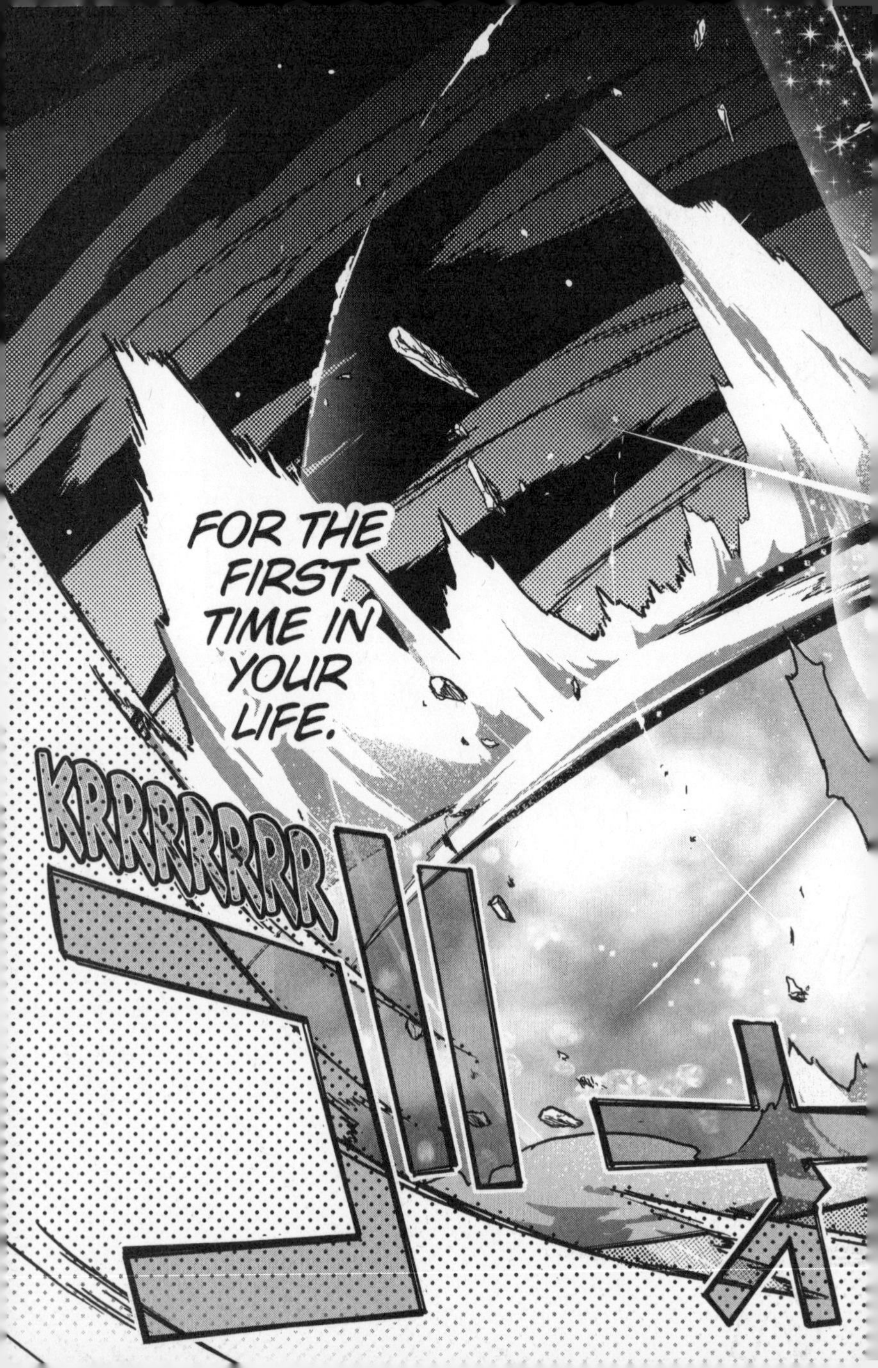
FOR THE FIRST TIME IN YOUR LIFE.
KRRRRRRRR

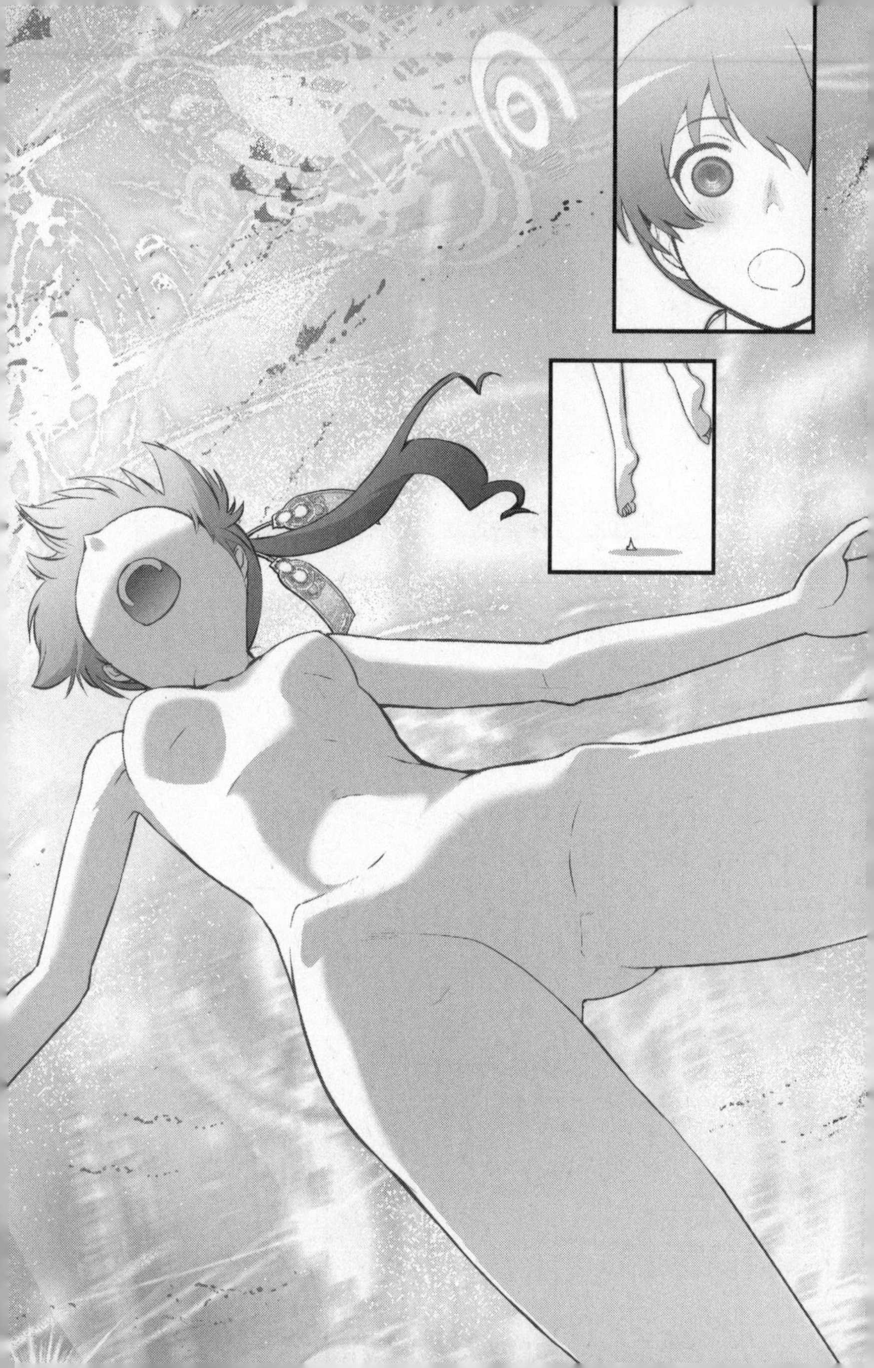

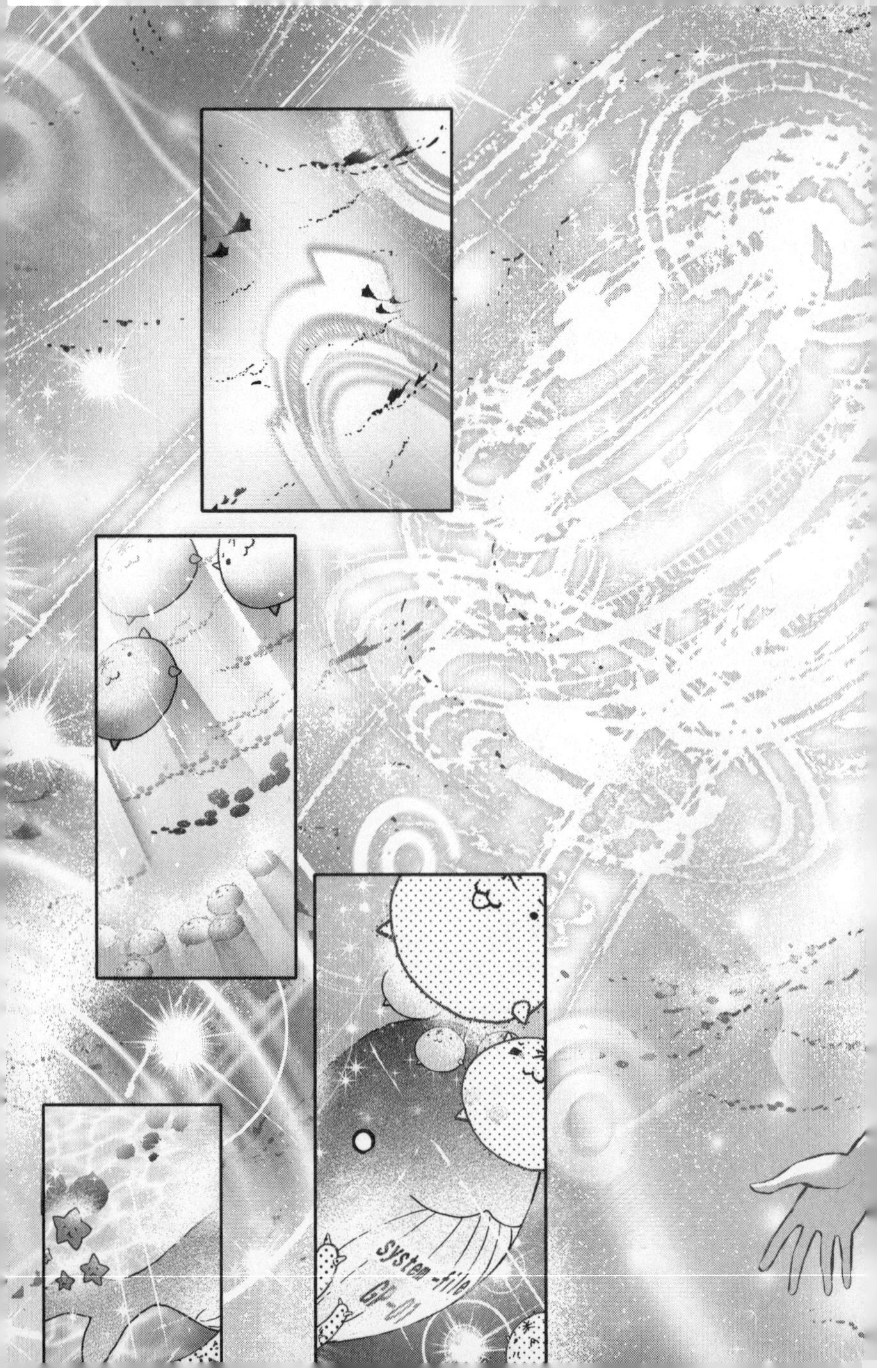
system-file
GP-01

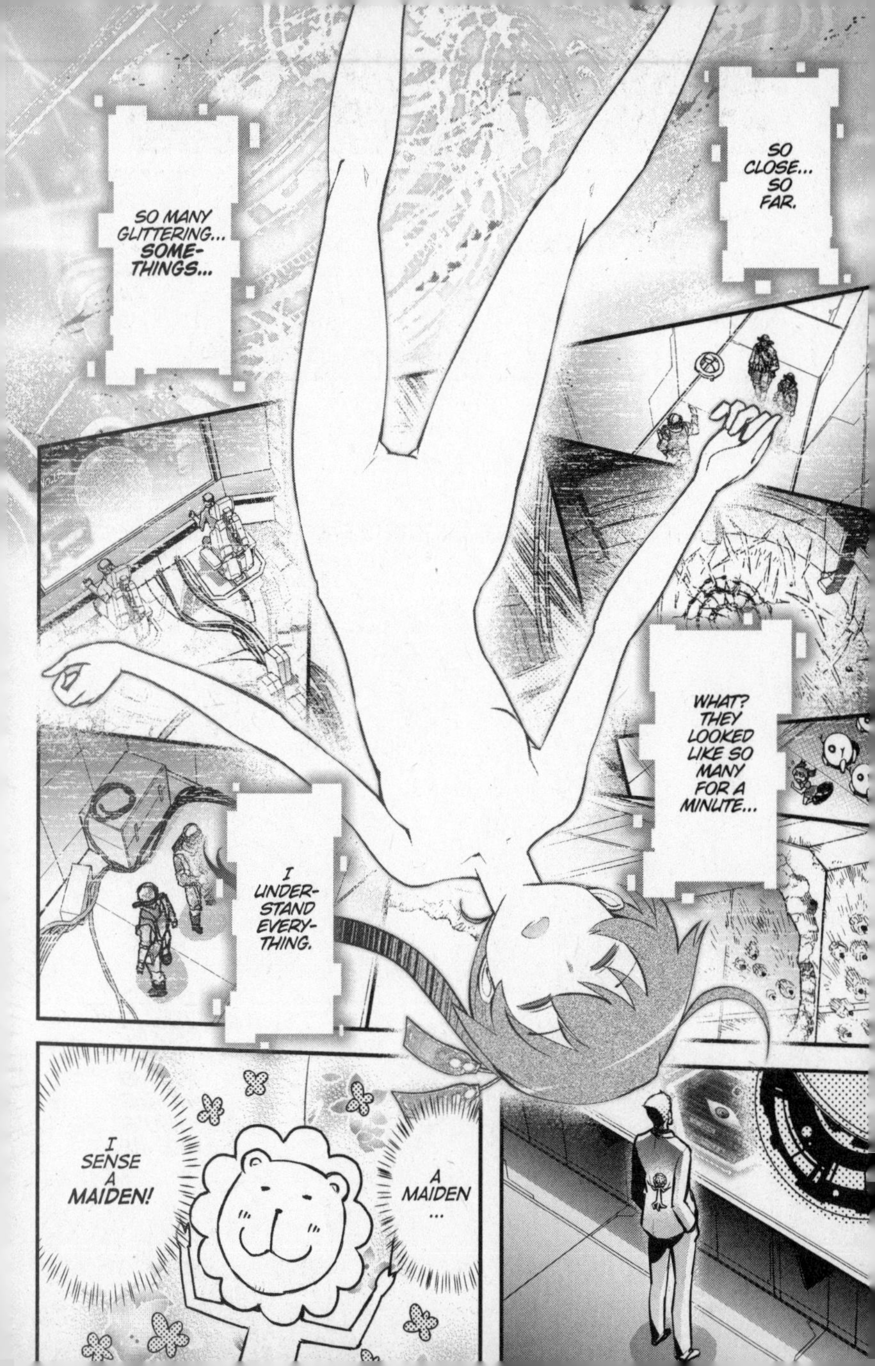
SO CLOSE... SO FAR.
SO MANY GLITTERING... SOME-THINGS...
WHAT? THEY LOOKED LIKE SO MANY FOR A MINUTE...
I UNDER-STAND EVERY-THING.
A MAIDEN ...
I SENSE A MAIDEN!

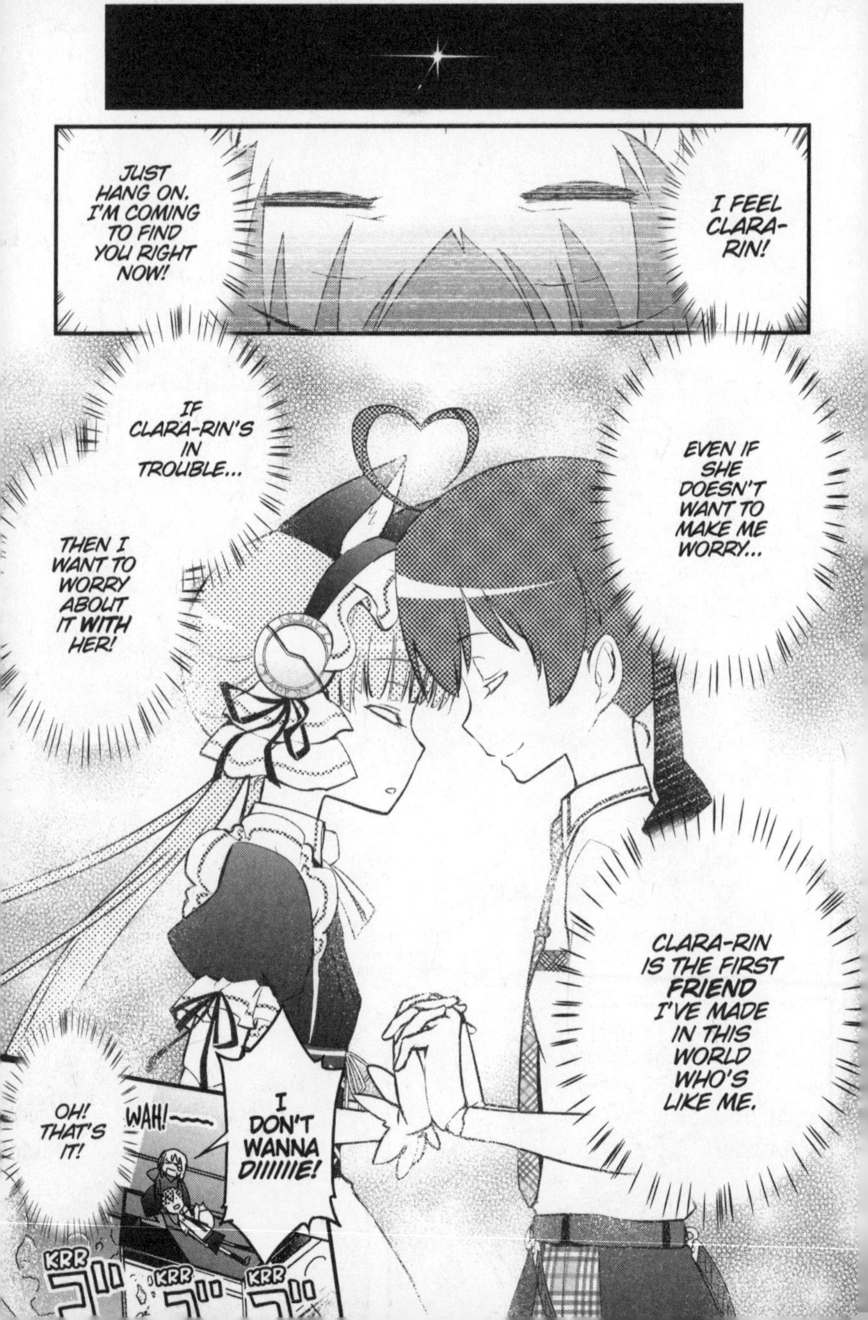
I FEEL CLARA-RIN!
JUST HANG ON. I'M COMING TO FIND YOU RIGHT NOW!
EVEN IF SHE DOESN'T WANT TO MAKE ME WORRY...
IF CLARA-RIN'S IN TROUBLE...
THEN I WANT TO WORRY ABOUT IT WITH HER!
CLARA-RIN IS THE FIRST FRIEND I'VE MADE IN THIS WORLD WHO'S LIKE ME.
I DON'T WANNA DIIIIIIE!
WAH!~~~
OH! THAT'S IT!
KRR
KRR
KRR

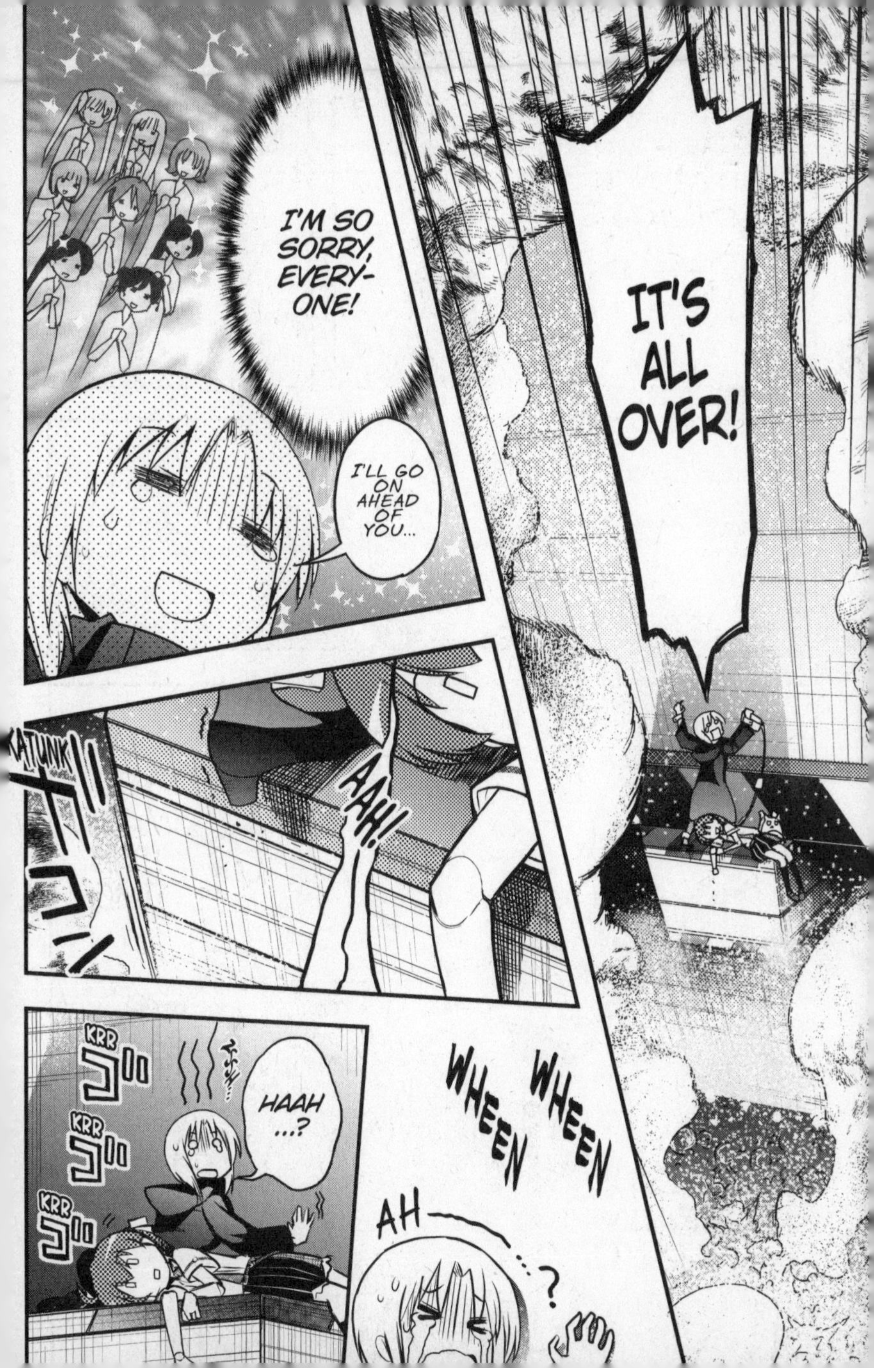
IT'S ALL OVER!
I'M SO SORRY, EVERY-ONE!
I'LL GO ON AHEAD OF YOU...
AAH!
KATUNK
WHEEN WHEEN
AH—...?
HAAH ...?
KRR
KRR
KRR

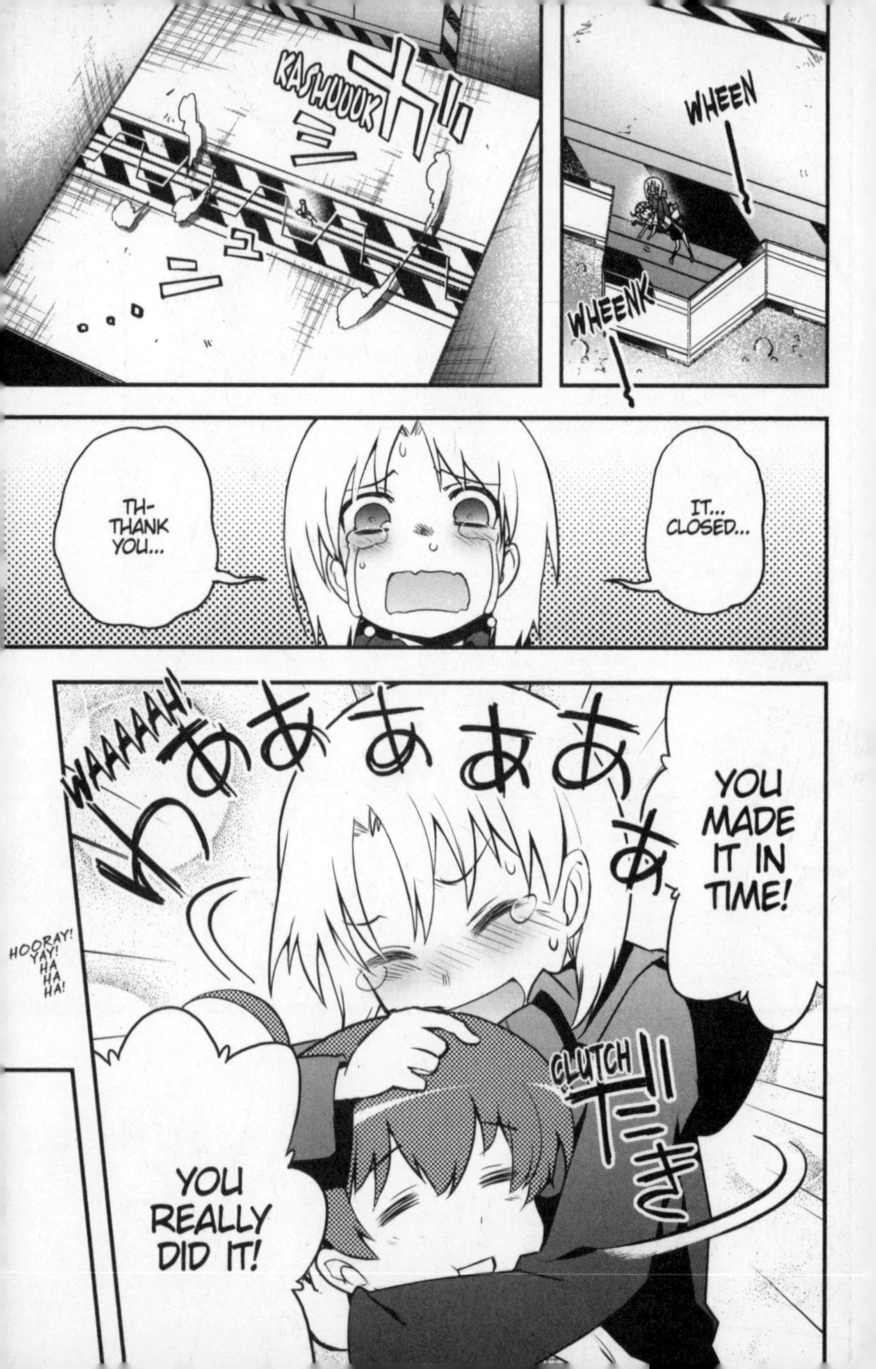
WHEEN
WHEENK
KASHUUUK
IT... CLOSED...
TH- THANK YOU...
YOU MADE IT IN TIME!
WAAAAAH!
わああああああ
HOORAY! YAY! HA HA HA!
CLUTCH
だき
YOU REALLY DID IT!

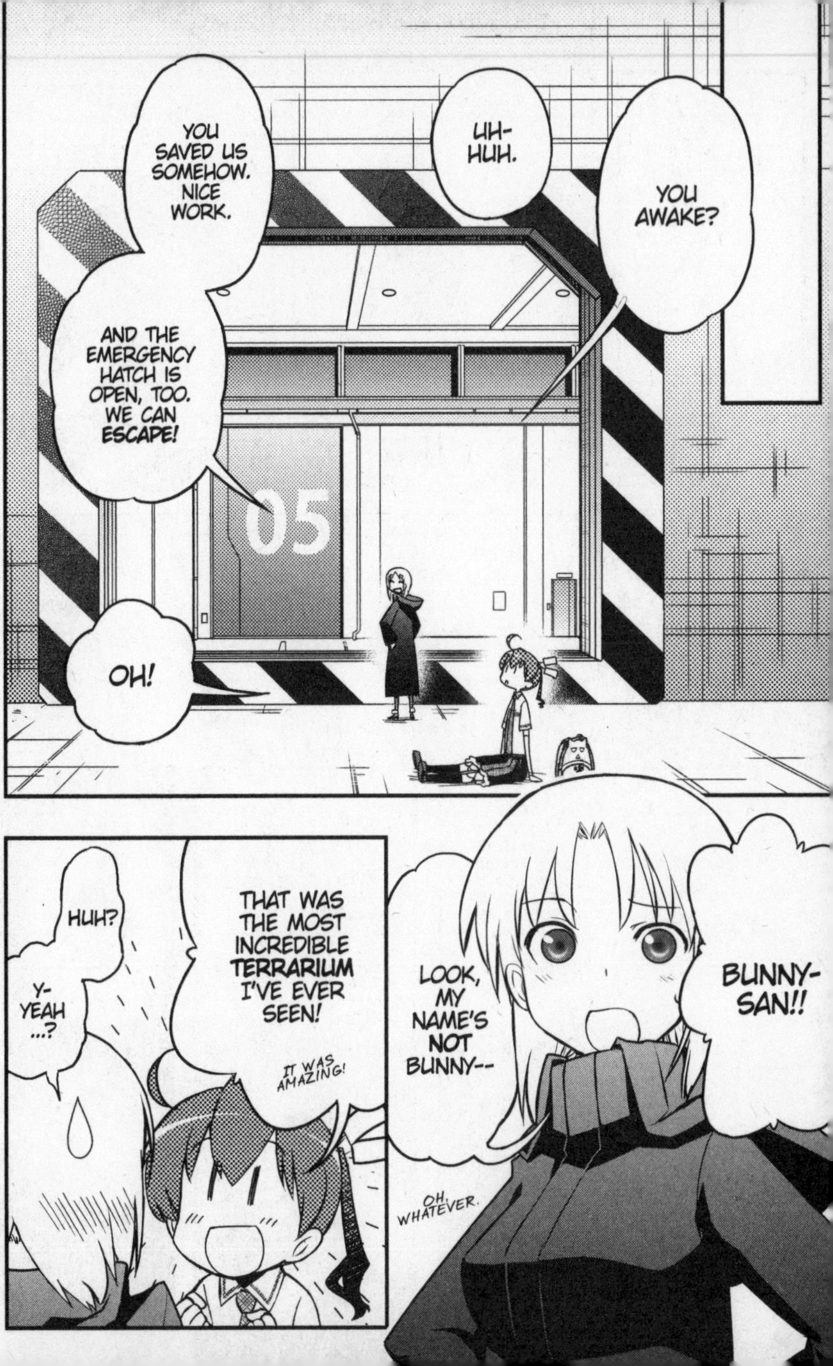
YOU AWAKE?
UH-HUH.
YOU SAVED US SOMEHOW. NICE WORK.
AND THE EMERGENCY HATCH IS OPEN, TOO. WE CAN ESCAPE!
05
OH!
BUNNY-SAN!!
LOOK, MY NAME'S NOT BUNNY--
OH, WHATEVER.
THAT WAS THE MOST INCREDIBLE TERRARIUM I'VE EVER SEEN!
IT WAS AMAZING!
HUH?
Y-YEAH ...?

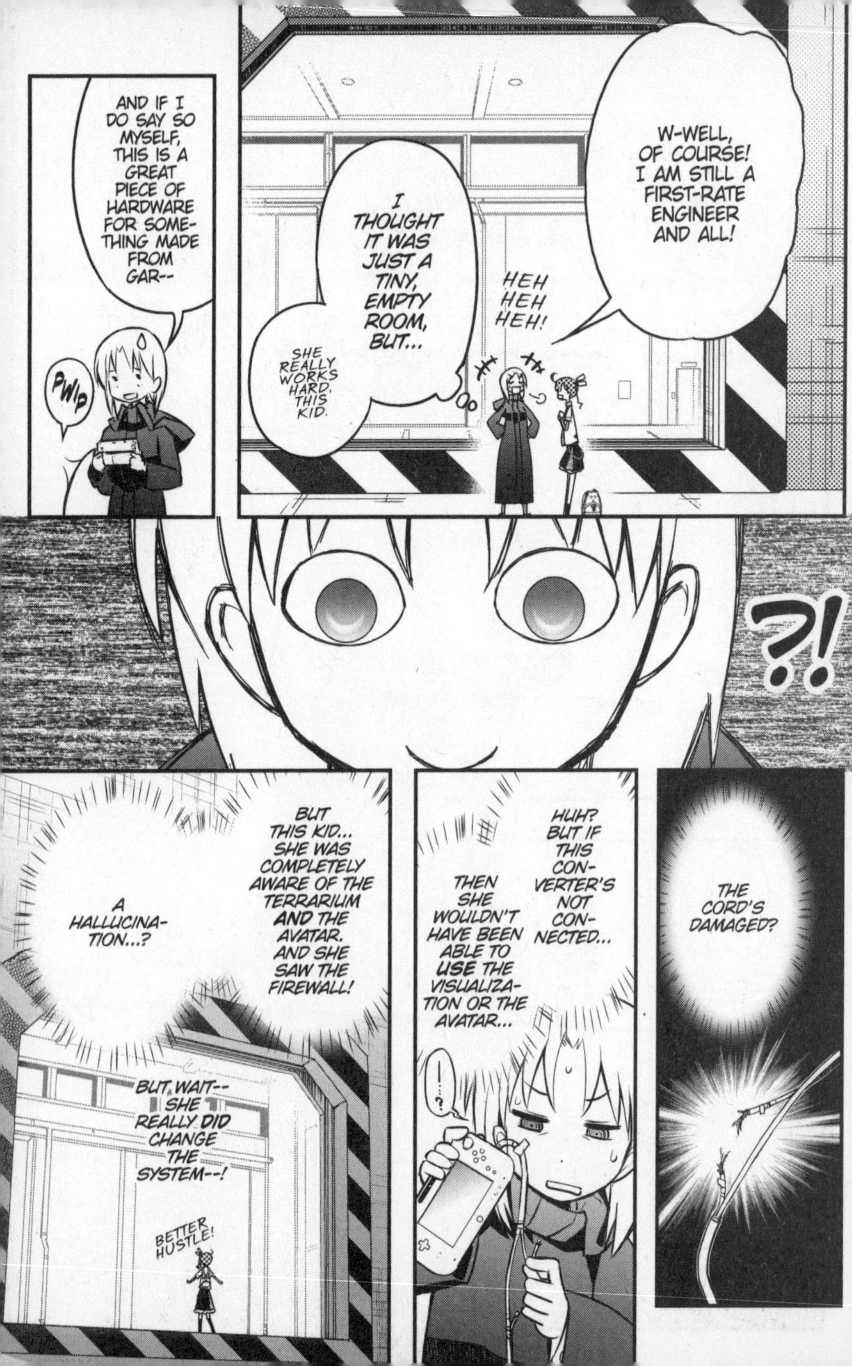
W-WELL, OF COURSE! I AM STILL A FIRST-RATE ENGINEER AND ALL!
HEH HEH HEH!
I THOUGHT IT WAS JUST A TINY, EMPTY ROOM, BUT...
SHE REALLY WORKS HARD, THIS KID.
AND IF I DO SAY SO MYSELF, THIS IS A GREAT PIECE OF HARDWARE FOR SOMETHING MADE FROM GAR--
PWIP
?!
THE CORD'S DAMAGED?
HUH? BUT IF THIS CONVERTER'S NOT CONNECTED...
THEN SHE WOULDN'T HAVE BEEN ABLE TO USE THE VISUALIZATION OR THE AVATAR...
!
?
BUT THIS KID... SHE WAS COMPLETELY AWARE OF THE TERRARIUM AND THE AVATAR. AND SHE SAW THE FIREWALL!
A HALLUCINATION...?
BUT, WAIT-- SHE REALLY DID CHANGE THE SYSTEM--!
BETTER HUSTLE!

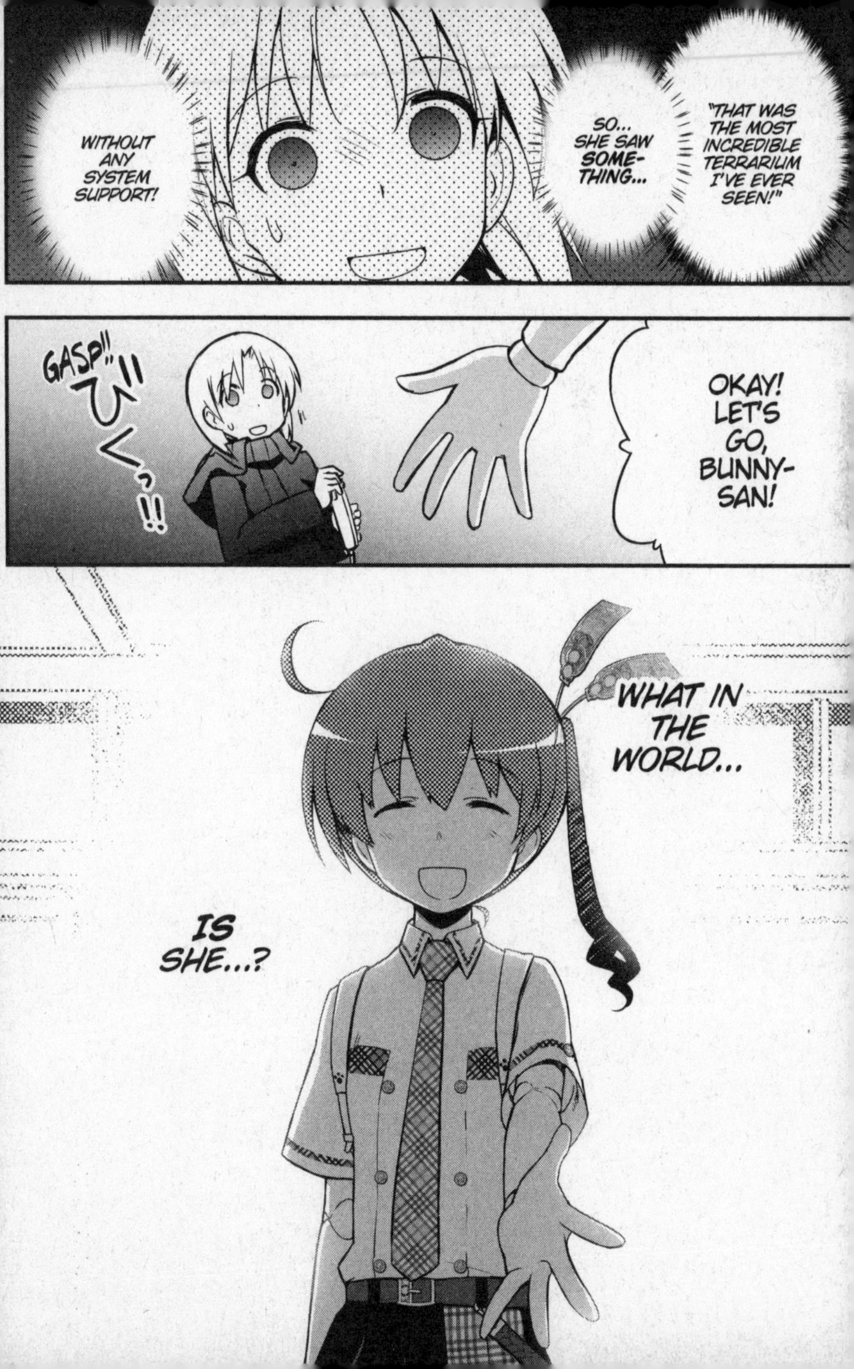
"THAT WAS THE MOST INCREDIBLE TERRARIUM I'VE EVER SEEN!"
SO... SHE SAW SOME-THING...
WITHOUT ANY SYSTEM SUPPORT!
OKAY! LET'S GO, BUNNY-SAN!
GASP!!
びくっ!!
WHAT IN THE WORLD...
IS SHE...?

GHOST URN

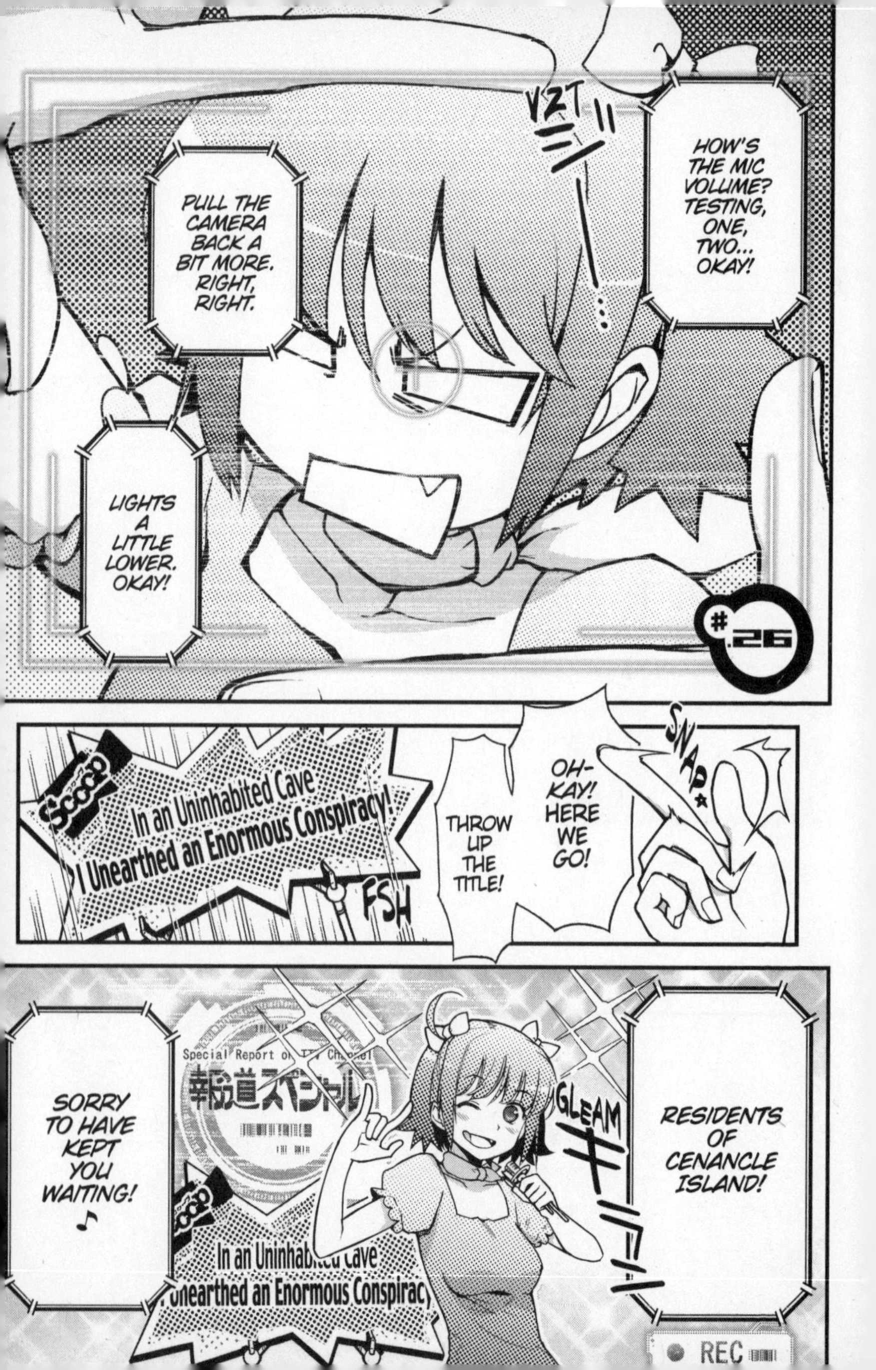
HOW'S THE MIC VOLUME? TESTING, ONE, TWO... OKAY!
VZT
PULL THE CAMERA BACK A BIT MORE. RIGHT, RIGHT.
LIGHTS A LITTLE LOWER. OKAY!
#.26
SNAP☆
OH-KAY! HERE WE GO!
THROW UP THE TITLE!
FSH
SCOOP
In an Uninhabited Cave I Unearthed an Enormous Conspiracy!
RESIDENTS OF CENANCLE ISLAND!
GLEAM
報道スペシャル
SORRY TO HAVE KEPT YOU WAITING! ♪
REC

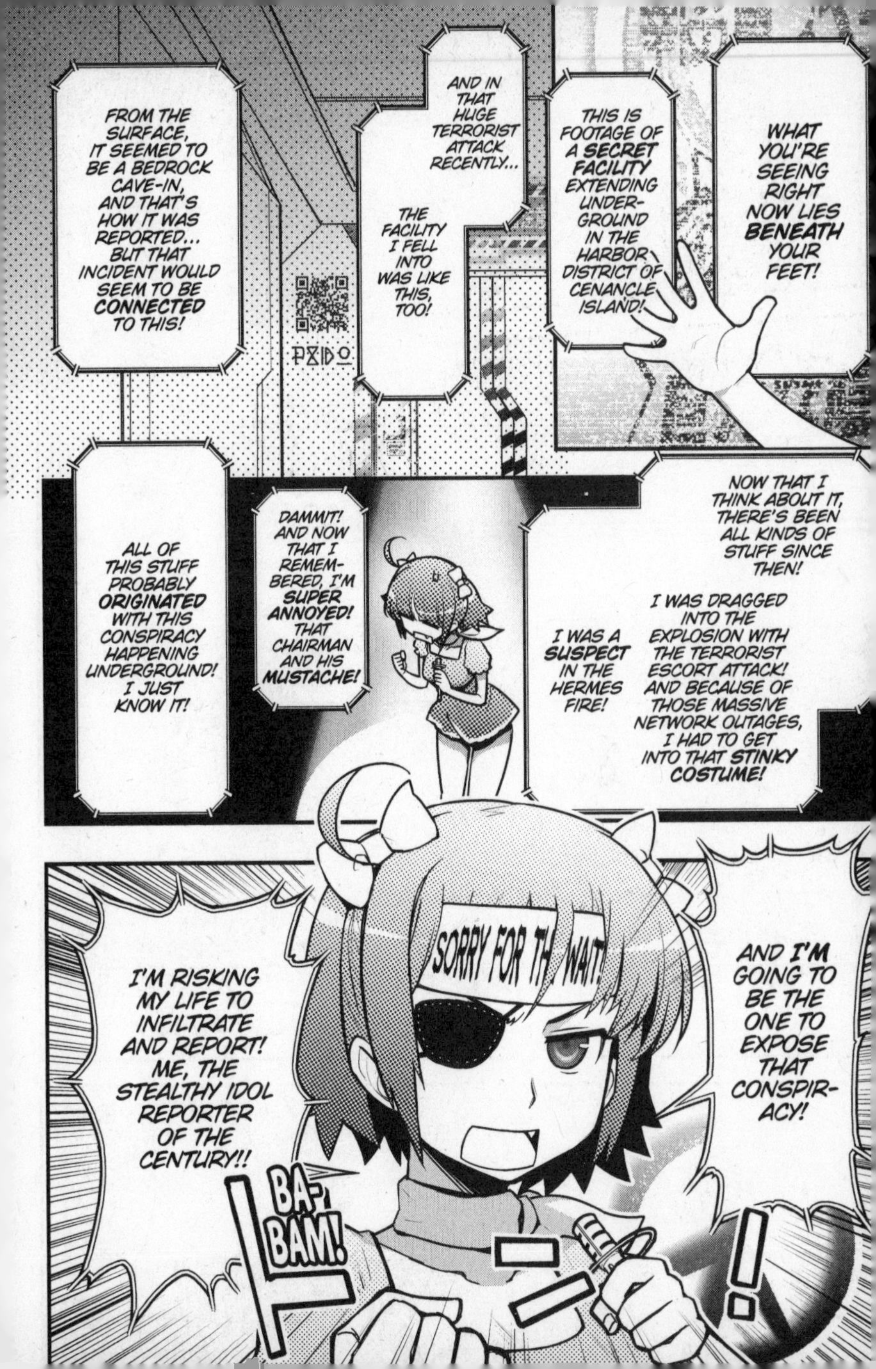
WHAT YOU'RE SEEING RIGHT NOW LIES BENEATH YOUR FEET!
THIS IS FOOTAGE OF A SECRET FACILITY EXTENDING UNDERGROUND IN THE HARBOR DISTRICT OF CENANCLE ISLAND!
AND IN THAT HUGE TERRORIST ATTACK RECENTLY...
THE FACILITY I FELL INTO WAS LIKE THIS, TOO!
FROM THE SURFACE, IT SEEMED TO BE A BEDROCK CAVE-IN, AND THAT'S HOW IT WAS REPORTED... BUT THAT INCIDENT WOULD SEEM TO BE CONNECTED TO THIS!
NOW THAT I THINK ABOUT IT, THERE'S BEEN ALL KINDS OF STUFF SINCE THEN!
I WAS DRAGGED INTO THE EXPLOSION WITH THE TERRORIST ESCORT ATTACK! AND BECAUSE OF THOSE MASSIVE NETWORK OUTAGES, I HAD TO GET INTO THAT STINKY COSTUME!
I WAS A SUSPECT IN THE HERMES FIRE!
DAMMIT! AND NOW THAT I REMEMBERED, I'M SUPER ANNOYED! THAT CHAIRMAN AND HIS MUSTACHE!
ALL OF THIS STUFF PROBABLY ORIGINATED WITH THIS CONSPIRACY HAPPENING UNDERGROUND! I JUST KNOW IT!
AND I'M GOING TO BE THE ONE TO EXPOSE THAT CONSPIRACY!
SORRY FOR TH WAIT!
I'M RISKING MY LIFE TO INFILTRATE AND REPORT! ME, THE STEALTHY IDOL REPORTER OF THE CENTURY!!
BA-BAM!

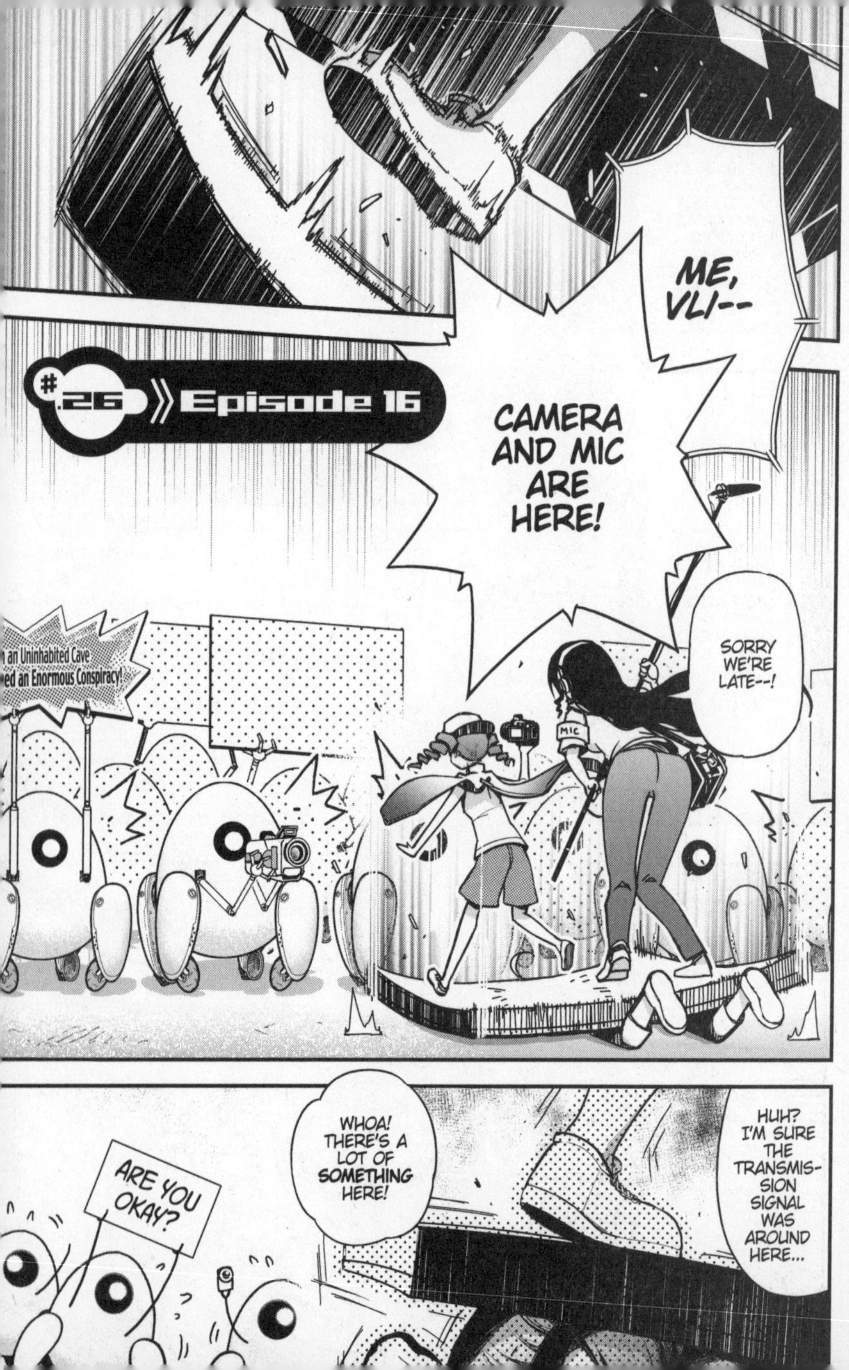
ME, VLI--
#.26 Episode 16
CAMERA AND MIC ARE HERE!
SORRY WE'RE LATE--!
an Uninhabited Cave
an Enormous Conspiracy!
HUH? I'M SURE THE TRANSMIS-SION SIGNAL WAS AROUND HERE...
WHOA! THERE'S A LOT OF SOMETHING HERE!
ARE YOU OKAY?

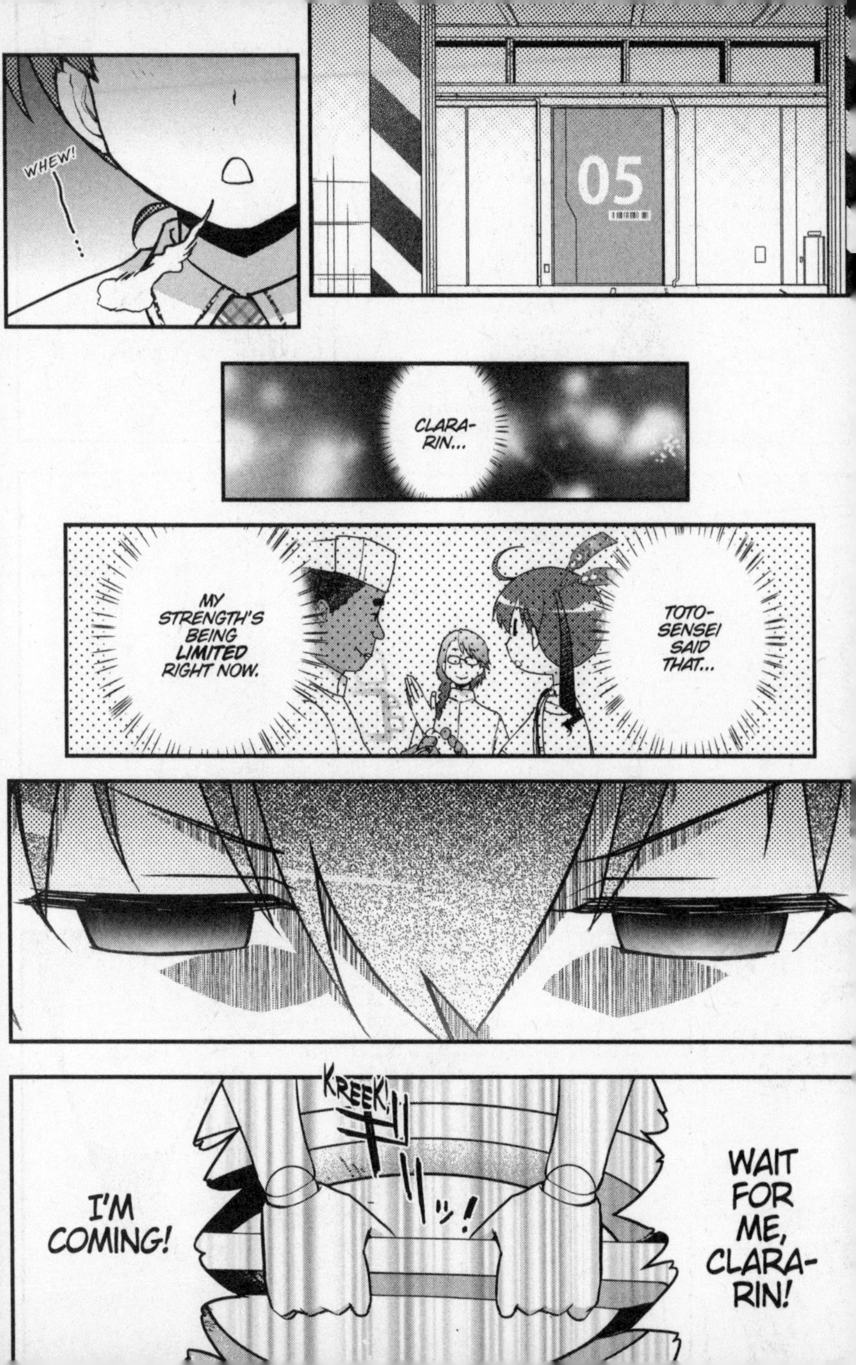

WHEW!
...
CLARA-RIN...
TOTO-SENSEI SAID THAT...
MY STRENGTH'S BEING LIMITED RIGHT NOW.
WAIT FOR ME, CLARA-RIN!
KREEK!!
I'M COMING!

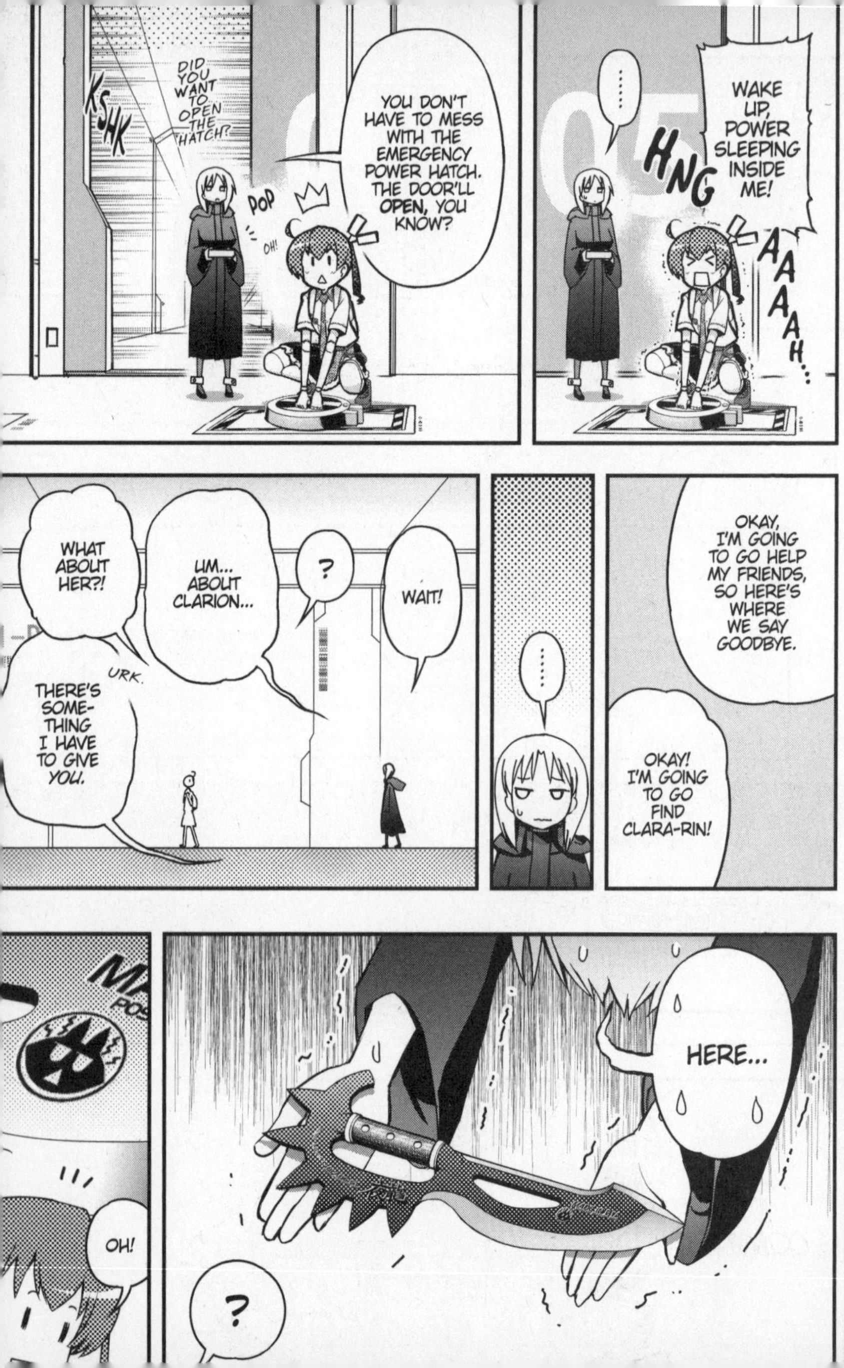

WAKE UP, POWER SLEEPING INSIDE ME!
......
HNG
AAAAAH...
YOU DON'T HAVE TO MESS WITH THE EMERGENCY POWER HATCH. THE DOOR'LL OPEN, YOU KNOW?
POP
OH!
DID YOU WANT TO OPEN THE HATCH?
KSHK
OKAY, I'M GOING TO GO HELP MY FRIENDS, SO HERE'S WHERE WE SAY GOODBYE.
OKAY! I'M GOING TO GO FIND CLARA-RIN!
......
WAIT!
?
UM... ABOUT CLARION...
WHAT ABOUT HER?!
URK.
THERE'S SOME-THING I HAVE TO GIVE YOU.
HERE...
?
OH!

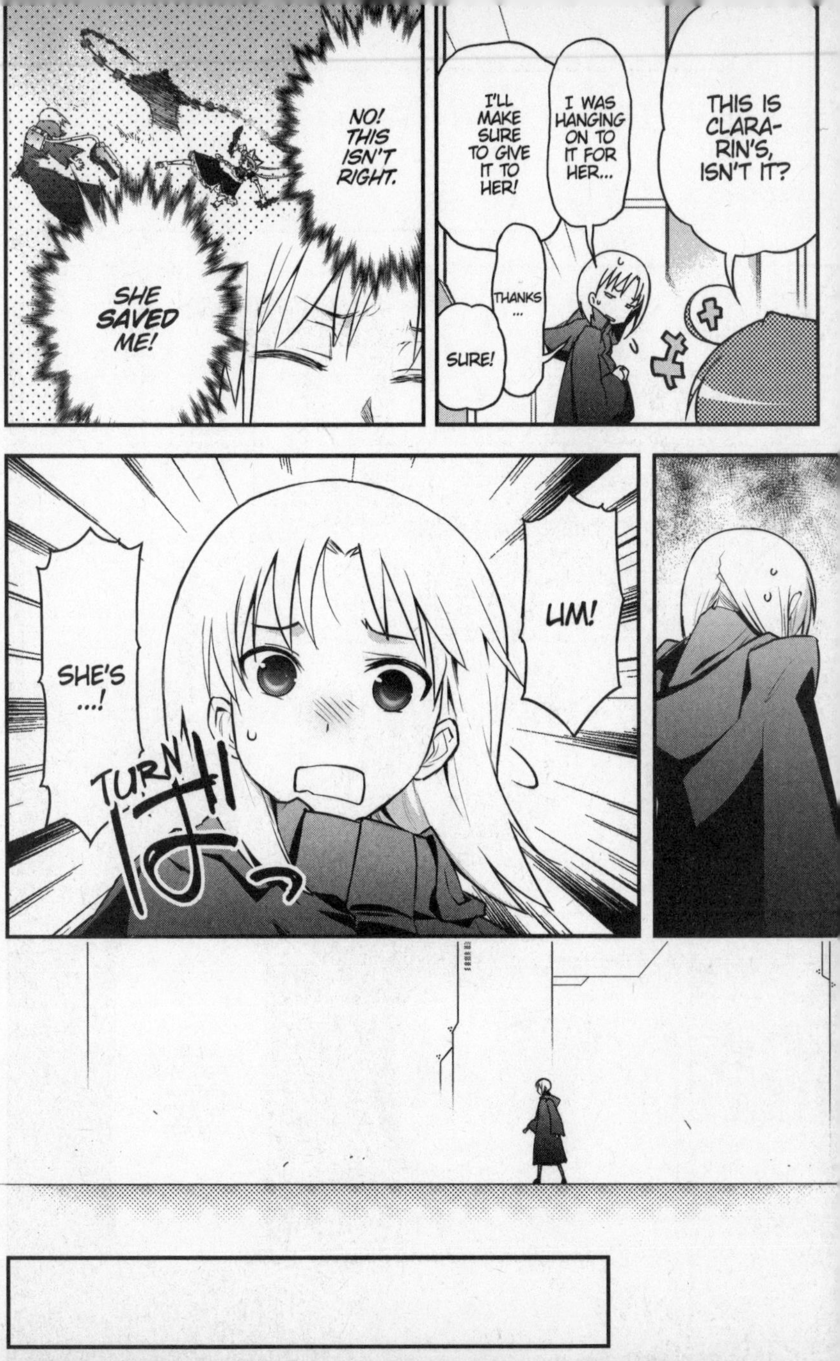
THIS IS CLARA-RIN'S, ISN'T IT?
I WAS HANGING ON TO IT FOR HER...
I'LL MAKE SURE TO GIVE IT TO HER!
THANKS...
SURE!
NO! THIS ISN'T RIGHT.
SHE SAVED ME!
UM!
SHE'S ...!
TURN
はっ

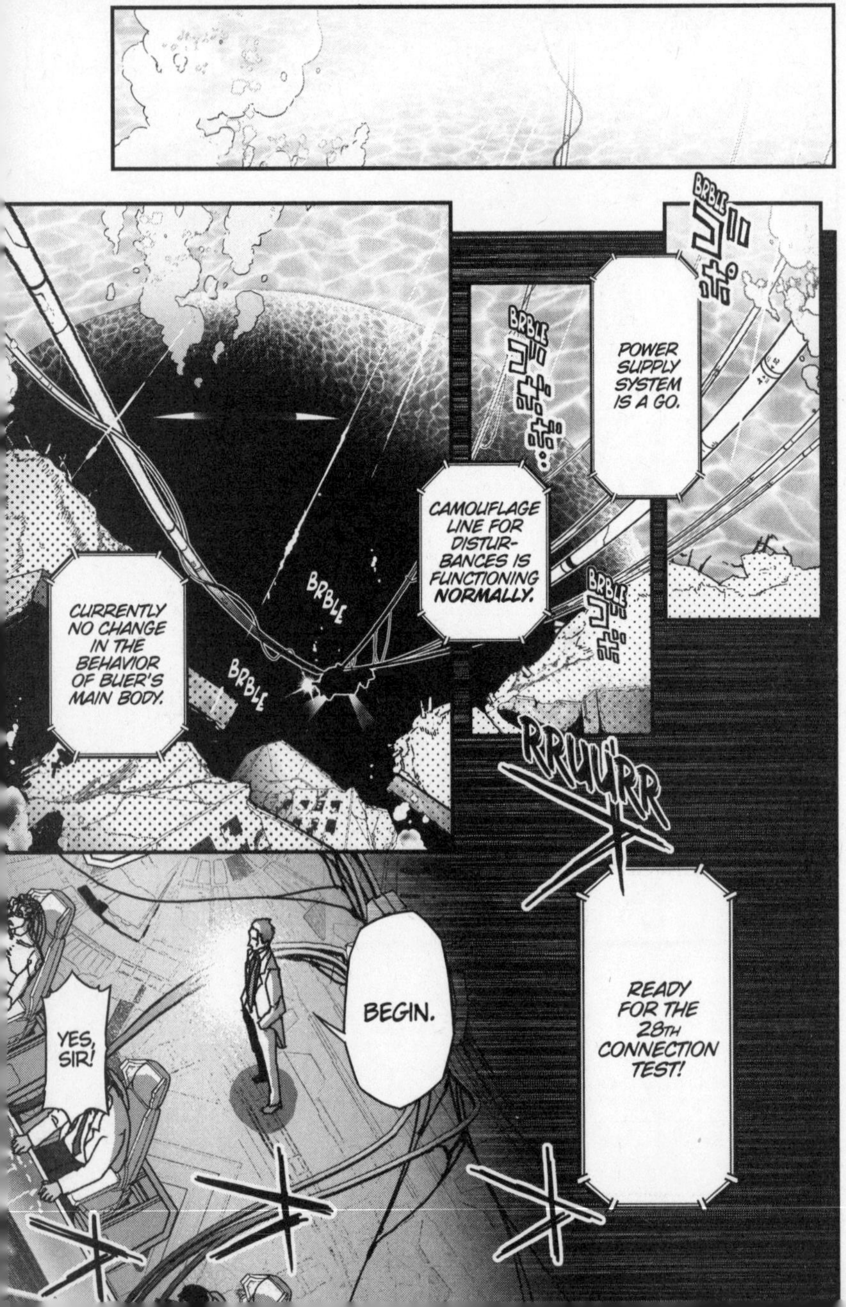
BRBLE
POWER SUPPLY SYSTEM IS A GO.
BRBLE
BRBLE
CAMOUFLAGE LINE FOR DISTURBANCES IS FUNCTIONING NORMALLY.
BRBLE
BRBLE
CURRENTLY NO CHANGE IN THE BEHAVIOR OF BUER'S MAIN BODY.
RRUURR
READY FOR THE 28TH CONNECTION TEST!
BEGIN.
YES, SIR!

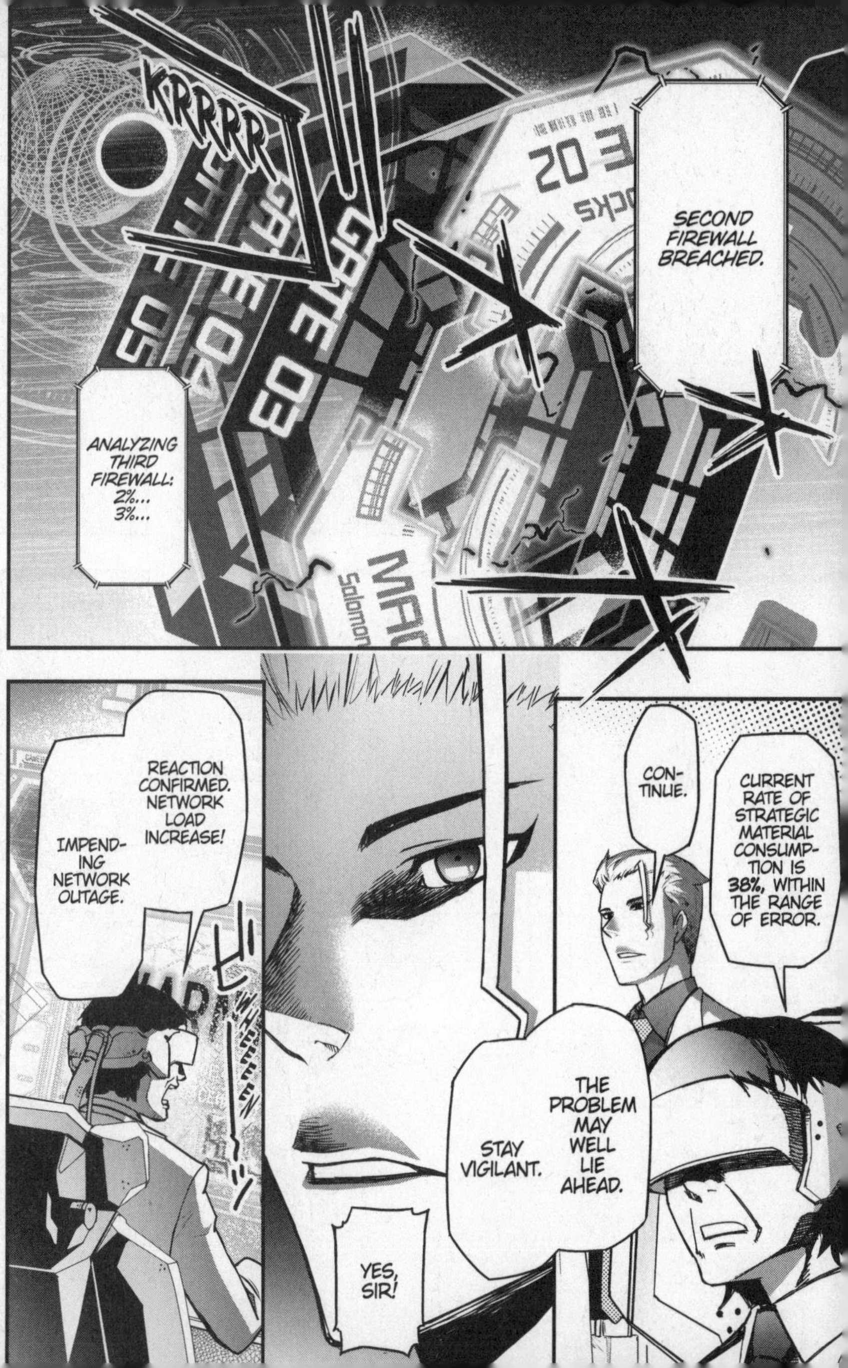
SECOND FIREWALL BREACHED.
KRRRRR
GATE 03
ANALYZING THIRD FIREWALL: 2%... 3%...
CURRENT RATE OF STRATEGIC MATERIAL CONSUMPTION IS 38%, WITHIN THE RANGE OF ERROR.
CONTINUE.
THE PROBLEM MAY WELL LIE AHEAD.
STAY VIGILANT.
YES, SIR!
REACTION CONFIRMED. NETWORK LOAD INCREASE!
IMPENDING NETWORK OUTAGE.

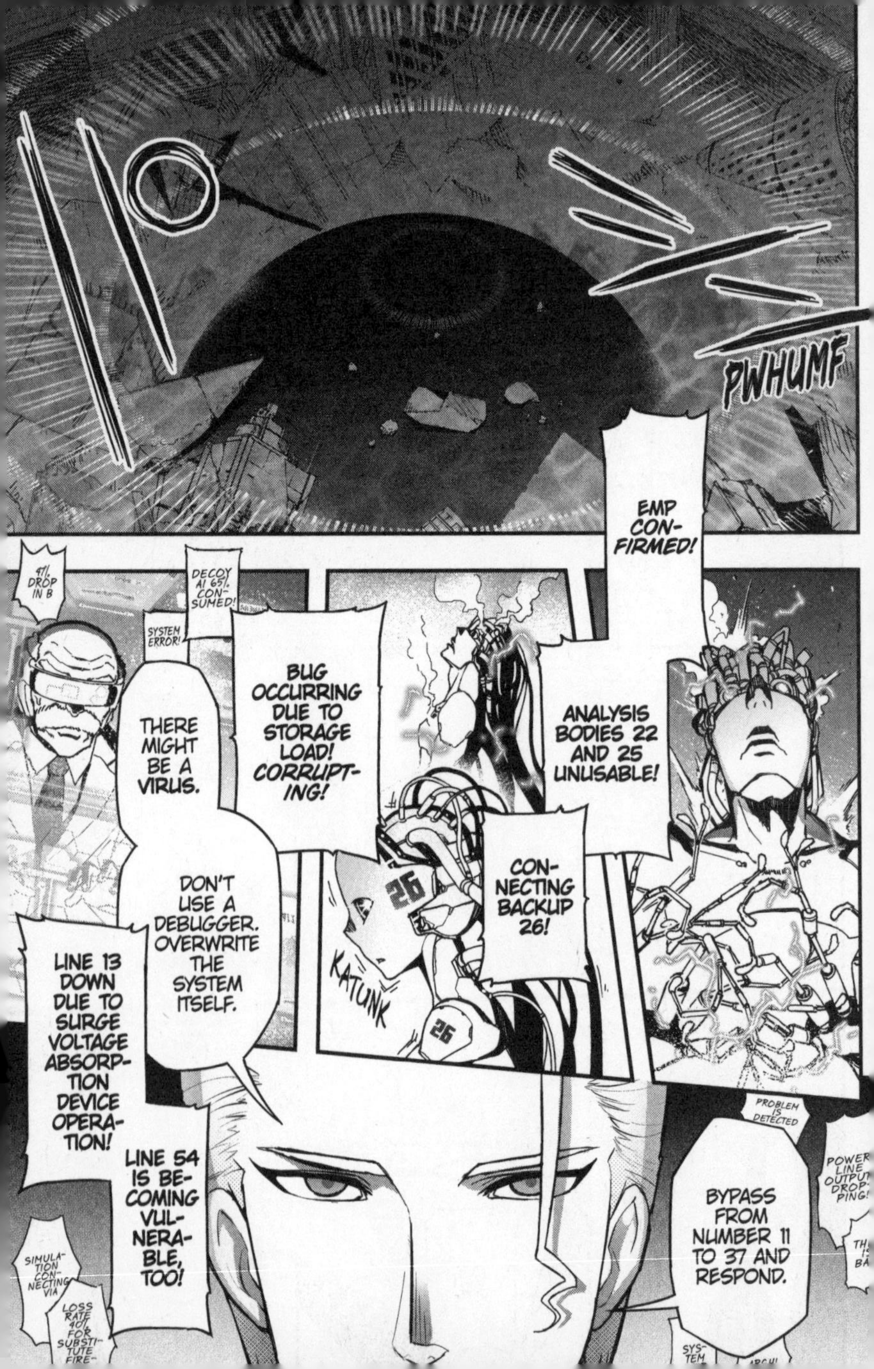
PWHUMF
EMP CONFIRMED!
ANALYSIS BODIES 22 AND 25 UNUSABLE!
BUG OCCURRING DUE TO STORAGE LOAD! CORRUPTING!
DECOY AI 65% CONSUMED!
SYSTEM ERROR!
47% DROP IN B
CONNECTING BACKUP 26!
KATUNK
THERE MIGHT BE A VIRUS.
DON'T USE A DEBUGGER. OVERWRITE THE SYSTEM ITSELF.
LINE 13 DOWN DUE TO SURGE VOLTAGE ABSORPTION DEVICE OPERATION!
PROBLEM IS DETECTED
POWER LINE OUTPUT DROPPING!
BYPASS FROM NUMBER 11 TO 37 AND RESPOND.
LINE 54 IS BECOMING VULNERABLE, TOO!
SIMULATION CONNECTING VIA
LOSS RATE 40% FOR SUBSTITUTE FIRE-
SYSTEM

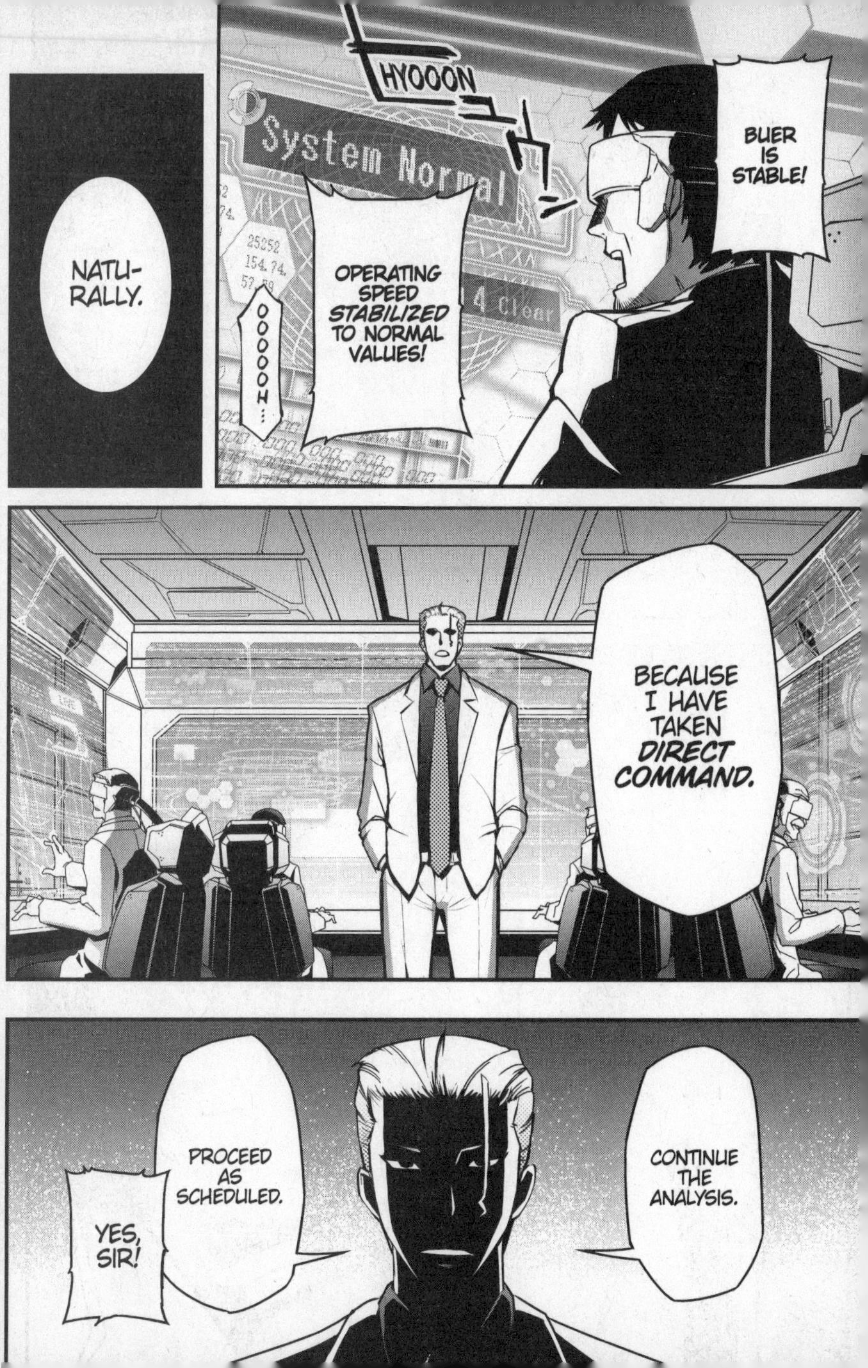
BUER IS STABLE!
HYOOON
System Normal
OPERATING SPEED STABILIZED TO NORMAL VALUES!
OOOOOOH...
NATU-RALLY.
BECAUSE I HAVE TAKEN DIRECT COMMAND.
CONTINUE THE ANALYSIS.
PROCEED AS SCHEDULED.
YES, SIR!

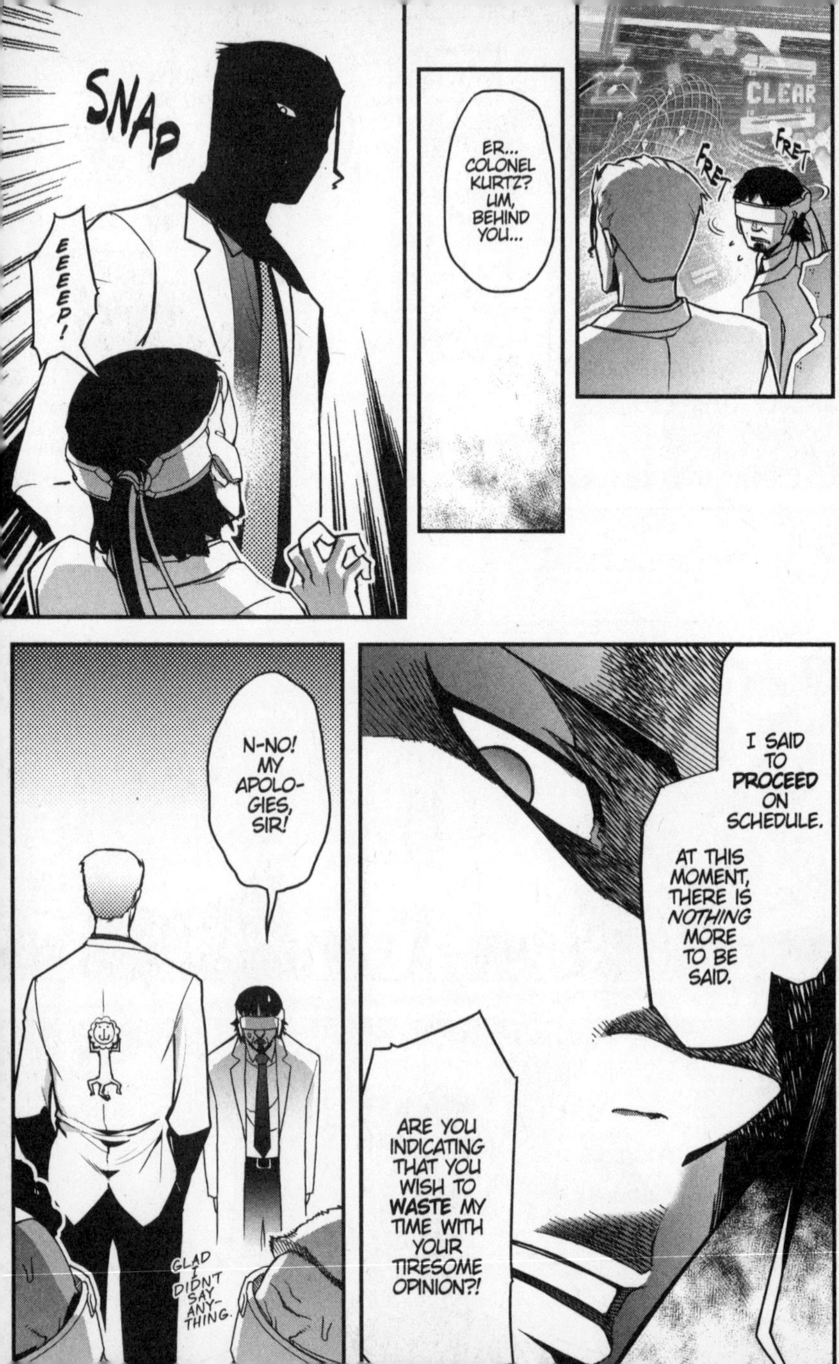
CLEAR
FRET FRET
ER... COLONEL KURTZ? UM, BEHIND YOU...
SNAP
EEEEEP!
I SAID TO PROCEED ON SCHEDULE.
AT THIS MOMENT, THERE IS NOTHING MORE TO BE SAID.
ARE YOU INDICATING THAT YOU WISH TO WASTE MY TIME WITH YOUR TIRESOME OPINION?!
N-NO! MY APOLO-GIES, SIR!
GLAD I DIDN'T SAY ANY-THING.

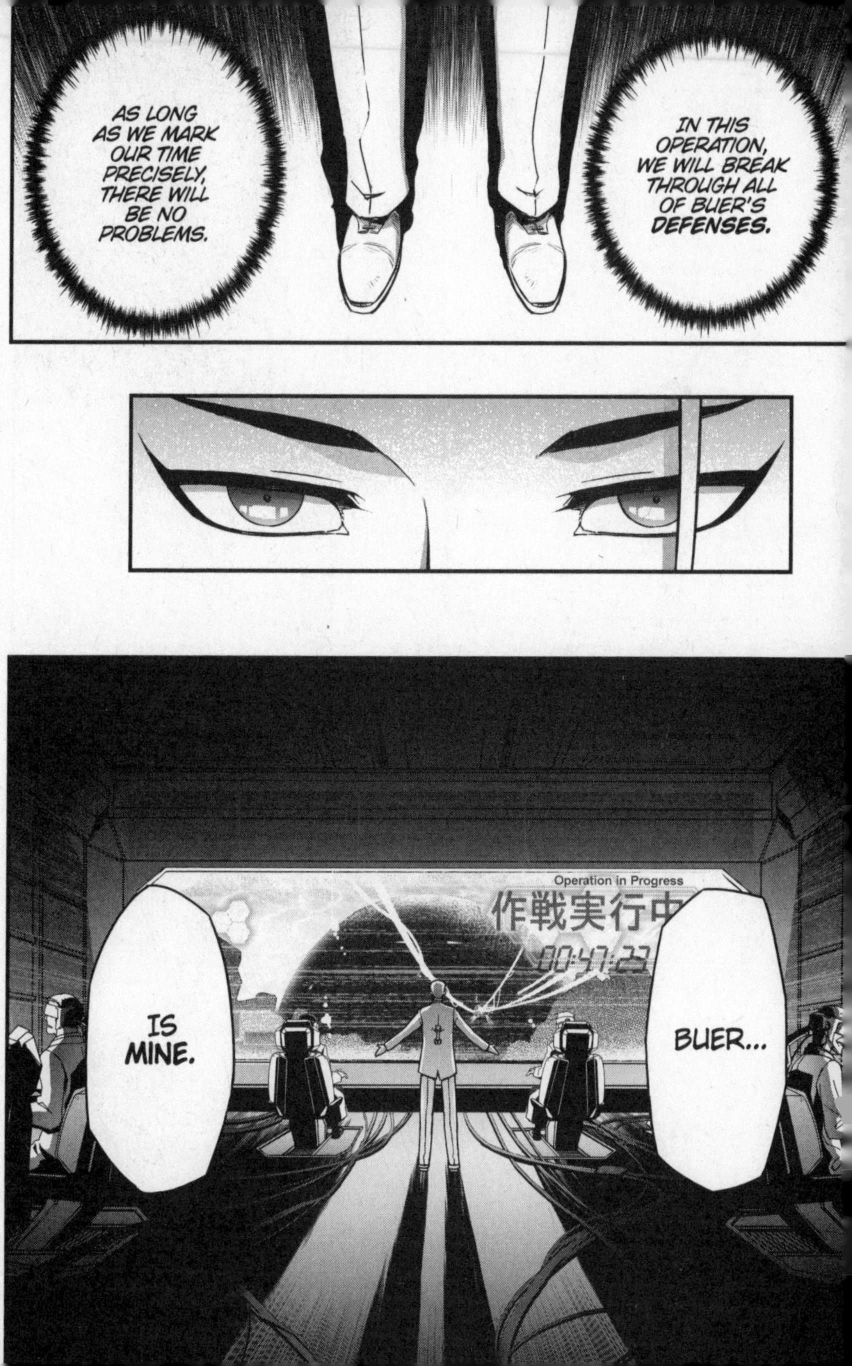
IN THIS OPERATION, WE WILL BREAK THROUGH ALL OF BUER'S DEFENSES.
AS LONG AS WE MARK OUR TIME PRECISELY, THERE WILL BE NO PROBLEMS.
Operation in Progress
作戦実行中
00:47:23
BUER...
IS MINE.

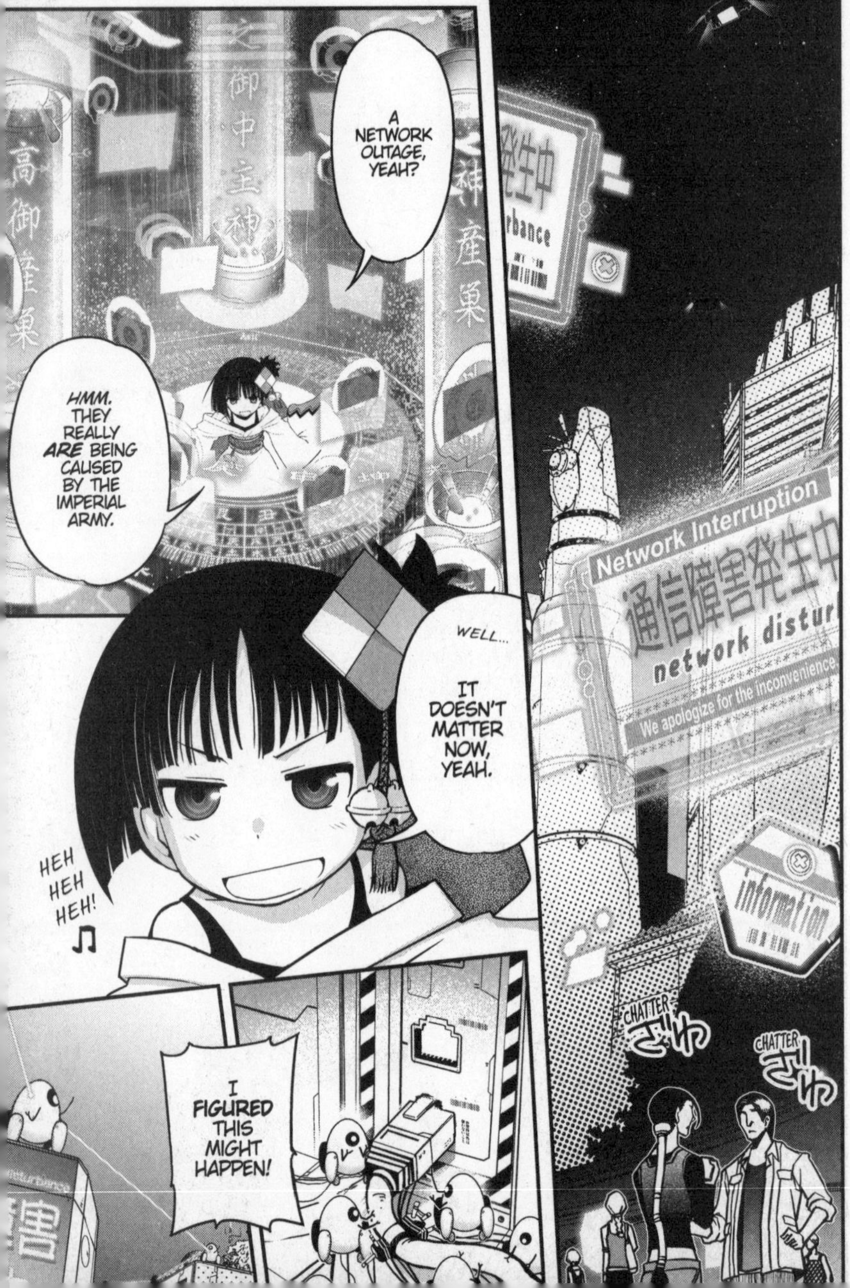
発生中
rbance
Network Interruption
通信障害発生中
network distur
We apologize for the inconvenience.
information
CHATTER ざわ
CHATTER ざわ
A NETWORK OUTAGE, YEAH?
HMM. THEY REALLY ARE BEING CAUSED BY THE IMPERIAL ARMY.
WELL... IT DOESN'T MATTER NOW, YEAH.
HEH HEH HEH! ♫
I FIGURED THIS MIGHT HAPPEN!

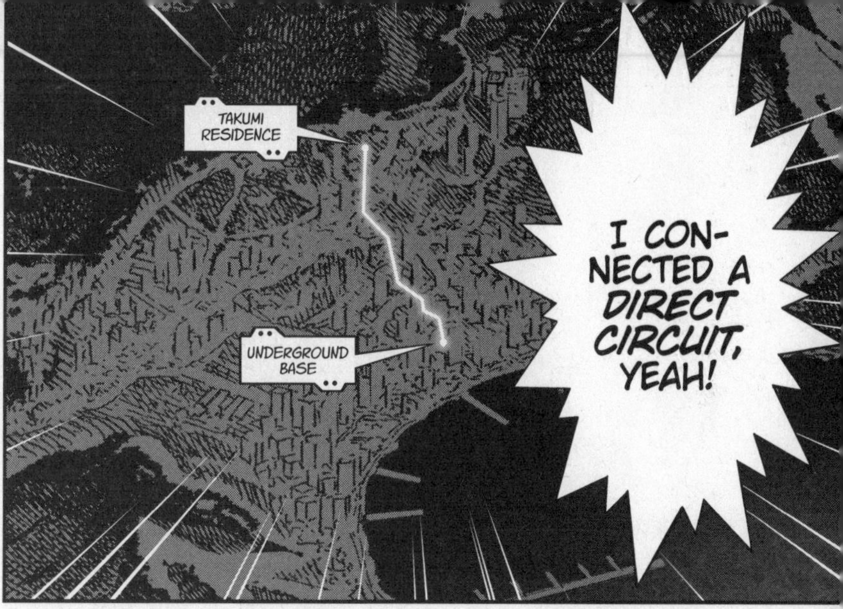
I CONNECTED A DIRECT CIRCUIT, YEAH!
TAKUMI RESIDENCE
UNDERGROUND BASE

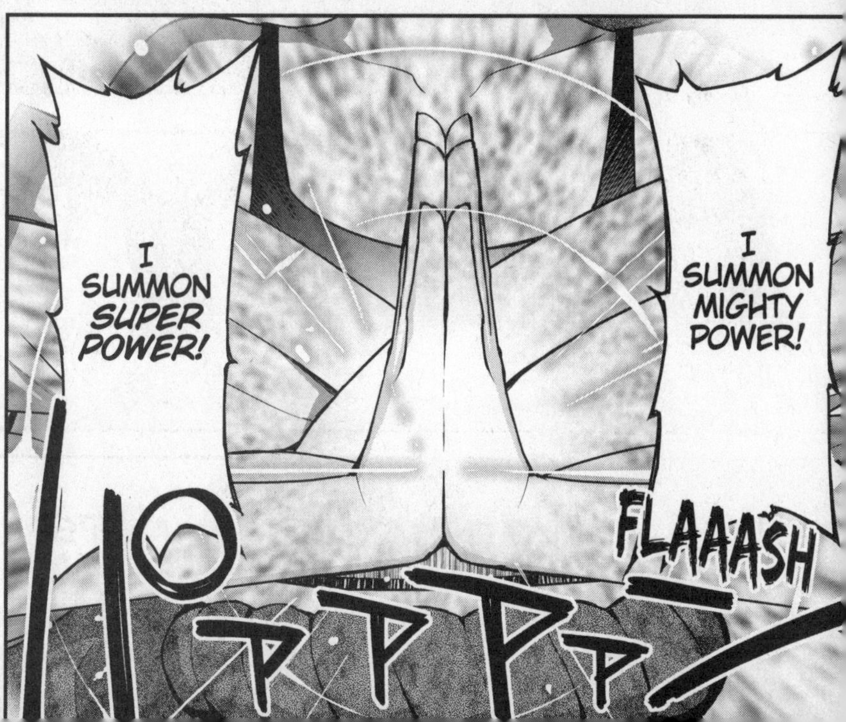
I SUMMON MIGHTY POWER!
I SUMMON SUPER POWER!
FLAAASH

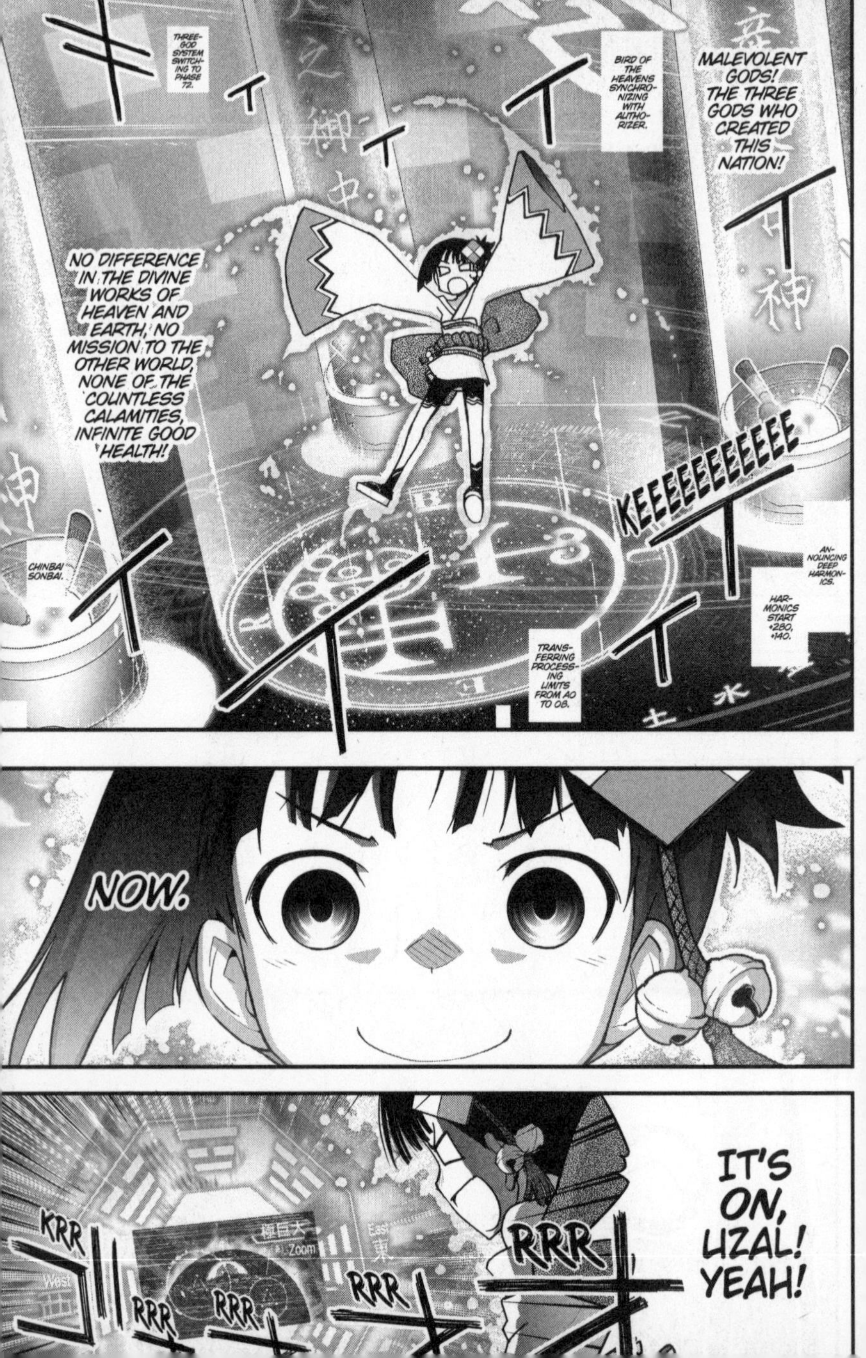
MALEVOLENT GODS! THE THREE GODS WHO CREATED THIS NATION!
BIRD OF THE HEAVENS SYNCHRONIZING WITH AUTHORIZER.
THREE-GOD SYSTEM SWITCHING TO PHASE 72.
NO DIFFERENCE IN THE DIVINE WORKS OF HEAVEN AND EARTH, NO MISSION TO THE OTHER WORLD, NONE OF THE COUNTLESS CALAMITIES, INFINITE GOOD HEALTH!
AN-NOUNCING DEEP HARMONICS.
HARMONICS START +280, +140.
KEEEEEEEEEEEE
TRANSFERRING PROCESSING LIMITS FROM A0 TO 08.
CHINBAI SONBAI.
NOW.
IT'S ON, UZAL! YEAH!
RRR
East
Zoom
KRR
West
RRR
RRR
RRR

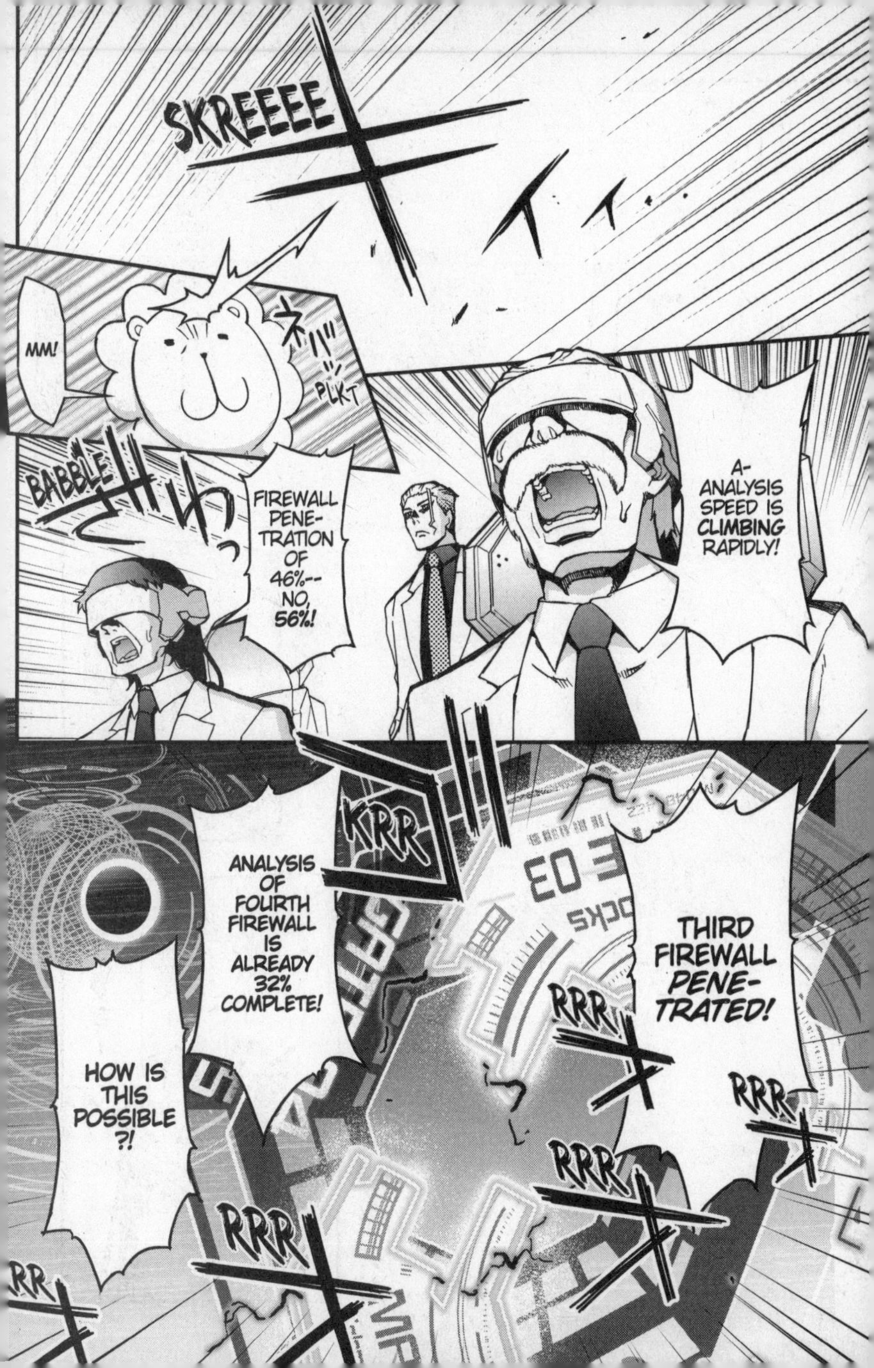
SKREEEE
A-ANALYSIS SPEED IS CLIMBING RAPIDLY!
PLKT
MM!
FIREWALL PENETRATION OF 46%--NO, 56%!
BABBLE
KRR
THIRD FIREWALL PENETRATED!
ANALYSIS OF FOURTH FIREWALL IS ALREADY 32% COMPLETE!
RRR
RRR
RRR
HOW IS THIS POSSIBLE?!
RRR
RR

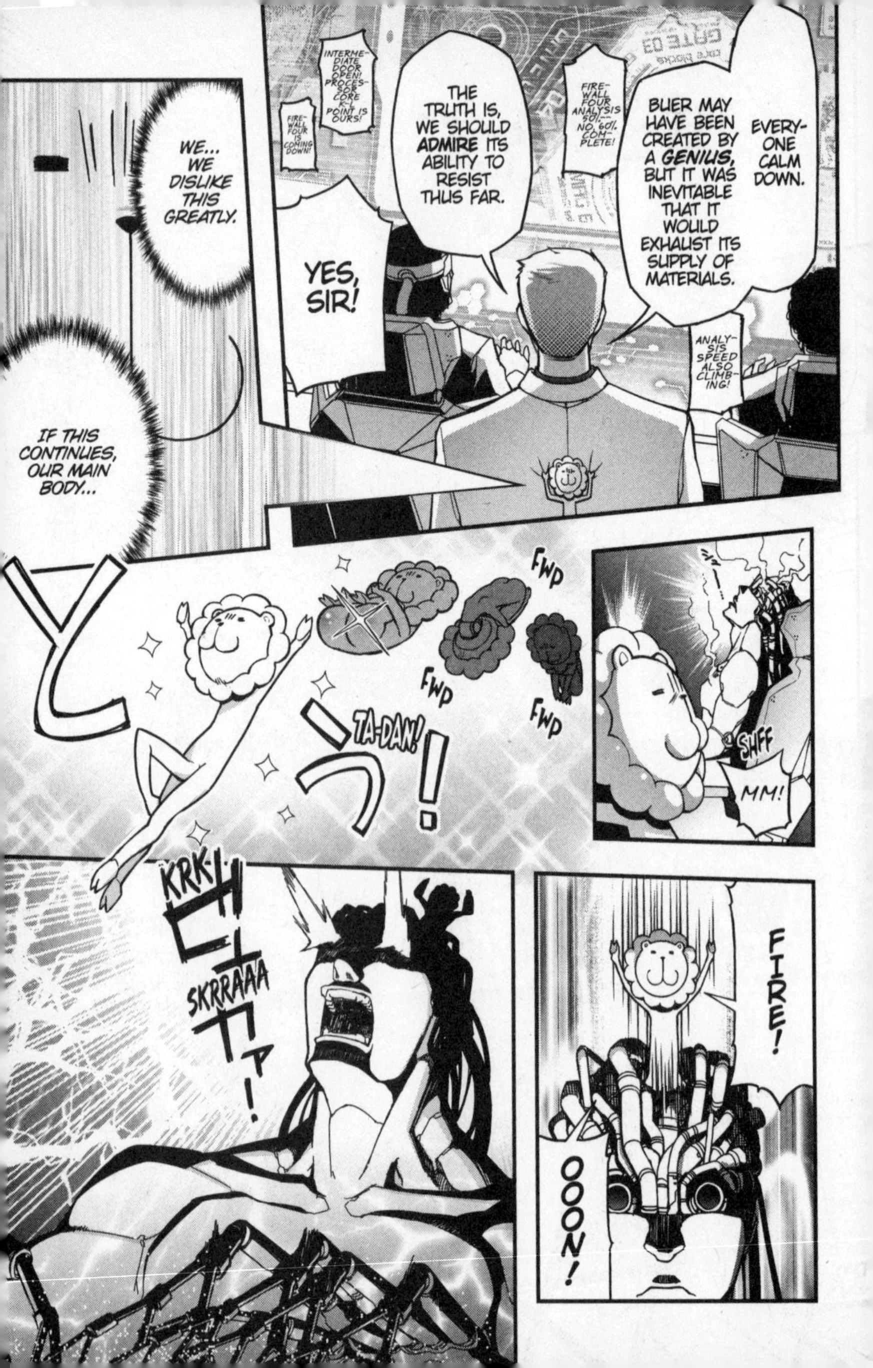
EVERYONE CALM DOWN.
BUER MAY HAVE BEEN CREATED BY A GENIUS, BUT IT WAS INEVITABLE THAT IT WOULD EXHAUST ITS SUPPLY OF MATERIALS.
FIREWALL FOUR ANALYSIS 50%... NO, 60% COMPLETE!
THE TRUTH IS, WE SHOULD ADMIRE ITS ABILITY TO RESIST THUS FAR.
INTERMEDIATE DOOR OPEN! PROCESSOR CORE K-1 POINT IS OURS!
FIREWALL FOUR IS COMING DOWN!
ANALYSIS SPEED ALSO CLIMBING!
YES, SIR!
WE... WE DISLIKE THIS GREATLY.
IF THIS CONTINUES, OUR MAIN BODY...
SHFF
MM!
FWP
FWP
FWP
TA-DAN!
FIRE!
OOON!
KRK-
SKRRAAA

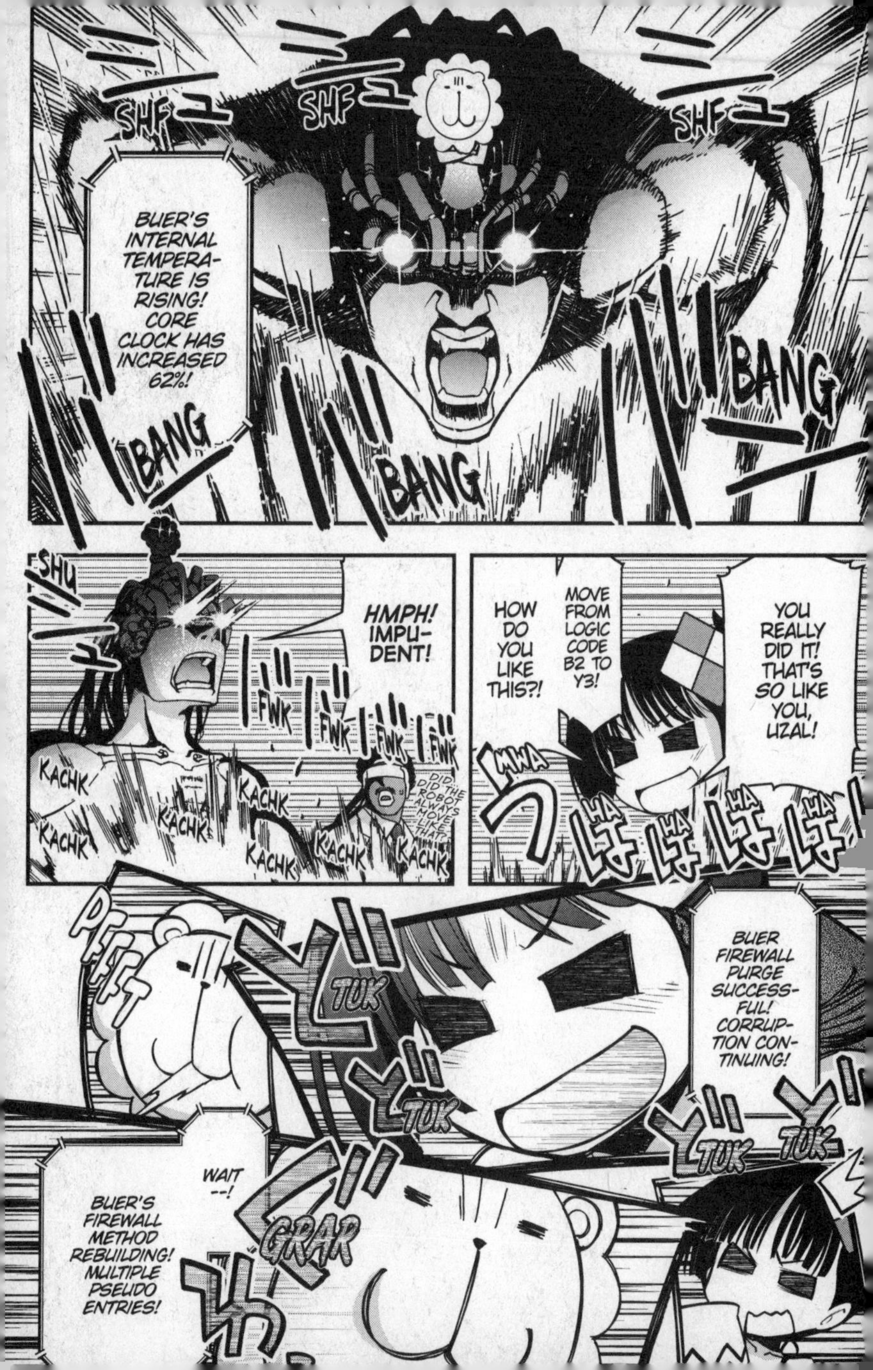
SHF
SHF
SHF
BUER'S INTERNAL TEMPERATURE IS RISING! CORE CLOCK HAS INCREASED 62%!
BANG
BANG
BANG
YOU REALLY DID IT! THAT'S SO LIKE YOU, UZAL!
MOVE FROM LOGIC CODE B2 TO Y3!
HOW DO YOU LIKE THIS?!
HA HA HA
MWA
HMPH! IMPUDENT!
SHU
FWK FWK FWK FWK
DID... DID THE ROBOT ALWAYS MOVE LIKE THAT?
KACHK KACHK KACHK KACHK KACHK KACHK KACHK
BUER FIREWALL PURGE SUCCESSFUL! CORRUPTION CONTINUING!
TUK TUK TUK TUK
PFFFT
WAIT --!
GRAR
BUER'S FIREWALL METHOD REBUILDING! MULTIPLE PSEUDO ENTRIES!

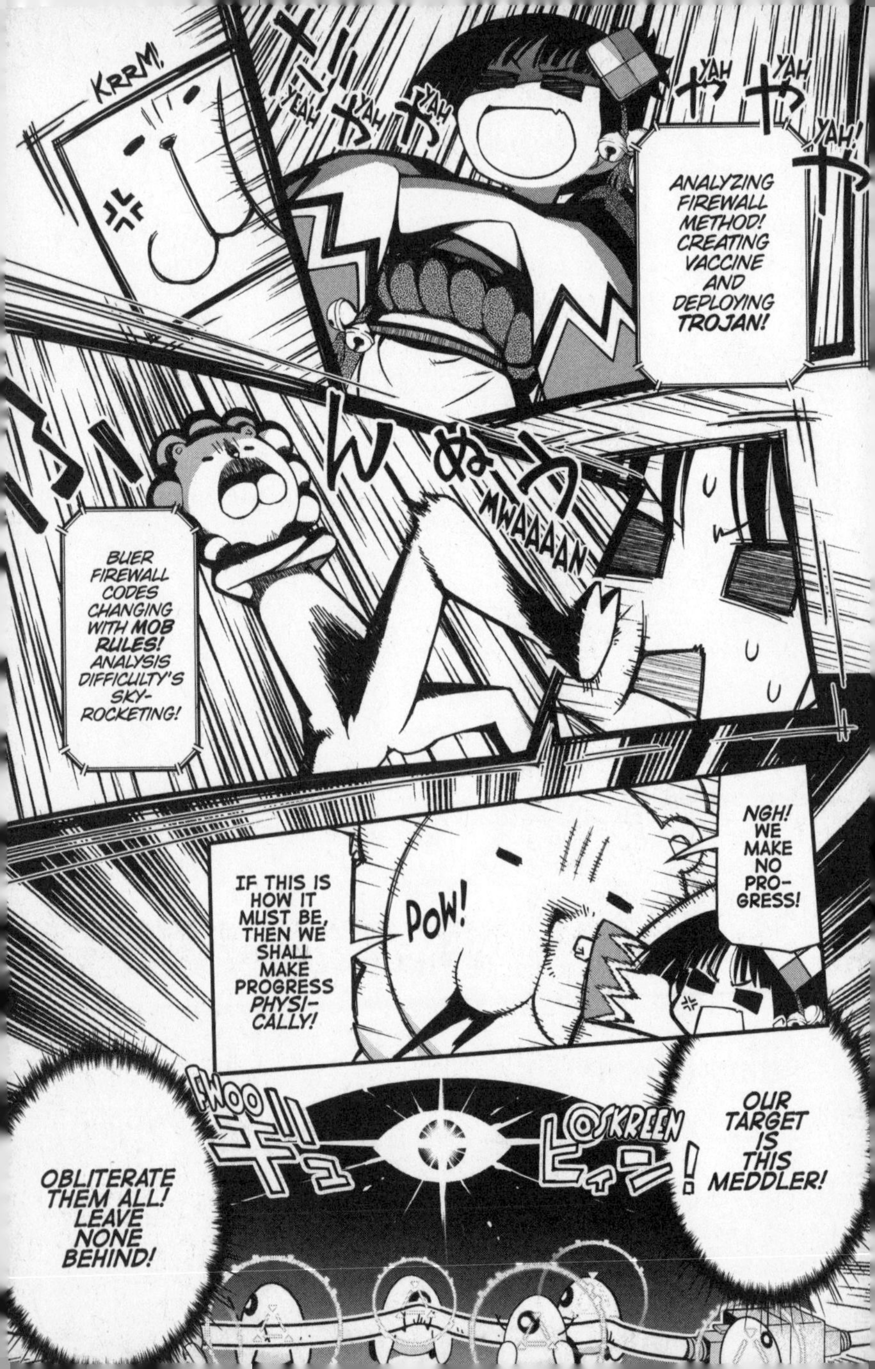
YAH YAH YAH!
ANALYZING FIREWALL METHOD! CREATING VACCINE AND DEPLOYING TROJAN!
YEAH YAH YAH
KRRM!
MWAAAAN
BUER FIREWALL CODES CHANGING WITH MOB RULES! ANALYSIS DIFFICULTY'S SKY-ROCKETING!
NGH! WE MAKE NO PRO-GRESS!
IF THIS IS HOW IT MUST BE, THEN WE SHALL MAKE PROGRESS PHYSI-CALLY!
POW!
OUR TARGET IS THIS MEDDLER!
SKREEN
SWOO
OBLITERATE THEM ALL! LEAVE NONE BEHIND!

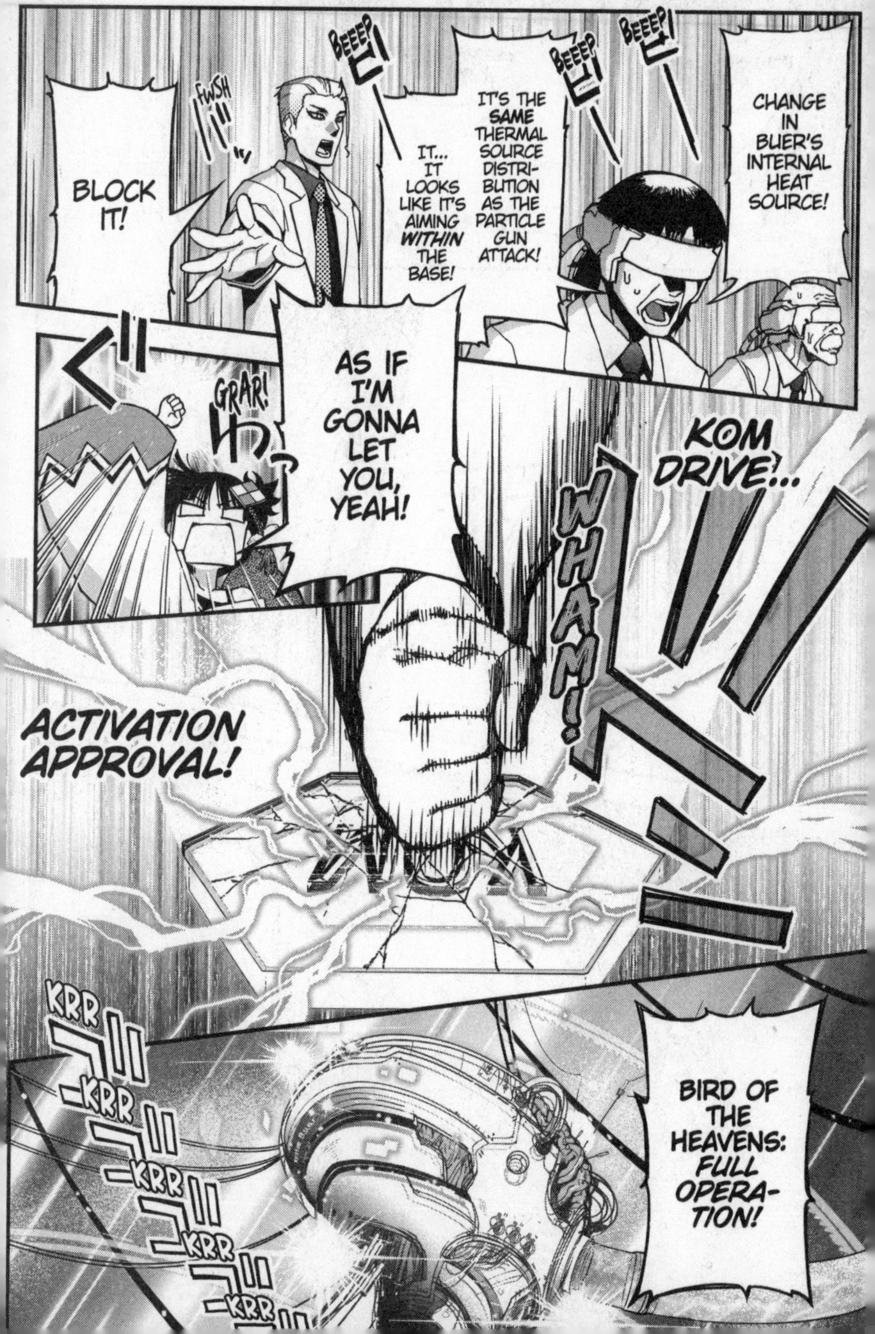
BEEEP!
CHANGE IN BUER'S INTERNAL HEAT SOURCE!
BEEEP
IT'S THE SAME THERMAL SOURCE DISTRI-BUTION AS THE PARTICLE GUN ATTACK!
BEEEP
IT... IT LOOKS LIKE IT'S AIMING WITHIN THE BASE!
FWSH
BLOCK IT!
KOM DRIVE...
WHAM!
AS IF I'M GONNA LET YOU, YEAH!
GRAR!
ACTIVATION APPROVAL!
BIRD OF THE HEAVENS: FULL OPERA-TION!
KRR
KRR
KRR
KRR
KRR

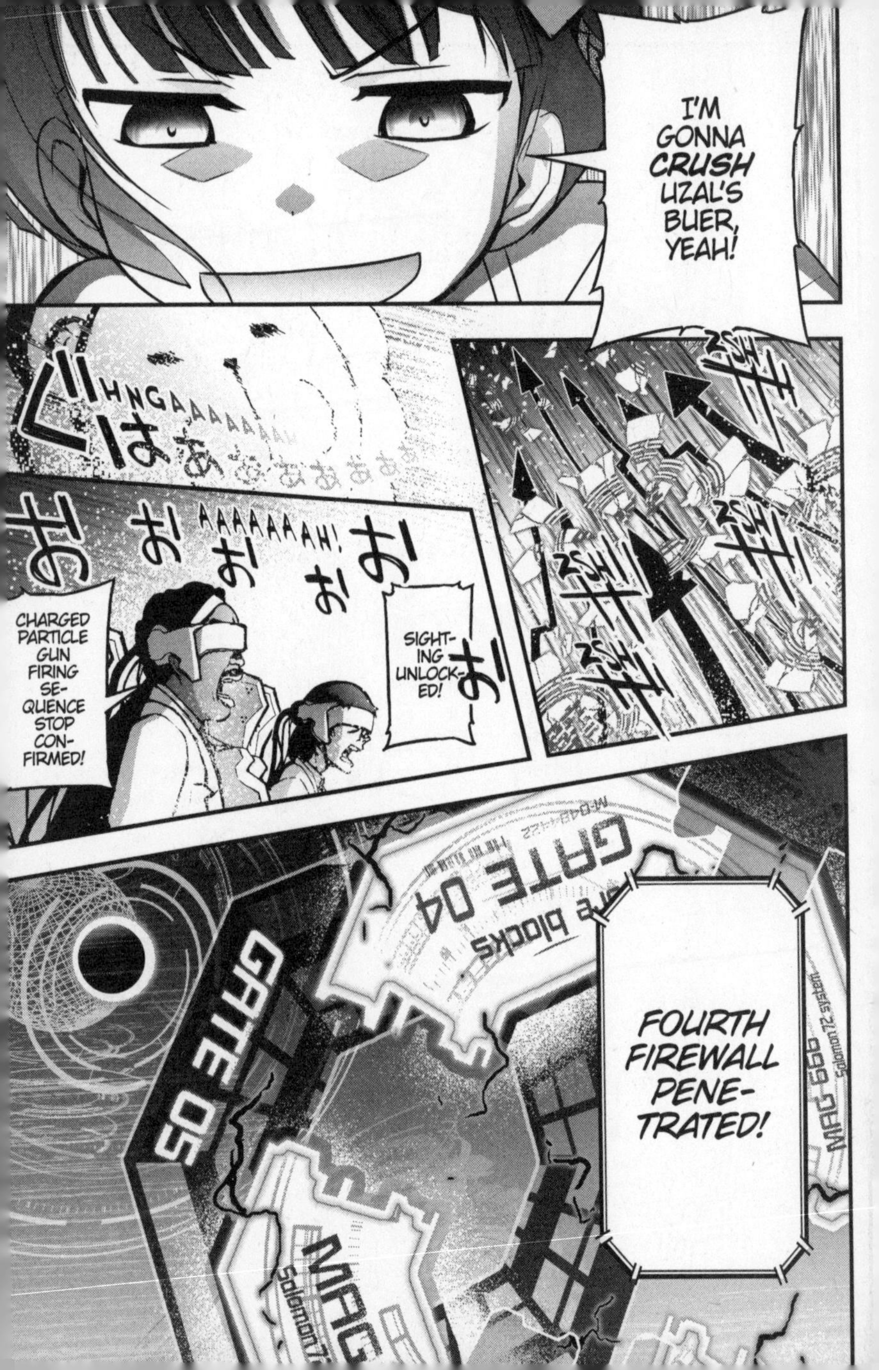
I'M GONNA CRUSH UZAL'S BUER, YEAH!
HSZ
HSZ
HSZ
HSZ
HNGAAAAAAAA
AAAAAAAH!
SIGHTING UNLOCKED!
CHARGED PARTICLE GUN FIRING SEQUENCE STOP CONFIRMED!
FOURTH FIREWALL PENETRATED!

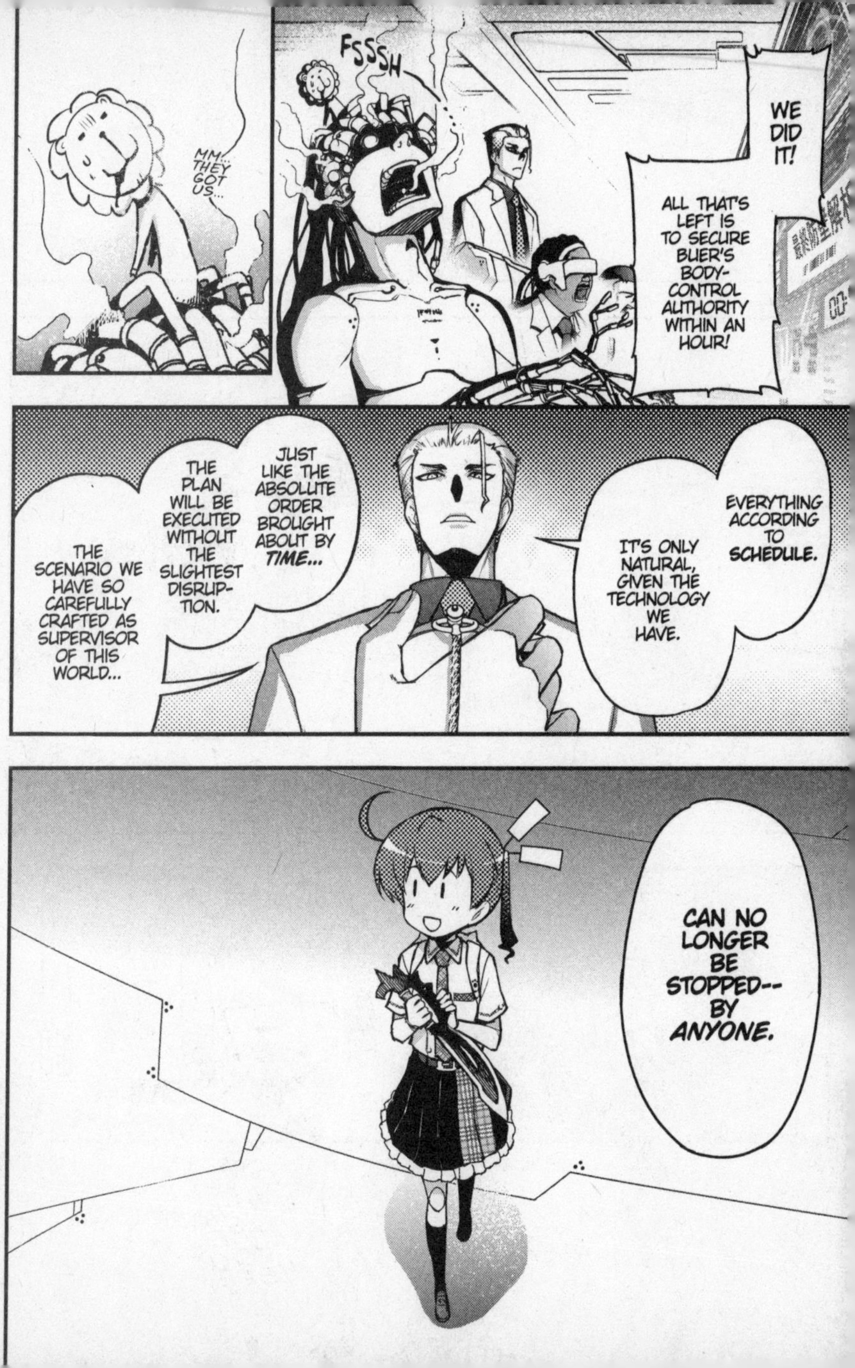
FSSSH
WE DID IT!
ALL THAT'S LEFT IS TO SECURE BUER'S BODY-CONTROL AUTHORITY WITHIN AN HOUR!
MM... THEY GOT US...
EVERYTHING ACCORDING TO SCHEDULE.
IT'S ONLY NATURAL, GIVEN THE TECHNOLOGY WE HAVE.
JUST LIKE THE ABSOLUTE ORDER BROUGHT ABOUT BY *TIME*...
THE PLAN WILL BE EXECUTED WITHOUT THE SLIGHTEST DISRUPTION.
THE SCENARIO WE HAVE SO CAREFULLY CRAFTED AS SUPERVISOR OF THIS WORLD...
CAN NO LONGER BE STOPPED--BY *ANYONE.*

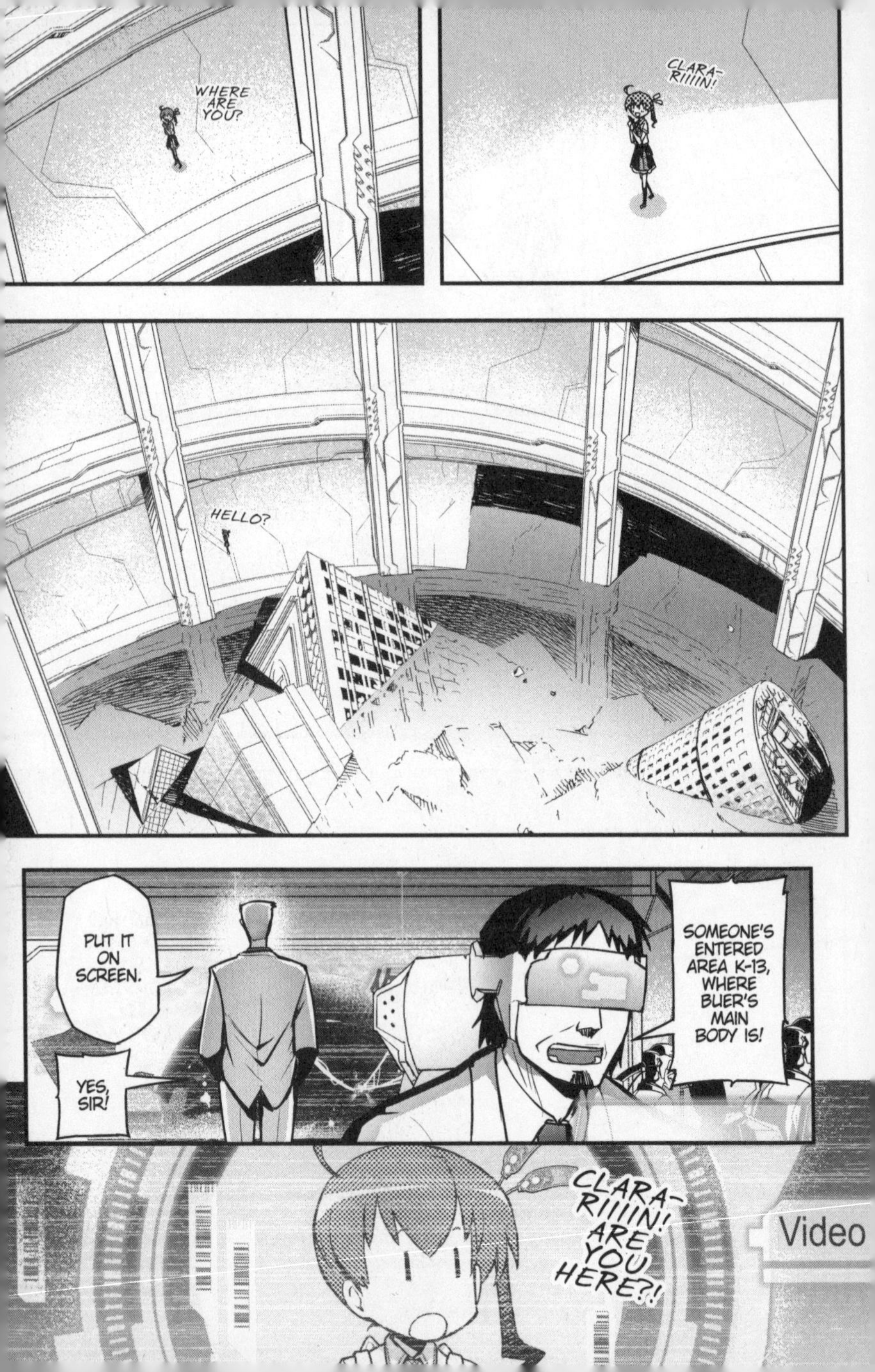
CLARA-RIIIIN!
WHERE ARE YOU?
HELLO?
SOMEONE'S ENTERED AREA K-13, WHERE BUER'S MAIN BODY IS!
PUT IT ON SCREEN.
YES, SIR!
CLARA-RIIIIN! ARE YOU HERE?!
Video

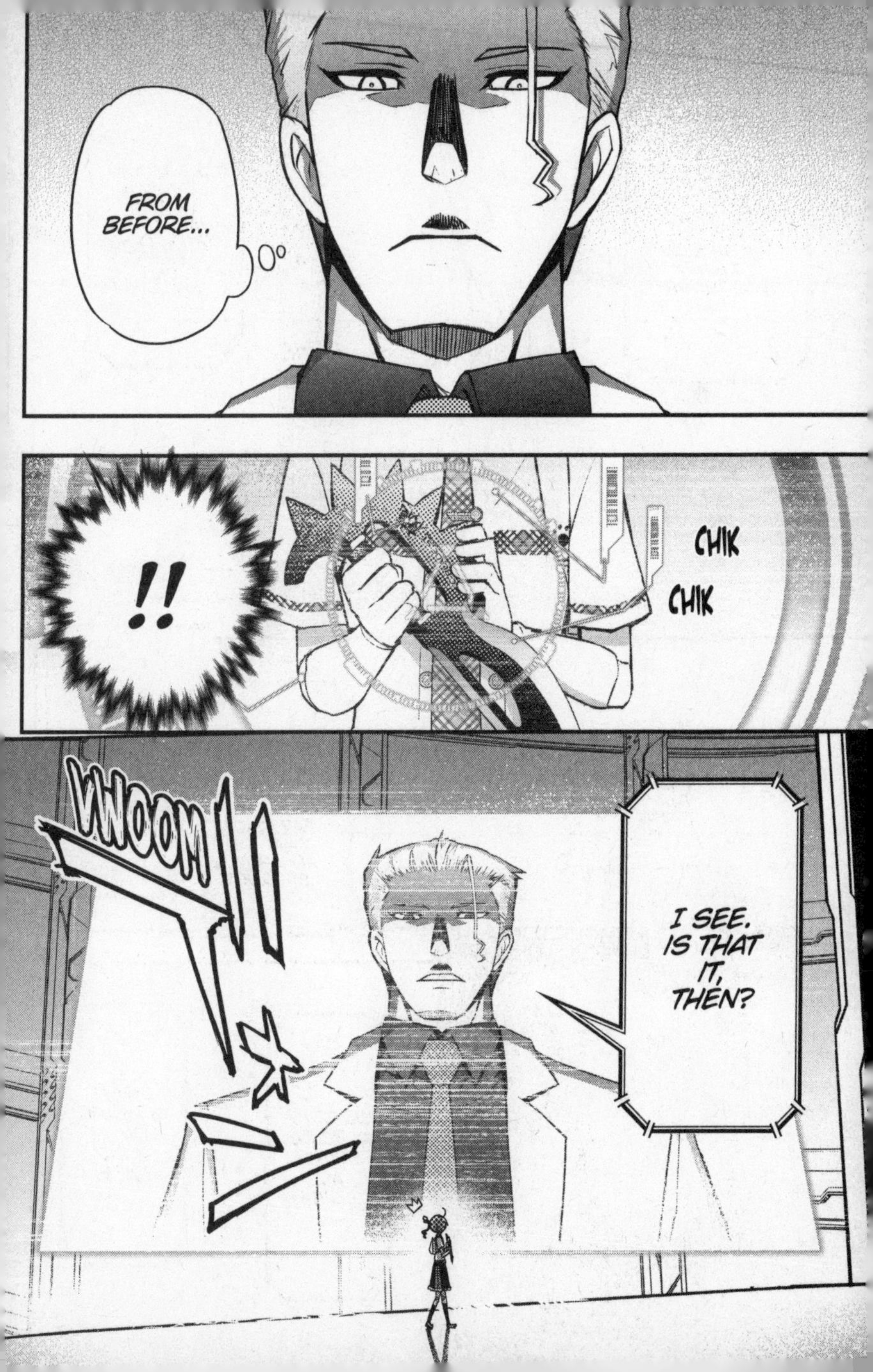
FROM BEFORE...
CHIK
CHIK
!!
I SEE. IS THAT IT, THEN?
VNOOM

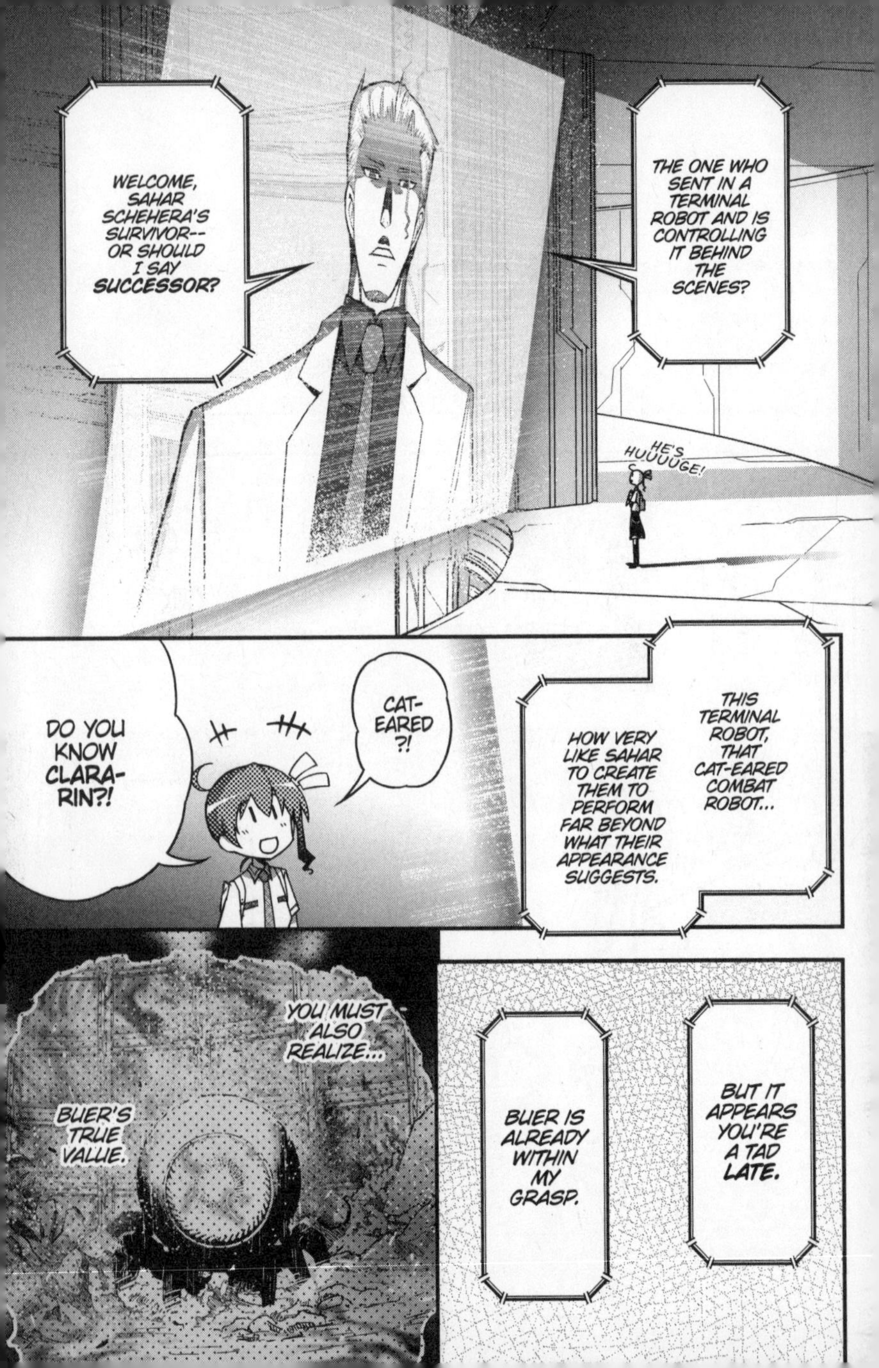
THE ONE WHO SENT IN A TERMINAL ROBOT AND IS CONTROLLING IT BEHIND THE SCENES?
WELCOME, SAHAR SCHEHERA'S SURVIVOR-- OR SHOULD I SAY SUCCESSOR?
HE'S HUUUUGE!
THIS TERMINAL ROBOT, THAT CAT-EARED COMBAT ROBOT...
HOW VERY LIKE SAHAR TO CREATE THEM TO PERFORM FAR BEYOND WHAT THEIR APPEARANCE SUGGESTS.
CAT-EARED?!
DO YOU KNOW CLARA-RIN?!
BUT IT APPEARS YOU'RE A TAD LATE.
BUER IS ALREADY WITHIN MY GRASP.
YOU MUST ALSO REALIZE...
BUER'S TRUE VALUE.

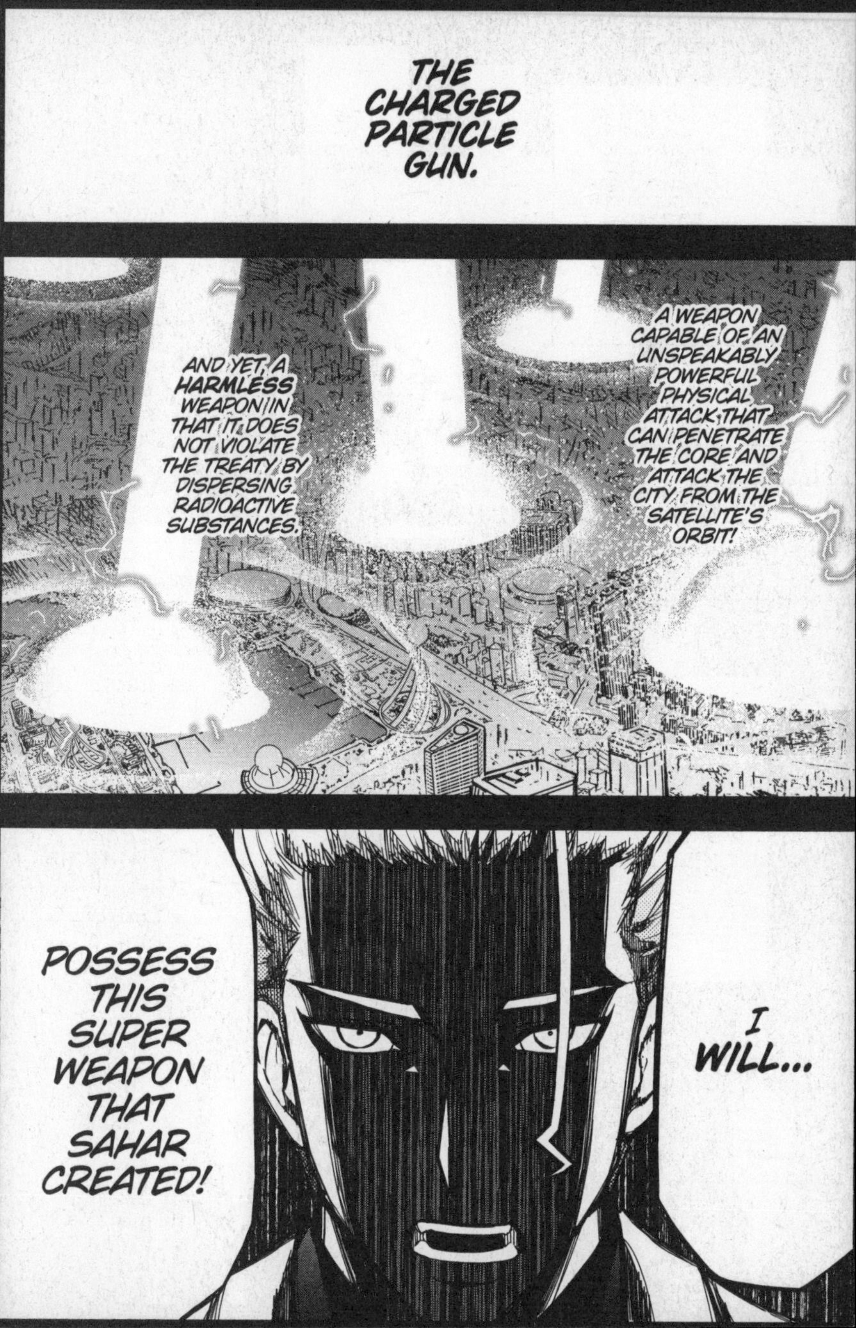
THE CHARGED PARTICLE GUN.
A WEAPON CAPABLE OF AN UNSPEAKABLY POWERFUL PHYSICAL ATTACK THAT CAN PENETRATE THE CORE AND ATTACK THE CITY FROM THE SATELLITE'S ORBIT!
AND YET, A **HARMLESS** WEAPON IN THAT IT DOES NOT VIOLATE THE TREATY BY DISPERSING RADIOACTIVE SUBSTANCES.
I WILL...
POSSESS THIS SUPER WEAPON THAT SAHAR CREATED!

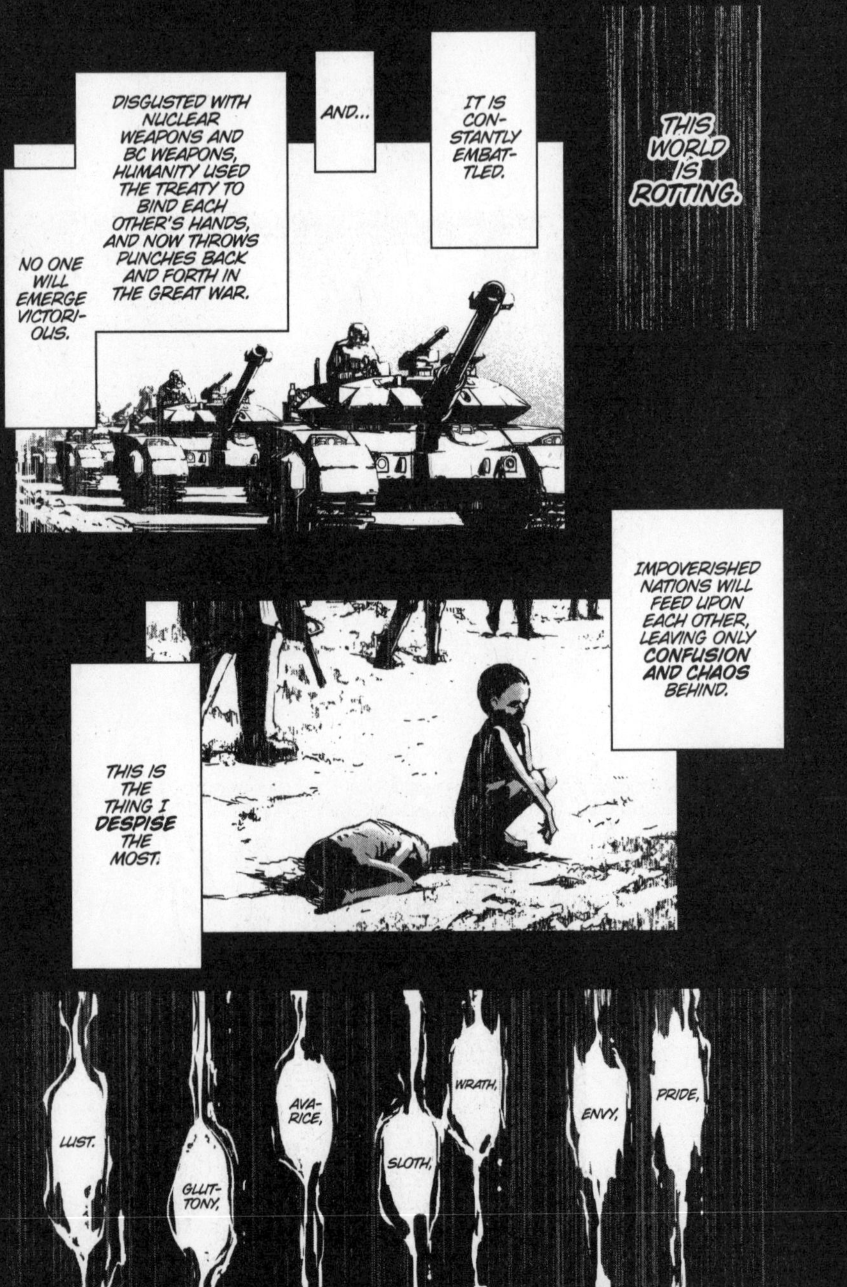
THIS WORLD IS ROTTING.
IT IS CONSTANTLY EMBATTLED.
AND...
DISGUSTED WITH NUCLEAR WEAPONS AND BC WEAPONS, HUMANITY USED THE TREATY TO BIND EACH OTHER'S HANDS, AND NOW THROWS PUNCHES BACK AND FORTH IN THE GREAT WAR.
NO ONE WILL EMERGE VICTORIOUS.
IMPOVERISHED NATIONS WILL FEED UPON EACH OTHER, LEAVING ONLY CONFUSION AND CHAOS BEHIND.
THIS IS THE THING I DESPISE THE MOST.
PRIDE,
ENVY,
WRATH,
SLOTH,
AVARICE,
GLUTTONY,
LUST.

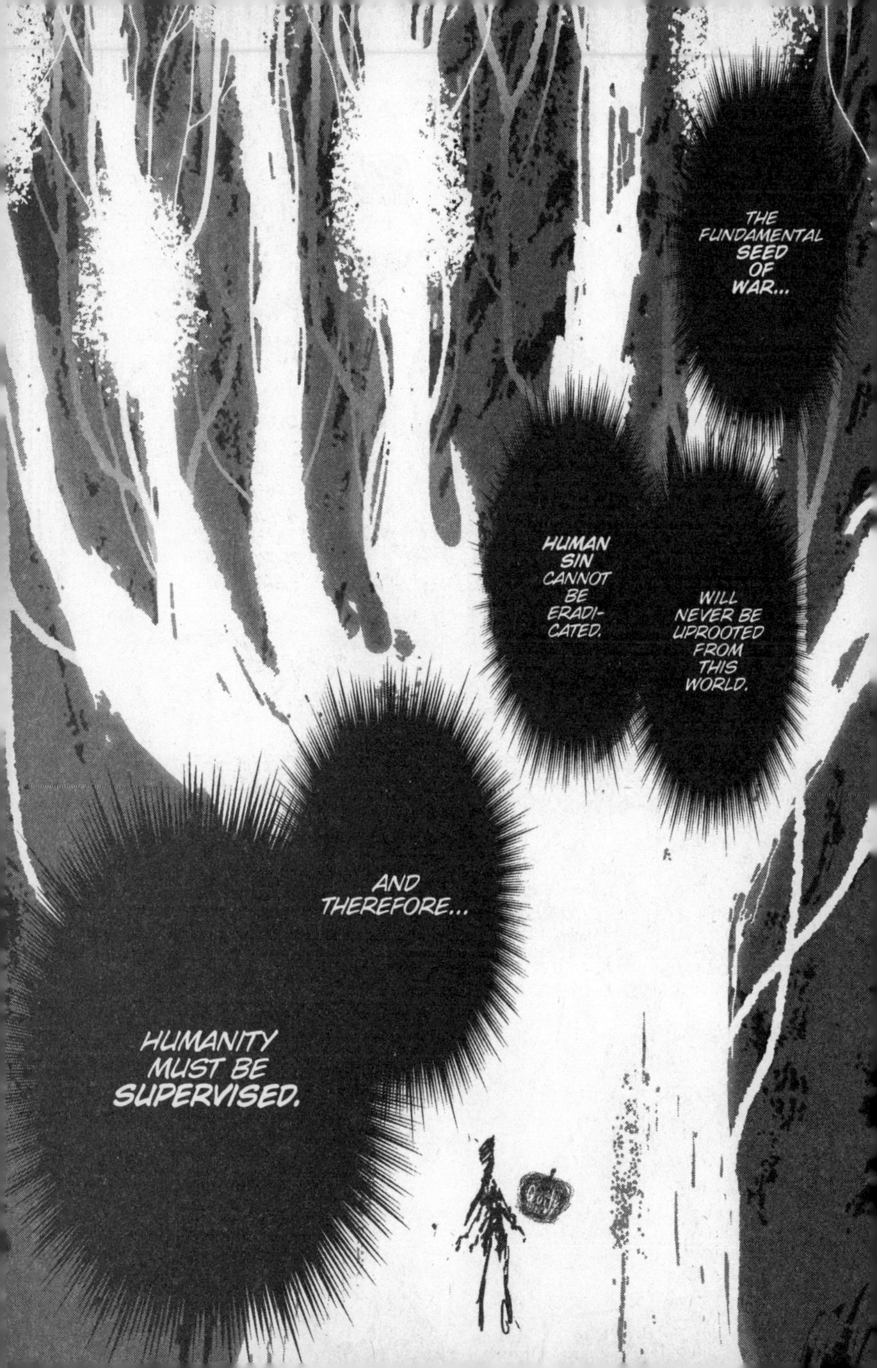
THE FUNDAMENTAL SEED OF WAR...
WILL NEVER BE UPROOTED FROM THIS WORLD.
HUMAN SIN CANNOT BE ERADICATED.
AND THEREFORE...
HUMANITY MUST BE SUPERVISED.

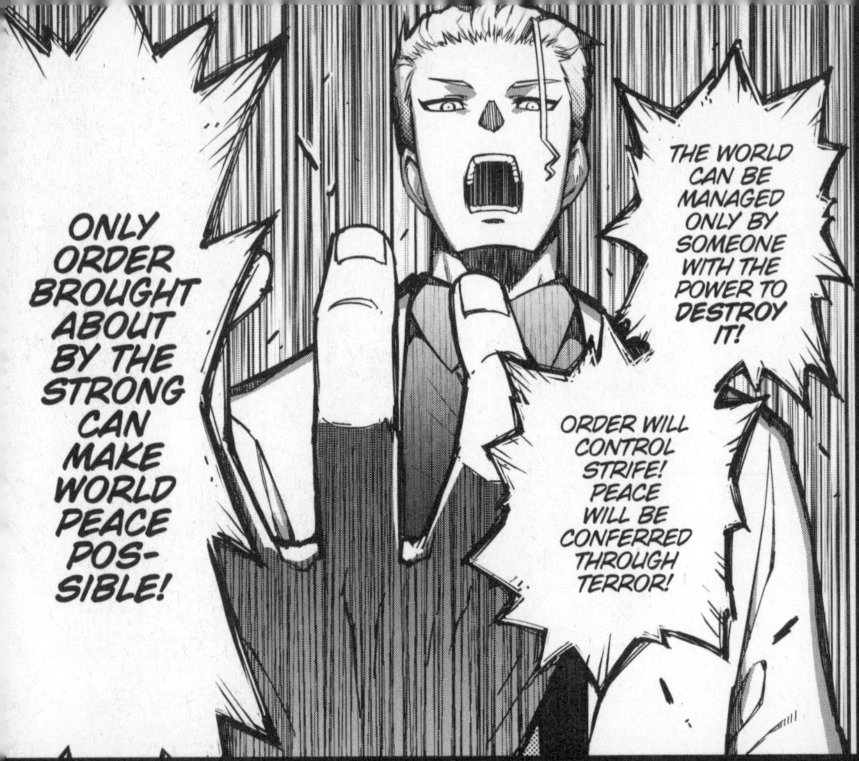
THE WORLD CAN BE MANAGED ONLY BY SOMEONE WITH THE POWER TO DESTROY IT!
ORDER WILL CONTROL STRIFE! PEACE WILL BE CONFERRED THROUGH TERROR!
ONLY ORDER BROUGHT ABOUT BY THE STRONG CAN MAKE WORLD PEACE POS-SIBLE!

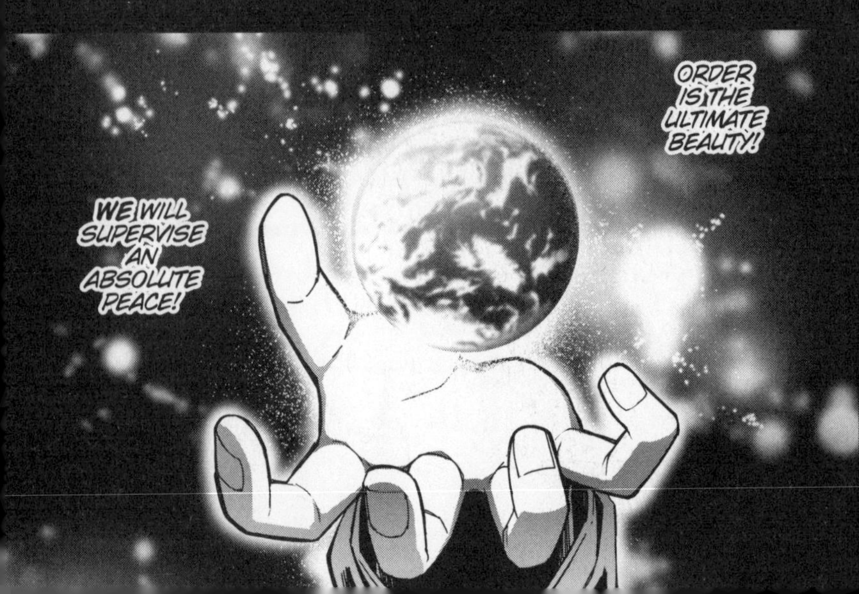
ORDER IS THE ULTIMATE BEAUTY!
WE WILL SUPERVISE AN ABSOLUTE PEACE!

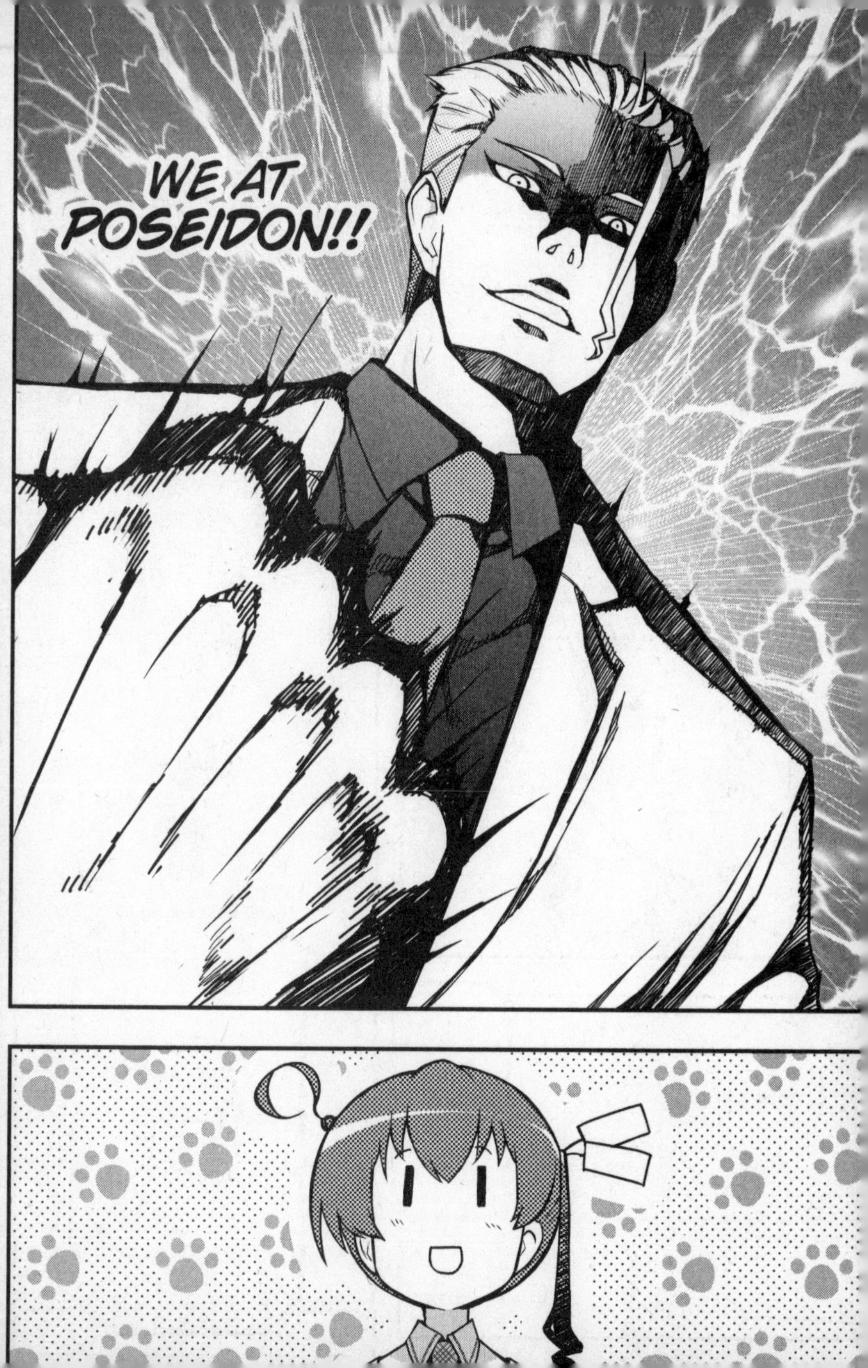
WE AT POSEIDON!!

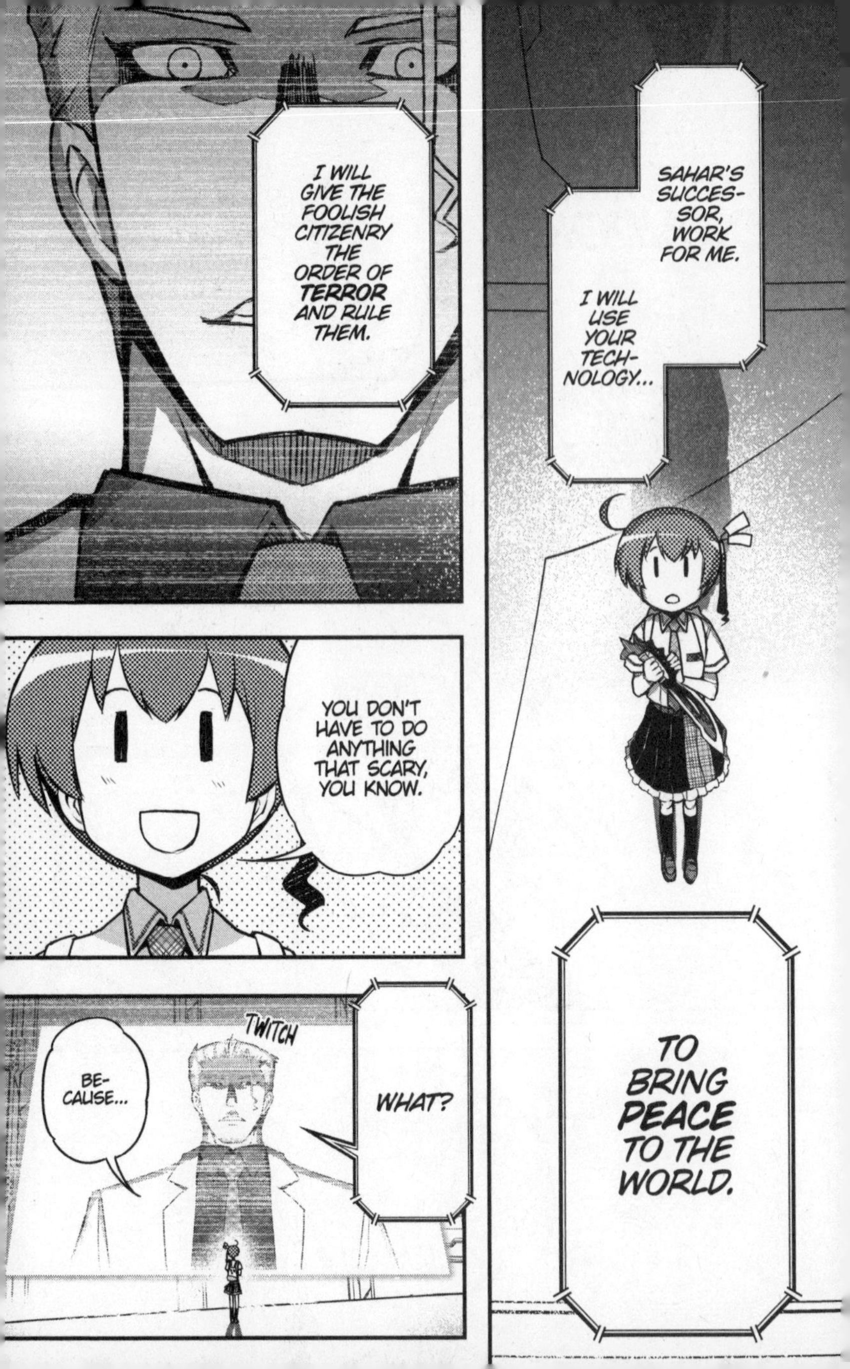
SAHAR'S SUCCES-SOR, WORK FOR ME.
I WILL USE YOUR TECH-NOLOGY...
TO BRING PEACE TO THE WORLD.
I WILL GIVE THE FOOLISH CITIZENRY THE ORDER OF TERROR AND RULE THEM.
YOU DON'T HAVE TO DO ANYTHING THAT SCARY, YOU KNOW.
WHAT?
TWITCH
BE-CAUSE...

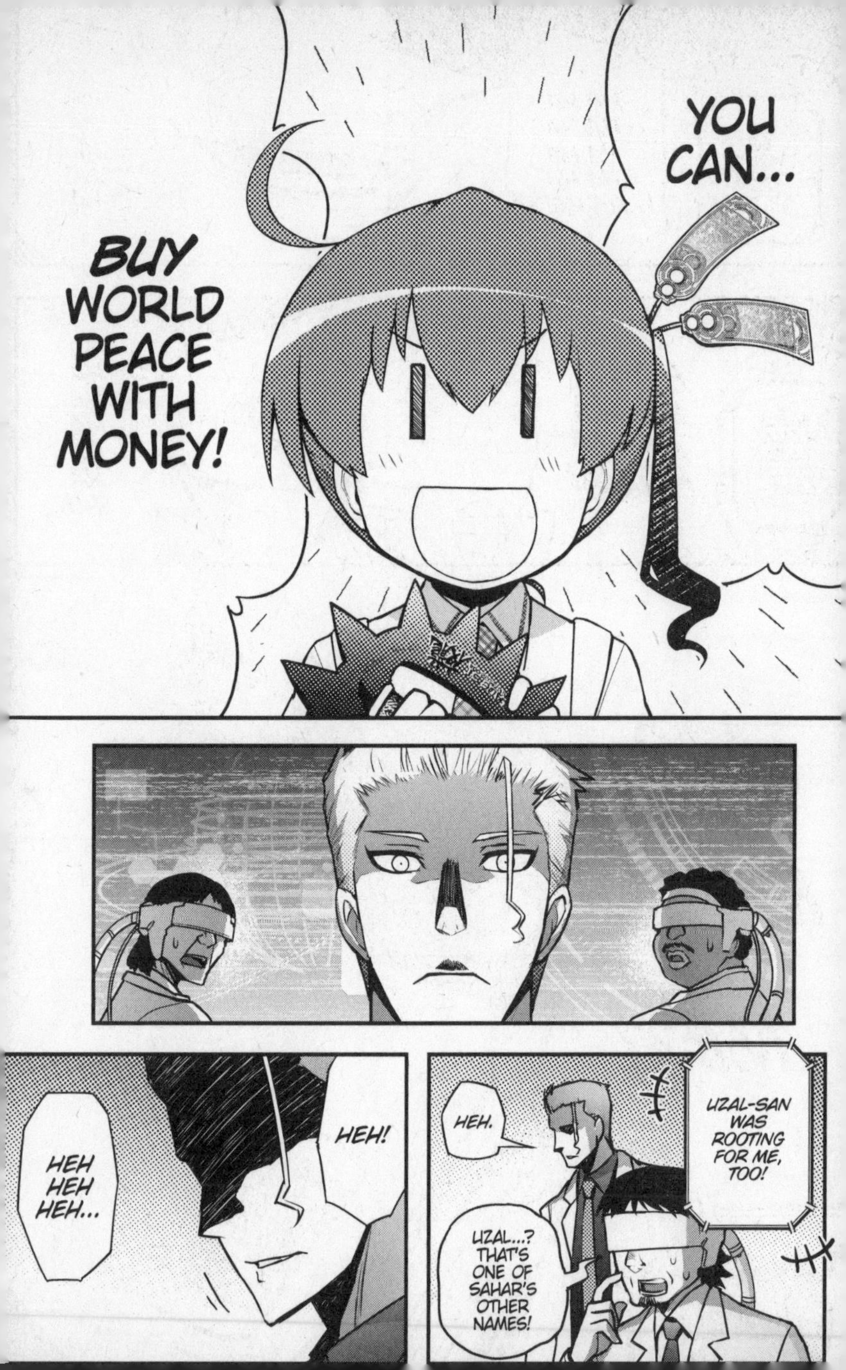
YOU CAN...
BUY WORLD PEACE WITH MONEY!
UZAL-SAN WAS ROOTING FOR ME, TOO!
HEH.
UZAL...? THAT'S ONE OF SAHAR'S OTHER NAMES!
HEH!
HEH HEH HEH...

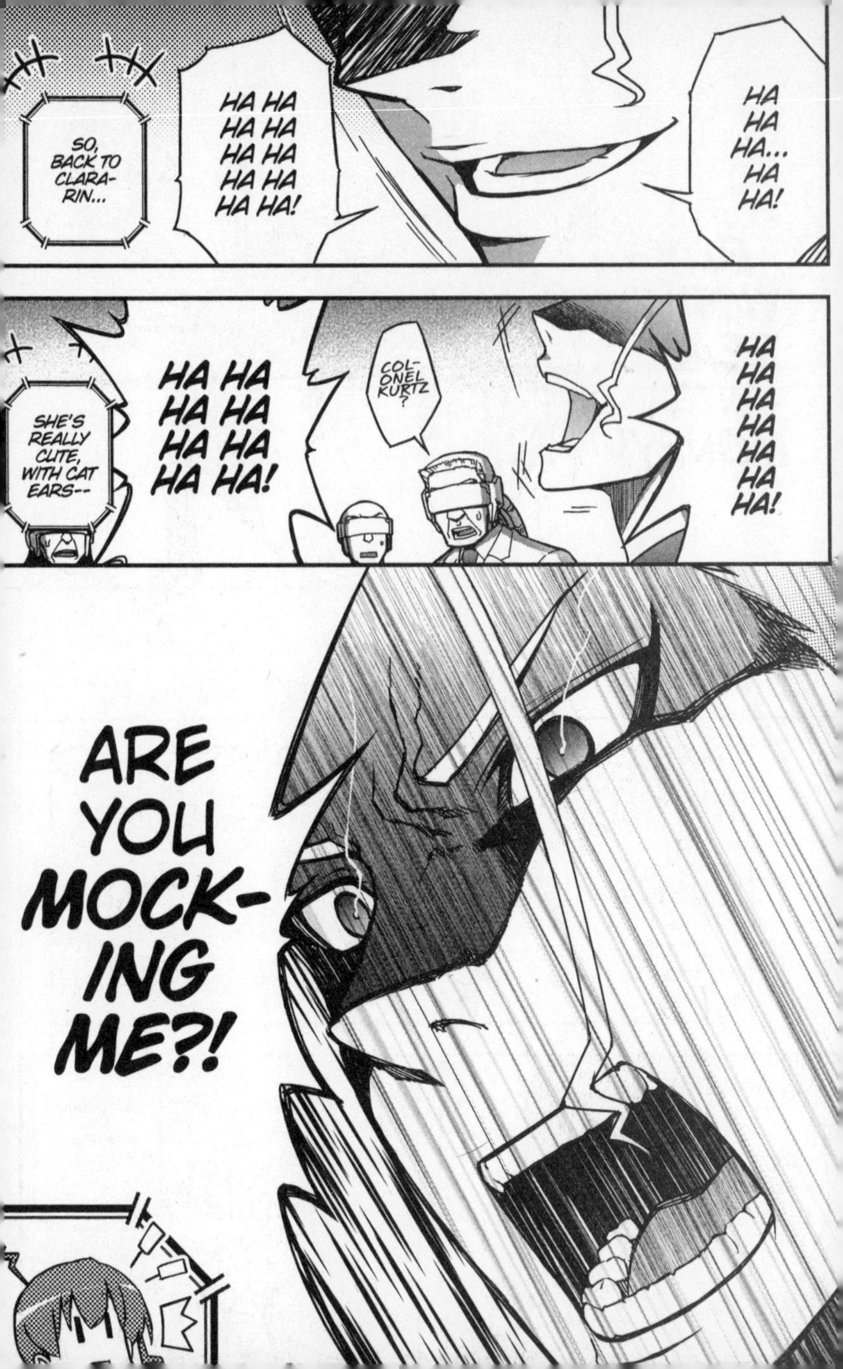
HA HA HA... HA HA!
HA HA HA HA HA HA HA HA HA HA!
SO, BACK TO CLARA-RIN...
HA HA HA HA HA HA HA!
COL-ONEL KURTZ?
HA HA HA HA HA HA HA HA!
SHE'S REALLY CUTE, WITH CAT EARS--
ARE YOU MOCK-ING ME?!

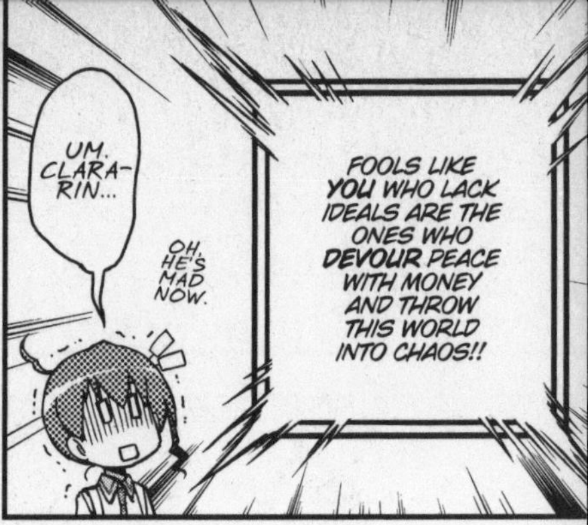
FOOLS LIKE YOU WHO LACK IDEALS ARE THE ONES WHO DEVOUR PEACE WITH MONEY AND THROW THIS WORLD INTO CHAOS!!
OH, HE'S MAD NOW.
UM. CLARA-RIN...
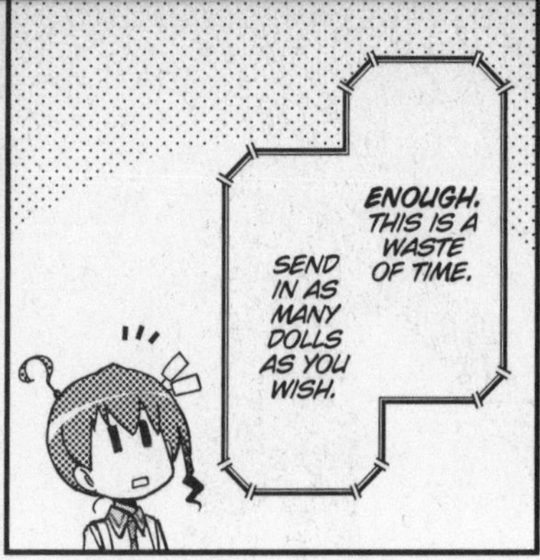
ENOUGH. THIS IS A WASTE OF TIME.
SEND IN AS MANY DOLLS AS YOU WISH.
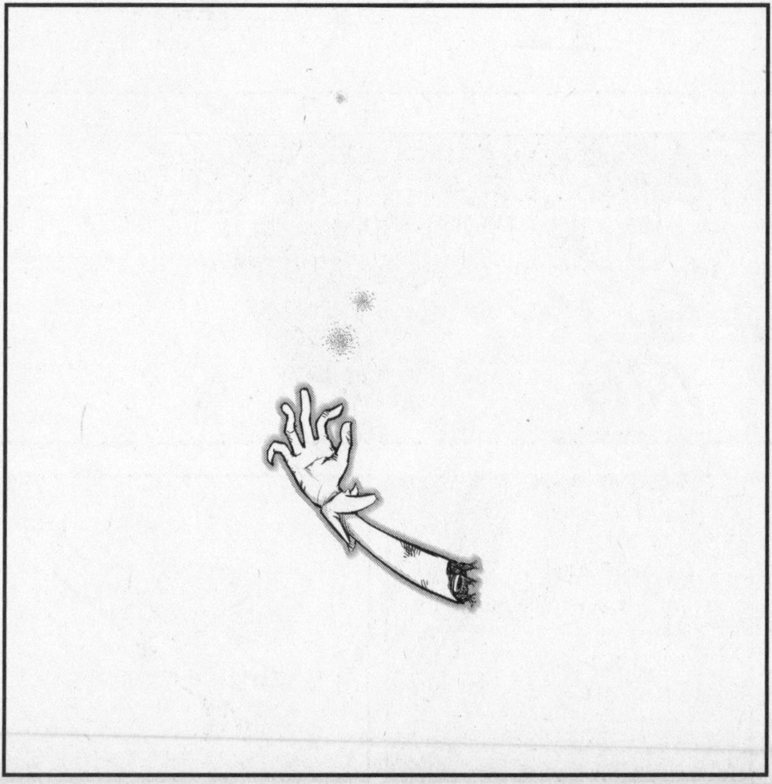

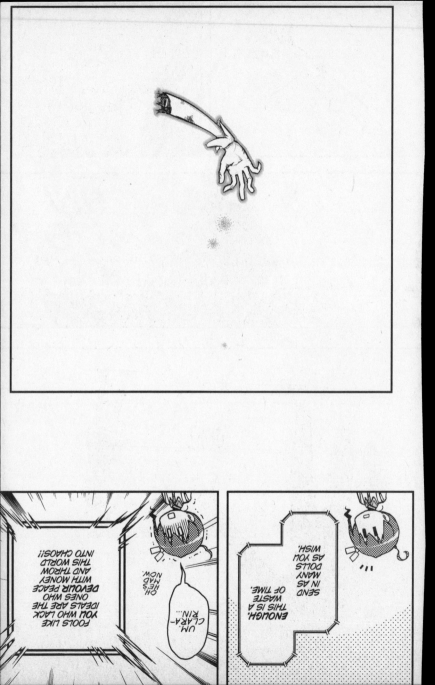

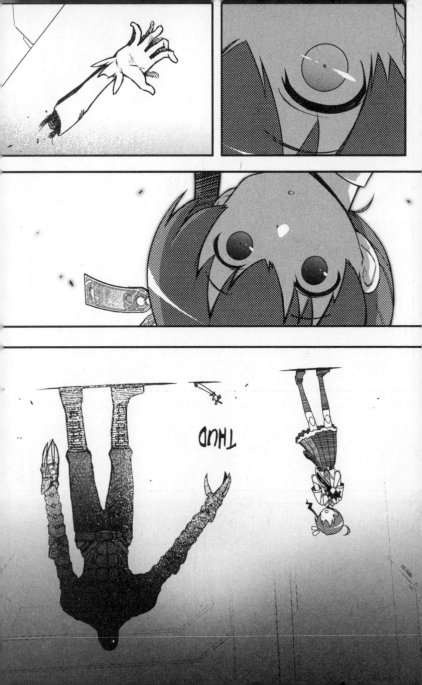

THUD

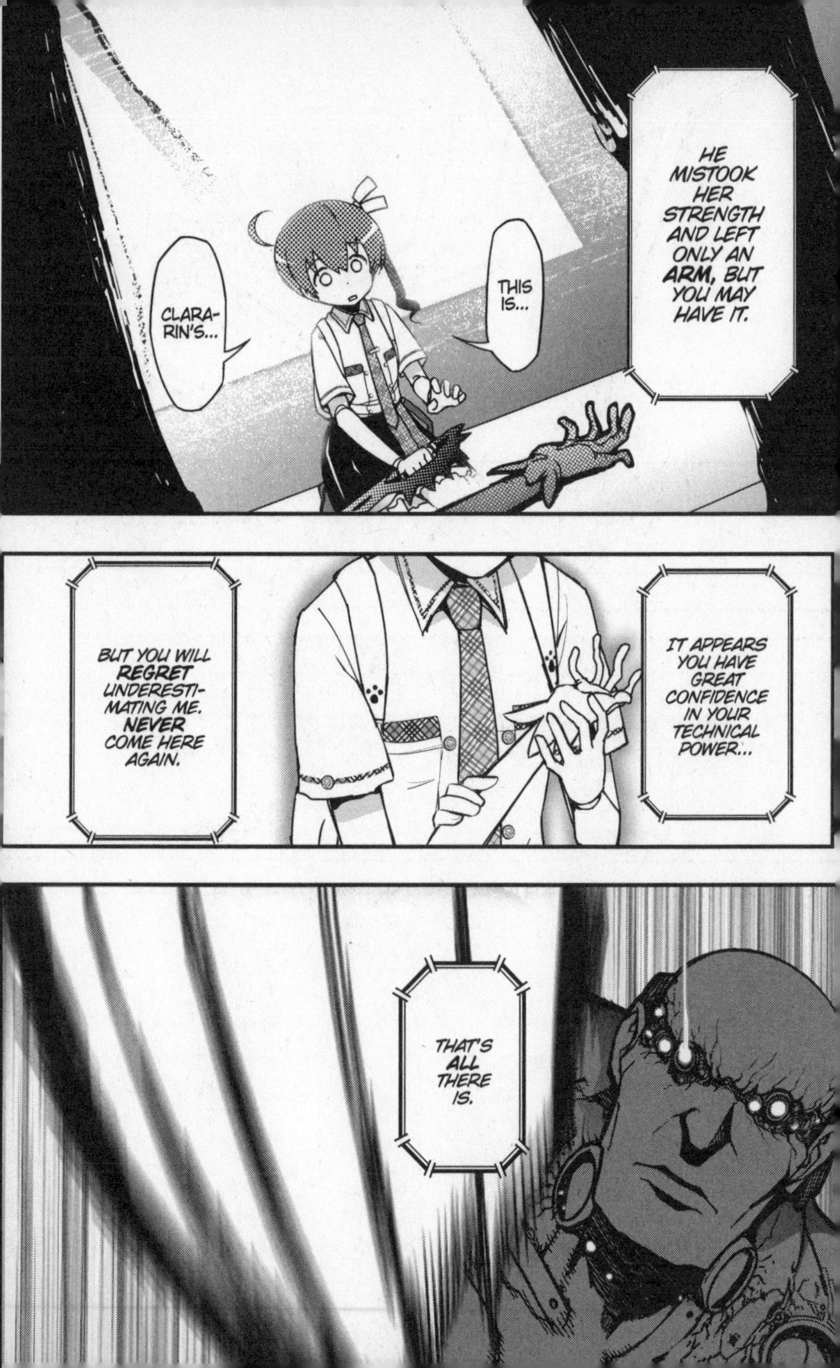
HE MISTOOK HER STRENGTH AND LEFT ONLY AN **ARM,** BUT YOU MAY HAVE IT.
THIS IS...
CLARA-RIN'S...
IT APPEARS YOU HAVE GREAT CONFIDENCE IN YOUR TECHNICAL POWER...
BUT YOU WILL **REGRET** UNDERESTI-MATING ME. **NEVER** COME HERE AGAIN.
THAT'S **ALL** THERE IS.

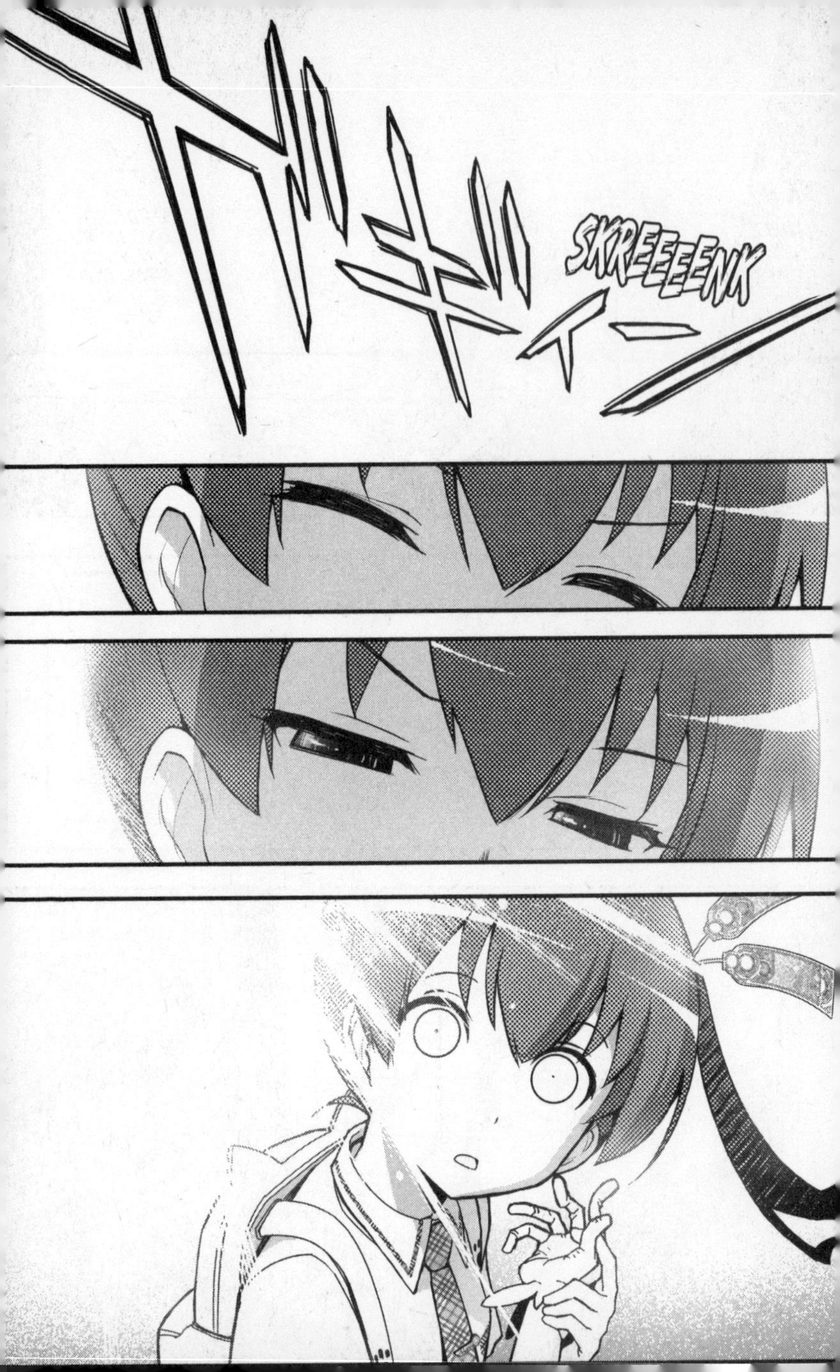
ズガギギィーン
SKREEEEENK

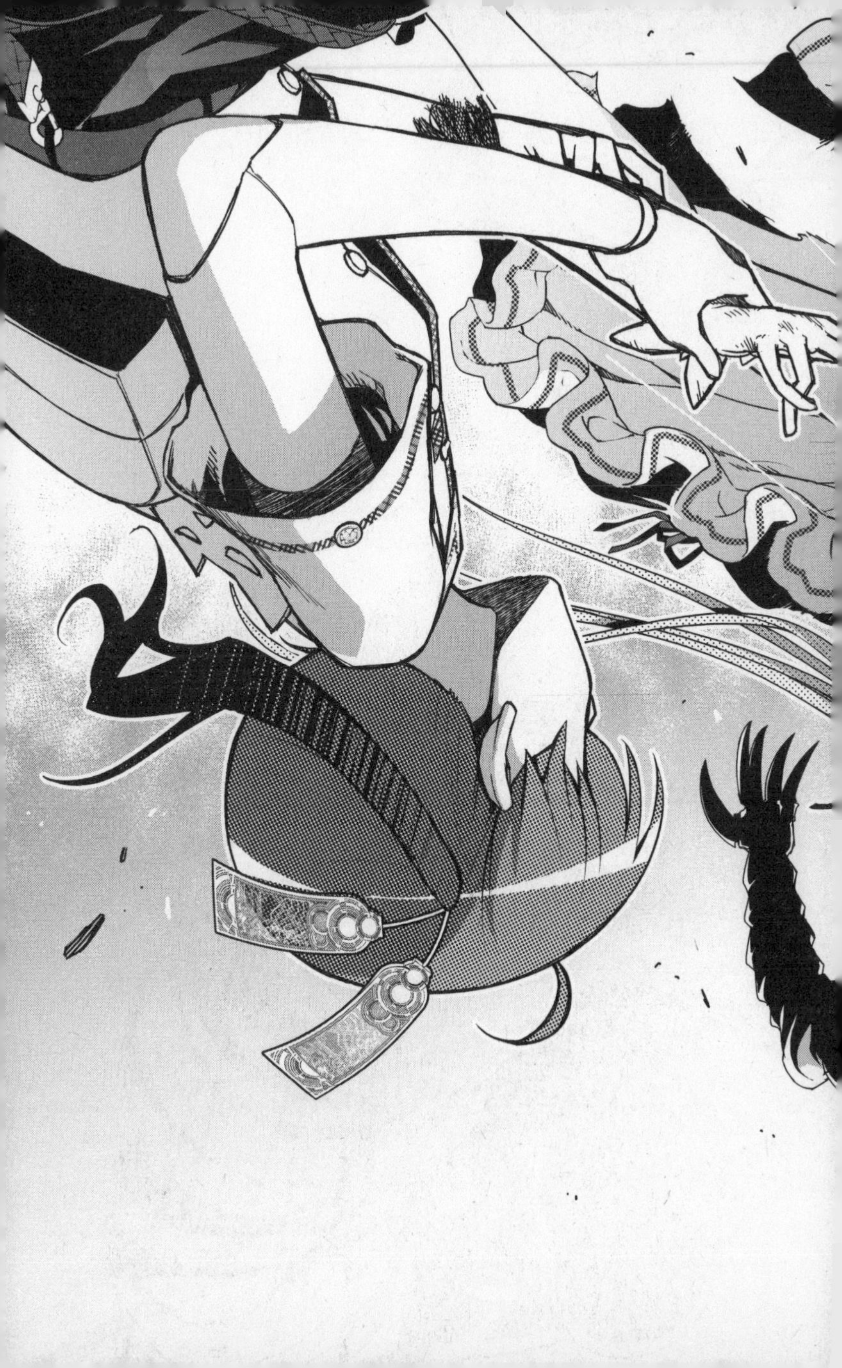

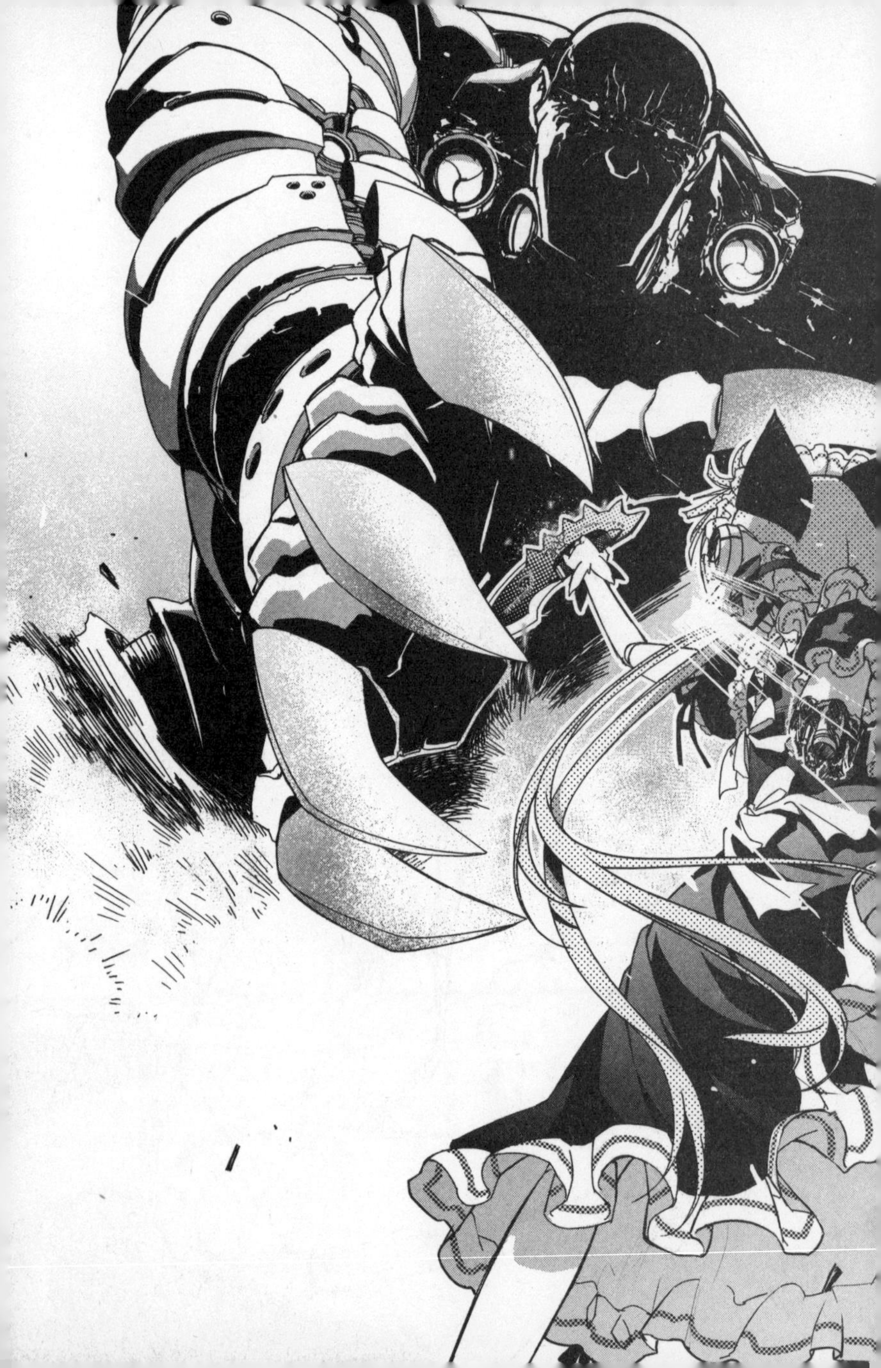

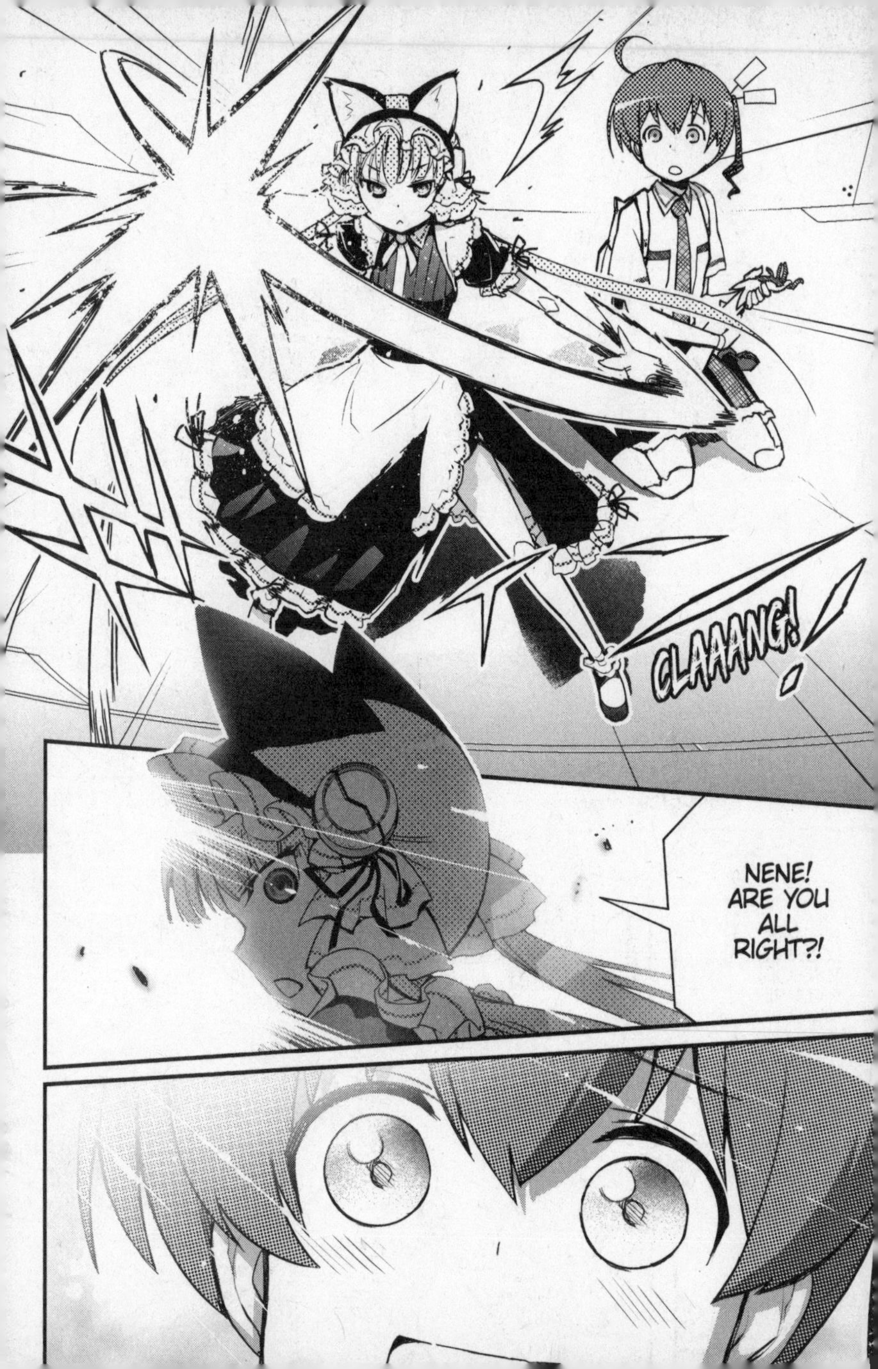
CLAAANG!
NENE! ARE YOU ALL RIGHT?!

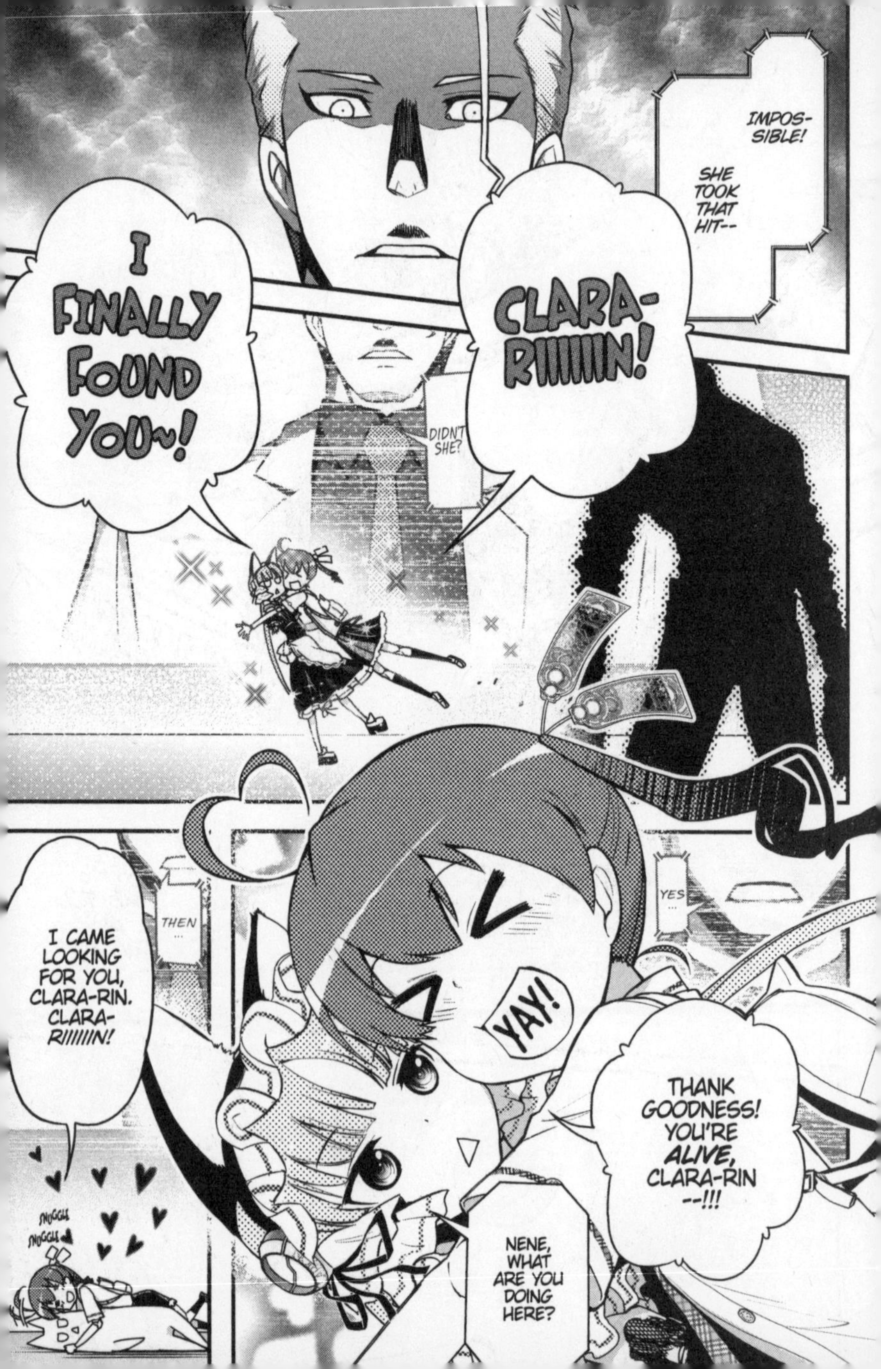
IMPOSSIBLE!
SHE TOOK THAT HIT--
DIDN'T SHE?
CLARA-RIIIIIIN!
I FINALLY FOUND YOU~!
YES...
THEN...
THANK GOODNESS! YOU'RE ALIVE, CLARA-RIN--!!!
YAY!
NENE, WHAT ARE YOU DOING HERE?
I CAME LOOKING FOR YOU, CLARA-RIN. CLARA-RIIIIIIN!
SNUGGLE
SNUGGLE

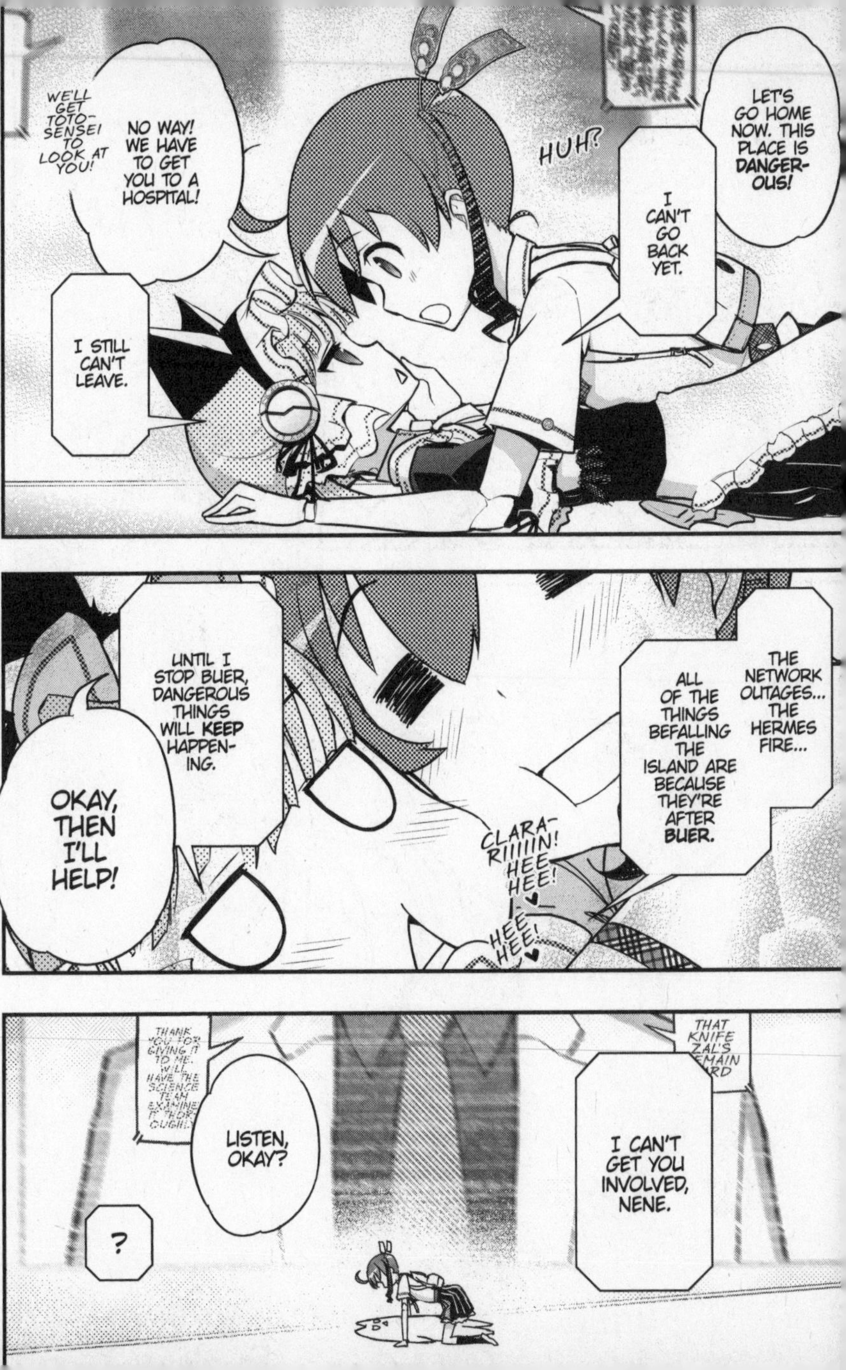
LET'S GO HOME NOW. THIS PLACE IS DANGEROUS!
HUH?
I CAN'T GO BACK YET.
NO WAY! WE HAVE TO GET YOU TO A HOSPITAL!
WE'LL GET TOTO-SENSEI TO LOOK AT YOU!
I STILL CAN'T LEAVE.
THE NETWORK OUTAGES... THE HERMES FIRE...
ALL OF THE THINGS BEFALLING THE ISLAND ARE BECAUSE THEY'RE AFTER BUER.
CLARA-RIIIIIIN! HEE HEE! HEE HEE!
UNTIL I STOP BUER, DANGEROUS THINGS WILL KEEP HAPPENING.
OKAY, THEN I'LL HELP!
THAT KNIFE ZAL'S
I CAN'T GET YOU INVOLVED, NENE.
LISTEN, OKAY?
THANK YOU FOR GIVING IT TO ME.
?

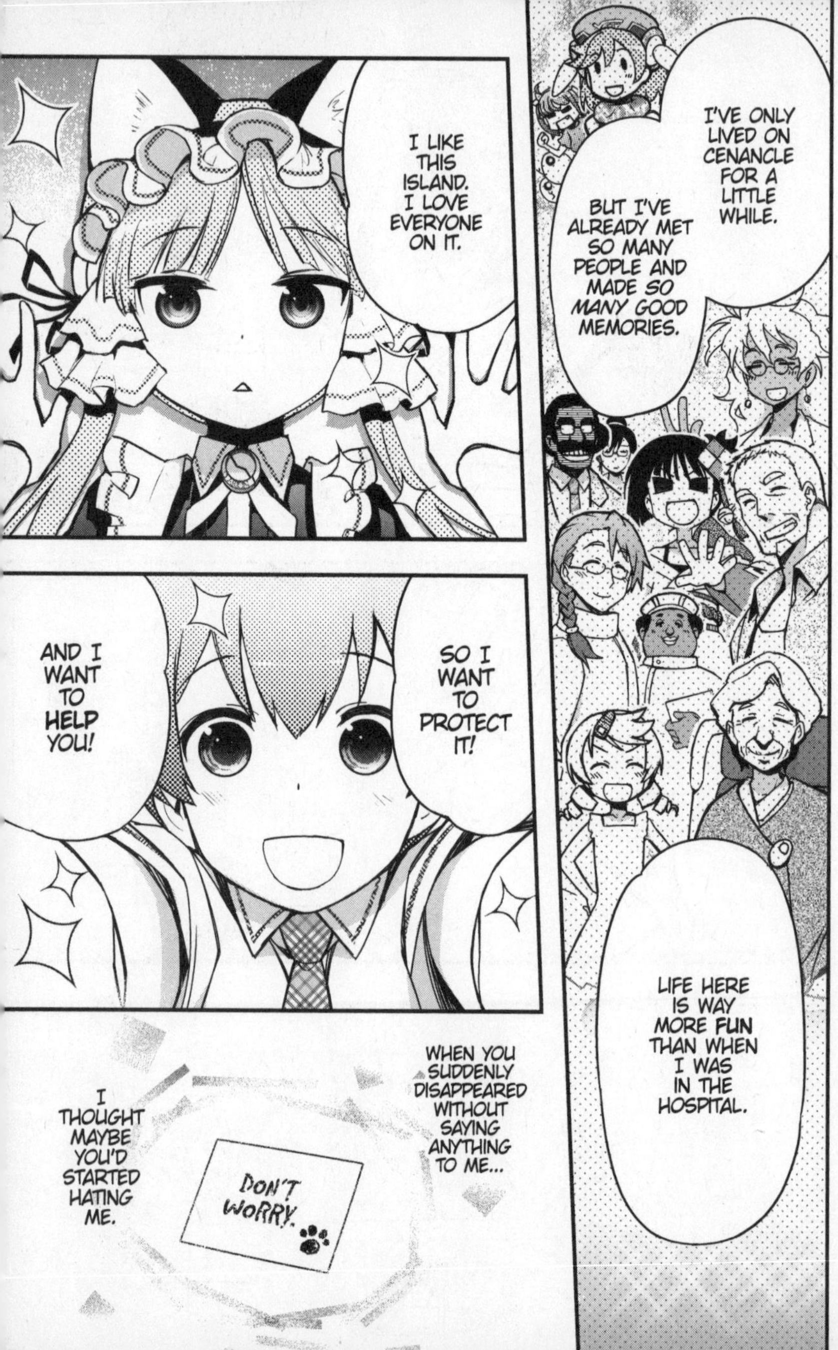
I'VE ONLY LIVED ON CENANCLE FOR A LITTLE WHILE.
BUT I'VE ALREADY MET SO MANY PEOPLE AND MADE SO *MANY* GOOD MEMORIES.
LIFE HERE IS WAY MORE FUN THAN WHEN I WAS IN THE HOSPITAL.
I LIKE THIS ISLAND. I LOVE EVERYONE ON IT.
SO I WANT TO PROTECT IT!
AND I WANT TO HELP YOU!
WHEN YOU SUDDENLY DISAPPEARED WITHOUT SAYING ANYTHING TO ME...
I THOUGHT MAYBE YOU'D STARTED HATING ME.
DON'T WORRY.

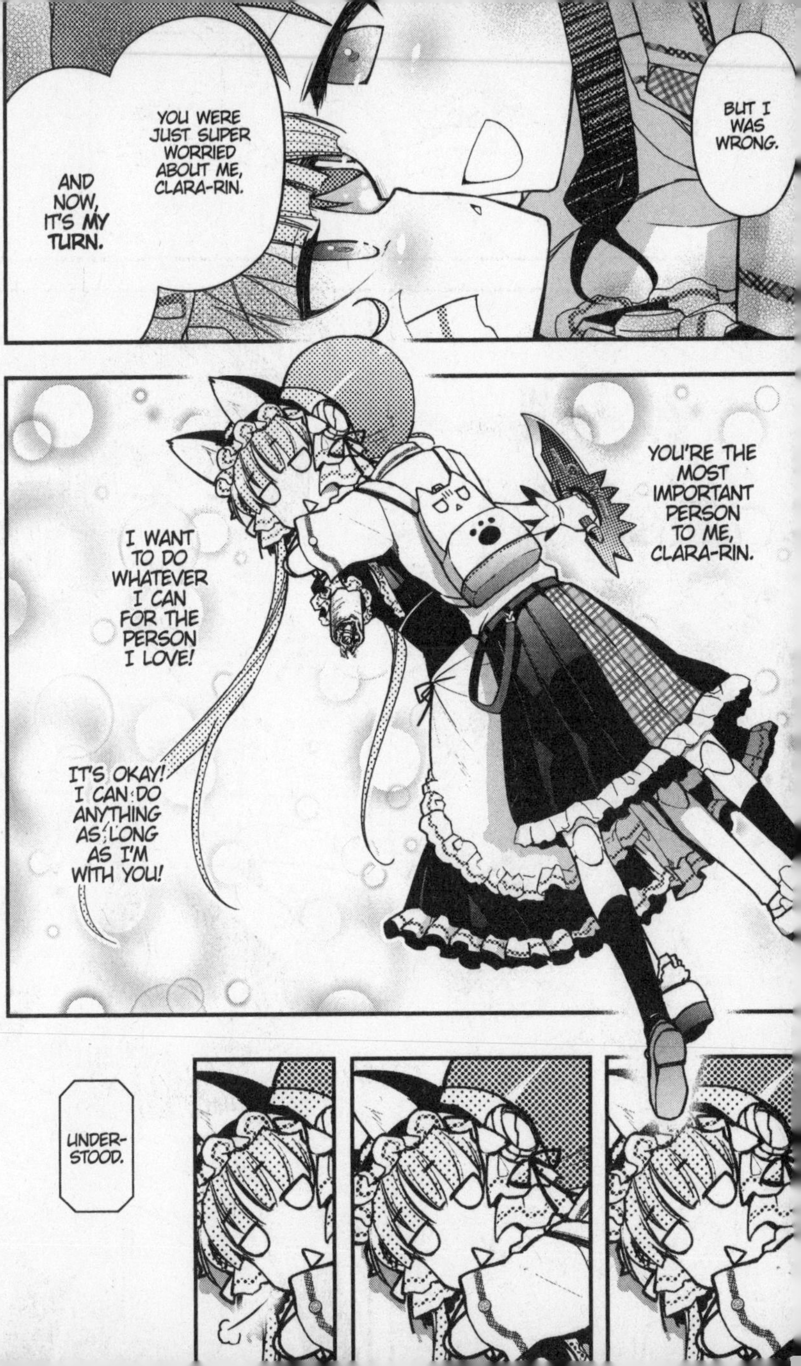
BUT I WAS WRONG.
YOU WERE JUST SUPER WORRIED ABOUT ME, CLARA-RIN.
AND NOW, IT'S MY TURN.
YOU'RE THE MOST IMPORTANT PERSON TO ME, CLARA-RIN.
I WANT TO DO WHATEVER I CAN FOR THE PERSON I LOVE!
IT'S OKAY! I CAN DO ANYTHING AS LONG AS I'M WITH YOU!
UNDER-STOOD.

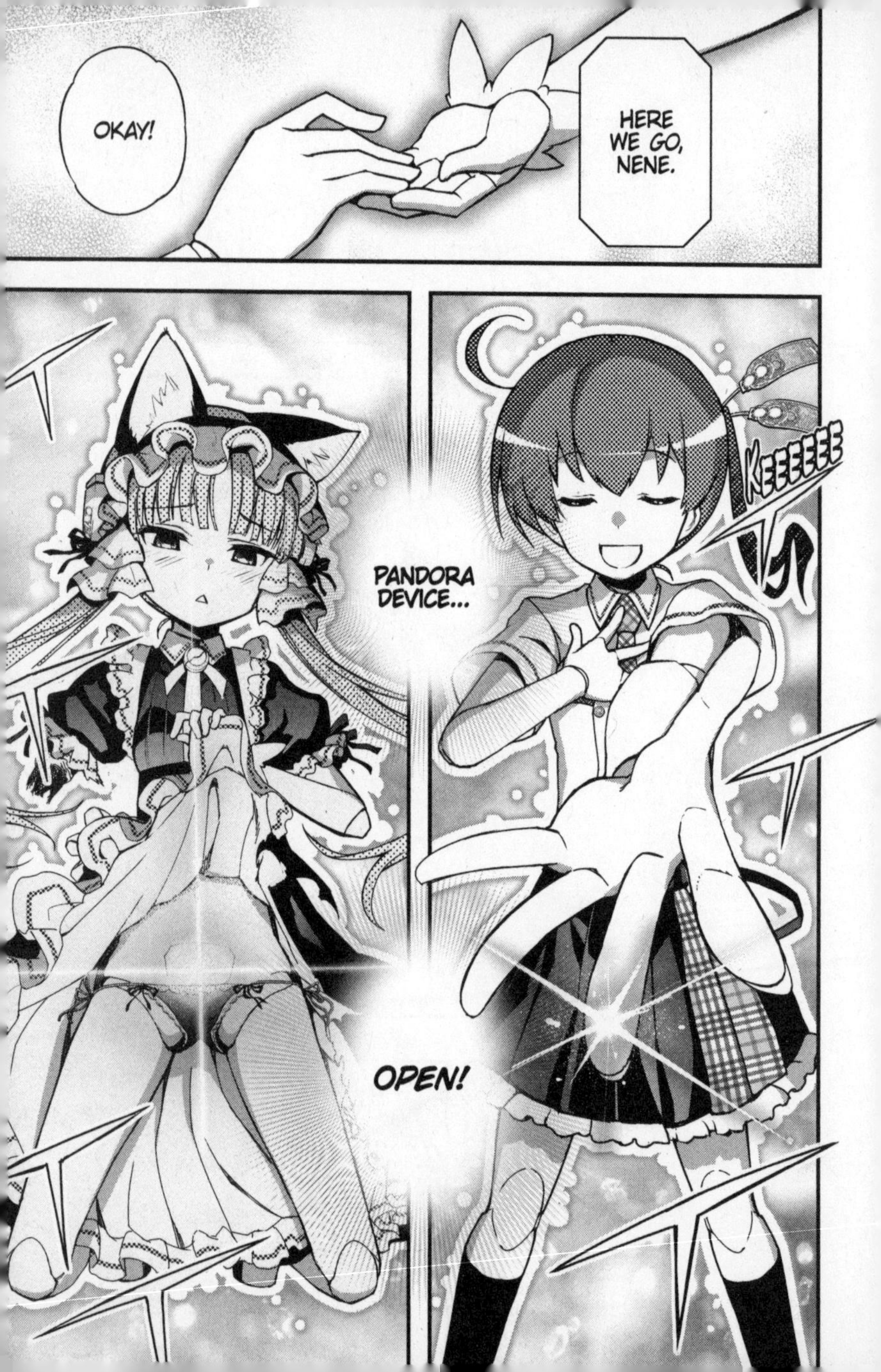
HERE WE GO, NENE.
OKAY!
KEEEEEE
PANDORA DEVICE...
OPEN!

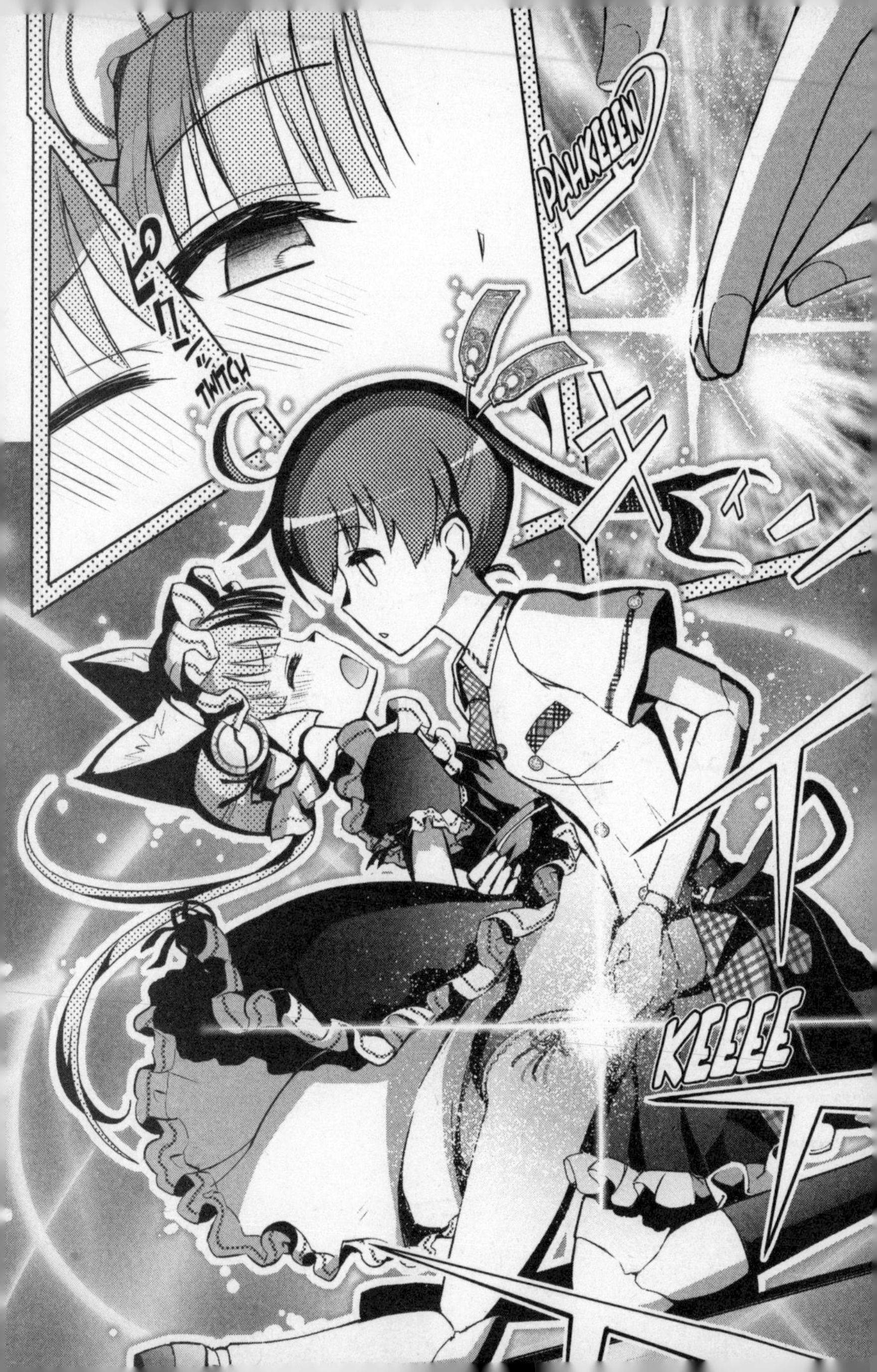
PAHKEEEN
TWITCH
KEEEE

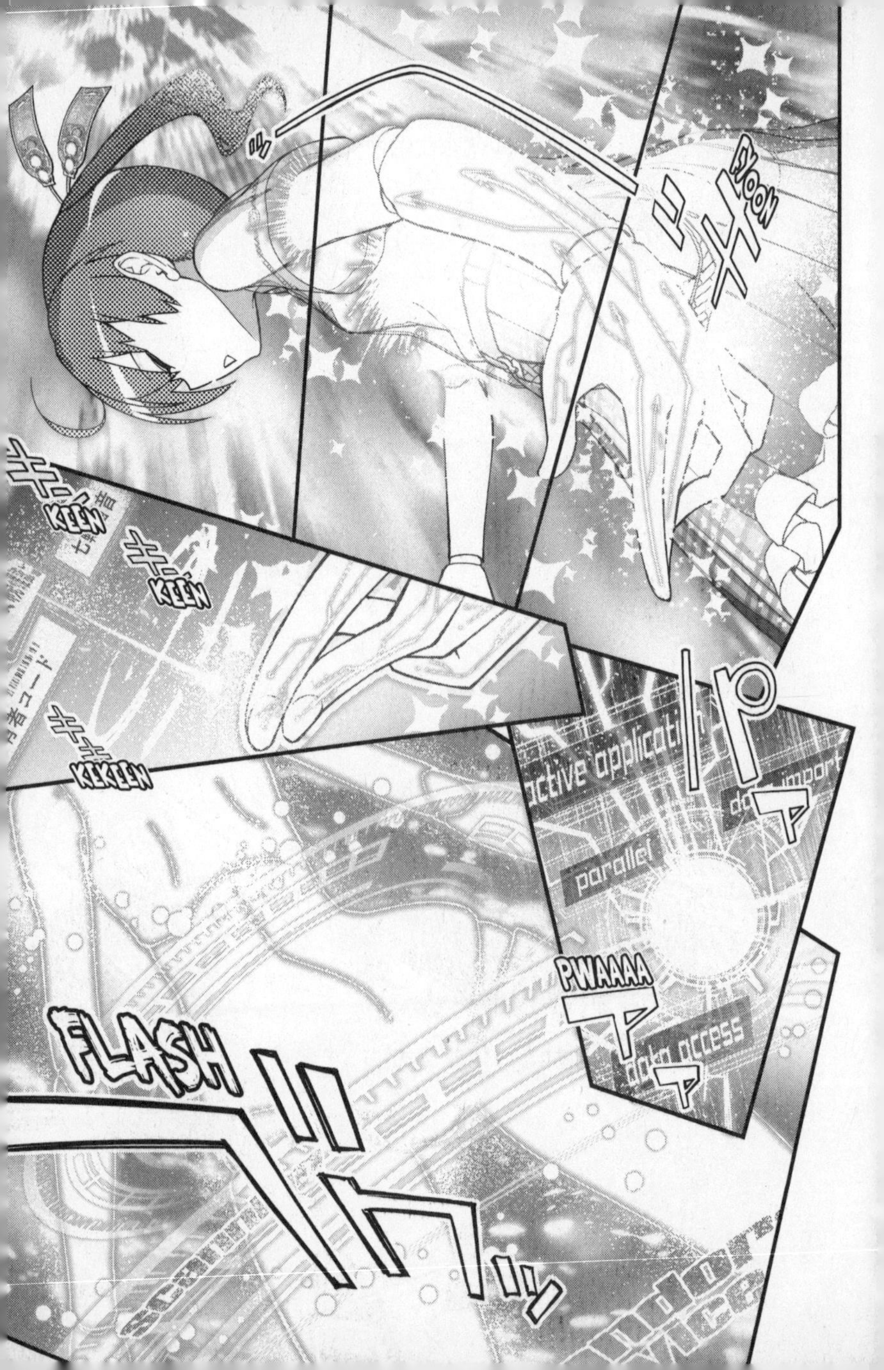
FYOON
KEEN
KEEN
KEKEEN
active applicati
parallel
import
PWAAAA
data access
FLASH

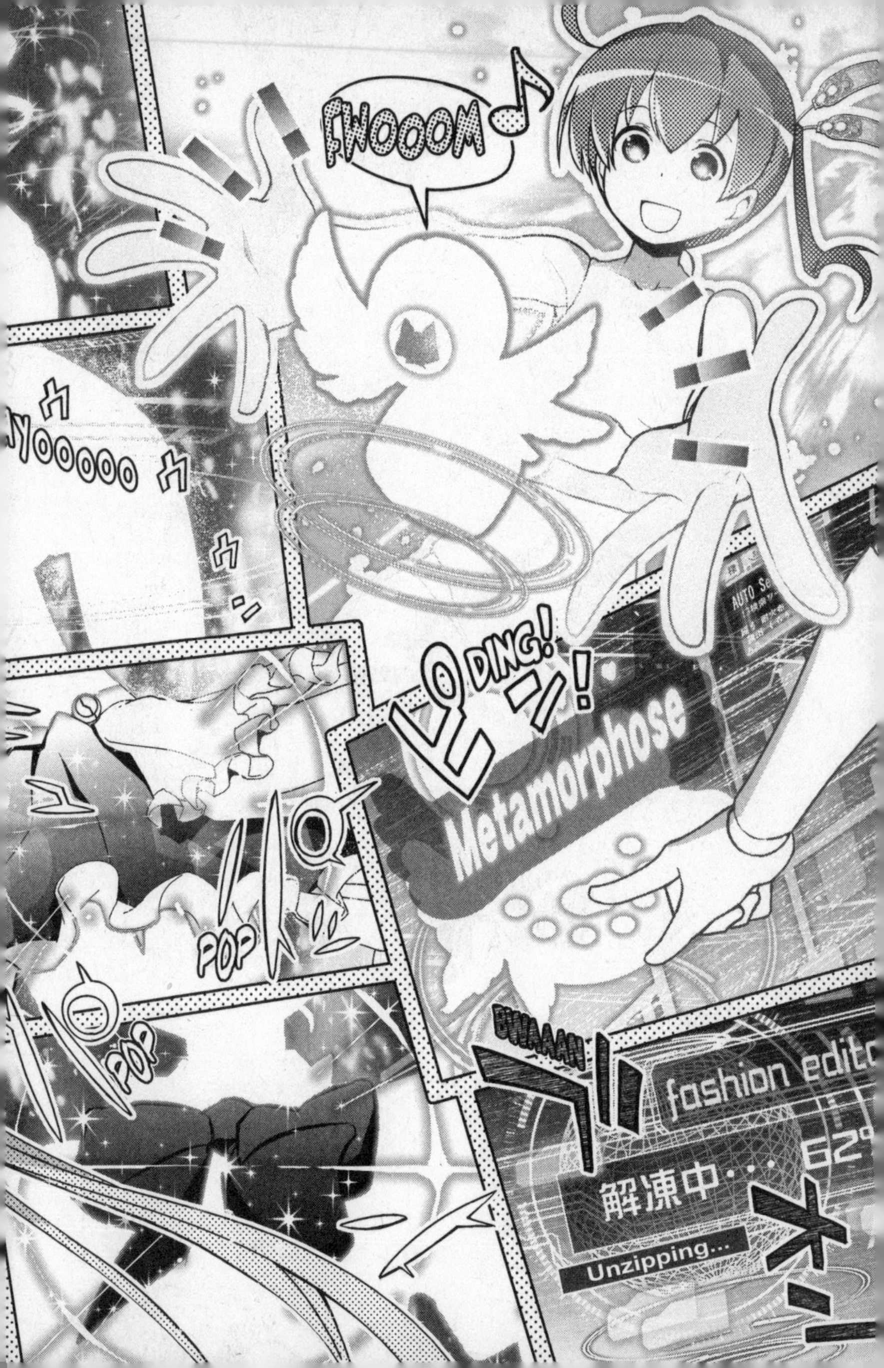
SWOOOM
DING!
Metamorphose
AUTO
POP
POP
BWAAAAN
fashion edito
62°
解凍中・・・
Unzipping...

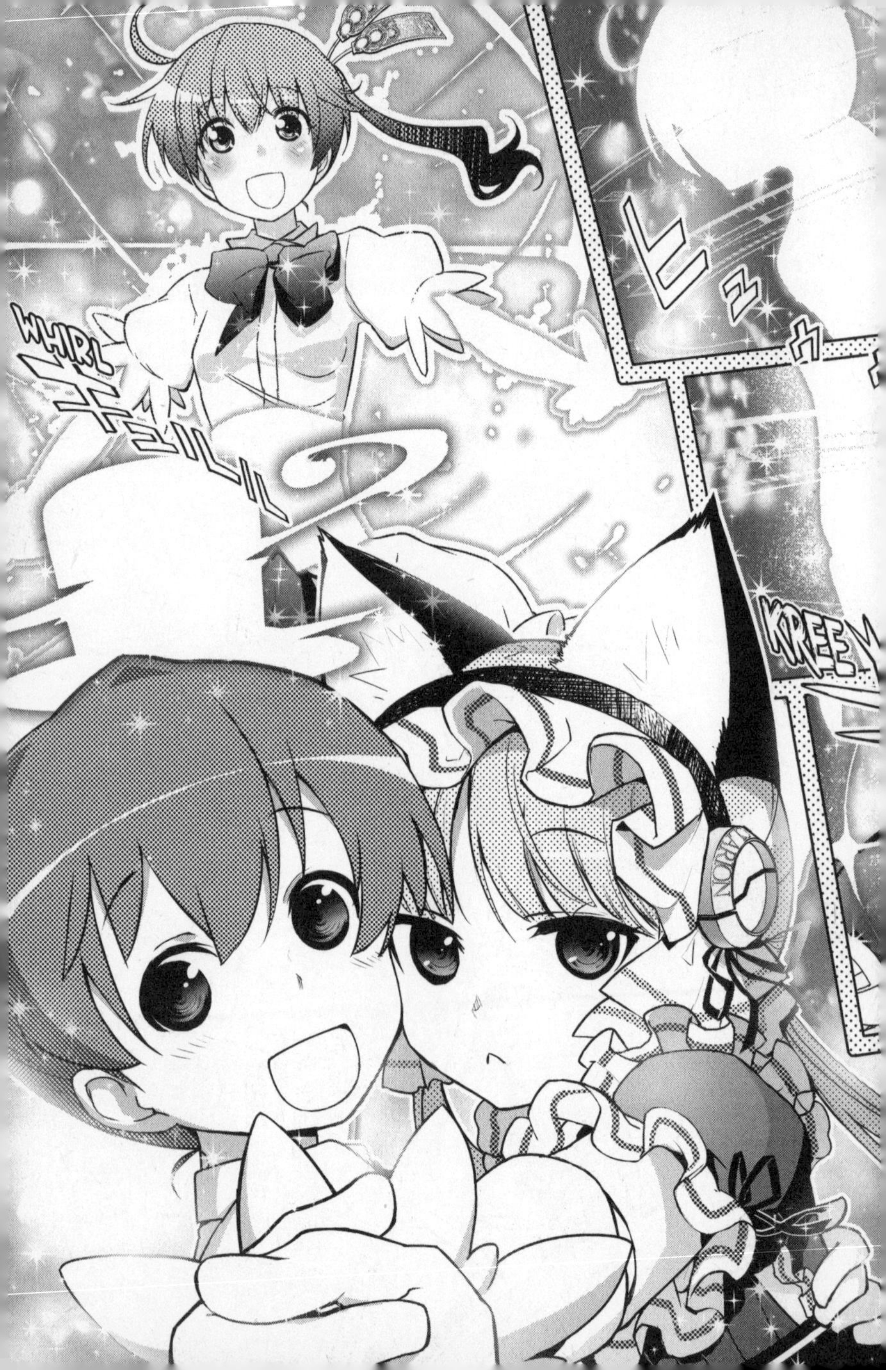
KREE
WHIRL

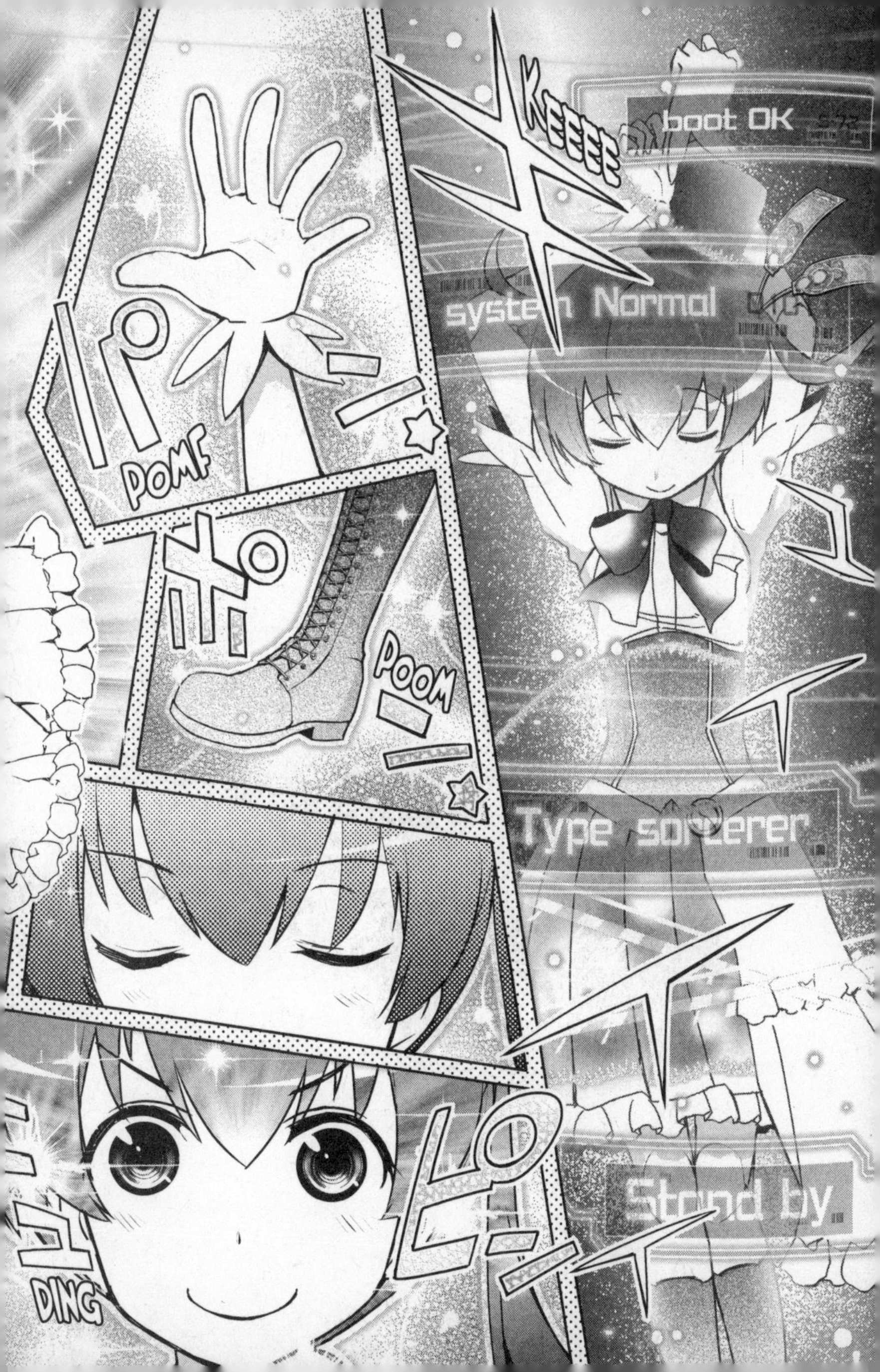
KEEEE
boot OK
system Normal
Type sorcerer
Stand by
POMF
POOM
DING

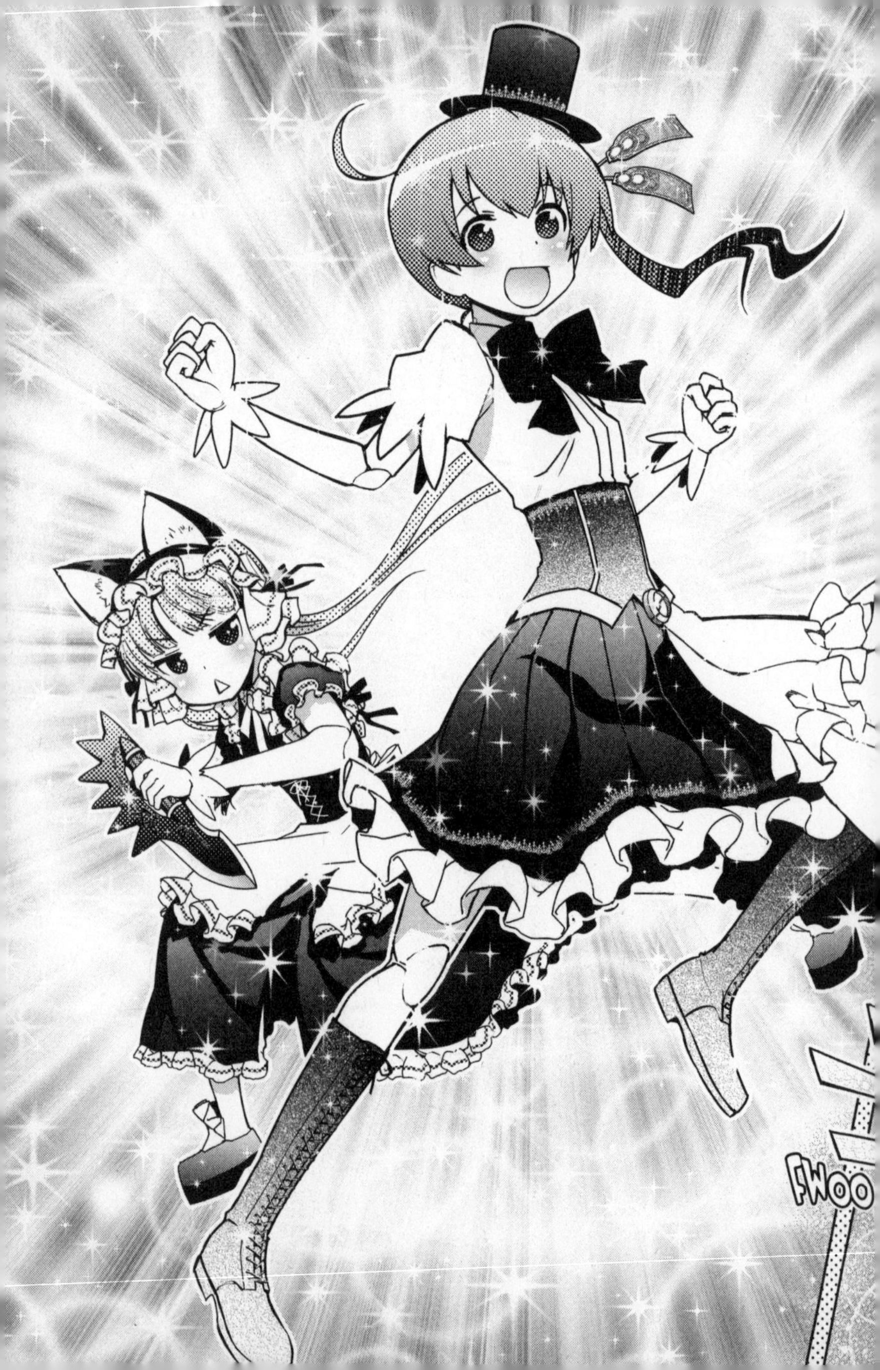
FWOO

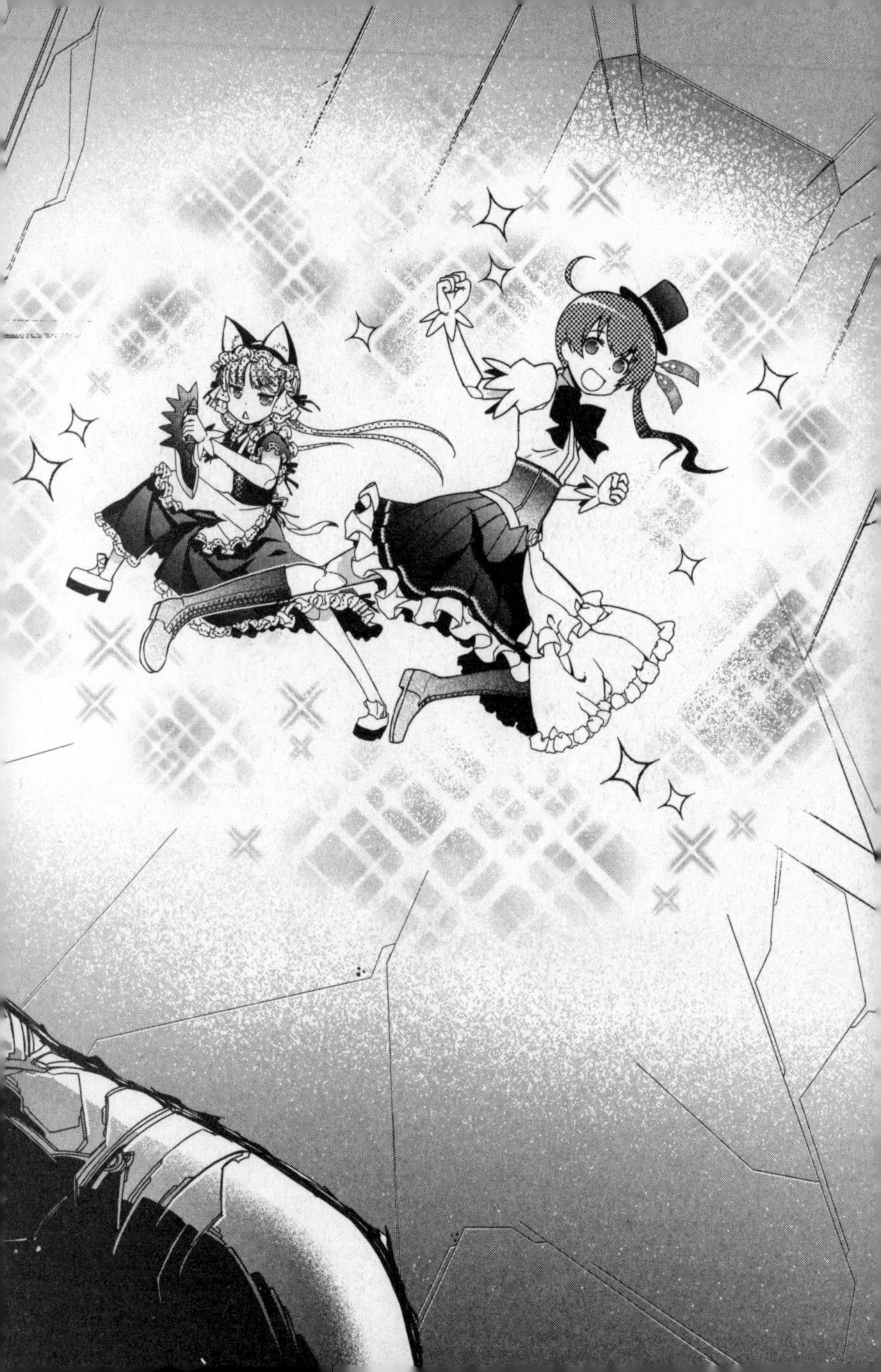

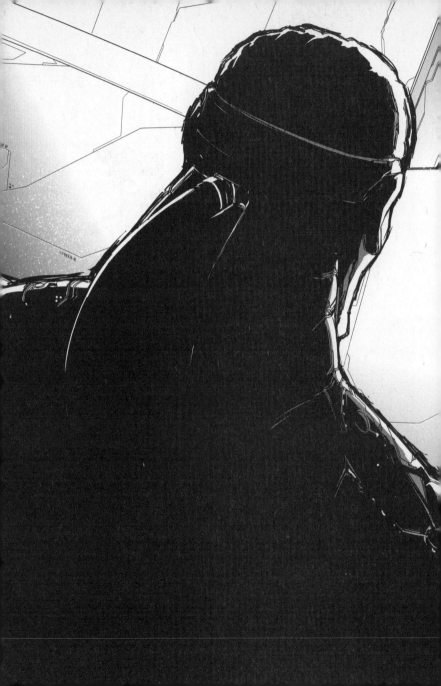

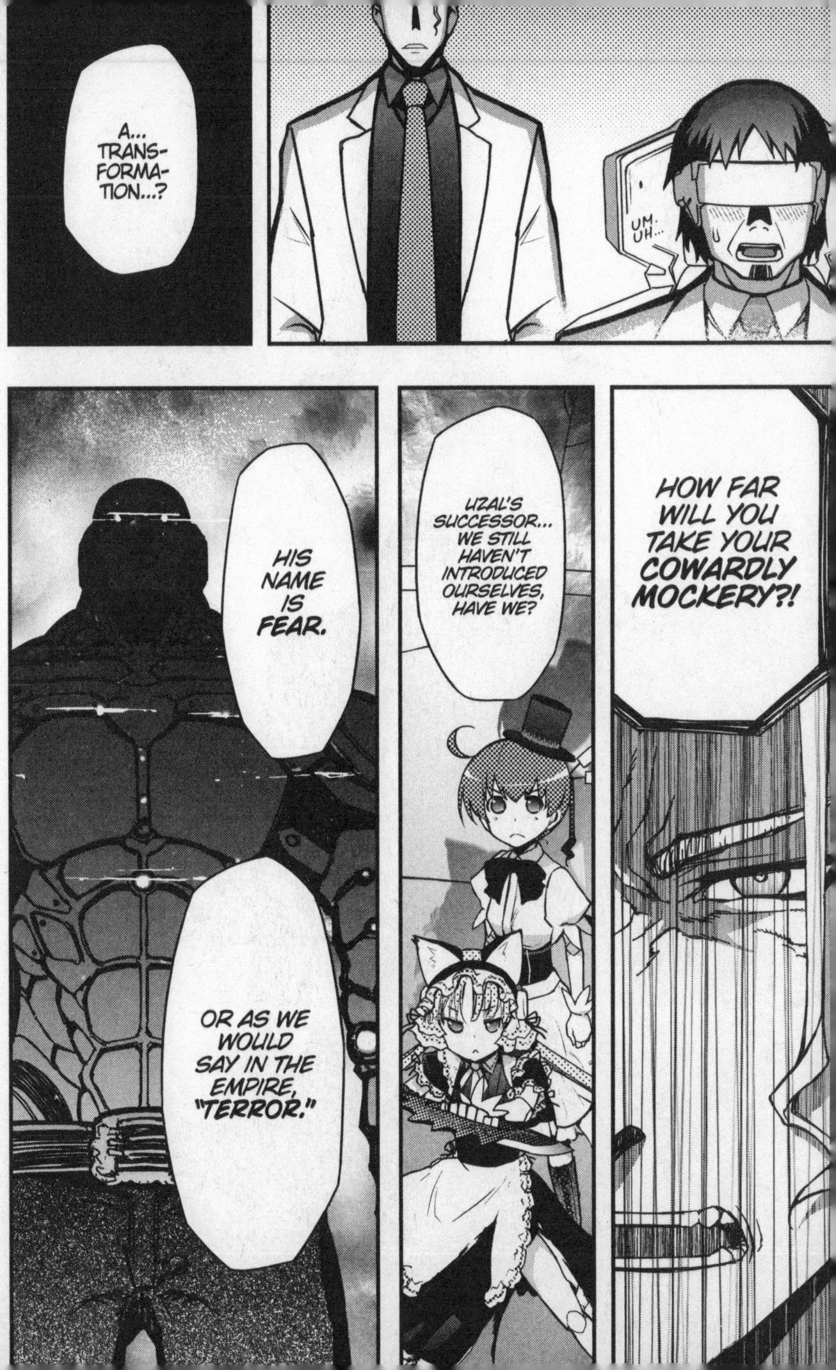
UM. UH...
A... TRANS-FORMA-TION...?
HOW FAR WILL YOU TAKE YOUR COWARDLY MOCKERY?!
UZAL'S SUCCESSOR... WE STILL HAVEN'T INTRODUCED OURSELVES, HAVE WE?
HIS NAME IS FEAR.
OR AS WE WOULD SAY IN THE EMPIRE, "TERROR."

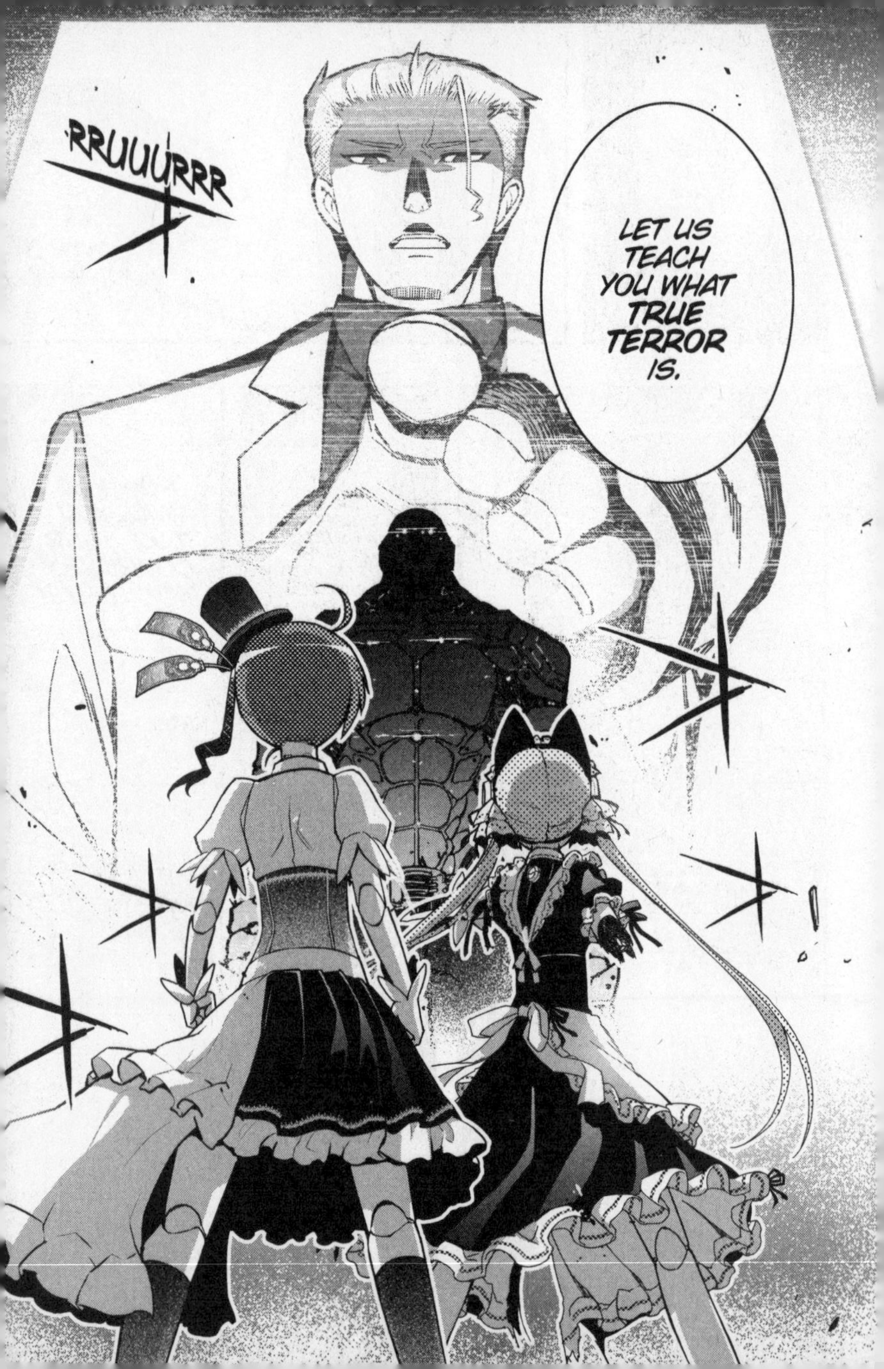
LET US TEACH YOU WHAT TRUE TERROR IS.
RRUUURRR

...TO BE CONTINUED

GHOST URN

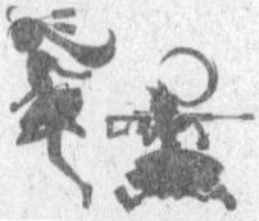

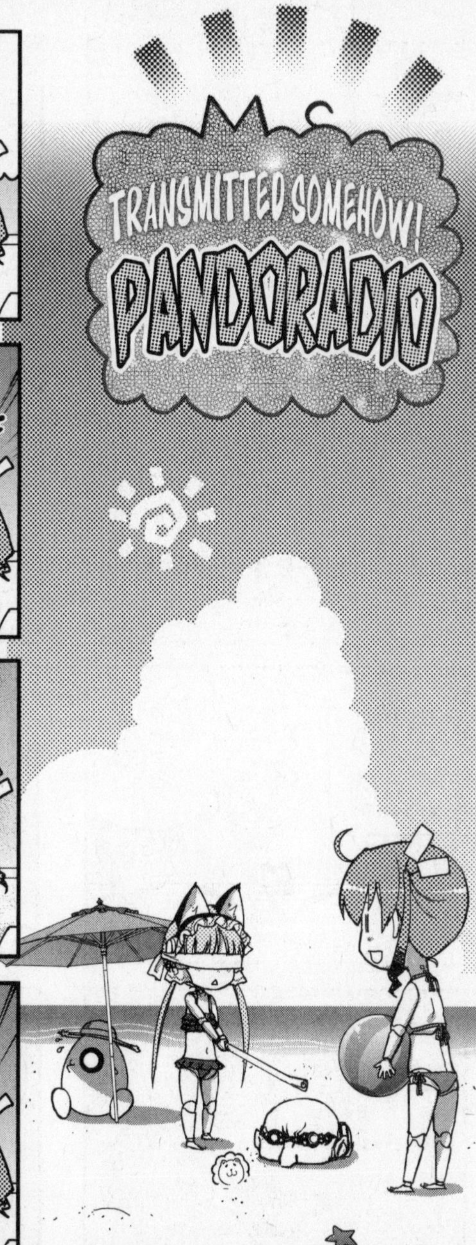
TRANSMITTED SOMEHOW!
PANDORADIO

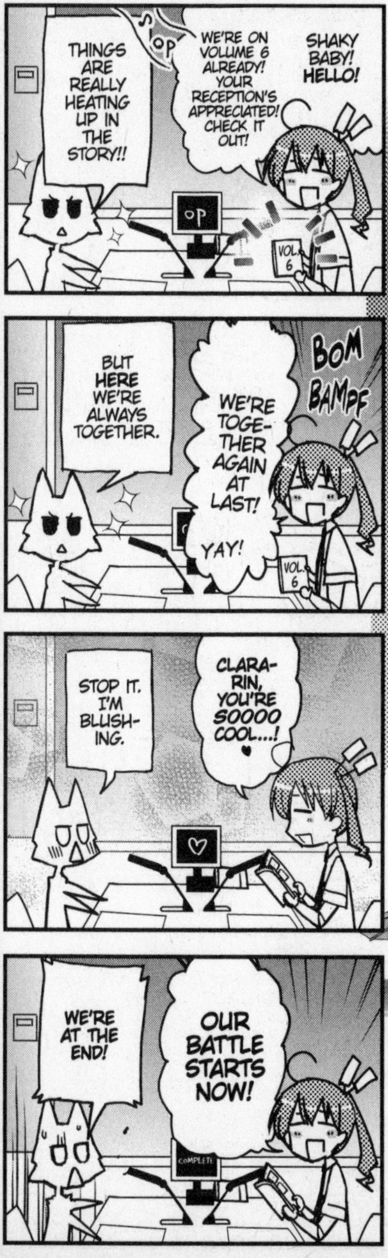
SHAKY BABY! HELLO!
WE'RE ON VOLUME 6 ALREADY! YOUR RECEPTION'S APPRECIATED! CHECK IT OUT!
♪ OP
THINGS ARE REALLY HEATING UP IN THE STORY!!
OP
VOL. 6
BOM BAMPF
WE'RE TOGE-THER AGAIN AT LAST!
YAY!
BUT HERE WE'RE ALWAYS TOGETHER.
VOL. 6
CLARA-RIN, YOU'RE SOOOO COOL...!
STOP IT. I'M BLUSH-ING.
OUR BATTLE STARTS NOW!
WE'RE AT THE END!
COMPLETE

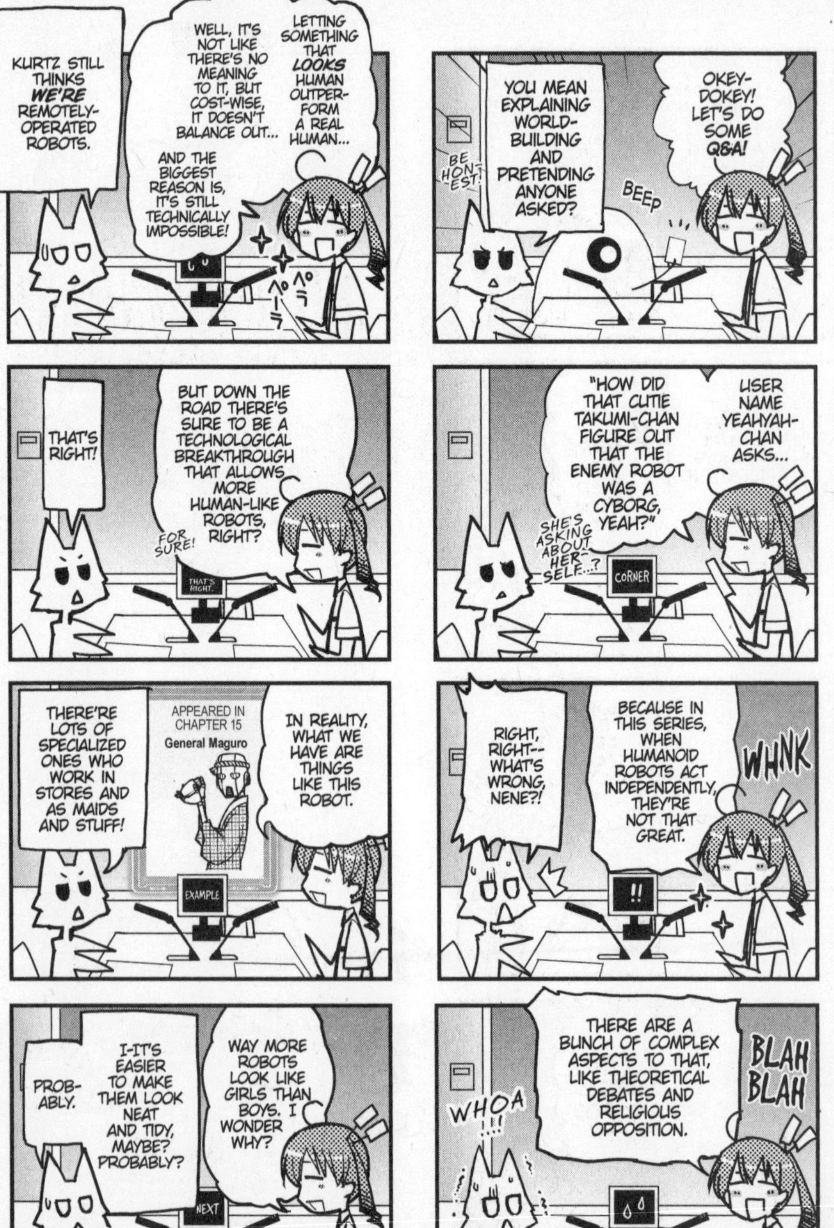
OKEY-DOKEY! LET'S DO SOME Q&A!
BEEP
YOU MEAN EXPLAINING WORLD-BUILDING AND PRETENDING ANYONE ASKED?
BE HON-EST!
LETTING SOMETHING THAT LOOKS HUMAN OUTPERFORM A REAL HUMAN...
WELL, IT'S NOT LIKE THERE'S NO MEANING TO IT, BUT COST-WISE, IT DOESN'T BALANCE OUT...
AND THE BIGGEST REASON IS, IT'S STILL TECHNICALLY IMPOSSIBLE!
KURTZ STILL THINKS WE'RE REMOTELY-OPERATED ROBOTS.
ヘラ ヘラ
USER NAME YEAHYAH-CHAN ASKS...
"HOW DID THAT CUTIE TAKUMI-CHAN FIGURE OUT THAT THE ENEMY ROBOT WAS A CYBORG, YEAH?"
SHE'S ASKING ABOUT HER-SELF...?
CORNER
BUT DOWN THE ROAD THERE'S SURE TO BE A TECHNOLOGICAL BREAKTHROUGH THAT ALLOWS MORE HUMAN-LIKE ROBOTS, RIGHT?
THAT'S RIGHT!
FOR SURE!
THAT'S RIGHT.
WHNK
BECAUSE IN THIS SERIES, WHEN HUMANOID ROBOTS ACT INDEPENDENTLY, THEY'RE NOT THAT GREAT.
RIGHT, RIGHT-- WHAT'S WRONG, NENE?!
!!
IN REALITY, WHAT WE HAVE ARE THINGS LIKE THIS ROBOT.
APPEARED IN CHAPTER 15
General Maguro
THERE'RE LOTS OF SPECIALIZED ONES WHO WORK IN STORES AND AS MAIDS AND STUFF!
EXAMPLE
BLAH BLAH
THERE ARE A BUNCH OF COMPLEX ASPECTS TO THAT, LIKE THEORETICAL DEBATES AND RELIGIOUS OPPOSITION.
WHOA
WAY MORE ROBOTS LOOK LIKE GIRLS THAN BOYS. I WONDER WHY?
I-IT'S EASIER TO MAKE THEM LOOK NEAT AND TIDY, MAYBE? PROBABLY?
PROB-ABLY.
NEXT

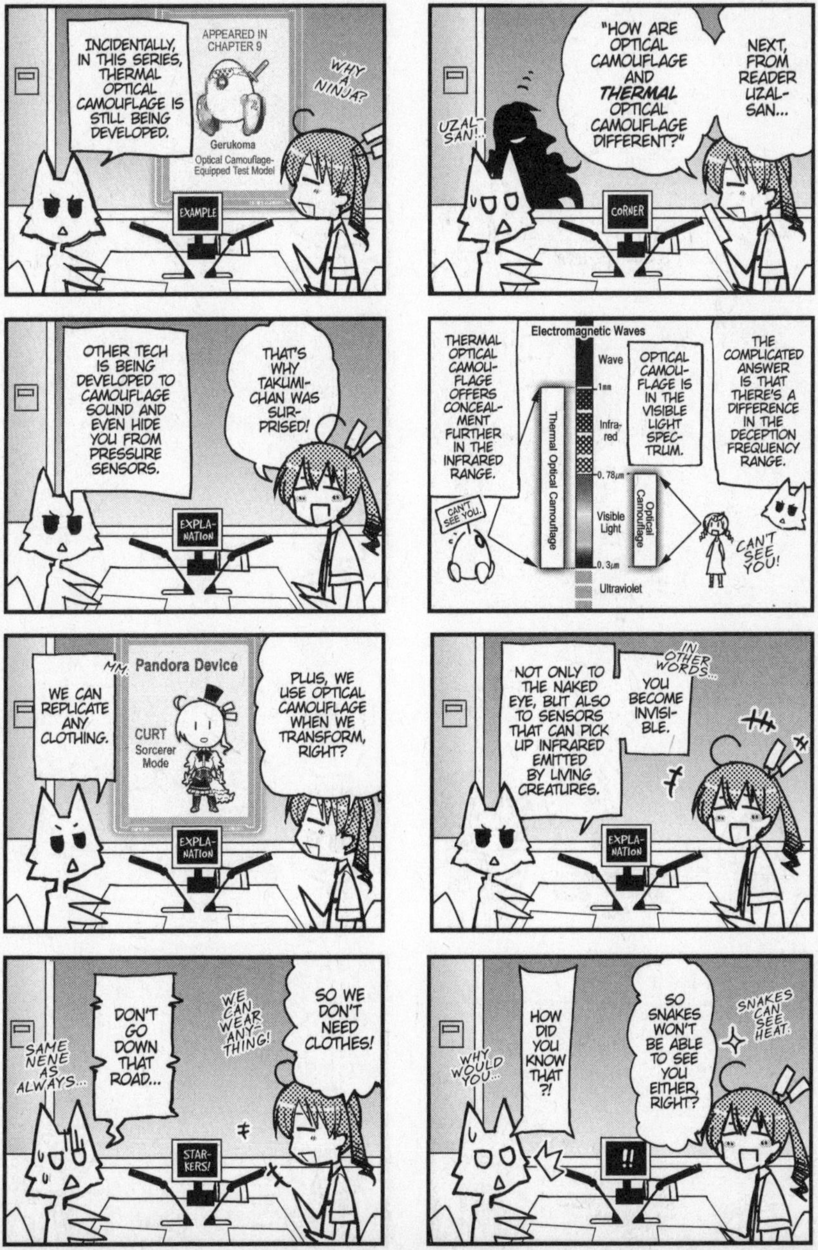
NEXT, FROM READER UZAL-SAN...
"HOW ARE OPTICAL CAMOUFLAGE AND THERMAL OPTICAL CAMOUFLAGE DIFFERENT?"
UZAL-SAN!
CORNER
WHY A NINJA?
APPEARED IN CHAPTER 9
Gerukoma
Optical Camouflage-Equipped Test Model
INCIDENTALLY, IN THIS SERIES, THERMAL OPTICAL CAMOUFLAGE IS STILL BEING DEVELOPED.
EXAMPLE
THE COMPLICATED ANSWER IS THAT THERE'S A DIFFERENCE IN THE DECEPTION FREQUENCY RANGE.
OPTICAL CAMOUFLAGE IS IN THE VISIBLE LIGHT SPECTRUM.
Electromagnetic Waves
Wave
1mm
Infrared
0.78μm
Visible Light
0.3μm
Ultraviolet
Optical Camouflage
Thermal Optical Camouflage
CAN'T SEE YOU!
THERMAL OPTICAL CAMOUFLAGE OFFERS CONCEALMENT FURTHER IN THE INFRARED RANGE.
CAN'T SEE YOU.
THAT'S WHY TAKUMI-CHAN WAS SURPRISED!
OTHER TECH IS BEING DEVELOPED TO CAMOUFLAGE SOUND AND EVEN HIDE YOU FROM PRESSURE SENSORS.
EXPLANATION
IN OTHER WORDS...
YOU BECOME INVISIBLE.
NOT ONLY TO THE NAKED EYE, BUT ALSO TO SENSORS THAT CAN PICK UP INFRARED EMITTED BY LIVING CREATURES.
EXPLANATION
PLUS, WE USE OPTICAL CAMOUFLAGE WHEN WE TRANSFORM, RIGHT?
Pandora Device
MM.
CURT
Sorcerer Mode
WE CAN REPLICATE ANY CLOTHING.
EXPLANATION
SNAKES CAN SEE HEAT.
SO SNAKES WON'T BE ABLE TO SEE YOU EITHER, RIGHT?
HOW DID YOU KNOW THAT?!
WHY WOULD YOU...
!!
SO WE DON'T NEED CLOTHES!
WE CAN WEAR ANYTHING!
DON'T GO DOWN THAT ROAD...
SAME NENE AS ALWAYS...
STARKERS!

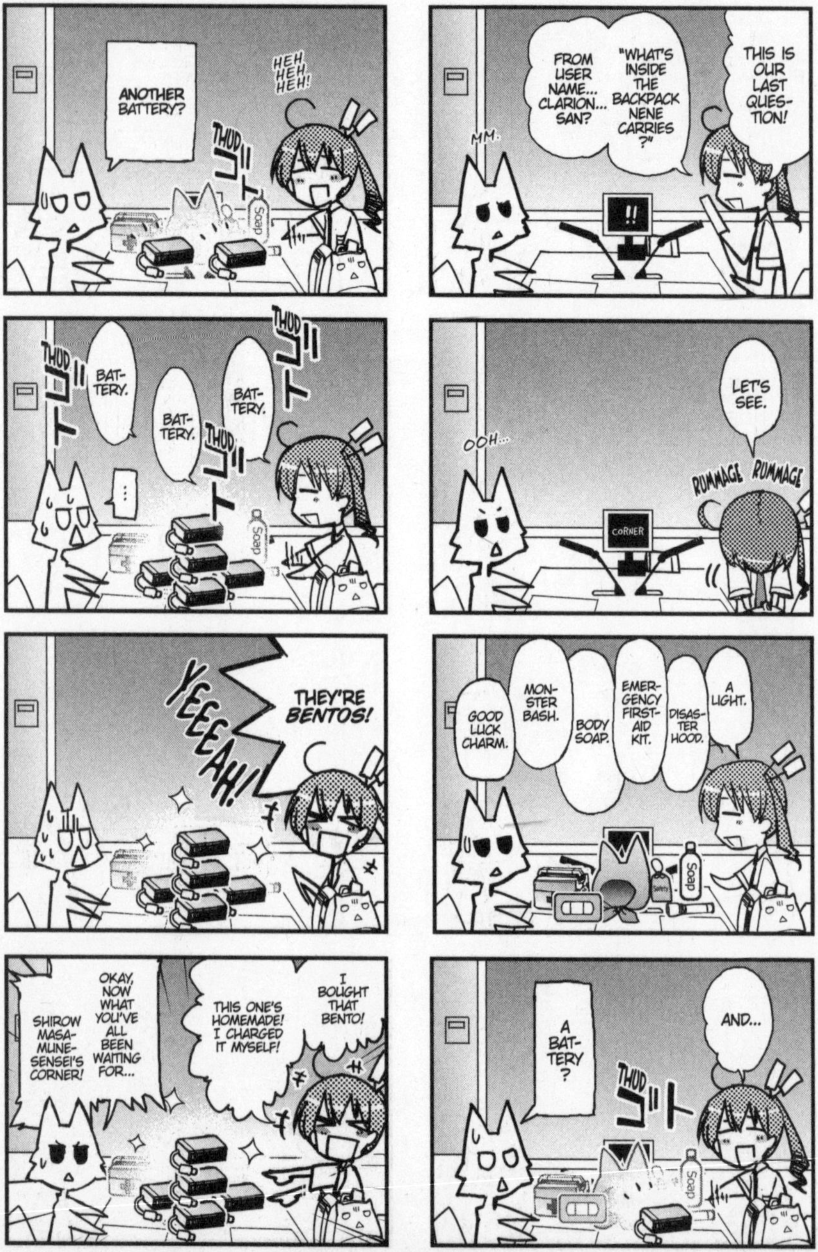
THIS IS OUR LAST QUESTION!
"WHAT'S INSIDE THE BACKPACK NENE CARRIES?"
FROM USER NAME... CLARION... SAN?
MM.
LET'S SEE.
RUMMAGE RUMMAGE
OOH...
CORNER
A LIGHT.
DISASTER HOOD.
EMERGENCY FIRST-AID KIT.
BODY SOAP.
MONSTER BASH.
GOOD LUCK CHARM.
Soap
AND...
THUD
A BATTERY?
Soap
HEH HEH HEH!
THUD
ANOTHER BATTERY?
Soap
THUD
BATTERY.
THUD
BATTERY.
THUD
BATTERY.
...
Soap
THEY'RE BENTOS!
YEEEAH!
I BOUGHT THAT BENTO!
THIS ONE'S HOMEMADE! I CHARGED IT MYSELF!
OKAY, NOW WHAT YOU'VE ALL BEEN WAITING FOR...
SHIROW MASAMUNE-SENSEI'S CORNER!

ORIGINAL CONCEPT DESIGN NOTES

I used these designs in *Ghost in the Shell: ARISE* as Amuri Noto and Instructor Ibachi (!), but the characters were originally created for this story. After coming ashore at Cenancle Island, terrorist Camelita Elchanpom and her subordinate (a mercenary with expertise in explosives) run into the protagonists, who are working part-time jobs on the beach. They try to eliminate the witnesses, but have an unexpected amount of trouble with it, and their terrorism plot goes off the rails... That's just their luck.

I decided the scar on her face was from that encounter with Clarion. (LOL)

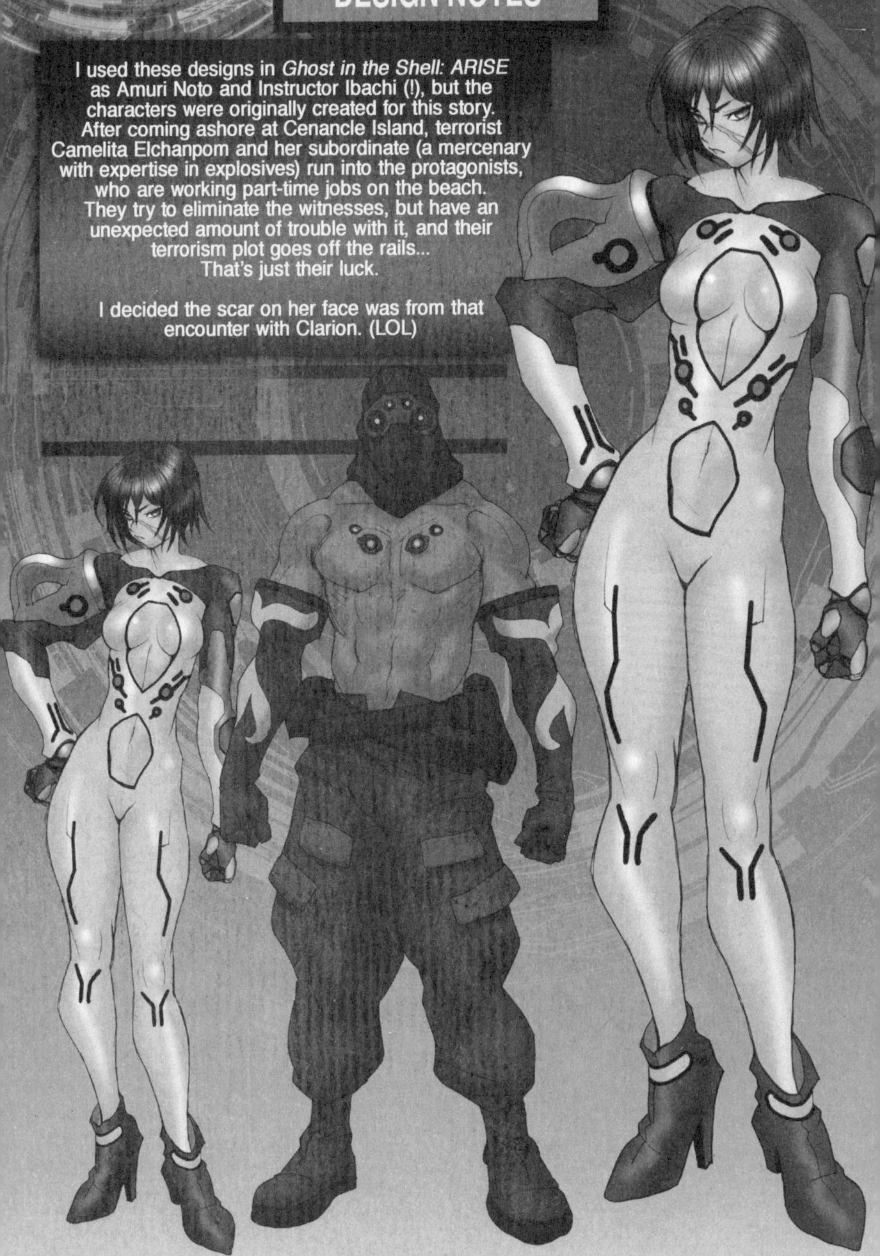

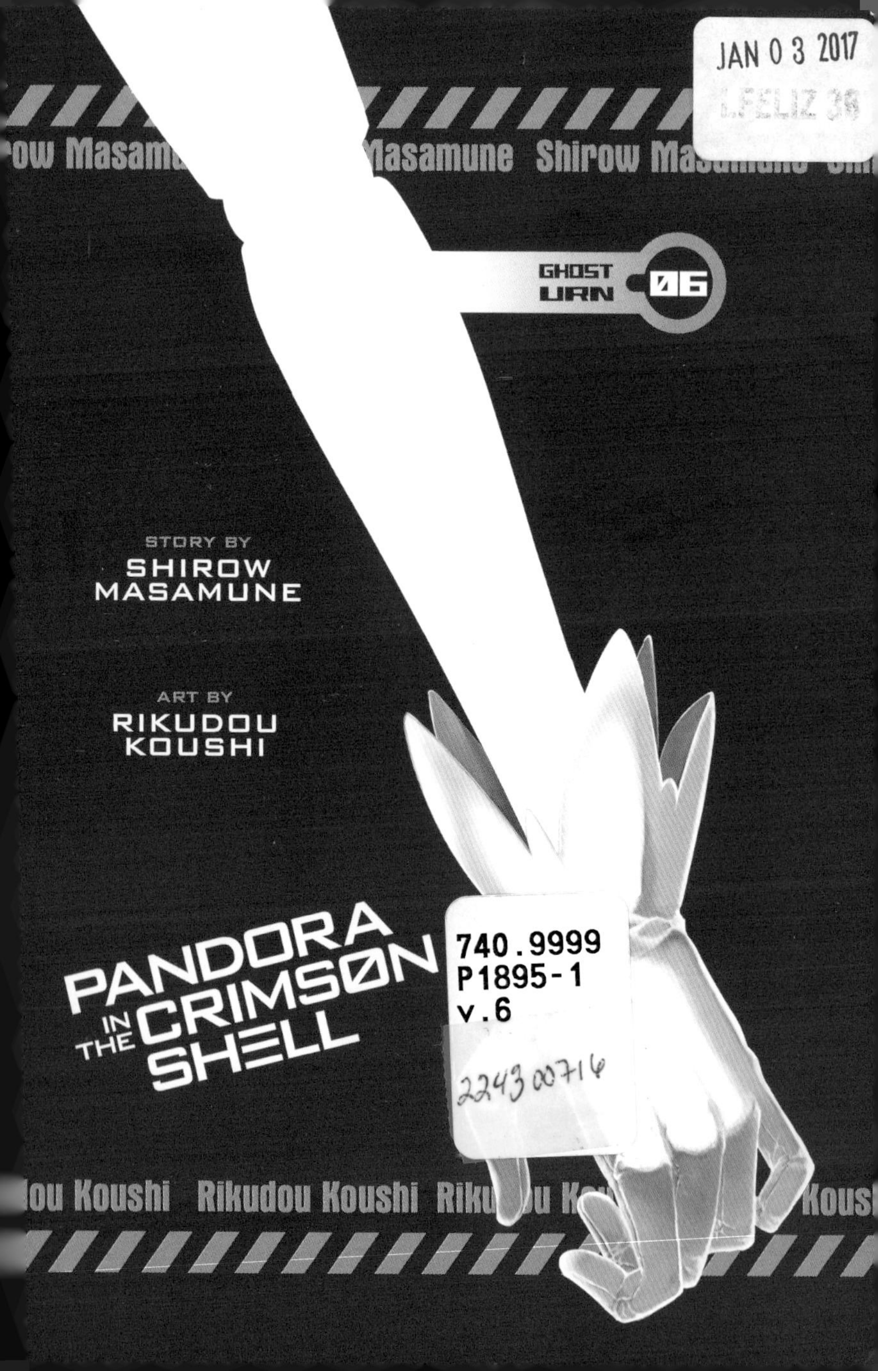
Shirow Masamune Shirow Masamune
GHOST URN 06
STORY BY
SHIROW MASAMUNE
ART BY
RIKUDOU KOUSHI
PANDORA IN THE CRIMSON SHELL
Rikudou Koushi Rikudou Koushi

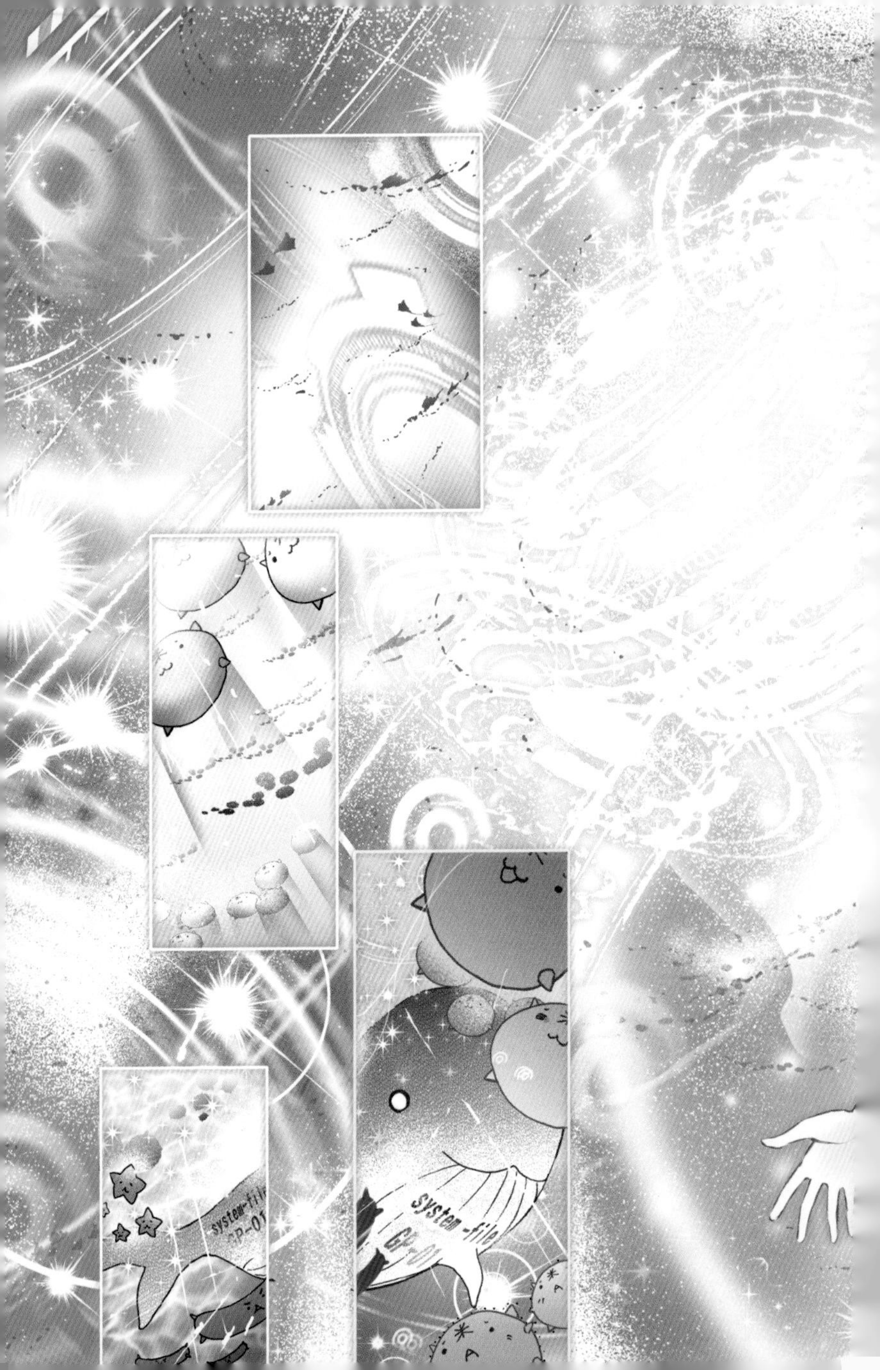
System-file

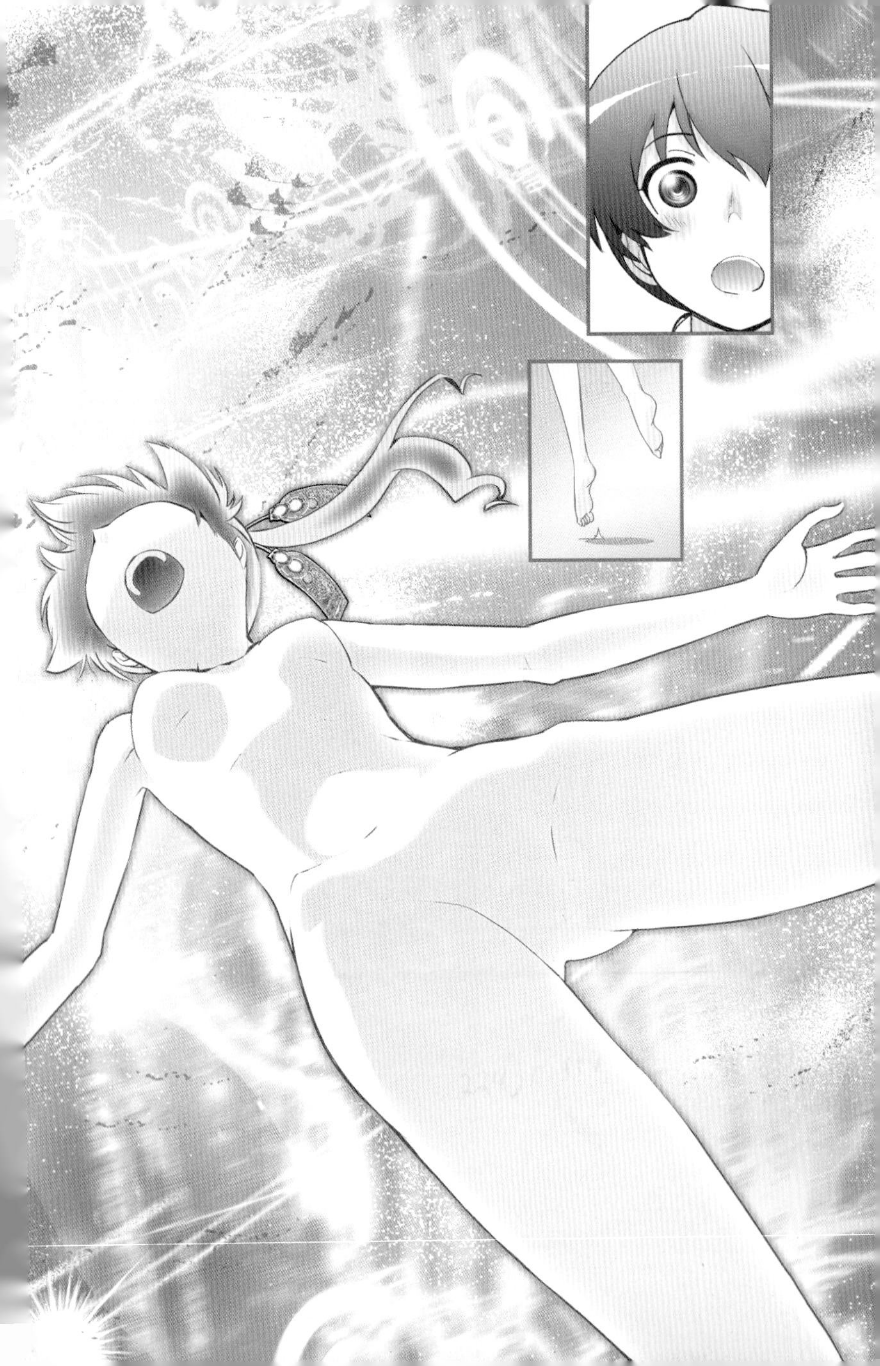

GHOST URN 06
SHIROW MASAMUNE
RIKUDOU KOUSHI